ARISTOTLE AND XENOPHON ON
DEMOCRACY AND OLIGARCHY

ARISTOTLE AND XENOPHON ON DEMOCRACY AND OLIGARCHY

ARISTOTLE'S
THE CONSTITUTION OF ATHENS

THE CONSTITUTION OF THE ATHENIANS
Ascribed to XENOPHON THE ORATOR

XENOPHON'S
THE POLITEIA OF THE SPARTANS

THE BOEOTIAN CONSTITUTION
From the OXYRHYNCHUS HISTORIAN

TRANSLATIONS WITH INTRODUCTIONS
AND COMMENTARY BY

J. M. MOORE

RADLEY COLLEGE

UNIVERSITY OF CALIFORNIA PRESS
BERKELEY · LOS ANGELES · LONDON

University of California Press
Berkeley and Los Angeles, California
University of California Press, Ltd.
London, England
© J. M. Moore 1975, 1983
Foreword to the 2010 Edition by Kurt A. Raaflaub
First paperback 1975
New edition in paperback 1986
ISBN 978-0-520-26605-6
Library of Congress Catalog Card Number 74-16713

17   16   15   14   13   12   11   10
     8   7   6   5   4   3   2   1

For

NICHOLAS
In the hope that he also may one day enjoy
the history of Greece

Contents

CONTENTS

MAPS

FOREWORD TO THE 2010 EDITION

The Greek word *politeia* is usually translated as "constitution." It is derived, like *politēs* (citizen), from *polis*, which initially designated a fortified settlement and later described a community comprising main settlement, territory, and people. Although traditionally understood as "city state," *polis* more properly means "citizen state": "The men are the polis *[andres polis]*," says an Athenian general in Thucydides. When we talk of a "constitution," we mean a comprehensive set of laws that regulates the operation of government and political institutions, political decision-making processes, rights and duties of citizens, and much more. The first time a constitution that approximates our modern use of the word was created in ancient Greece was at the very beginning of the fourth century BCE, after Athens had lost the Peloponnesian War with Sparta and suffered through five constitutional changes in less than ten years. Before then, the laws in use were in part those given the Athenians by Draco in the last third of the seventh century and by Solon at the beginning of the sixth, in part those passed in the assembly over almost two hundred years after Solon, whenever there was need for them. Although Solon's laws had been inscribed and were displayed in a public place, there is reason to think that over time much was attributed to Solon that was not among his original laws. Moreover, the Athenians initially made no systematic distinction between decrees that were valid for a particular situation or need (later called *psēphismata*), and laws with general validity *(nomoi)*, much as modern Americans do not distinguish between these two categories when they use the word *bill* to refer to both. To our knowledge, no systematic review had ever been undertaken to determine what laws were still valid and appropriate. The oligarchic coups that forcefully removed some of the inscribed laws (such as those of Ephialtes recorded on the Areopagus Hill) and democratic restorations did much to add to the confusion.

3

Hence already in 410, when the short-lived regimes of the radical Four Hundred and the more moderate Five Thousand had been overthrown, the Athenians appointed a committee to collect, revise, and codify *(anagraphein)* the laws that were in force at the time. This committee had apparently just completed the task of reviewing and republishing the laws of Draco and Solon when in 404 Athens was defeated and Sparta imposed on it the rule by thirty men who soon became infamous as the "thirty tyrants." One of their first acts was to remove the republished laws. They were soon attacked by an army of exiled democrats, and when real civil war threatened, the Spartans negotiated a settlement and democracy was restored again, bolstered by a remarkable reconciliation agreement. A new committee of *anagrapheis,* perhaps led by the same person as before, took up the constitutional review, and in 399 the set of laws they presented was examined and passed, not by the assembly that previously had been in charge of legislation, but by a specially selected board of five hundred "lawgivers" *(nomothetai).* This was the first step in the process of separating legislation and political decision making—crucial in creating a more moderate and stable democracy. Moreover, the law code of 399, apparently unlike the laws of Draco and Solon, contained not only the traditional sets of law of procedure, criminal, and private law but also a range of what we would properly call "constitutional law," that is, regulations concerning political institutions and procedures.

The *Athēnaiōn politeia* written by Aristotle or, many think, one of his pupils was part of a great project (mentioned at the end of *Nicomachean Ethics*): to collect a large number (158, to be precise) *politeiai* that were to provide the empirical material for the master's great synthesis of constitutional theory and analysis he offered in *Politics.* This particular piece, the only one preserved almost completely, was produced early in the last third of the fourth century, decades after the publication of the Athenian law code. This date, and the purpose and context of its production, explain why here *politeia* really means "constitution": the piece offers first a survey of constitutional developments from the earliest remembered stage in the late seventh to the final stage in the early fourth century, then a (probably not quite complete) sketch of the functioning of the Athenian constitution in the author's time. Its discovery on various pieces of papyrus in the late nineteenth century was exceptionally lucky. That it concerns, of all places, Athens is invaluable for our understanding of this *polis* that cannot but occupy a central place, because of its role not only as the cradle of Greece's

Golden Age of culture and the arts but also as the birthplace of the most fully developed democracy that was possible under the conditions of the ancient world.

Of the anonymous "Oxyrhynchus historian," who continued Thucydides' history, much as Xenophon did, only a few excerpts survive, among them a description of the peculiar oligarchic constitution that operated in Boeotia in the early fourth century and had some parallels in drafts of constitutions that were considered in Athens at the time of the first oligarchic coup of 411. Here too, of course, *politeia* means "constitution," and this piece, short though it is, has singular value because it is the only extant and unbiased sketch of an oligarchy. We hear about oligarchies in other authors too, especially Thucydides and Xenophon, but their narratives focus not on the working of this constitution but on its emergence, struggles, and disappearance in Athens (that is, in especially unfavorable soil), and they show the distorted face of a system desperately fighting for survival from the beginning and with all available means, including deception and terror. *The Boeotian Constitution* thus offers a most precious different perspective.

The two other *politeiai* assembled in this volume belong to another category. They were probably written in the 430s or 420s (Pseudo-Xenophon) and the second decade of the fourth century (Xenophon). They reflect an earlier and much broader understanding of *politeia* that, in fact, continued to be used along the more specific "constitutional" meaning. For when Athenians and other Greeks talked of *politeia,* they did not primarily—or only—think of a set of laws. They thought of everything that characterized a polity as a community of people and affected its functioning and well-being. This certainly included laws but also norms, customs, ways of relating to each other (citizens and noncitizens, free and slaves, men and women, rich and poor) and to the gods, behavior patterns, preferences, military institutions, oddities that distinguished one community from others, and so on. In short, *politeia* described the entire nature, makeup, and way of life of a polity.

Hence Xenophon focuses, not on the working of the Spartan political institutions and decision-making processes—in fact, he almost completely ignores these—but on those aspects of communal life that distinguish this particular *polis* from most others: its citizens' unique way of life, their rigid military regime, their upbringing and tough training designed to produce the very best soldiers, their strange marriage customs, and their extraordinary relations to the helots (their large slave population), to mention only some of the most important issues. In Xenophon's time, Sparta was of great interest to many Greek aristocrats who, dissatisfied with democratic egalitarianism, looked to it as an ideal form of an aristocratic community. Xenophon initially embraced this view, but signs of disillusionment are clearly visible toward the end of his piece. Together with Plutarch's *Life of Lycurgus,* which retrojects much later conditions into the founding hero's past, Xenophon's *Lakedaimoniōn politeia* offers most precious insights into the relations and customs prevailing in this exceptional, secretive, and influential *polis.*

The anonymous author of the *Athēnaiōn politeia* that was preserved among Xenophon's works presents similarly revealing and important observations on Athenian communal life. We have no idea who he was or why, or to whom, he wrote this pamphlet. He wrote as an outsider and insider at the same time, that is, most probably, as a member of the Athenian elite who was thoroughly disenchanted with conditions in his city but knew them well enough and was able to appreciate them for what they were. He too is not primarily interested in the political institutions and "constitutional law." Rather, he offers a highly critical but insightful analysis of why democracy, operated (in the view of elite opponents) by the most incompetent and "crazy" part of the citizen body, both served the interests of the majority of the *dēmos* and was surprisingly successful—so much so that he sees no reasonable prospect of overthrowing it, although he knows exactly what would need to be done to replace this "bad order" *(kakonomia)* with a "good order" *(eunomia)* run exclusively and in their own interest by the best and noblest citizens. Eerily, only a few years later his ideas were realized by the oligarchs of 411.

One might say, therefore, that Pseudo-Xenophon's pamphlet at least indirectly deals with constitutional issues because it critically explores the impact of democracy on Athenian communal life. Modern observers sometimes tend to see Athenian democracy in almost teleological ways as the ultimate realization of a potential inherent in the Greek polis. This perspective obscures the fact that democracy, especially in the fully developed form we see in Athens in the fifth and fourth centuries, was an exception in the ancient constitutional landscape, made possible by rather unique conditions. It was unprecedented and, although more moderate democracies existed in many *poleis,* judged negatively by most contemporaries and by posterity well into the modern period. Echoes of an intense discussion about the merits and vices of democracy and about *the* best constitution are pervasive already in late fifth-century literature. The most famous example is the "Constitutional Debate" in Herodotus (included in an appendix in the present volume), which has a parallel in Euripides' *Suppliant Women.*

Each of the texts assembled in the present volume thus has particular and exceptional value for the historian, whether from political, cultural, or more narrowly constitutional perspectives. Together, they complement in many important ways the information we can gather from historians and other writers (such as dramatists or philosophers). They are uniquely important also for teaching purposes because they lead students right into the center of ancient intellectuals' major concerns about the nature of communal order and life, the evolution and differentiation of constitutions, and the citizens' ability to take charge and shape the communal order in which they wanted to live.

To have these texts collected, translated, introduced, and commented upon between two covers is extremely useful and a great service to the profession. To have all this done by an expert, J. M. Moore, who has the required broad knowledge, keen insight, and deep understanding of the needs of his readers is priceless. When this collection was first published in 1975, nothing comparable existed. True, individual pieces are available elsewhere—for example, Xenophon and Pseudo-Xenophon in the bilingual Loeb collection, Aristotle and Xenophon's works on Sparta in Penguin volumes—but no other volume combines them all. To have this collection, which has long been an indispensable standard work for scholars and students alike, reissued is most commendable. Among the books in my own personal library this one ranks, with Homer, Herodotus, and Thucydides, among those that I have used most often: both my copies are falling apart, and I am glad that a new edition will soon replace them.

Kurt A. Raaflaub

PREFACE

The aim of this book is to make some of the basic texts written on political practice by authors in Ancient Greece available to those who cannot read them in the original. All translations are my own, and are intended to reproduce the Greek texts as faithfully as may be; the Commentary is designed to make them comprehensible to those not intimately familiar with the history of the period and the society for which they were written. In so far as it was possible, I have tried to write a running commentary rather than disjointed notes on individual points; the nature of the texts has made some of the latter inevitable, but I hope that it may be possible to read a chapter or group of chapters followed by the relevant section of the Commentary as consecutive units, rather than refer backwards and forwards continuously.

Naturally, the works translated were not constructed in the way in which such treatises would be written to-day; I have taken them as they are, and explored the ideas which the authors were discussing, resisting the temptation to branch out into topics which may be fascinating but are not raised by the passage under consideration. Different types of constitution and forms of society must have something of interest for modern readers; the study of what succeeded or failed in the past can contribute to contemporary debates, and also to the consideration of politics and constitutional practice at other periods of history. It is with this field in view, as well as the study of the Ancient World itself, that this book has been written.

Each work has been treated in a self-contained section of the book so that the reader who wishes to consult only one may do so without inconvenience; at the same time, there are some cross-references where they are appropriate, and it is hoped that the Index will assist those studying topics rather than individual works. There is no separate index of passages from ancient authors which are translated or referred to in the Commentary, but pages where such quotations or references are to be found are listed under the author's name in the Index. Each section contains a Select Bibliography; the standard histories of Greece are not included, since the Bibliography concentrates on works specifically concerned with particular topics raised by the text. I have restricted references wherever possible to works in English; those wishing to explore further will find references to the foreign publications which are relevant in the bibliographies of the books cited here. The abbreviated form used for reference to works repeatedly cited in the Commentary will be found in the relevant Bibliography. The writings of ancient authors have been referred to by English titles, the abbreviations of which should be self-explanatory; the only other abbreviations used are the normal ones for periodicals and standard collections.

All dates, apart from that at the end of this preface and otherwise where stated, are B C. It is not infrequently necessary in giving dates from the classical period to express them in the form '478/7'. This arises from the fact that the Athenian year started about halfway through our year; therefore if we can only date an event to an Athenian year, it is impossible without any further guidance to be sure in which of the two half-years according to our reckoning it occurred. I have transliterated Greek proper names precisely except where it seemed to me that the name is so well known in a different form that this would cause unnecessary difficulties. The result is inevitably a somewhat unhappy compromise, and to a certain extent arbitrary, but to 'Latinise' all names seems an unnecessary violence, and it would certainly cause many readers disproportionate trouble when consulting other books if all the names had been precisely transliterated.

My debts are many. To those who have written on these subjects before me I owe a very great deal which will be clear to those who know, or are led to look at, the works listed in the bibliographies. The format prevents detailed reference to the work of predecessors in footnotes, and this general acknowledgment must suffice; such small points as there may be in this book which are original spring largely from the ideas and researches of others. My second debt is to the Warden of Radley College for the generous grant of a year's leave of absence, without which the writing of this book would have been even more delayed than it has been already. To Professor Bernard Knox and the Center for Hellenic Studies in Washington, DC, I owe more than I can say for their welcome, and for a year spent in idyllic surroundings and an atmosphere of friendliness and critical scholarship which makes an incalculable contribution to any period of research. All the Junior Fellows of 1970–71 have contributed something to the ideas behind this book; Oliver Taplin, in particular, read two sections in draft, and made many useful suggestions. Professor Knox himself also read sections in draft, and his penetrating and kindly acumen saved me from many errors and suggested many fruitful lines of development.

To Professor M. I. Finley I owe not merely the original suggestion of the topic but also a great deal for guidance and patience throughout the long period of gestation. Professor A. Andrewes read the book in typescript, and his detailed and generous criticism was invaluable. John Roberts also read the typescript, and contributed much; I am grateful to him, as also to Professor G. Bowersock for discussion of the *Constitution of the Athenians*. For the faults which remain I am naturally responsible; they would have been many more but for the generous help which I have received.

My wife remains, as always, remarkably patient of my distractions in the midst of so many other calls on our time.

Radley College
September 1972   John M. Moore

PREFACE TO SECOND EDITION

In this second edition, I am glad to take the opportunity to correct some errors which crept into the first, and to take account of some of the work published since the book was first issued. I am grateful to friends and reviewers for kind and constructive comments which have contributed to this process.

November 1982   JMM

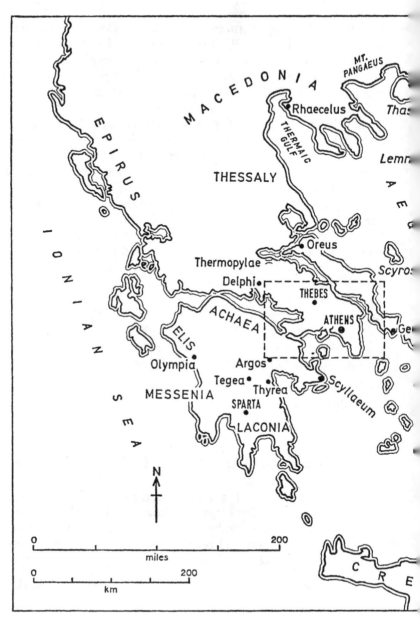

Map I. ANCIENT GREECE

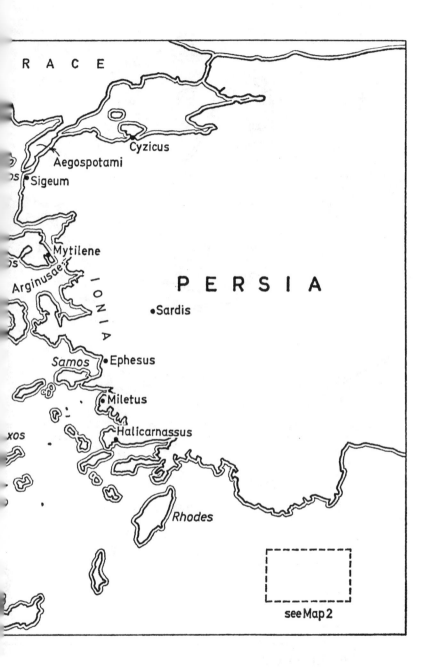

RACE

Cyzicus

Aegospotami

Sigeum

Mytilene

IONIA

Arginusae

PERSIA

•Sardis

Samos •Ephesus

•Miletus

Halicarnassus

Rhodes

see Map 2

Map 2. BOEOTIA AND ATTICA

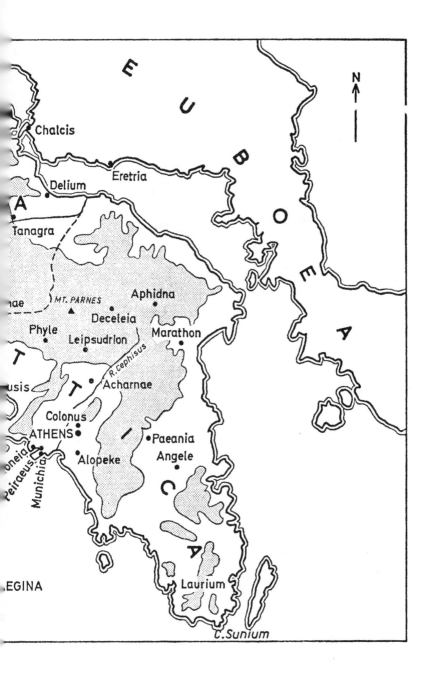

N

Chalcis

E U B O E A

Eretria

Delium

A

Tanagra

MT. PARNES ▲   Aphidna

nae

Phyle   Deceleia

Leipsudrion   Marathon

R.Cephisus

usis   T   Acharnae

Colonus

ATHENS

Alopeke   Paeania
Angele

oneia

Peiraeus

Munichia   C

A

EGINA   Laurium

C.Sunium

PART I

The Constitution of the Athenians
ascribed to
XENOPHON THE ORATOR

The Politeia of the Spartans
by
XENOPHON

The Boeotian Constitution
from
THE OXYRHYNCHUS HISTORIAN

The Constitution of the Athenians

INTRODUCTION

The *Constitution of the Athenians* was preserved in antiquity among the writings of the historian Xenophon, but it has long been accepted that he cannot have written it; the point was made originally by Demetrius of Magnesia in the first century BC. Apart from the obvious differences of style from the genuine works of Xenophon, the latest possible date which has been proposed for the composition of the treatise is about 415–12, at which time Xenophon was not yet grown up; a more likely date is some years earlier. The author has been almost universally referred to in English as the 'Old Oligarch'; the origin of this soubriquet is unknown, but the effect is unfortunate and prejudicial —it can appear cosy and condescending or contemptuous and condemnatory, depending on how it is read. The title preserved in the manuscripts, like the titles of other similar works, probably goes back to the Hellenistic libraries; it is unlikely to have originated with the author. Both the present work and Aristotle's *Constitution of Athens* are called 'Constitution of the Athenians' in the manuscripts; 'of the Athenians' would be the normal way for a Greek to refer to Athens in a context such as this. The traditional English title, *Constitution of Athens*, has been retained for Aristotle's work, and the present work referred to as the *Constitution of the Athenians* in order to make a distinction between the two for ease of reference, while retaining titles which are close to the Greek.

The treatise was not written in Athens. The author refers to Athens as 'there', and surely cannot include himself amongst those he condemns so strongly at I I,20; in only one section does he include himself among the Athenians by saying 'we'—otherwise he refers to 'the Athenians' or 'they'. His first paragraph makes it clear that he disapproves of the democratic constitution in Athens, and yet he shows an intimate understanding of many sides of life there. It appears therefore that the author was an Athenian of oligarchic sympathies living outside Athens; this lends point to his stated intention of demonstrating how well the Athenians have designed their constitution to survive, since he is, at least ostensibly, explaining the workings of Athens to those who were less familiar with the details than he, and therefore puzzled by what they took to be the surprising success of the Athenian constitution. All attempts to identify the author by name have been unconvincing, and it is not even certain that the work was ever 'published' in the sense of being given more than the most limited circulation in the fifth century. Indeed, its attribution to Xenophon suggests that it was not widely known at that time; if it had been, the name of the author would probably have been preserved, unless, of course, it had been circulated anonymously. It has been suggested that Xenophon inherited the treatise among his father's papers, and so it was eventually wrongly included among his own works after his death. The suggestion must remain pure hypothesis, but is not implausible in view of the known oligarchic sympathies of the family; similar documents circulated privately among dissidents at Athens under the democracy.* It is equally possible that Xenophon acquired the work during his long residence in the Peloponnese (c394–65).

The date of composition cannot be firmly fixed. It must have been after 446 because of the reference to the failure of Athenian policy in Boeotia (III,11); it is generally, though not universally, agreed that the passage about the impossibility of long overland expeditions (II,5) could not have been written after the expedition of Brasidas to Thrace in 424, which so manifestly disproved the assertion made there. Since specific historical events are mentioned only in III,11, it is not easy to be more precise. Proponents of an early date argue that the events referred to in Miletus were probably over by 443, and that it is remarkable to find no reference to the Samian revolt of 441 in III,11; it is not strictly parallel to the other events mentioned, but there is a point here. Those in favour of a later date argue that the work must have been written at a time when Athens' sea power was bringing great success, (e.g. II,2–7), during a war against a major land power with recurrent invasions of Attica and sea-borne reprisals (e.g. II,13–16). Further, they point out that the whole picture of Athens given by the author matches the period after the death of Pericles far better than the 440s, and is remarkably similar to the impression of those years which we get from Thucydides and Aristophanes. The discussion can obviously be applied to the Peloponnesian War situation, but it is very theoretical in tone and to my mind need not have been written in war time; such speculations could well have been current in the period immediately after the loss of the Athenian Land Empire, and the strategy envisaged is certainly implicit in Athenian thinking of the earlier period, not least in the building of the Long Walls (completed 456). However, on balance, the later date seems the more likely, and the years 425–4 the most probable within that period.†

It is not clear to what literary type the work should be ascribed. The opening is such that it could well be a fragment of a larger treatise,

* A. Lesky, *A History of Greek Literature*, 452.

† See also on II,2–6 below. For references to works with full discussion of dating and authorship, see the Bibliography; the argument accepted above is that of Forrest, who states the case fully and clearly.

though this is not a necessary conclusion. The structure is in some respects carefully thought out, and shows evidence of planning, in particular in the way in which the main argument is bracketed by almost identical sentences (I,1 and III,1). In other places the author repeats himself or splits what could have been a single, integral discussion between two widely separated passages, and the end of the work is surprisingly disjointed; it almost reads like a lecture (I–III,1), followed by answers to questions put to the speaker, in which he expands on points made before or amplifies the argument (III,1–13). Ostensibly the author addresses a hearer in the second person, and gives the impression that the hearer lives, or normally lives, in Sparta (I,11), but it is not at all clear that this is meant to be taken literally.

The *Constitution of the Athenians* is one of the earliest extant pieces of Greek prose which is complete or reasonably so. The style is simple and direct, and the transitions from one subject to another often harsh and sudden; there is no sign of the studied interest in antithesis or word order which became fashionable in the later fifth century under the influence of the Sophists. That is not to say that there is no Sophistic influence at all; one may see in the discussion of strategy in war time the effect of their interest in analytical thinking. However, the level of analysis is not very profound, and is at all times subject to the prejudices of the author. These perhaps show at their clearest at II,20, where he condemns as having criminal purposes anyone who is not of the common people but is willing to live under a democracy rather than an oligarchy. He must have known from his own experience that, while it was theoretically possible for any Greek to move to another city and live there, if he did so he had no hope of becoming a citizen, barring the most exceptional circumstances. Therefore he would be placed under very real disadvantages in his everyday life; these normally included heavier taxation and inability to go to law, own land or make any contract except through a citizen as intermediary. This important factor the author omitted, as did Socrates in the *Crito*, where the same subject is discussed at greater length and with greater insight. Further, not merely was it not a simple choice, but also it was a ridiculous and implausible slur to cast doubts on the motives of someone who was aristocratic and chose to live under a democracy. Did the author really believe, or expect his hearers to believe, that all the leading statesmen of Athens who were of the wealthier classes were 'preparing to do wrong' because 'it is easier to get away with being wicked under a democracy'? Such an allegation smacks of the wildest accusation of a modern election campaign.

Clearly, then, this work is an attempt by an Athenian exile to explain Athens to other Greeks; it may have been written early in the Peloponnesian War, possibly in the Peloponnese; any attempt to speculate further must be pure hypothesis.

Whatever the motives and exact time and place of composition, the work is of first-class importance as a historical source. The author is manifestly prejudiced, but because his prejudice is so manifest it is easy to identify it and make allowances accordingly. In analysing why the democracy at Athens is so successful he gives us an invaluable insight into its workings at or near its peak, for the author is in many ways shrewd and clear-sighted, and the comments which he makes illuminate not only the world of politics but also many facets of the everyday life of Athens. This is as valuable to us as it was inevitable for him. To an Athenian, whatever his political persuasion, politics formed a central and vital part of his whole life, as is shown most clearly in Pericles' Funeral Speech (Thucydides II, 35–46), particularly in the following excerpt: 'The same people are concerned with private and public affairs, and, despite their varied activities, have an adequate understanding of public affairs; for we alone hold that the man who takes no part in politics is not one who minds his own business, but a useless citizen' (40,2). In the speech and elsewhere Thucydides gives us his conception of the strength and greatness of Periclean democracy and why it worked; the *Constitution of the Athenians* gives us a picture of the same thing seen from a very different point of view.

It is not the duty of a translator to improve on his material, but rather to attempt to convey as faithfully as he can the content and tone of the original. The author of the *Constitution of the Athenians* had a rather turgid and repetitive style, and on occasions produced effects which are distinctly awkward to the English ear; I have attempted to reproduce this in my rendering, and at the same time to resist the temptation to introduce 'elegant variation' not justified by the original. There is one further point which complicates the task of translating this work: certain words, which had started as terms of approval or disapproval, came in the fifth century to have political overtones also, particularly in oligarchic circles; for example, the Greek words *chrestoi* and *poneroi* meant 'useful' and 'troublesome', and so 'good' and 'evil' respectively, but in oligarchic thought they also had the overtones of 'decent' and 'worthless', i.e. 'respectable people' and 'the masses' or 'the mob'. Therefore, when such words are used, the question arises of whether they are being used in their basic sense or with the developed political overtone; it may often be that both senses are there. In a recently published translation* the authors decided on a single rendering for each of these words, and used it whenever the word appeared. Such a practice not only leads to awkwardness on occasions, but is a misrepresentation of the original: it cannot be said that the political meaning was uniformly uppermost in the author's mind whenever he used such words, particularly in the case of *demos* ('the people', 'democracy' or 'the mob'). I have therefore decided on a particular rendering for each of these words when it appears to me that the political meaning is dominant in the author's mind, but have not felt bound to use it whenever the word appears.

Because of the somewhat disjointed structure of the work, the discussion of the *Constitution of the Athenians* has been divided into two sections:

* *The Old Oligarch*, Lactor 2 (London Association of Classical Teachers).

before the text will be found an analysis of the main themes of the work, with references to the relevant sections, while after it there is a commentary explaining points of detail.

Three Greek words have been transliterated: *strategos* (plural *-oi*) meaning 'general', but with wider connotations because the holders of the post were the nearest Athens had to chief ministers at this time; *Boule*, the Council of 500 members who supervised the day-to-day administration, and prepared all business for the *Ekklesia*, the assembly of all adult male Athenian citizens. Note that 'metic' is the technical term for a Greek residing in a state other than that of which he was a citizen; 'hoplite' is the name for the heavily-armed foot-soldier who formed the backbone of Greek armies in the fifth century; a trierarch commanded and maintained at his own expense a trireme in the Athenian navy.

THE MAIN TOPICS

INTRODUCTION

I,1   In the opening paragraph the author states his position
bluntly: he disapproves of the Athenian democracy because
by its very nature it ensures that the common people are more
powerful than the 'respectable' citizens, by which he means
those of oligarchic sympathies and almost certainly also of
'upper class' families. That the oligarchs were numerically
very much in the minority and politically so weak as to be of
very little consequence for almost all the period of Athens'
greatness is shown by the fact that an oligarchic government
held power in Athens only twice in the period 508–322: in
411–10 under the pressure of the Sicilian disaster, and in
404–3 on the orders of the victorious Spartans. Both regimes
were imposed, and neither lasted more than a few months.
This illuminates the second section of his opening statement,
'how well they preserve their constitution'. This must be a
prejudiced remark since nearly two centuries of history
demonstrate that it was the wish of an overwhelming majority
of Athenians to live under a democracy.

         The same prejudice may be amply illustrated at many
I,13–15 other points, notably in the author's approach to cultural and
III,10   athletic activities, and his discussion of the relation between
the Athenian people and the wealthy class among the allies.
However, despite his prejudice, he is aware of the success of
Athens and of the realities of the political situation, as is
shown by the end of the opening paragraph; he recognises the
skill of the Athenians and the fact that they handle affairs
well. It is not easy to decide exactly what he refers to as
'affairs for which the other Greeks criticise them'. It is less
likely to refer to the acquisition and maintenance of Athenian
domination in the Delian League, in which they were
manifestly successful at the time of writing (whatever date is
accepted for the work) than to the day-to-day administration
of Athens. If so, this again is a misleading generalisation;
there were other democracies in Greece, notably in Argos and
Syracuse, whose supporters presumably approved of the
Athenian constitution.

ATHENIAN POLITICS

1,2–9 The discussion of the details of the democratic constitution opens with the earliest known version of the principle later stated by Aristotle, that 'the class that does the fighting is the most powerful' (*Politics*, 1279 b 3; cf. 1321 a 5–14); the fleet is the basis of Athens' power rather than the hoplites, and the common people man the fleet.

The paragraph raises a most important point of theory in the radical Athenian democracy. As many offices as possible were filled by those selected by lot on the basis of rotation, the aim of which was that nobody should hold any office for a second time until all eligible citizens had held it once. To have any form of election involved 'aristocracy' in the Greek sense—the selection of the *best* men for the job—and this was not democratic. Therefore office holders were selected by lot from the body of those who were eligible and put themselves forward; most offices could be held only once during a man's life. Since a large number of Athenians were not wealthy enough to be able to devote a significant part of their time to politics without losing an unacceptable proportion of their income, a system of so-called 'pay' for office was introduced; this would be more accurately described as 'compensation for loss of earnings' to avoid any suggestion that a man could earn a living by doing what was regarded as his duty as a citizen. Thus the Athenians equalised as nearly as was possible every individual's chance of playing his part in the running of the state. The details of those who received 'pay' for office are set out in Aristotle's *Constitution of Athens*, XXIV,3 and LXII,2, the latter applying to the late fourth century.

At the same time, the Athenians recognised that certain posts, notably that of *strategos*, had to be held by experts; for obvious reasons, this principle was never questioned. How-
1,3 ever, the author casts the remainder of the paragraph in such a way as to insinuate that the populace did not attempt to hold such offices because there was no payment attached to them.

1,4–9 The author is now moving from sound factual description into the field of motives. He condemns the democrats as self-interested, while at the same time naïvely admitting that the upper classes, if given the power, would certainly organise things in their own interests at the expense of the common people. He has an arguable point when he says that an aristocratic constitution might produce a better city in some ways, but it would be at the expense of the essential element of democracy and equality which the majority want. The double meaning of some of the terms used affects the argument: the abstract noun translated as 'badness' in I,7 is from the same root as the adjective translated as 'a member of the mob' in I,6. This ambiguity of meaning has led to a confusion of thought, in that the author cannot see how a 'member of the mob', because of the 'bad' overtones of the word used, could contribute usefully to political discussion.

II,17–19 The theme is taken up again later, where it is alleged that democracies are less likely to keep their word or shoulder responsibility for their actions than oligarchies. The detailed argument is specious in that those directly responsible for any proposal could be as easily identified in Athens as in any oligarchy; it has a shred of truth in it only in so far as it is easier to disclaim responsibility as an anonymous member of a large voting body like the *Ekklesia* than it is in a small oligarchic government. Here, as elsewhere, the author suggests that the mass of Athenians 'hate' the 'respectable' classes, which is hardly born out by the facts: if they had done so, they could have persecuted and exiled them, a fate suffered by the aristocrats of numerous Greek cities. Further, the contribution to the greatness of Athens made by the wealthier classes, who were often also the more aristocratic, can perhaps best be seen in the fact that the *strategoi* were effectively the leaders of Athens from 487, and yet were never paid, although they must have been engaged on public affairs for most of their time while in office. There are also many records of wealthy men throughout the history of Athens willingly undertaking costly projects for the public benefit even when not forced to do so. The real picture is very different from the impression of almost deliberate persecution and exploitation which is a recurrent theme of the work, notably in the

I,13 discussions of the financing of cultural and athletic pursuits
I,14–15 and of relations with the upper classes in allied states. The suggestion might almost be made that fifth-century Athens was effectively an oligarchy between 508 and 429, so dominant was aristocratic leadership; the democratic answer to this would be that the final decisions were taken by the *Ekklesia*, and all magistrates had to account for their actions to the people. In the same way, the imputation of incompetence against the democrats can hardly be sustained in the light of history. Granted that the democracy made mistakes, nevertheless over a period of two hundred years the record of Athens under their guidance will bear comparison with that of any other Greek state.

Within this context of class prejudice are summarised the benefits which the ordinary people get from the democratic
I,3–4 constitution. Apart from 'pay' for office and political power in general (the attractiveness of which is clearly appreciated),
I,13 there is payment for taking part in cultural activities, choral

26

and otherwise, and for service in the fleet, the earnings and
1,16–18 sense of importance arising from the legal system of the
11,9–10 empire, the pleasures and profits from public buildings and
11,11–12 festivals, the financial benefits attendant on being an imperial
11,7–8 power, not to mention the gastronomic pleasures and
cosmopolitan nature of the culture which sprang from being
the centre of a widespread trading network. These are all
actual benefits resulting from Athens' position, but to imply
that the democracy was deliberately organised in order to
produce them for the common people is absurd, and even
more absurd is the suggestion that they were in part moti-
1,13 vated by an almost socialistic desire to redistribute wealth.

SOCIAL ATTITUDES

e.g. 1,5 On the whole the tone of the author is one of frustrated
superiority; he is convinced that he and his class are much
better qualified to govern than the democracy and morally
superior to its individual members, and yet without any hope
111,12 of achieving political power. He is perhaps surprised by the
success of the democracy himself, and ascribes it by implication
to cunning rather than wisdom.

In particular, the author is offended by the indiscipline of
1,10–12 the slaves and metics in Athens. The paragraph contains a
corrupt sentence, and is otherwise not altogether clear, but
1,10 the meaning appears to be as follows. First, slaves in Athens
are protected to an unusual degree by the law in that one
may not strike them; the result is that they behave arrogantly
('nor will a slave step aside for you'). The reason given is full
of class prejudice—so poor is the ordinary Athenian's dress
that it is impossible to distinguish him from a slave, and therefore one might strike an Athenian in error. Thus he casts a
slur on the ordinary Athenian, whereas he could equally well
have concluded from his next statement (that slaves are
allowed to live in luxury, and some in considerable magni-
ficence) that the lack of differentiation of dress sprang from
the relative wealth of the slaves rather than the poverty of
1,11 the free citizens. The second point is that in a naval state
slaves must work for hire. It is true that slaves cannot work
directly for an owner who is on foreign service in a trireme,
but no note is taken of the fact that a large number of the
slaves who worked for hire worked in the mines at Laurium
(see Xenophon, *Ways and Means* IV,4); they would have been
very badly off—but they were not the slaves one would see
in the streets.*

To install slaves in separate establishments with trades of
their own was probably one of the more lucrative methods of

* On the position and treatment of slaves in general, see Ehrenberg, *People*, 184ff.

27

getting a good return on the investment represented by the slave. If this system was to work, there had to be some incentive for the slave, which was provided by allowing him to keep his earnings beyond a certain sum which his owner took, and so eventually making it possible for him to buy his freedom. This arrangement arose from sound commercial sense, not the fact that Athens was a naval power. Inevitably in such a system some slaves would choose to use a part of their earnings to make life more comfortable while they were still slaves, and therefore might dress in a fashion no different from, perhaps even superior to, that of the lower-class Athenian citizen. A regime based on fear cannot be applied to such a situation, but the sea-based democracy had little to do with the behaviour of the slaves, except in so far as Athens' position encouraged some industries. The statement that fear

I,11 might induce a slave to 'spend some of his money' must presumably refer to the possibility of blackmail which arose when a slave had money; although the exact point that is being made is obscure, here is one of the many interesting sociological observations contained in this passage, for all its superficial prejudice.

I,12 The author then says that slave and citizen enjoy equal rights of free speech. He uses the term *isegoria*, which includes full rights to address the Ekklesia and take part in political life. This is obviously an overstatement, a deliberate exaggeration of the fact that slaves, perhaps as a result of their greater freedom if living in separate establishments, tended to be less servile than elsewhere. Finally, the discussion comes full circle to its starting-point, the metics, and correctly explains their relatively privileged position in Athens, though here again freedom of speech cannot be taken in the full sense of *isegoria*. Metics were free men, and the author's attitude to them is almost feudal. There were a large number of them in Athens, demonstrating that many people found it well worth their while to put up with inferior status and lack of political rights in order to have the compensating benefits. Presumably most of them were traders or skilled craftsmen.*

FESTIVALS

I,13 To the author, the Athenian festivals were either a cause
III,2,4,8 of expense to the rich or an interference with the administration of justice and the running of the state; also, by implica-
II,9–10 tion there were too many of them. Only once does he recognise in passing that they added something to the quality of life in Athens, and then in a context where he lays the

* On metics and their position, see also the Introduction, above, and Ehrenberg, *People*, 150ff.

main stress on the way in which the common people are getting something which they have not paid for. Nothing here of the glories of the temples, the drama, and the choruses, or of the Panathenaic procession so beautifully recorded in the Parthenon frieze. A Philistine indeed! Interestingly, Plutarch also in general followed the aristocratic tradition in describing these things (*Pericles* 11–14), but he was honest enough to admit and admire the artistic and cultural achievements of the Periclean age.

The statement that there are twice as many festivals in Athens as in other states sounds a typical exaggeration, but is factually accurate according to our sources. Maximus of Tyre made a comment in the second century AD which might be freely paraphrased as: 'All Attica stinks of incense.'

THE COURTS

Aristotle regarded control of the lawcourts as the key to control of the state (*Constitution of Athens*, IX), and the author III,8 of this treatise makes the same assumption implicitly at the end of the long passage dealing with delays in the transaction of business at Athens. The same point is made at 1,13, but 1,16–18 shortly afterwards he goes on to develop the theme that the courts are essential both in retaining control over the empire and in keeping this control in the hands of ordinary people. The points are well taken. The resentment caused by the imposition of Athenian justice on the allies, and the fact that they often had to come to Athens to receive it, are made clear in the defence of Athenian conduct which Thucydides puts into the mouth of the delegation at Sparta before the beginning of the Peloponnesian War (1,76–7), though Thucydides there offers a plausible justification of what they had done, while the present author offers a cynical list of the material benefits which flow from the practice.

Neither author really makes clear the distinction between civil and criminal justice. In civil cases it was normal for Athens to make treaty arrangements with her allies which put allied and Athenian citizens virtually on an equal footing. Cases would be decided either in Athens or in allied cities; it was normal to sue in the state of the defendant because it was then easier to execute judgment. Presumably this is what Thucydides refers to when he says: 'We are at a disadvantage in commercial cases affecting our allies' (1,77,1), and the 'disadvantage' refers to the fact that Athens was prepared for her citizens to be bound by decisions of courts other than her own. The implication is that such an attitude was unusual for a state when dealing with subject allies. Criminal cases, and cases involving death or loss of rights of citizenship, were increasingly referred to Athens, either for trial or for confirmation of sentence. Thucydides says: 'Although when we conduct trials at Athens we are bound by the same laws as they are, we are accused of a passion for litigation' (*ib.*), which glosses over the essential infringement of the autonomy of the allied states, and the possible bias involved in trying cases before an Athenian jury. However, the author of the *Constitution of the Athenians* is under no illusions about the

1,13 approach of an Athenian jury: 'In the courts too, they are as much interested in their own advantage as they are in justice.' Although this generalisation is not specifically applied to relations with the allies, it is instructive, particularly when compared with the long list of the benefits which

1,16–18 Athens derived from the fact that the allies had to come to Athens for cases to be tried.*

III,2–9 In the final section of the treatise the author returns to the subject of the courts from a different angle, discussing the multifarious business wihch came before them and the consequent delays. Disregarding the slightly utopian suggestion

III,6 that if judicial business could be transacted more efficiently crime would be prevented, the interesting point in this

III,7–8 discussion is the conclusion that any modification of the legal system would make the decisions of the courts much less just, and take away something from the democracy. Such a tribute from an opponent of democracy has illuminating implications for the standard of legal practice in oligarchic states, and

1,13 also presents an interesting contrast with the earlier statement that the Athenians are as concerned with their own interests as they are with justice in their courts.

THE WORKING OF ATHENIAN DEMOCRACY

III,1–9 The long passage dealing with the delays experienced in conducting business in Athens reads rather like an Appendix or the answer to a question. The author has rounded off the main discussion at III,1, but nothing has as yet been said of practice as opposed to theory, a subject raised in the opening lines of the work. The answer given to the objector is that there is just too much to be done for the democratic machine to handle it expeditiously, whether in politics, where he concentrates on the *Boule*, or in the courts. In addition, there are

III,2 a large number of religious festivals, which, as was normal, prevent the transaction of all but emergency public business.

III,8 There are twice as many festivals as in other states, and this impedes the administration of justice in particular, but even if the number were drastically reduced, they still could not

III,3 keep up with the pressure of business. In a parenthesis there

---

* For further details, see G. E. M. de Ste. Croix, 'Notes on Jurisdiction in the Athenian Empire', *CQ* NS 11 (1961), 94–111 and 268–80.

is the admission that bribery plays its part—it would be surprising if it did not—but even unlimited bribery would not solve the problem. Throughout the passage the administrative and judicial sides are interwoven; while this is to a certain extent comprehensible because so much of the *Boule's* business was either quasi-judicial or led to judicial hearings, none the less this paragraph is not as clear as it might be. It looks rather as if the points were put down just as they

III,5 occurred to the writer; a particular example is the afterthought about the tribute. When disentangled, the section gives a good summary list of the main duties of the *Boule*, and shows why it was so overburdened that it was always behind schedule. Similarly, it refers to the main administrative

III,8 matters which led to trials. Finally he comes round again to his starting-point with the conclusion that you could not change anything significantly without radically affecting the democracy.

III,12–13 Almost as an afterthought comes the final paragraph, on the question of the disfranchised. Whereas III,1–9 appear to be the answer to the sort of question which an oligarch might have asked, this paragraph begins with a question which is either that of a convinced democrat who thinks that the Athenian judicial system could do no wrong, or else is heavily ironic. However this may be, the author makes an important amplification of his main thesis: not only is Athenian democracy well designed to preserve the democratic system internally, but also there is no hope of fostering a successful revolt from outside based on people who have been disfranchised under circumstances which would give them a legitimate grievance, and who could therefore reasonably be expected to attract some support.

The Empire and Athens' Military Position

All Greeks paid lip service to the idea of freedom, and any state which established an empire was bound to interfere with the freedom of the member states. However, the Greek idea of the highest form of freedom tacitly included the ruling of others, and thus implied an essential contradiction.* Therefore Thucydides can have the Corinthians accuse Athens of enslaving states (I,68,3), a plausible and useful allegation for stirring up feeling before a war, but the Athenians can reasonably reply that the Spartans would have done the same or worse if they had been in the same position as Athens (I,75,2–76,3), and point out that it has always been accepted in practice that the weaker will be controlled by the stronger (I,76,2). The imperial power may be hated; this is not,

---

* Thucydides VIII,68,4.

however, a good reason for abandoning an empire, but, if anything, for keeping it (Pericles in Thucydides II,63,2, and Cleon in Thucydides III,37,2). The author of the *Constitution of the Athenians* appears to accept this view completely. He may attack a good deal of what Athens does in administering eg I, her empire, but he never questions the right of Athens to have 14–18 an empire at all. This basic assumption underlies his whole discussion of the way in which the empire is run and the strategic position of Athens in time of war.

His theme in discussing the empire is the same as it is in the rest of the work: the efficiency with which the democracy does what is necessary to maintain its position. The most offensive thing to him is the way in which, in the allied states, I,14–15 the upper classes are legally and financially oppressed, and III,10–11 the Athenian people back the common people in times of political strife. An example of the harrying of the rich and of the techniques employed is to be seen in Aristophanes, *Peace* 639ff: 'Then they [the speakers in the *Ekklesia*] would harass the substantial and rich men among the allies, alleging a leaning towards Brasidas [i.e. treachery], and you would tear the man apart like a pack of little hounds.' A similar theme may be seen throughout the *Knights*, though there Aristophanes is more concerned with the position of the upper classes in Athens itself. The accusation levelled here at the democracy is, no doubt, reasonably well founded, and cases of such oppression must have been more common during the Peloponnesian War, particularly towards the end of it, when the general leaning of the wealthy towards a more oligarchic type of constitution would naturally lead to suspicions of treachery. Thucydides once takes a uniquely contradictory point of view at VIII,48,6, where he blames the upper class at Athens for oppression, and credits the people with defending the oppressed in the empire; the present work adopts a more conventional line.

However, the author does less than full justice to the Athenian approach, at least in the earlier period of the Delian League. There is no evidence that Athens interfered in the internal affairs of allied states unless factional strife inside a city threatened its stability, and therefore its continued useful membership. In such cases the Athenians did tend to favour the establishment of democratic rather than oligarchic governments, for the sound practical reason that a democratic regime established by Athens was more likely to remain loyal to the Athenian democracy, since it could count on support should the oligarchs try to seize power, whereas an oligarchic faction tended to look naturally to the Spartans or Persia. Miletus had an oligarchic constitution which remained undisturbed until there was political strife there in 454–3, and an inscription shows that after the first revolt was quelled they were left under a form of controlled oligarchy; it was only after a second revolt that the oligarchic leaders were expelled, probably in about 443.* Samos did not have a democracy imposed on her until after the revolt of 441–0, but the democracy then remained loyal even during the actual siege of Athens in 404. Thus, while the statements made in this passage are strictly true, they are only one side of the picture; there is at least some truth in the view expressed by Lysias in the fourth century (*Funeral Speech* 55–6): 'The Athenians ruled the sea for seventy years, and saved their allies from faction fighting; they did not require the masses to yield to the dominance of the few, but compelled all to live on terms of equality . . . and they did not make their allies weak but strong.' Thucydides makes his Athenian speaker claim that Athens was worthy of her empire and ruled it well.

1,16–18   Equally, while there is no question that some allied delegates were humiliated when they had to appear in court or as ambassadors to Athens, it is hard to believe that the empire would have remained relatively peaceful and loyal for so long if the picture had always been as black as it is painted in 1,16–18. Ideally, no doubt, the allies would have wished to be free and fully independent, but granted the proximity of Persia and the economic benefits of membership, it is probable that the majority were reasonably content to tolerate their position. The 'hostility' referred to was presumably mainly that of the oligarchic and wealthy classes in the allied cities, on whom the main burden of the tribute would have fallen. The author of the *Constitution of the Athenians* would naturally have been in touch with them; it is too often forgotten that such people made friendships which were not limited by national boundaries, the best example perhaps being the friendship between the Spartan king, Archidamus and both Pericles and (apparently) Thucydides the son of Melesias (Thucydides II, 13, 1; Plutarch, *Pericles* 8).

II,1   The general discussion of Athens' military position opens with a brief look at land forces. The exact interpretation of this passage is a matter of dispute, but the rendering given makes a sound observation which, if anything, underestimates the effectiveness of the Athenian land forces. They were not in the same class as the Spartans, but man for man could hold their own with many of the armies of Greece. Since Athens' power rested mainly on her control of the sea, it was wise to put the main effort into the fleet. The chief function of the

---

* See Barron, 'Milesian Politics and Athenian Propaganda', *JHS* 82 (1962), 1–6.

THE CONSTITUTION OF THE ATHENIANS

Athenian army, according to the author, was to deal with recalcitrant allies, and Athens was certainly a match for them individually by land. However, this accurate assessment led the author to a less effective second point. It is true that it

II,2 would be difficult for the islanders to concentrate their *land* forces, and that if they did so supplies could pose a problem, but he takes no account of the threat of a combined allied *navy*, or for that matter, of a combined effort by land and sea, when the allied naval forces would have been strong enough to cause Athens some concern, and could cover the supply routes for a combined army. This, however, is an assessment as theoretical as the analysis of the author. In fact, Athens' allies did not work together in this way in the Peloponnesian War, and revolts did not threaten over a wide area until after the Syracuse disaster; then it was the presence of a strong Peloponnesian fleet which provided the focus, not a combination of dissident allies. Something nearer to such a combined effort may be seen in the collapse of the Second Athenian Confederacy (357-5).

II,2-6; In this context, the author launches into an assessment of
13 the wider strategic implications of Athens' position, and sums up well the advantages of a sea power as opposed to a land power in Greece. Perhaps Themistocles and Aristides were the first to appreciate this point, which was well demonstrated by the fact that Athens was willing to continue the war against Persia in 478/7 while Sparta was not. The author fails to note one great limitation on the freedom of movement of a fleet: a trireme, as opposed to a merchant ship, had to stop for the night; it had not the room to carry food and water for more than a day or two, the endurance of a crew rowing was limited, and there was no space on board for them to sleep. Therefore, for any long voyage, they had to have either friendly or neutral staging posts, or at the least an area devoid of hostile troops, so that they could beach their ships and make camp.*

II,11-12 The commercial strength of Athens is discussed next, but
cf. II,3 the author only draws the conclusion that Athens has in it a weapon to hold down her empire and a unique means of amassing wealth. He does not display even the fairly basic consciousness of the importance of financial resources to Athens in time of war which is shown by Thucydides (II,13), still less the sort of budgetary awareness which must have lain behind the management of Athens' finances in the period when Cleon was in the ascendant.

II,14-16 That Athens was a mainland city, not an island, was a basic

---

* See Thucydides VI,42,1 and Gomme, 'A forgotten factor of Greek Naval Strategy', *JHS*, 53 (1933), 16-24 (= *Essays in Greek History and Literature*, 190-203).

weakness in her position, and the advantages which would have followed from being an island are fully discussed. The only flaw is a slight imprecision about the terms used, in that the 'common people' in II,14 apparently must be the city dwellers since they stand to lose least if Attica is ravaged, and yet in II,16, where the subject is clearly the 'common people', the author considers the possibility of their losing property in raids; here he must be including the country dwellers, since those who lived in the city and went out of it to till their land would presumably have had very little to lose if they had 'deposited all their property on the islands'.

The position is discussed at length in Thucydides in various passages in Books I and II, particularly 1,140–4, II,13 and II,60–64; see especially 1,143,5: 'Just consider; if we were islanders, who could be more impregnable? Now we must behave as much as possible as if we were, abandoning our land and houses . . .' The analysis offered in the *Constitution of the Athenians* agrees in the main outline with that in Thucydides; however, again it gives only one side of the picture; as noted above, there is no consideration of the importance of financial resources, nor are the Long Walls specifically mentioned. The author makes the point that the produce of Attica is expendable, though not in the vivid phraseology of Pericles in Thucydides: 'Our (naval) power is not to be compared with the loss of homes and land, great though these losses should seem to you to be; you should not be upset, but rather regard them as a pleasure garden, a decorative luxury in comparison with your real power, and therefore disregard them' (II,62,3). The very building of the Long Walls indicated a strategy under which Athens was prepared to abandon Attica, and therefore rely on imported produce and such of her own livestock as she could move to nearby islands, but the assessment is not complete until the practicability of doing this is recognised and taken into consideration; with the Long Walls Athens was virtually impregnable as long as she controlled the sea. It is perhaps to be expected that the author should here follow the natural leanings of the land-owning hoplite or cavalry class to which he belongs; he not merely puts a little more stress on the position of Athens' hoplite force than Thucydides does, but also refrains from spelling out the logic which could lead to the ruin of the source of wealth of much of his own class. This is not, of course, because he cannot conceive of the common

II,16 people being responsible for such a thing—he makes it very clear that he can. Of its psychological effects neither he, nor Thucydides in his more theoretical passages, takes any account. The amount of persuasive power which Pericles is represented as having to use to induce the people to follow his policy consistently makes one suspect that, before the outbreak of the war, the idea was considered more amongst a relatively small circle than accepted by the common people as a whole, as is implied in II,16.

CONCLUSION

Here, then, we have a contrast to the eulogistic, idealised picture of Athens at her height painted by Thucydides in the relevant speeches in Books I and II. The author is thoroughly disillusioned, and not prepared to work within the system. The study is valuable because he does succeed in some measure in his stated aim of showing why the democracy was successful and wherein a contemporary opponent thought its strength lay. Thus we get a partial and prejudiced but highly illuminating picture of Athens.

THE CONSTITUTION OF THE
ATHENIANS

1 Now, in discussing the Athenian constitution, I cannot commend their present method of running the state, because in choosing it they preferred that the masses should do better than the respectable citizens; this, then, is my reason for not commending it. Since, however, they have made this choice, I will demonstrate how well they preserve their constitution and handle the other affairs for which the rest of the Greeks criticise them.

2 My first point is that it is right that the poor and the ordinary people there should have more power than the noble and the rich, because it is the ordinary people who man the fleet and bring the city her power; they provide the helmsmen, the boatswains, the junior officers, the look-outs and the shipwrights; it is these people who make the city powerful much more than the hoplites and the noble and respectable citizens. This being so, it seems just that all should share in public office by lot and by election, and that any citizen who wishes should be able

3 to speak in the Assembly. On the other hand, there are offices which bring safety to the whole people if they are in the hands of the right people, and danger if they are not; the people demand no share in these—they do not suppose that they ought to be able to cast lots for the post of *strategos* or commander of the cavalry, for they realise that they gain greater advantage from not holding these offices themselves but allowing the most capable to hold them. However, they are eager to hold any public office which brings pay or private profit.

4 Again, some people are surprised at the fact that in all fields they give more power to the masses, the poor and the common people than they do to the respectable

elements of society, but it will become clear that they preserve the democracy by doing precisely this. When the poor, the ordinary people and the lower classes flourish and increase in numbers, then the power of the democracy will be increased; if, however, the rich and the respectable flourish, the democrats increase the

5 strength of their opponents. Throughout the world the aristocracy are opposed to democracy, for they are naturally least liable to loss of self control and injustice and most meticulous in their regard for what is respectable, whereas the masses display extreme ignorance, indiscipline and wickedness, for poverty gives them a tendency towards the ignoble, and in some cases lack of money leads to their being uneducated and ignorant.

6   It may be objected that they ought not to grant each and every man the right of speaking in the *Ekklesia* and serving on the *Boule*, but only the ablest and best of them; however, in this also they are acting in their own best interests by allowing the mob also a voice. If none but the respectable spoke in the *Ekklesia* and the *Boule*, the result would benefit that class and harm the masses; as it is, anyone who wishes rises and speaks, and as a member of the mob he discovers what is to his own advantage and that of those like him.

7   But someone may say: 'How could such a man find out what was advantageous to himself and the common people?' The Athenians realise that this man, despite his ignorance and badness, brings them more advantage because he is well disposed to them than the ill-disposed respectable man would, despite his virtue and wisdom.

8 Such practices do not produce the best city, but they are the best way of preserving democracy. For the common people do not wish to be deprived of their rights in an admirably governed city, but to be free and to rule the city; they are not disturbed by inferior laws, for the common people get their strength and freedom from

9 what you define as inferior laws. If you are looking for an admirable code of laws, first you will find that the ablest draw them up in their own interest; secondly, the respectable will punish the masses, and will plan the

city's affairs and will not allow men who are mad to take part in planning or discussion or even sit in the *Ekklesia*. As a result of this excellent system the common people would very soon lose all their political rights.

10   Slaves and metics at Athens lead a singularly un-disciplined life; one may not strike them there, nor will a slave step aside for you. Let me explain the reason for this situation: if it were legal for a free man to strike a slave, a metic or a freedman, an Athenian would often have been struck under the mistaken impression that he was a slave, for the clothing of the common people there is in no way superior to that of the slaves and metics, nor is

11   their appearance. There is also good sense behind the apparently suprising fact that they allow slaves there to live in luxury, and some of them in considerable magni-ficence. In a state relying on naval power it is inevitable that slaves must work for hire so that we may take profits from what they earn, and they must be allowed to go free.* Where there are rich slaves it is no longer profitable for my slave to be afraid of you; in Sparta my slave would be afraid of you, but there, if your slave is afraid of me, he will probably spend some of his own money to free

12   himself from the danger. This, then, is why in the matter of free speech we have put slaves and free men on equal terms; we have also done the same for metics and citizens because the city needs metics because of the multiplicity of her industries and for her fleet; that is why we were right to establish freedom of speech for metics as well.

13   The practice of physical exercises and the pursuit of culture has been brought into disrepute by the common people as being undesirable because they realise that these accomplishments are beyond them.* However, for the staging of dramatic and choral festivals, the super-intending of the gymnasia and the games and the provision of triremes, they realise that it is the rich who pay, and the common people for whom such things are arranged and who serve in the triremes. At all events,

---

* Corruption of the text makes it impossible to be sure of the exact meaning of this sentence.

they think it right to receive pay for singing, running and dancing, and for sailing in the fleet so that they may have money and the rich may become poorer. In the courts too, they are as much interested in their own advantage as they are in justice.

14 As to their relation with their allies, it is clear that they sail out and bring charges against the respectable elements among them, as they seem to do,* and hate them. They realise that it is inevitable that an imperial power will be hated by its subjects, but that if the rich and respectable elements in the subject states are strong, the rule of the Athenian people will only last for a very brief period; that is why they disfranchise the respectable elements, and fine, exile and kill them, but support the masses. Respectable Athenians, however, protect the interests of the respectable people in the allied cities, realising that

15 it is always in their interests to do so. Some might maintain that the strength of Athens lies in the allies being wealthy enough to pay tax, but to the common people it seems more advantageous for individual Athenians to possess the wealth of their allies and for them to retain enough to live on, and to work without being in a position to plot.

16 There is a feeling that the Athenians are ill advised to compel their allies to sail to Athens for legal proceedings. In reply, the Athenians enumerate the resulting benefits for the Athenian people: first, the legal deposits finance state pay for the year; secondly, they control the allied cities while staying at home without the necessity of going on voyages, and in the lawcourts they support the democrats and destroy their opponents, while if each state held its trials in its own city, because of their hostility towards Athens they would ruin those of their own citizens who appeared to be particularly in favour

17 with the ordinary people of Athens. There are also other benefits which the Athenian people reap from the fact that cases involving the allies are heard at Athens: first, the 1 % tax levied in the Peiraeus brings in a greater

---

* This phrase is probably corrupt.

revenue; then, individuals who own rooms to let, a carriage, or have a slave for hire make a greater profit; thirdly, the heralds make more because of the visits of

18 the allies. In addition to this, if the allies did not come for trials, they would only respect those Athenians who go abroad—the *strategoi*, the trierarchs and the ambassadors; but as it is, each individual ally is compelled to flatter the common people of Athens, realising that, having come to Athens, the penalty or satisfaction that he receives at law depends solely upon the common people; such is the law at Athens. Therefore he is compelled to plead humbly in the courts and to seize people's hands as a suppliant as they enter. This situation has increased the subjection of the allies to the people of Athens.

19 Moreover, because the Athenians own property abroad and public duties take them abroad, they and their attendants have learnt to row almost without realising it; for it is inevitable that a man who goes on frequent voyages will take an oar, and learn nautical

20 terminology, and the same is true of his servant. Experience of voyages and practice makes them good helmsmen, some learning in smaller boats, others in merchantmen, and others graduating to triremes; the majority are competent rowers as soon as they board their ships because of previous practice throughout their lives.

II Their hoplite force, which seems to be the least effective arm at Athens, is based on the following principle: they realise that they are inferior to their enemies in skill and numbers, but compared with their tribute-paying allies they are the strongest by land as well as by sea, and they think that their hoplite force is

2 sufficient if they maintain this superiority. There is a further factor which happens to affect them: it is possible for small subject cities on the mainland to unite and form a single army, but in a sea empire it is not possible for those who are islanders to combine their forces, for the sea divides them, and their rulers control the sea. Even if it is possible for islanders to assemble unnoticed on one

3 island, they will die of starvation. Of the mainland

cities which Athens controls, the large ones are ruled by fear, the small by sheer necessity; there is no city which does not need to import or export something, but this will not be possible unless they submit to those who control the sea.

4   Further, it is possible for the rulers of the sea to do what land powers cannot always do; they can ravage the land of more powerful states. They can sail along the coast to an area where the enemy forces are few or non-existent, and if the emeny approach they can embark and sail away; in this way they get into less difficulty than those

5 operating on land. Then again, the rulers of the sea can sail as far as you like from their own land, but land powers cannot make lengthy expeditions from their own territory, for marching is slow, and it is not possible to take provisions for a long period when travelling on foot. Also, a land force must march through friendly territory or win a passage by force, but a naval force can disembark where it is stronger and not do so where it is not, but sail on until it reaches friendly territory or a less

6 powerful state. Further, the strongest land powers are badly affected when disease strikes their crops, but sea powers are not troubled, for the whole world is not affected simultaneously, and they can import from a prosperous area.

7   To turn to less important matters, because of their control of the sea, the Athenians have mingled with peoples in different areas and discovered various gastronomic luxuries; the specialities of Sicily, Italy, Cyprus, Egypt, Lydia, Pontus, the Peloponnese or any other area have all been brought back to Athens because of their

8 control of the sea. They hear all dialects, and pick one thing from one, another from another; the other Greeks tend to adhere to their own dialect and way of life and dress, but the Athenians have mingled elements from all Greeks and foreigners.

9   The common people realise that it is not possible for each of the poor to sacrifice, hold feasts and build shrines and to run a beautiful and great city, but they have found a way of having sacrifices, rites, festivals and

sanctuaries: they make frequent public sacrifices as a city, but it is the people who enjoy the feasts and to whom
10 the victims are allotted. There are some private gymnasia, baths and changing-rooms belonging to the rich, but the people have built many wrestling-places, changing-rooms and public baths for their own use, and the rabble get more benefit from them than the few who are well off.

11 They alone of Greeks and foreigners can be wealthy: where will a city rich in timber for ship-building dispose of its goods without the agreement of the rulers of the sea? If a city is wealthy in iron, copper or flax, where will it dispose of its goods without the consent of the rulers of the sea? But these are just what I need for ships — wood from one, iron from another, and copper, flax and
12 wax from others. In addition, exports to any city hostile to us will be forbidden on pain of being barred from the sea. Although I do nothing, I have all these products of the land because of the sea, while no other city has two of them; no city has both timber and flax, but where there is an abundance of flax the ground is level and treeless, nor do copper and iron come from the same city, nor any two or three of the other products from one place but one from one city, another from another.

13 In addition to this, every mainland state has either a projecting headland or an offshore island or a narrow strait where it is possible for those who control the sea to put in and harm those who dwell there.

14 There is one weakness in the Athenian position: as rulers of the sea, if they lived on an island, it would be open to them to harm their enemies if they wished while remaining themselves immune from devastation of their land or invasion as long as they controlled the sea; in the present situation the farmers and the wealthy Athenians are more inclined to make up to the enemy, but the common people live without fear and do no such thing because they know that none of their property will be
15 burnt or destroyed. In addition to this, if they lived on an island, they would also be freed from the fear of the city being betrayed by oligarchs, or the gates opened,

or the enemy being let in; for how could this happen if they lived on an island? Again, there would be no chance of anyone's staging a coup against the common people; in the present situation, if anyone planned a coup, he would do so in the hope of bringing in the city's enemies by land; if Athens were an island, this fear also
16 would be removed. Since it happens that the city was not founded on an island, they handle the situation as follows: they desposit all their property on islands, relying on their control of the sea, and they disregard any devastation of Attica, realising that if they allow themselves to be moved by this, they will be deprived of other greater benefits.

17 Further, it is essential for oligarchic cities to observe treaties and oaths; if they do not abide by agreements, or if injustice is committed, the names of those responsible are available in a small body. But when the whole people makes an agreement, it is possible for them to lay the blame on the man who spoke and the man who put it to the vote, and for the others to deny that they were present or approved of an agreement which they discover was made by the whole citizen body;* if it seems inadvisable for a decision to be followed, there are a thousand excuses available for not doing what they do not want to do. If a decision of the people turns out badly, they blame a few men acting against their interests, but if things go well, they take the credit for themselves.

18 They do not allow comedians to attack the people so that they may not be abused themselves; they encourage personal attacks if anyone wishes, knowing that the butts of comedy are not for the most part of the common people nor from the masses, but rich or noble or powerful; only a few of the poor, ordinary citizens are attacked in comedy, and they only because they meddle in everything or try to become too influential; therefore the people do not object even to the ridiculing of such men.

19 Therefore it is my view that the common people at

---

* Corruption of the text makes it impossible to be sure of the exact meaning of this sentence.

Athens know which citizens are respectable and which are wicked; realising that the latter are useful to them and help them, they like them despite their wickedness, but they tend to hate the respectable citizens. They do not think that their virtue exists for the common people's advantage but the opposite. On the other hand, there are some who are truly of the common people, but are
20 not by nature on the side of the common people. I do not blame the common people for their democracy, for anyone is to be pardoned for looking after his own interests; but a man who is not of the common people and chooses to live in a city that is ruled by a democracy rather than one with an oligarchy is preparing to do wrong, and realises that it is easier to get away with being wicked
III under a democracy than under an oligarchy. As far as the Athenian constitution is concerned, I do not commend its type; since they chose a democratic form of government, it seems to me that they preserve their democracy well in the manner which I have described.

I notice that people also find fault with the Athenians because there are occasions when it is impossible to get a matter dealt with by the *Boule* or the *Ekklesia* although one waits for a year. This happens at Athens solely because there is such pressure of business that it is not
2 possible to deal with everyone who raises a point. How could they do so when they have so many obligations? They celebrate more festivals than any other Greek city, during which there is even less possibility of transacting public business; they handle more public and private lawsuits and judicial investigations than the whole of the rest of mankind; the *Boule* has multifarious business to deal with concerning war, revenue, legislation, the day-to-day affairs of the city and matters affecting their allies, and has to receive the tribute and look after the dockyards and shrines. Is it remotely surprising if, with so many matters to deal with, they cannot settle every-
3 one's business? Some say that if you approach the *Boule* or the people with money, then things get considered. Now I would agree that money plays a considerable part in getting things done in Athens, and it would be even

more influential if more people employed it; however, I am absolutely sure that the city could not deal with all the requests that come before it, however much gold and
4 silver were offered. The courts are also involved if someone does not refit a ship or builds on public land; in addition, every year they have to settle disputes about the provision of choruses at the Dionysia, the Thargelia, the Panathenaia, the Promethia and the Hephaestia. Four hundred trierarchs are appointed every year, and they must judge any appeals which arise. Further, they must examine magistrates and decide on their conduct,
5 examine orphans, and appoint guards for prisoners. This, then, happens every year. They also have to decide cases of avoidance of military service when they arise, and any other crime which suddenly occurs, such as unusual violence or impiety. I am omitting a great deal of public business, but I have listed the most important items apart from the assessments of the tribute, which
6 generally occur every four years. Well then, ought one to suppose that all these cases ought not to be dealt with? If so, let someone suggest what ought to be omitted. If then, one must agree that all these matters have to be decided, the courts must sit throughout the year, since even now when they do sit throughout the year they cannot prevent crime because of the numbers involved.
7 Well then, someone will suggest that the courts ought to sit, but the juries ought to be smaller; however, it is inevitable that, unless they have only a few courts, there will then only be a few jurors in each, with the result that it will be easy to prepare oneself to handle a small jury and bribe them; the decision will be much less just.
8 In addition to this, one must consider the fact that the Athenians have to hold festivals, during which no trials can take place, and they have twice as many as other states. However, even if one were to assume for the sake of argument that they only held as many as the state which holds fewest, even then it would be impossible in my view for affairs at Athens to be arranged other than they are now, except for minor changes here and there; significant alterations cannot be made without taking

9 away something from the democracy. Many suggestions can be made for improving the constitution, but it is not easy to find satisfactory ways of improving it while preserving the democracy intact, except, as I have just said, for minor changes.

10 There seems to be a further way in which the Athenians are ill advised, in that they support the lower classes in cities involved in civil strife. There is, however, a reason for what they do: if they supported the more reputable citizens, they would not be supporting those with the same views as their own, for there is no city where the aristocrats are well disposed to the common people, but in each city the lowest element is well disposed to them. After all, like favours like; therefore the Athenians support those sympathetic to themselves.

11 Whenever they tried to support the aristocrats it was not to their advantage; it was not long before the people were enslaved in Boeotia, and when they supported the aristocrats in Miletus, within a short time they revolted and massacred the common people; again, when they supported the Spartans instead of the Messenians, within a short time the Spartans had overcome the Messenians and were at war with the Athenians.

12 It might be suggested that nobody has in fact been unjustly deprived of his citizenship at Athens; it is my view that there have been some cases, but not many. However, it would need a considerable number to launch an attack on the democracy at Athens; since this is so, one must not consider those who have been justly disfranchised, but any who have lost their rights unjustly.

13 How could anyone suppose that the majority had been unjustly disfranchised in Athens where it is the common people who hold the magistracies? People lose their rights for offences during their tenure of magistracies or for saying or doing what is not just. From these considerations one must conclude that those who have been disfranchised at Athens pose no threat.

COMMENTARY

I,1 The words translated as 'masses' and 'respectable people' are *poneroi* and *chrestoi* respectively; there is no doubt that here they are meant to have their basic as well as their class connotations; see the Introduction above.

I,2 The natural ladder of promotion for a sailor is set out in Aristophanes *Knights* 541ff: 'He should first be an oarsman before assisting at the steering oars, then act as look-out in the bows and study the weather, and then finally steer by himself.' Note that not all will rise to the fighting fleet (the triremes), and compare with this passage I,20 and Thucydides I,143,1. There is a curious mixture of admiration and contempt in the attitude to what Aristotle called 'the trireme democracy' (*Politics* 1291 b 21ff).

I,5 The faith in the virtues of the aristocracy expressed here echoes the old-fashioned views of Pindar, and is probably typical of the generations brought up in the first half of the fifth century. Thucydides the son of Melesias (not the historian) was connected with the 'international' elite of aristocratic athletes for whom Pindar wrote; his father was one of the great wrestling masters of his age.

The strictures on the masses* are not borne out by historical evidence. The fleet displayed at least as good a sense of discipline as the army which was composed of the more upper-class hoplites and cavalry (Xenophon, *Memorabilia* III,v,18–21). Secondly, while poverty certainly made it more difficult for an Athenian to get an education, evidence suggests that in the fifth century the level of basic literacy for men was very high—probably at least as high as it is in the twentieth century AD, and certainly significantly higher than it was under the Roman Empire. Direct democracy depended for its efficient working on the citizens being able to read: both draft decrees and agenda, and decisions of the *Ekklesia* were published in writing. For a full discussion, see Harvey, 'Literacy in the Athenian Democracy', *REG* 79 (1966), 585–635.

I,8 *Eunomeisthai*, here rendered as 'admirably governed', comes from *eunomia*, another of the terms which came to have a prejudiced political

---

* cf. Herodotus III,81, below p. 136.

48

overtone. At first the word meant simply a situation where the laws were well conceived and obeyed, but this was early equated by political theorists with the Spartan system (as in Thucydides I,18,1), and hence the word acquired an oligarchic meaning; in this passage I suspect that both meanings are present in the author's mind.

I,10 There are many instances of cheeky and disobedient slaves in comedy, perhaps the best known of which are the slaves of Strepsiades in Aristophanes, *Clouds*, and Xanthias in his *Frogs*; presumably such slaves existed or the joke would have misfired, but allowances must always be made for comic exaggeration.

I,13 The opening sentence cannot be taken, as has been traditional, as a statement that there was a legislative ban on physical exercise and the pursuit of culture; this is not merely denied immediately below and in II,10, but is also contrary to all the evidence, e.g. Plato, *Crito* 50 d 9, where the Laws say that they had specifically required Socrates' father to teach him these subjects. The Greek must be taken, as in the translation, in the metaphorical sense of bringing such pursuits into disrepute. This then fits well, not merely with the facts, but also with the prejudices of the author. Athletics had always been especially the interest of the wealthier, since they had the leisure for it, and it is clear that the ordinary citizens of Athens not merely did not have time for it, but also despised it. The Knights of Aristophanes say 'do not grudge us our baths and oil' (580), that is, 'let us pursue our athletic interests unhindered', in the old way. One would expect the present author to resent any interference with the traditional way of doing things. Frisch sees a passage in the Funeral Speech as a covert answer to this attitude: 'They (the Spartans) from early childhood try to attain bravery by laborious training, while we live a more relaxed life . . .' (Frisch, 213; Thucydides II,39,1).

The list of duties undertaken by the rich includes some of the more common liturgies; the liturgy was a form of taxation of the wealthy in Athens, by which from time to time they were required to undertake certain public duties at their own expense. This had the advantage that they were personally involved: the trierarchs who maintained the triremes also sailed on them, and their own safety therefore depended, at least to some extent, on not 'economising'. Men doing liturgies also took a pride in what they did—the *choregoi* who had provided the winning choruses erected the monuments which commemorated the victories, and their names were prominent. Modern tax-payers have not become notorious for boasting of their contributions to the state! To provide a tragic chorus could well cost half a talent, a dithyramb distinctly more, and to maintain a trireme could cost nearly a talent; by comparison, a poor family could live on $\frac{1}{20}$th of a talent a year.* A

---

* For a discussion of liturgies, see J. K. Davies, 'Demosthenes on Liturgies; a note', *JHS* 87 (1967), 33–40, with my note, *JHS* 91 (1971), 140–41.

minimum expenditure was probably laid down for each liturgy, since some men boasted of having spent more than was required of them. This is symptomatic of the public spirit which was so evident in Athens in the fifth century, and directly disproves the contention of the *Constitution of the Athenians* that the population was divided into the poor, grasping masses and the rich who were universally exploited and therefore resentful. See also below on III,1–9.

I,14–15   The general questions raised about the relation between Athens and her allies in this section have been discussed above. On points of detail: it is hard to know how many Athenians went out 'to bring charges'; since they would be private individuals, they would not be included in Aristotle's 700 citizens serving abroad (*Constitution of Athens* XXIV,3 — and a suspect figure anyway). Aristophanes mentions a man who was clearly harassing the islanders by bringing charges against them (*Birds* 1422); these would have been criminal charges, and potential accusers would have been attracted by the rewards. A successful prosecutor received a proportion of the property of the condemned man; this would have tempted them to concentrate on the wealthy, and presumably to bring false charges on occasions. If such oppression was widespread, it is surprising that it is not mentioned in Thucydides, for example by the Mytileneans when they are justifying their revolt to the Peloponnesians (III,9–14).

The Greek words translated as 'pay tax' have normally been taken as referring to the tribute which the allies paid to Athens; this seems to me doubtful since the remainder of the paragraph implies that it is *not* in the interests of the Athenian people for them to be able to do whatever this phrase means — yet the allies have been paying tribute for years, the level was not extortionate, and it manifestly was in the interests of the ordinary Athenian for the tribute to continue to come in, as the author recognises throughout the treatise. The meaning might be ironic — 'If they go on extorting money like this, they will end up with no tribute, and so be weaker' — or, more likely, it may refer to the idea that Athens would be stronger if she left the wealthy citizens with enough money to be able to pay some extra tax in a crisis, perhaps along the lines of the *eisphora*, a capital levy which was a source of revenue by no means confined to Athens.

I,16   'The legal deposits finance state pay for the year.' This cannot be so: while the figure of 150 talents a year given by Aristophanes (*Wasps* 663) for the pay of the jurors alone must be rejected as a deliberate exaggeration to suit the context, none the less the total for them must have been in the region of 60 talents, and for all state pay perhaps 100+ talents. Such a sum could not be raised from the deposits, relatively small sums paid before a civil case which went to the state after its conclusion. Since the deposit was only 30 drachmae in a major case involving 1,000 to 10,000 drachmae, only a proportion of the jurors' pay could possibly have been raised in this way: to raise 60 talents would require 12,000 cases with at least 1,000 drachmae at stake in each case.

Behind this paragraph lies the implicit accusation that the Athenian democracy was parasitic on the empire. The internal revenue of Athens in 431 was probably about 400 talents a year, or possibly even 540; by 422 it had reached about 800 talents (*Wasps* 660); 400 talents was more than enough to cover all internal expenditure and significant expenses on the fleet. In the early fourth century, when Athens had no empire, she not merely continued all payments made in the fifth century, but also added a new and expensive charge, payment for attendance at the *Ekklesia*. (For the figures, see Gomme, *Commentary* II,26–33, and Jones, *Athenian Democracy* 5f.) Athens, of course, profited considerably from having an empire, but these figures suggest that the holding of an empire was not an essential prerequisite for financing the democracy in the Athenian manner. On the other hand, no other city is known to have had a system of pay for office, and it can be shown that the Syracusan democracy did not. It is at least open to question whether Athens would have instituted such a system had she not had the significant extra income which came from the empire; once the system was established, it was naturally continued.

I,17–18 We do not know on what this 1% tax in the Peiraeus was levied. The hiring out of carriages and of slaves, here regarded as similar operations, should be compared with I,11, where the author was interested in a very different side of slavery. The point made about the allies' respect for the common people is a sound one—the officials listed who went abroad tended to be from the more well-to-do classes.

The way in which jurors were normally flattered is described by Aristophanes (*Wasps* 550ff), and even allowing for comic exaggeration, it bears out the point made here: 'Is anyone more to be envied and congratulated than a juror today? . . . As soon as I creep out of bed, I find great tall men waiting for me at the entrance. As soon as I approach, a man thrusts into my hand his own delicate fingers which have dipped into the public purse. They beg and they bow, they whine and they plead: "Pity me, good sir, if ever you made something on the side when in office or running the mess on foreign expeditions." He wouldn't have known me from Adam if it hadn't been for his previous acquittal!' Forensic speeches surviving from the fourth century suggest that all methods of exciting pity were used in order to win one's case, and Plato's *Apology* shows that they were normal and expected (34 b–35 d). This is an interesting comment on the point made in III,7–8 that any change in the system would be to the detriment of justice.

I,19–20 This is a curious paragraph. The property referred to may be private holdings or land allocated to cleruchs (settlers who were sent out officially by Athens to land confiscated abroad but retained Athenian citizenship); the attendants will have been slaves, whose presence is taken as normal. The contrast being drawn is between a naturally seafaring city and others—Athenian crews still had to be trained for naval warfare, but they started with the enormous initial advantage of having 'pottered about in boats' since they were children, and many had widened their experience as adults. The naval policy of Athens, however, was not an accident, as the author implies—presumably only semi-seriously. See also above, I,2 note.

II,2-6 For the main ideas, see the discussion above. The whole passage is couched in very general terms; it is not essential to see a reference here to the synoecism of Olynthus in 432, still less to the revolt of Mytilene in 428, nor must the discussion of the possibility of sea raiding (II,4) be referred either to the expeditions of Pericles in 431 and 430, or to the Pylos affair in 425. They may have been in the author's mind, but this seems to be an abstract discussion; hence the generalised form in which it is presented. On the other hand, it is surprising that II,6 could have been written after the plague had struck Athens in 430-29 and 427; after such a catastrophe, it is remarkable to discuss disease striking crops and make no mention of human disease, particularly as the Athenians must have been uncomfortably conscious of the fact that the plague struck them and not their enemies; the average man would have been likely to suspect some form of divine punishment in so selective an epidemic.

The fact that all Greek states relied on some import or other, and that this strengthened Athens' position was noted also by Thucydides (I,120,2). It is a little surprising to find no mention here or elsewhere in the work of the importation of corn to Attica, which had been essential to her survival for some considerable time. Here was a potential weakness in her position, but, as in his discussion of the military threat from the allies, the author does not anticipate a serious challenge to Athens' naval supremacy, and therefore sees no possibility of a blockade being used against her.

II,7-8 No doubt the central position of Athens, and even more of the port of the Peiraeus, must have made them cosmopolitan centres, resulting inevitably in the introduction of foreign foods and the adoption of words from other languages. On luxury foods imported, which included almonds, scallops and silphium, see French, *The Growth of the Athenian Economy*, 122ff, Knorringa, *Emporos*, 42ff; 132ff, and Ehrenberg, *People*, 319ff. The addition of foreign words to Attic is likely, but evidence is lacking; it is probable that the pure Attic of literature differed considerably from the language spoken around the docks of the Peiraeus, and it was the latter which included foreign loan-words. This would provide a social, as well as a purist, reason for the author to object to what was happening. However, it is hardly sense to imply that these changes were the result of deliberate policy on the part of the common people. Changes of dress were commented on by Thucydides (I,6,3-4), and also Aristophanes (*Clouds* 961-1104); the latter provides a mass of information on the contrast between new and old ways of life.

Surprisingly absent from II,7–8 is any real condemnation of the changes; it can only be read into the Greek word *barbaroi*, translated as 'foreigners' above, and I doubt whether it is strong there.

II,9–10 This paragraph is very awkwardly inserted here, particularly as the author returns to the theme of the benefits of being a maritime power at II,11; it would be much better placed in association with I,13. Further, the thought is not very clear or logical. However, there is nothing to suggest that it should be moved to another context beyond the awkwardness of its present position, and this is probably an indication of the author's uncertain grasp of structure rather than a fault in the transmission of the work.

The feasts associated with all the major religious festivals were not merely an extra ornament in a display which was meant to impress, but also an important contribution to life, since it was probably only at such feasts that the poorer citizens ate meat. The sacrificial victims were distributed and cooked, as the gods conveniently required only the totally inedible sections to be burnt in the actual sacrifice. The connexion between this passage and I,13 makes clear again the point that the rich pay for the luxuries of the poor. On the other hand, the logic of II,10 has gone astray. Apparently it is meant to be another slur on the people's profiteering, but the innuendo gets lost. How could one take exception to the people getting more from the buildings which they have erected?

This passage is early evidence for public baths, although a little later Aristophanes mentions baths to which entrance could be obtained for a small fee; the Serangeion public bath at the Peiraeus was functioning by 422. Perhaps we should translate 'washing facilities' rather than 'public baths', for the great gymnasia (the Academy, the Lyceum and Cynosarges) all had changing accommodation attached, and there were simple washing arrangements for use after taking exercise attached early in the fifth century if not before.* Similarly, private houses probably had fairly elementary bathing arrangements until the fourth century, usually consisting of a pedestal basin and bowls for pouring water over the body. There is clearly an element of exaggeration in the *Constitution of the Athenians* here, and the passage should be treated with caution.

II,11–12 Here again, the generalised style leads to an overstatement of the strength of the Athenian position, and the thought is not absolutely accurate. While other cities 'have' raw materials in the sense that they are the producers of them, Athens only 'has' them by virtue of her control of the sea—she was no better off than most Greek cities in terms of natural resources in her own territory, with the important exception of the Laurium silver mines. Athens is in a position to get ship-building materials, and it is implied that her potential opponents

---

* See Wycherley, *How the Greeks built Cities*², 218, note 7.

are not. Thucydides also has this suggestion at 1,80–81, and the tone of the Corinthian speech at 1,121,3 is clearly over-optimistic. When it came to the test of war, shortage of raw materials does not appear in fact to have hampered the Peloponnesians, although Athens was in a good position to attack their communications with all the main timber-producing areas of the Greek world, Thrace, south Italy, Cilicia and Cyprus. It should be noted that Cyprus exported both copper and iron in the Classical period; the author presumably disregards this in order not to spoil the effect of the contrast which he is drawing. Equally, using a blockade against the Peloponnese was clearly a sound possibility, and that it could be effective is shown by the aftermath of the Megarian decrees; presumably Aristophanes' picture of a starving Megarian must have some basis of fact behind the comedy (*Acharnians* 729ff). However, the Peloponnese in general did not turn out to be as vulnerable in this way as the author of the *Constitution of the Athenians* expected, nor does he take account of the opposite possibility, a blockade of Athenian corn imports. As so often in the treatise, these are theoretical assessments which have not been tested; the phrasing makes this clear when it discusses cities which are 'hostile', that is rivals of Athens; the Greek does not imply that they are actually at war.

Frisch argues from this passage and others that the surprising enthusiasm shown by the author for the Athenian navy, and the detailed knowledge he has of its functioning, suggest strongly that he was an ex naval officer—a trierarch or even *strategos*.

II,14–16 The prevailing tone of confidence in II,16 is in marked contrast to the account, presumably first-hand, given by Thucydides of the state of Athens as soon as the first Spartan invasion took place in 431: 'The removal was hard for them to tolerate because the majority had always lived in the country' (II,14,2; cf. 16,1); 'When they saw the (Spartan) army only seven or eight miles from the city, at Acharnae, it was intolerable; they saw their own land being devastated, which the younger men had never seen, and their elders only during the Persian invasion; this seemed a terrible thing . . . , and the whole city was infuriated and angry with Pericles, forgetting all his previous advice' (II,21,2–3). Compare the implacable anger of the Acharnians as portrayed by Aristophanes in the play of that name, particularly lines 180–5, 230–2. In addition, Thucydides shows that the implication of II,14 that the common people (used in a different sense from that of II,16) will lose nothing in an invasion is not a tenable point of view. See Ehrenberg, *People*, 136ff.

Similarly, the chances of oligarchic treachery cannot have been very high, as is implied throughout the *Constitution of the Athenians*, particularly in III,12–13. The discussion is again pure theorising, and is only slightly impaired by the intrusion of the author's favourite distinction between the attitudes of the wealthy and the common people, which will not fit easily into the argument.

II,17 The transition to this paragraph is very abrupt, and the argument specious, as shown above. It is not possible to draw any useful distinction in relative political virtue between democracies and oligarchies in Greece. However, the author has indirectly hit upon an important psychological point; in a direct democracy it is not logical to blame 'the government' or 'them' for a disaster, as one can in a modern state; any active participant in politics must feel partially responsible, which can be a very considerable strain—hence hostility to the authors of disastrous decisions, and the search for scapegoats, for example after the failure of the Sicilian expedition (Thucydides VIII,1,1).

II,18 Some scholars have seen in this passage a reference to a specific law banning attacks on 'the people' in comedy, but this is not necessary linguistically, and poses serious problems historically. No connection need be seen either with the decree of 440 (repealed in 437) which restricted some of the freedom of criticism of comic writing, or with the personification of 'the People' in Aristophanes, *Knights* (produced in 424). The decree of 440 was apparently connected with the revolt of Samos, and aimed at restricting critical comment on the handling of the empire at a time when relations were strained; one must not forget that comedies were performed at the Great Dionysia, and that the allies' representatives, and probably many tourists, were present in the theatre. The point the author is in fact making here is that the people disliked being abused as a body; this contrasts well with the preceding remark, where the people 'take the credit', and should not be read as anything but a typically cynical remark. In general, Athenians reacted with great tolerance to comedy; individuals faced some biting criticism, but evidence suggests that on the whole they took it in good part. The audience clearly distinguished between comedy and real life: they could award first prize to the *Knights*, a bitter attack on Cleon, and still elect him *strategos* for the next year.

II,19-20 The aristocratic prejudice against the people shows again here, in particular in the allegation that the people suspect those who are respectable because of their virtue. The ironic disclaimer that the author 'does not blame the people' for their democracy sums up his attitude well as he nears the end of his main discourse. However, the facts do not bear him out, since many wealthy men and many aristocrats had a distinguished place in the history of Athens throughout the fifth century. Similarly, the imputation of sinister motives to any wealthy man who chooses to live in a democracy is absurdly prejudiced.* Interestingly, Plutarch has a similar passage: 'Pericles went over to the democratic side, choosing to support the poor and the masses, instead of the rich oligarchs; this was against his natural

---

* But see Aristophanes, *Knights* 864ff where it is suggested that profiteering is easier under a democracy.

inclination which was not remotely democratic' (*Pericles* 7). There is probably some truth in the tradition that Pericles was aloof, but there is no need to ascribe base motives to his conduct, or that of others in a similar position. See also the Introduction, above.

III,1 With this first sentence, the author comes full circle to an almost exact repetition of his opening, thus marking the end of the main part of the treatise.

III,1–9 Here the author fulfils the undertaking of 1,1 to discuss the actions of the Athenians, as opposed to their constitution. However, as noted above, this is a curiously involved and unsatisfactory passage, in which are woven together three points, all of which spring from the observation that the transaction of public business is undesirably slow; they are the mass of political and legal business which has to be handled, and the fact that Athens celebrates a very large number of festivals, during which virtually nothing can be done. The nearest thing to a structure in the passage is that the author lists the topics in the order: festivals, courts, administration, and then discusses them in reverse order; this is not, however, uniform.

The qualification 'there are occasions when' does a great deal to soften the impact of the discussion, and it remains on an almost consistently objective plane until the end. The author passes rapidly over the main fields of responsibility of the *Boule* with the one serious omission of the preparation of business for the *Ekklesia*, which is probably not included in the term translated as 'legislation'; if it is, the word is being used very freely (III,2). For the details of the various institutions and processes mentioned see Aristotle's *Constitution of Athens* XLIII–XLIX. The omission of the *Ekklesia* from this whole paragraph is not really surprising, important as it was in Athens; the main delays did not occur there.

The clear reference to bribery (III,3) comes in at the point where there is a transition from the administrative acts of the *Boule* to matters which come before the courts. The author opens with a number of possible disputes about liturgies (see above, 1,13 note), with the apparently trivial matter of building on public land intruding into the list; for details, again see Aristotle, *Constitution of Athens*, particularly LIII–LXIX. The question of refitting a ship refers to the duty of a trierarch to hand over a seaworthy vessel at the end of his year of office, exemption from doing so being granted only if he could prove that the damage was caused by storm, enemy action or some similar cause beyond his control; this could clearly give rise to extensive argument. The choruses referred to were dramatic (Lenaia, Dionysia), dithyrambic (Dionysia, Thargelia, Panathenaia), or 'heroic' (Promethia, Hephaestia). The Promethia belonged to a hero cult, and choral singing was an essential part of hero cults. The altar of Hephaestus stood close to that of Prometheus in the Academy, and as the divine craftsman he was assimilated to Prometheus. Hence it is right to take this passage at face value, and accept that there were choruses involved in both these last two festivals; they were celebrated in October/November, and both included torch races. The Dionysia referred to is presumably the Great, or City, Dionysia, celebrated in March/April; the Thargelia was celebrated in May/June in honour of Apollo, and involved both men's and boys' choruses. The Panathenaia was celebrated every year in July/August, and once every four years with extra splendour as the Great Panathenaia.

Finally amongst the liturgies comes the slightly surprising reference to 400 trierarchs. Thucydides lists 300 seaworthy triremes as Athens' naval strength, and Aristophanes confirms this; many editors have therefore wished to emend the figure given here. However, the manuscripts of Andocides, *On the Peace* 9 confirm the figure 400, and the explanation may perhaps be found in Thucydides himself: at II,24,2 he says: 'They set aside 100 triremes which were the best in the fleet every year and assigned trierarchs to them; they were not to be used for any purpose except in conjunction with the emergency reserve if it became necessary.' In other words, Thucydides is probably thinking in terms of 400 available hulls in the first year of the war, and also is familiar with the possibility of trierarchs not having to sail in the course of their year of office. Others have explained the figures by referring the extra 100 trierarchies to horse transports and other such ships; they existed, and are mentioned by Thucydides, but it is not certain that trierarchs were assigned to them. Thucydides VI,44,1 is by no means decisive on this point.

The final sentence of III,4 deals with questions which were mostly handled in the first instance by the *Boule*. The conduct of magistrates could be questioned once a month before the *Boule*, who also examined the credentials of their successors in office; similarly, they checked on the eligibility of the orphans who were maintained at the expense of the state; any disputes were decided by the courts. On guards for prisoners cf. Aristotle, *Constitution of Athens*, XXIV,3.

'This then happens every year' (III,5) is a sentence which carries very important implications: once a new *Boule* had entered office, all the administrative arrangements made by the preceding *Boule* had to be reviewed and confirmed or altered; there was no necessary continuity. The remainder of the section is a somewhat fragmentary list of other business dealt with by courts and the *Boule*, including a warning that the list is not intended to be exhaustive; hence there is no reason for attacking the author for leaving out this or that subject, least of all ostracism, as some have done, since it was a matter exclusively for the *Ekklesia*.

Having thus indicated the pressure of business, the author discusses its impact on Athens. The choice is clear: either the amount of business must be reduced, or the number of jurors involved in each case must be cut, or delays will have to be tolerated. The first is rejected by implication as impossible, the second because it would open the way to corruption, and the third is left as the only possibility consistent with maintaining the full democracy (III,8–9). The *Boule* appears to have slipped into the background, though they were as liable to delays as the courts. The author also takes account of the argument that a reduction in the number of festivals, and therefore of public holidays, might mend the situation; this was in practice unthinkable, and the author says that it would not solve the problem anyway. This whole section is perhaps the most impartial piece of analysis in the work, the impartiality showing particularly in the rejection of a reduction in the size of juries; evidence from Aristophanes and elsewhere shows that this was a standard aim of the more aristocratic or oligarchic factions, but the argument against it here is effective; compare Aristotle, *Constitution of Athens* XLI,2: 'a small number are more open to corruption by bribery or favours than a large.'

III,10–11 The general import of this passage has been discussed above; it fits well into the main stream of the author's attitude to the Athenian empire, but is awkwardly placed at this point in the work. It is noteworthy that this is the only section in which he mentions actual historical events as opposed to relying on generalisations. The events in Boeotia are to be placed somewhere in the period 457–47 during the Athenian Land Empire, though it is not easy to see exactly where Athens backed an oligarchic regime during that period. Gomme suggests that initially Athens supported democracies in the liberated towns of Boeotia, and then about 450 was forced (or induced) to support moderate oligarchies; these then readmitted the extreme anti-Athenian oligarchs in 447.* Alternatively, the Athenians may have originally supported oligarchs opposed to Thebes, who then turned on the common people in their own cities. The events in Miletus are to be dated to the period 446–3, while the reference to Messenia is to Cimon's ill-starred intervention on the side of the Spartans in the Messenian revolt of the late 460s. The classic description of the effects of internal strife in Greek cities is Thucydides' account of the events at Corcyra (III,70–85), though the present author has hinted at the possibility even at Athens (II,15), optimistic though this may have been.

III,12–13 The final paragraph of the work discusses *atimia*, the loss of political rights, which could be partial or total. The main causes of *atimia* were: debt to the state, whether as the result of non-payment of fines or of embezzlement while in office; theft, burglary or other serious crimes (*atimia* here applied also to a man's descendants); and some fairly serious military offences (cowardice, avoiding military service, desertion etc.) or misbehaviour in the courts. Exact disabilities varied, but the common feature was that the disfranchised were banned from speaking in the *Ekklesia* or taking a seat in the *Boule*; for details, see Andocides, *On the Mysteries* 73–76. The argument advanced is that it is the people who hold the offices and also control the courts; therefore

---

* Gomme, 'The Old Oligarch', in *HSCP* Suppl. 1 (1940), 230, note 1, = *More Studies in Greek History and Literature*, 55, note 31.

the majority of the decisions are just; there is no need to assume, with Frisch, that there is an intermediate step omitted from the argument, 'that most offices are badly discharged'. The author is merely stating that there is not a vast body of dissidents in Athens who are ripe for a change of constitution; rather than being sardonic, the argument is, if anything, slightly idealistic in that he implies that those who have been justly condemned will accept their punishment and not attempt to recover their position by a change of constitution. Alcibiades demonstrated that this was not always the case in the negotiations of 411–10 (Thucydides VIII,48,4). However, the stability of Athenian politics supports the general conclusion, that there was no reason for oligarchs to hope for a significant body of support from those inside Athens.

SELECT BIBLIOGRAPHY

The present translation has been made from a conflation of the texts of the following editions:

Xenophontis Opera Omnia, Vol. v; *Opuscula*, edited by A. C. Marchant, (Oxford, Oxford University Press, 1920);

The Constitution of the Athenians (Classica Mediaevalia, Dissertationes II), (Copenhagen, Hartvig Frisch, 1942) (with translation; cited as 'Frisch');

Xenophon, Vol. vII; *Scripta Minora*, Loeb Classical Library, (London, Heinemann and Cambridge, Mass., Harvard University Press, 1968); *Constitution of the Athenians* edited and translated by G. W. Bowersock.

Frisch includes a long and exhaustive introduction and commentary, and is of considerable importance; Bowersock has an introduction and notes on a smaller scale, but contains much useful material, including a full bibliography.

Of the ancient sources referred to, Thucydides, Aristophanes and much of Plutarch are available in Penguin translations. For Aristotle's *Constitution of Athens* see Part II of this volume.

A starting-point for the investigation of problems raised by the text is often provided by Frisch. A stimulating analysis is given by A. W. Gomme, 'The Old Oligarch', *Harvard Studies in Classical Philology* (*HSCP*) Suppl. Vol. 1 (1940), 211–45, reprinted in *More Essays in Greek Literature and History*, (Oxford, Blackwell, 1962); he is in favour of a very late date for the work. W. G. Forrest, 'The Date of the Pseudo-Xenophontic Athenaion Politeia', *Klio* 52 (1970), 107–116, contains much useful information, and argues well for a late date; an earlier date is supported by Frisch, Bowersock, and Jacoby, *Atthis*, 292, n. 13.

J. K. Davies, *Democracy and Classical Greece* (London, Fontana, 1978), and V. Ehrenberg, *The People of Aristophanes* (2nd ed., Oxford, Blackwell, 1951) cast much light on issues raised by this work.

The following books may also be found useful on individual points:

A. W. H. Adkins, *Merit and Responsibility*, (Oxford, Oxford University Press, 1960), and *Moral Values and Political Behaviour in Ancient Greece*, (London, Chatto & Windus; New York, Norton, 1972).

J. Barron, 'Milesian Politics and Athenian Propaganda', *JHS* 82 (1962), 1–6; vital for the dating of the events referred to in III,11.

R. J. Bonner and G. Smith, *The Administration of Justice from Homer to Aristotle*, (Chicago, Chicago University Press, 2 vols 1930–38); on courts.

J. de Romilly, *Thucydides and Athenian Imperialism*, translated by P. Thody, (Oxford, Blackwell, 1963); a detailed, if extreme, analysis of the subject.

M. I. Finley, *The Ancestral Constitution*, (Cambridge, Cambridge University Press, 1971) and 'Athenian Demagogues' *Past and Present* 21 (1962), 3–24.

A. French, *The Growth of the Athenian Economy*, (London, Routledge and Kegan Paul, 1964); to be used with caution.

SELECT BIBLIOGRAPHY

A. W. Gomme, A. Andrewes, K. J. Dover, *A Historical Commentary on Thucydides*, i–v, (Oxford, Oxford University Press, 1945–81); valuable wherever Thucydides is covering parallel material.

A. W. Gomme, 'A Forgotten Factor of Greek Naval Strategy', *JHS* 53 (1933), 16–24, reprinted in *Essays in Greek History and Literature*, (Oxford, Blackwell, 1937); valuable on naval tactics.

F. D. Harvey, 'Literacy in the Athenian Democracy', *Revue des Etudes Grecs*, 79 (1966), 585–635; illuminating both on the subject and on its social implications.

A. H. M. Jones, *Athenian Democracy*, (Oxford, Blackwell, 1957); of great importance.

H. Knorringa, *Emporos*, (Amsterdam, 1926; reprint Amsterdam, Hakkert, 1961); sources on trade.

A Lesky, *A History of Greek Literature*, translated by J. Willis and C. de Heer, (London, Methuen, 1966); pp. 452ff. on the *Constitution of the Athenians*.

R. Meiggs, *The Athenian Empire* (Oxford, Oxford University Press, 1972).

P. J. Rhodes, *The Athenian Boule*, (Oxford, Oxford University Press, 1972).

Apart from these works, readers are referred to the standard histories of the fifth century, with their bibliographies, and the second edition of the *Oxford Classical Dictionary*.

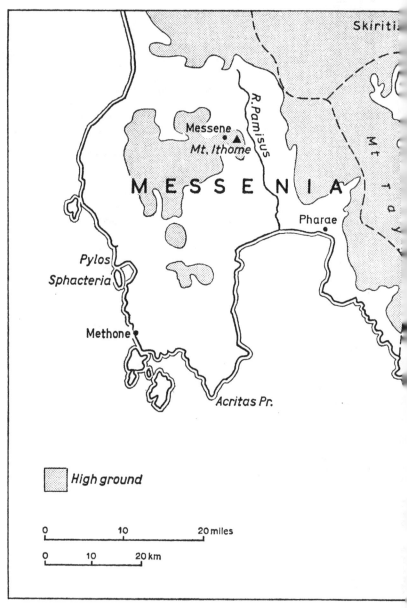

Map 3. MESSENIA AND LACONIA

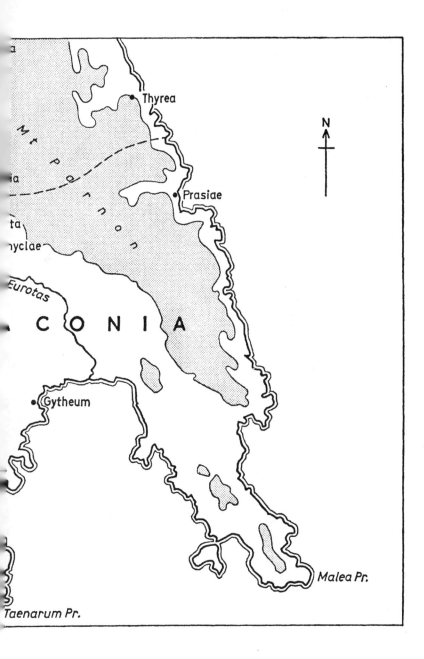

The Politeia of the Spartans

GLOSSARY

The following Greek words and technical terms are used in the text; references after the brief definitions are to passages in the commentary where the words are more fully discussed. Plurals are given in brackets.

Agoge   The Spartan educational system.

aulos (-oi)   A wind instrument; XIII,6–11.

chous (choes)   A liquid measure between five and six imperial pints.

Eiren   A Spartiate at least twenty years old; II,5–8.

Ephor   One of a board of five Spartan magistrates; VIII.

Eunomia   Literally 'good rule'; in practice, a technical term for an oligarchic form of government, usually referring specifically to the Spartan system.

Gerousia   The council of Spartan elders, plus the two kings; X.

Harmost   A Spartan officer, either in command of detached Spartan forces abroad, or in charge of a city or area under Spartan control.

Hellanodikai   Legal officers whose exact function is obscure.

Helot   A member of the subject population in the area ruled by Sparta.

Hippagretes (-ai)   Spartan officials in charge of a picked body of 300 young men; IV,1–6.

Homoios (-oi)   'Equal', the Spartan name for a full citizen of Sparta.

Krupteia   A force of selected young Spartiates mainly concerned with internal security.

Melleiren   A Spartan a little younger than an Eiren; II,5–8.

Mina/Mna   A measure of weight, either 431 or 630 grammes; it is not certain which standard Xenophon uses.

Mothakes or *Mothones* (both plural)   Inhabitants of Sparta under some civil disability; see the Introduction, p. 69.

paidagogos (-oi)   A slave responsible for supervising a child during his education—not customary in Sparta.

Paidonomos   A Spartan official in charge of education; II,2–4.

Perioikoi (plural)   The inhabitants of towns and villages around Sparta, subject to Sparta in a general sense, but free within their own communities.

Skiritai (plural)   Perhaps light armed troops in the Spartan army; XII.

Spartiate   A full citizen at Sparta, one of the *Homoioi*.

sussition (-ia)   The communal 'mess' where adult male Spartans ate until the age of sixty; V,1–6.

Other transliterated Greek words are explained in the commentary.

INTRODUCTION

The *Politeia* of the Spartans preserved among the works of Xenophon has been generally accepted as genuine by modern scholars, and rightly so, despite a detailed and ingenious attack on the attribution made by K. M. T. Chrimes.* There seem no convincing stylistic grounds for rejecting it, and, while the content differs in some significant points from the views expressed in other works by Xenophon, there is no discrepancy which cannot reasonably be accounted for when one takes account of the various dates of composition, and the differing purposes lying behind different works. The title is normally translated 'The Constitution of the Spartans';† I have deliberately avoided the traditional word 'constitution', because there is very little here which we would normally class as constitutional history; rather, it is a discussion of the way of life of the Spartans, and only some aspects of it at that, a valid meaning for the word *politeia* which covers 'how the *polis* (city) is arranged' in the widest sense. This is a social document of considerable importance, but those looking for an analysis of organs of government will be disappointed.

Xenophon was probably born about the beginning of the Peloponnesian War, and came of a wealthy family. The well-to-do were often out of sympathy with the radical democracy of Athens, and Xenophon himself was no exception. In his youth, he was also a friend of Socrates. In 401, when he was probably about twenty-seven years old, he joined a force of mercenaries in Asia Minor who aided an abortive revolt by Cyrus against the Persian throne. Thereafter he saw a good deal of fighting during the extrication of the 'Ten Thousand' from central Asia Minor, and subsequently with various Spartan armies campaigning in Ionia. In the course of this period he became friendly with Agesilaus, the Spartan king; when Agesilaus was recalled to Greece in 394, Xenophon returned with him, and was with him at the battle of Coronea, when the Spartan forces fought a confederation including the Athenians. A formal decree of banishment had probably been pronounced against him in Athens before this, and he was not free to return to his native city until about 368. During this period he and his family lived first at Sparta, and then on an estate which he was given

* K. M. T. Chrimes, *The* Respublica Lacedaemoniorum *ascribed to Xenophon*, Manchester University Press, 1948.

† The title is unlikely to go back to Xenophon himself; see above, Introduction to the *Constitution of the Athenians*.

by the Spartans near Olympia, and finally at Corinth. He occupied his time with the normal pursuits of a 'gentleman farmer' and also with writing extensively.

The *Politeia of the Spartans* concentrates almost entirely on the education of the Spartiate, his life from beginning to end, and the army which the system produced; this naturally involves a discussion of the kings, who were the commanders in chief of the army in the field. In writing on these subjects, Xenophon combined his two major interests, warfare, of which he had wide practical experience, and education; his interest in the latter is seen also in his *Education of Cyrus*, which is more a theoretical treatise on how to educate a ruler than a historical document about Cyrus. His grasp of practical detail is superior to his theoretical and philosophical discussions, just as might be expected in a reasonably educated, professional army officer today; there is little theorising in the *Politeia*, and one therefore sees the more competent side of his writing.

Virtually the whole Spartan system is ascribed by Xenophon to Lycurgus; the assertion cannot be accepted as historically accurate. Even Plutarch, writing a life of Lycurgus in the early second century AD, opens with the cautious remark: 'Concerning the lawgiver Lycurgus it is totally impossible to make any undisputed statement; his birth, travels, death and the whole of his work on the laws and constitution are recorded in conflicting reports by different historians, and there is the greatest dispute about his date.' The earlier the writer, the less detail they allege, until one reaches the Spartan poet Tyrtaeus (seventh century), who apparently did not even mention him in a context where it would have been highly appropriate to do so. An oracle recorded by Herodotus (1,65) may well be interpreted as being the answer to an inquiry as to whether Lycurgus had been divine or human. Xenophon takes an extreme position in ascribing so much to Lycurgus, and also in dating him to the time of the sons of Heracles (x,8), by which he must mean the time of the original Dorian conquest of the Peloponnese. That this is absurd goes without saying, since there would hardly then have been a system to reform. Further, there was a firm tradition that, before a period of reforms, Sparta went through a period of severe civil upheaval (e.g. Herodotus 1,65); Thucydides (1,18,1), dates the stabilisation of Sparta 400 years before his own day, that is a little before 800. Speculation as to the actual date of Lycurgus, assuming that he was a historical figure, is as profitless as most other attempts to reconstruct the details of archaic Spartan history. However, it is known that Sparta went through a period of considerable stress and turmoil connected with her expansion in the Peloponnese, and that this period, came to an end about 600; when she emerged into a period of stability, her constitution and way of life were more or less established in the form known in the fifth and fourth centuries. Many elements were probably traditional and long-established; the whole was organised and tightened up at this time. The Spartan constitution was subject to repeated modifications for much of her history, some of which, affecting her army, were considerable; the Greeks were deluded into describing it as unchanging because the basic structure was *relatively* archaic, and the alterations were much less drastic and less violent than those affecting other states in the same period.

It follows, then, that we should disregard Xenophon's attribution of the system to Lycurgus. Fortunately, the main interest of the *Politeia* lies in its description of the established social order of classical Sparta; therefore the false ascription to Lycurgus does not seriously affect the value of what he records. It must be read as a piece of social analysis, not a historical account of one man's work. Similarly, the claim of originality (1,2) must be read as a claim that the established Spartan system was without parallel in Greece, not as a claim of special inventive genius for a historical person—a valid assertion, despite the fact that many individual aspects of the Spartan way of life could be paralleled elsewhere; the whole ensemble was unique.

There are further limitations which must be noted. Xenophon is concerned throughout solely with the relatively small group of full Spartan citizens and their families, the Spartiates; they are the core of the army, the people with full rights in the Assembly, and those from whom magistrates and members of the *Gerousia* were drawn. They were often referred to as *Homoioi*, 'Equals', which represents an important theoretical principle in Sparta. In practice, this equality was illusory, as is shown not merely in the hints in our sources that some Spartan families were more influential than others (a common feature of an aristocratic society), but also in the wide disparity of wealth, seen most clearly in the contrast between a number of Spartans who were too poor to pay their compulsory contributions to the *sussitia* and therefore lost the status of full citizens, and the record of a significant number of Spartans who were victors in the chariot races at Olympia in the Fifth century (e.g. Pausanias, VI,2,1–2); horse-racing is always an expensive hobby.

It was primarily the *Homoioi* who went through the full rigours of the *Agoge*, but others took part also. A mysterious group referred to as the *Mothakes* or *Mothones* are variously described as slaves sent out by their masters to accompany their children in the gymnasia (Aelian, *Var. Hist.* XII,43), or foster-brothers of the Lacedaemonians (Phylarchus Jacoby *F.Gr.H.* 81 F 43). In fact, since distinguished Spartans including Lysander and Gylippus are described as *Mothakes*, it is probable that this group did not consist of slaves but of the sons of those who had lost their full status for some reason—Lysander claimed to be a descendant of the sons of Heracles, and Gylippus' father was a very distinguished Spartan, Cleandridas, who had been exiled. This tallies with the fact that these people could achieve full citizenship after passing through the *Agoge*. Sparta was always short of manpower, and it would be surprising if she refused to accept the children of Spartiate fathers who had fallen into disgrace. Remembering that there were other reasons for failing to complete the *Agoge* (with its attendant disqualification from the status of the *Homoioi*), such as physical injury which prevented a man from fighting as a hoplite, it becomes eminently reasonable that there should be some means whereby their children could regain membership of the élite.

Throughout the discussion, Xenophon looks at general considerations, and keeps criticism to a minimum. This leads to certain implausibilities, as when he praises the system of competition on which so much of Spartan education was based, without considering the fact that there must have been losers as well as winners; one cannot believe that all Spartans reacted in the way Plutarch describes: 'When Paidaretos was not selected amongst the three hundred best men [see IV,3–5], he went away looking very cheerful, delighted that the city had three hundred men better than him.' (*Lycurgus* 25,4). In addition, the whole sequence which broke down family life at the age of seven and grouped children by age for their education, and then broke down this element of stability in their lives by forcing individuals to join different *sussitia* in which there would be virtually none of their contemporaries, admirable as it may have been for preventing any form of seditious combination, must have left many without roots or security, with severe attendant psychological problems for some. The tight restrictions which inhibited any form of real home life in the early years of marriage cannot have helped either: by the time a man came to spend more than the odd, stolen hour at home, he must have felt like a visitor in his own house, while his wife would have got used to running the place herself; at the same time he would have risen to a position of some status in his *sussition* and in the all-male society in which he had been used to living; the inherent problems are obvious.

Equally, Xenophon has virtually nothing to say of the great majority of those who lived in Laconia—Helots, *Perioikoi*, and inferiors who were free Spartans who did not qualify as *Homoioi*. Without these people, the élite few could never have lived the life which Xenophon so much admired; for instance, it is obvious from VII,2 that the *Homoioi* did not make their own armour.

When the limitations of content are realised, it is easier to attempt to assess Xenophon's aims in writing. From references to Sparta as 'there' (e.g. II,2), his intended audience was clearly not Spartan. His attitude was not that of the ordinary Greek of his own day. The inherent pro-Spartan bias of a small, upper-class minority at Athens has combined with the fact that so much of the literature which has survived came from this class to give us a disproportionately favourable picture of Sparta; in particular, many philosophers approved of her constitution because of its efficiency, without pausing to think of the quality of life resulting from it. It is worth considering the following passage from Euripides; granted it was written during the Peloponnesian War, at a time when anti-Spartan feeling was presumably at a higher pitch than usual, and that the dramatic context is very hostile to Sparta, none the less it probably represents in an extreme form feelings which were widely held in Greece at large: 'Most hateful of all mankind, dwellers in Sparta, plotters of treachery, lords of the lie, schemers of evil, your success in Greece is a crime. What wickedness is not found among you? Murder rampant; greed and dishonesty; treacherous thoughts and treacherous deeds; to hell with you!' (*Andromache* 445ff.); cf. Thucydides v,105,4. There was much for Xenophon to be on the defensive about, whether facts or deeply held prejudices. From the way in which he discusses such topics as friendships between men and boys at Sparta (II,13) and Spartan eugenics (I,6–10) he appears to be answering what were standard points of attack against the Spartan way of life. Combined with this, he is writing a general and fairly uncritical defence of the best in Sparta—hence the slightly odd combination of broad general themes without the details which we could often wish he had included, and some surprising concentration on matters which we regard as relatively trivial. His own tastes as an experienced officer no doubt led him to include some slightly disjointed minutiae on every-day military life; this was particularly interesting to him, and the sort of thing which the rest of Greece was less likely to know about. Xenophon's own tastes probably also lie behind the stress on Lycurgus as the author of virtually all the institutions discussed; throughout his writings, he showed a weakness for the 'great man', and tended to build his work around such figures. In Xenophon's day the myth of Lycurgus was not fully developed in the form in which it is recorded by Plutarch and others—indeed, in Plato, Aristotle and Isocrates he figures far less than he does in Xenophon. One may reasonably guess that it was Xenophon's liking for a single central character which led him to accord so much importance to Lycurgus, combined with the added respectability lent to all that he discusses (in his own eyes at any rate) by the resultant antiquity of the institutions. It is tempting to guess that Xenophon saw the ideal Spartan as a man not unlike himself.

If the work is conceived as a eulogy of Spartan virtues, one may perhaps be more precise about its date. That Spartan morale and 'civic virtue' began to decline very soon after 404 is indisputable; however, much of the decline may have been hidden from Xenophon, or he may have closed his eyes to it because of the old-fashioned ways of his close associate, King Agesilaus. Further, Sparta was under severe pressure in Greece during the Corinthian War (396–86), and this would have been a likely moment at which to conceive a defence of Spartan values and an explanation of her success, despite her relatively small size. However, a work praising the virtues and successes of the Spartan system could surely not have been written after the crushing disaster of Leuctra (371), and the decline became obvious at any rate by 378, when the Spartan Harmost of Thespiae, Sphodrias, staged a treacherous and abortive attempt to seize the Peiraeus; this must have offended Xenophon not only for the treachery involved, but also as an Athenian, however pro-Spartan. In addition, Sphodrias was tried and acquitted, and the part of Agesilaus in the process was not remotely honourable. It is probable, in fact, that Xenophon wrote even earlier than 378; in 383 the Spartan Phoebidas seized the Cadmea, the citadel of Thebes, in an act of gross treachery; the Spartans recalled and punished him, but kept the Cadmea, an action hardly in tune with Xenophon's picture of Spartan virtue. Since it is extremely unlikely that he started writing before settling in Sparta some time after 396, the period of composition falls in the years 396–83; the years around 388 have been held to be the most likely period.

Chapter XIV cannot have been written at the same time. The whole tone is one of disillusion at the way in which the leaders of Sparta have abandoned the old ideas, and the fabric of Lycurgan society has broken down with disastrous consequences. An ingenious theory has recently been propounded by Chrimes* suggesting that this was originally the opening chapter of the work, containing an apology for writing on Sparta at her best at a period when she was clearly degenerate; the suggestion is supported by an extremely complex set of palaeographical arguments which aim to explain the position in which the chapter was in fact transmitted in surviving manuscripts. It is indeed odd to find an attack like chapter XIV half-way through what appears to be a single analysis of the position of the Spartan kings, and the conclusion that it is misplaced is inescapable. However, the theory which restores it as the opening chapter of the whole work is so complicated, and depends on such a chain of very precise coincidences of length and structure in the supposed copy where the damage is alleged to have taken place, that the theory is very difficult to accept. It seems much more likely that Xenophon wrote the main part of the work, and then added a brief note attempting to explain the reasons for the decline that had become manifest in the meantime. This hypothesis in its turn involves an assumption: either the work had not been 'published' at all, and therefore Xenophon was in a position to add the modification, or, if it had been 'published', our manuscripts are all ultimately derived from Xenophon's own copy which he had retained and could therefore modify. The former is obviously the more likely hypothesis. It is not difficult to conceive of Xenophon writing the work and not publishing it in the sense of letting people have copies of it; the ancient world did not share the modern urge to spread its ideas to a wide audience, and anyway it is more than likely that Xenophon would have become increasingly aware of the faults in contemporary Sparta as he crystallised his own ideas, and that he would therefore have been reluctant to give wide circulation to a document which could only harm his own position. One must remember that he was a guest of the Spartans, and they could well have felt that he was either drawing invidious comparisons or attempting to interfere in their politics; the views expressed would have made him more unpopular in Athens, and indeed in all the Greek states allied against Sparta in the Corinthian War. He could only lose from the circulation of the work in the 380s, and at any later period, in view of what had happened to Sparta, it would hardly be appropriate unless it was radically redrafted; XIV is in the nature of a brief note, and would not meet the purpose at all. If the work did

* *op. cit.*

remain unpublished, it is easy to assume that it was found in Xenophon's papers after his death, and published then. How xiv reached its present position must remain a matter for guesswork, though it is not inconceivable that it was on a separate piece of papyrus and carelessly added in the wrong place by those who sorted Xenophon's papers; this is essentially more plausible than the suggestion that it was written in the margin of the original work, which implies the availability of remarkably large margins. There is some evidence that the editing of Xenophon's papers was not of a high order: it is difficult to see how anyone at the time of his death could have believed that he wrote the *Constitution of the Athenians* which has come down to us under his name.

THE COMMENTARY

In the Commentary I have tried to amplify and clarify obscure references to institutions or customs, while avoiding excessive detail. Further, I have attempted to point out to the reader where Xenophon's laudatory purpose has led him to exaggeration or over-simplification; it is fair to say that he is not, as far as we can tell, guilty of direct falsehood about Sparta itself, although his claims for the uniqueness of certain institutions will not stand up to scrutiny. After considerable thought, I have continued to refer to Lycurgus as the author of reforms which Xenophon ascribes to him; manifestly false as this is, it would be absurd to burden the text with inverted commas whenever the name occurs, and to retain it aids brevity in discussion. The reader should by now be warned sufficiently clearly that we do not know enough about Lycurgus to ascribe anything to him, let alone the detailed social system here described. The use of his name is merely convenient shorthand.

Since this is not a 'Constitution' in the normally accepted sense, the reader will look in vain in the commentary, just as in the text, for a general discussion of the Spartan political machine; for this he should consult the books listed in the bibliography. What Xenophon has given us is an extremely valuable insight into the way of life of the Spartiates; this I have attempted to clarify where necessary, and above all to amplify with details from other classical authors. In doing so, I have drawn extensively on Plutarch's *Life of Lycurgus*; for all its late date, it contains material which goes back to reputable fourth-century sources such as Ephorus. There are occasions when he is anachronistic, as for example in his treatment of the curious ceremonies in the temple of Artemis Orthia (ii, 9), where he must in part at least be referring to practices of Roman times. I have attempted to exclude the most blatant anachronisms, but where the matter is open to doubt, I have included Plutarch's account if it added materially to the information in Xenophon. The comparison of historical sources is a useful and stimulating exercise which should illuminate the ideas being investigated. Those who wish for further guidance on the historical reliability of Plutarch are referred to A. W. Gomme, *Commentary*, i, 54–84 for an admirable and judicious assessment.

THE POLITEIA OF THE SPARTANS

1　　I was reflecting one day on the fact that, although Sparta has one of the smallest populations, it has become the most powerful and famous of all Greek states, and I wondered how this could have come about. However, when I examined the way of life of the Spartiates, I

2　ceased to be surprised. None the less I do admire Lycurgus, the man who established the laws under which they flourished; I consider him a remarkably wise man. Not merely did he not imitate other states, but he adopted opposite institutions to the majority with outstandingly successful results.

3　　Let us begin our survey at the very beginning, with the begetting of children. In other cities, the girls who are to become mothers, and are brought up in the approved fashion, are reared on the simplest possible diet, and with a minimum of luxury foods; they either drink no wine at all, or only drink it diluted. Girls are expected to imitate the usually sedentary life of craftsmen, and to work their wool sitting quietly. How could one expect girls brought up in such a way to produce

4　outstanding offspring? Lycurgus felt that slave girls were perfectly capable of producing garments, and that the most important job of free women was to bear children; he therefore decreed that women should take as much trouble over physical fitness as men. Moreover, he instituted contests of speed and strength for women parallel to those for men, on the grounds that if both parents were strong the offspring would be more sturdy.

5　He saw that, generally, husbands spent a disproportionate amount of time with their wives when they were first married, and decreed the opposite here too, for he made it disgraceful for a man to be seen entering or leaving his

75

wife's apartment. Thus their desire would inevitably be heightened when they did meet, and any offspring which might result would therefore be stronger than if the 6 parents were surfeited with each other. Furthermore, he did not allow men to take wives as and when they wished, but decreed that marriage should take place at the period of physical prime, thinking that this also was 7 likely to produce fine children. He realised that old men with young wives tend to be particularly jealous, and again made the opposite customary, for he made it possible for an old man to introduce to his wife a man whose appearance and character he approved and so 8 have children. Further, if a man did not wish to live with a wife, but wanted children worthy of note, Lycurgus made it legal for him to select a woman who was noble and the mother of fine children, and, if he obtained the 9 husband's consent, to have children by her. He approved many such arrangements, for the women wish to run two households, and the men to get more brothers for their children—brothers who will share in the honour and position of the family, but will make no financial 10 claims. Lycurgus thus took the opposite position to the rest of the Greeks on the begetting of children; it is up to the observer to decide whether he managed to make the Spartans outstanding in stature and strength.

11 Having discussed the subject of birth, I wish to turn to the educational systems of Sparta and the rest of Greece. Outside Sparta, those who claim to educate their children best put servants in charge of them as *paidagogoi* as soon as the children can understand what is said to them, and immediately send them to teachers to learn to read and write, to study the arts, and to practise gymnastics. Moreover, they soften their children's feet by giving them shoes, and weaken their bodies by changes of clothes; their diet is limited only by their capacity. 2 Instead of leaving each man to appoint a slave *paidagogos* privately for his children, Lycurgus put in charge of all of them a man who was drawn from the same class as those who hold the major offices of state; he is called the

Paidonomos, and Lycurgus gave him authority to assemble the boys, inspect them and punish any faults severely. This official was also given a group of young men provided with whips for floggings where necessary; the result is considerable respect and obedience there.

3 Instead of softening their feet with shoes, Lycurgus decreed that they should harden them by going barefoot; he believed that if this were their practice, they would climb more easily, go downhill more sure-footedly, and that a man would leap, jump up and run more swiftly barefoot than wearing shoes, as long as his feet were

4 accustomed to it. Instead of pampering them in matters of dress, he decreed that they should habitually wear one garment all the year round to make them more tolerant

5 of heat and cold. He laid down each Eiren's contribution at such a level that nobody should be burdened by overeating or be without experience of going short. He thought that those brought up under such a regime would be better able to labour on without food if the situation demanded it, and to hold out longer on the same rations if ordered to do so; they would miss delicacies less, be less interested in food altogether, and live a healthier life. He thought that food which tended to produce slimmer figures would make them grow

6 taller, rather than that which produces fat. To prevent their being too distressed by hunger, while he did not make it possible for them to take whatever they wanted without trouble, he did permit them to steal something

7 to alleviate their hunger. As I am sure everyone realises, he did not allow them to feed themselves through their own resourcefulness because he lacked the means of providing for them. Obviously, a man who intends to steal must stay awake at night, and deceive and lie in ambush during the day, and if he is to succeed he must also have spies out. It is clear then that he included this element in their education to make the boys more resourceful in obtaining the necessities of life, and more

8 suited for war. Someone may ask why, if he thought theft a good thing, he decreed a severe flogging for anyone who was caught. My answer is that this is parallel

to the way in which punishment is always handed out for not carrying out well what one is taught—those who
9 are caught they punish for stealing badly. Lycurgus made it honourable to steal as many cheeses as possible from the altar of Artemis Orthia, and detailed others to whip the thieves in the process, wishing to demonstrate in this way that a brief moment's pain can bring the joy of enduring fame. This shows that where speed is needed
10 the idler gains nothing except a mass of trouble. To prevent the children being without control even if the supervisor left them, Lycurgus laid it down that any citizen who was present could give the boys whatever instructions seemed necessary, and punish any misconduct. By this means he produced more respect in the boys; in fact, adults and boys alike respect nothing more
11 than the men who are in charge of them. In order that they might not be without someone in charge even when there was no adult present, he put the keenest of the Eirens in charge of each company; therefore boys at Sparta are never without someone to control them.
12   It seems that I must say something also about affection for boys since this too is relevant to education. Elsewhere there are varying practices: in Boeotia, men and boys live together as if they were married; in Elis, they attract a young man by favours;* again, there are states where men are absolutely forbidden even to speak
13 to boys in these circumstances. Lycurgus yet again took a totally different course; if an honourable man admired a boy's character, and wished to become his friend in all innocence, and spend time with him, he approved, and thought this a very fine form of education. If, however, a man was clearly physically attracted to a boy, he classed this as a heinous disgrace, and so ensured that in Sparta there is no more physical love between men and boys than there is between parents and children or
14 brother and brother. I am not surprised that some find this difficult to believe, for many cities tolerate love between men and boys.

* Or possibly: 'in Elis they win short periods with young men by favours.'

Such, then, are the educational systems of Sparta and of the other Greek States; which of them produces men who are more obedient, respectful and self-controlled is again for the reader to decide.

III When a boy begins to grow up, the other Greeks release him from his *paidogogos* and no longer send him to school; no one controls him, and he is totally his own
2 master. Lycurgus again chose the opposite. Realising that at this age pride is greatest, insolence at its height and temptations towards pleasures most insistent, he selected this period in which to subject them to the most demanding regime, and arranged for them to have as
3 little free time as possible. By adding the provision that if anyone should avoid this stage of the training he should be deprived of all future privileges, he ensured that not merely those appointed by the state but also those who cared for each individual would take care that the boys did not, by shrinking from these duties, utterly destroy
4 their standing in the city. Apart from this, because he wanted modesty to be firmly implanted in them, he decreed that they should keep their hands inside their cloaks in public, walk in silence, and not look about them, but keep their eyes fixed on the ground in front of their feet. Here it has become clear that in self-control as well as other fields men are stronger than women—
5 you would be more likely to hear a stone statue speak than them, more likely to catch a wandering glance from a bronze figure, and would think them even more modest than the pupil of the eye.* At the common meals you have to be content if you can even get an answer to a question.

Such, then, was his care for those who were growing up.

IV He took by far the greatest care about those who had just reached manhood, thinking that if they became the

* Accepting a reading found only in ancient quotations, this sentence contains an untranslatable (and very frigid) play on words; the Greek word translated 'pupil' normally means 'maiden'—hence Xenophon plays on the modesty of a 'maiden' who has no chance of being anything but modest, and also gives a strict parallel to the other two illustrations.

sort of people they ought to be, they would have a very
2 great influence for good in the city. He realised that the
greater the rivalry involved, the better choruses are to
listen to and athletic contests to watch; therefore, he
thought that if he could induce a spirit of competition
among the young in the field of virtue, this would bring
them to the highest levels of manliness. I will explain
3 how he brought it about. The Ephors pick three men in
their prime who are called *Hippagretai*; each of these
chooses a hundred men, giving his reasons for choosing
4 some and rejecting others. Those who do not achieve
this honour are at odds with those who rejected them and
with those selected instead of them, and keep a close
watch on each other for any lapse from the accepted
5 standards of honour. This is the strife most favoured by
the gods and most beneficial to the city, since it demonstrates what a good man ought to do; each group
individually aims at being outstanding, and collectively
they protect the city with all their might if the need
6 arises. They are compelled to take care of their physical
fitness, for this strife leads to scuffles wherever they meet;
however, any passer-by has the right to separate the
combatants. If such an order is disobeyed, the *Paidonomos* takes the offender to the Ephors, who punish him
severely, wishing to ensure that passion never becomes
stronger than obedience to the laws.

7 The men who have reached maturity, who also fill the
highest offices in the state, are relieved by the other Greeks
of the duty of preserving their fitness, although they are
still required to undertake military service. Lycurgus,
on the other hand, established the principle that hunting
was the noblest occupation for them, unless prevented by
public duties, so that they, no less than the young men,
should be able to stand the strain of campaigning.

v   After this description of the occupations laid down by
Lycurgus for each stage of a Spartan's development, I
will now try to describe the type of life which he arranged
2 for everyone. The Spartiates were in the habit of living
at home like the other Greeks, and he realised that this led

to considerable neglect of duty; he therefore instituted public messes, believing that this would be the most
3 effective check on disobedience. He specified a quantity of food which would not be too much nor leave them short; however, many unexpected additions come from hunting, and rich men sometimes contribute wheat cakes instead. The result is that as long as they are together their table is never without food, and yet is
4 not extravagant. He stopped anything involving compulsory drinking, which harms the body and fuddles the wits, but permitted each to drink when he was thirsty, believing this to be the least harmful and most pleasant form of drinking. When men live together like this, how could anyone ruin himself or his family through gluttony
5 or drunkenness? In other cities it is usually contemporaries who meet, and in their company there is the minimum of restraint; Lycurgus mingled the age groups in Sparta so that the younger learn from their more
6 experienced elders.* It is customary for noble deeds in the city to be recounted in the messes, with the result that there is the minimum of insolence, drunkenness,
7 wickedness or foul talk there. The custom of eating in public has a further beneficial consequence, in that men are compelled to walk home; they know that they will not spend the night where they eat, and must be careful not to stumble through drink; they must walk during the night as they do by day, and men of military age may not even use a torch.
8 Lycurgus realised that the same food gives someone who is working a good colour, health and strength, but makes an idle man fat, flabby and feeble. He did not neglect this either, but, noticing that even when someone works hard of his own free will in doing his duty, he clearly stays satisfactorily fit, he required the senior members of each gymnasium to ensure that the rations were not out of proportion to the exercise undertaken.†

* There appears to be an omission in this sentence; a suggested restoration has been incorporated in the translation.
† The text of this sentence is uncertain; the translation contains a possible free interpretation.

9 In my judgement he was again right; it would be difficult to find a healthier or physically more well-developed people than the Spartans, for they exercise their legs, arms and necks equally.

VI   Another field in which Lycurgus' institutions differed from the normal was that of authority; in other cities each man controls his own children, servants and property, but Lycurgus, because he wished the citizens to benefit from each other without doing any harm, gave fathers equal authority over all children, whether their
2 own or those of others. When a man realises that such men have the authority of fathers, he will inevitably control those he has authority over as he would wish his own sons to be controlled.* If a boy tells his father that he has been beaten by another man, it is a disgrace for his own father not to beat him too—to such an extent do they trust each other not to give improper
3 commands to the children. Lycurgus made it possible for someone to use another man's servants in case of need, and established a similar system of sharing hunting dogs; those who need dogs invite the owner to join them, and if he has not time himself, he lends his pack with pleasure. Similarly with horses, when someone is ill, needs a carriage, or has to get somewhere quickly, if he sees a horse, he takes it, uses it carefully
4 and returns it. Another unique custom concerns hunting parties which are caught out late and need food but, have none prepared; they open sealed caches of food which others, according to Lycurgus' rule, have left ready after eating, take what they need, and reseal them.†
5 Because they share in this way, even those who are not well off have some part in all the resources of the country when they need something.

VII   There is yet another respect in which Lycurgus' institutions are unique in Greece. In other states, every-

---

* The text of this sentence is uncertain; the translation contains a possible free interpretation.
† Freely translated to make the sense clear.

one, I suppose, makes as much money as he can; one farms, another is a ship-owner, another is a merchant, and
2 others follow trades for their living. In Sparta Lycurgus forbad the free citizens to have anything to do with making money, and ordered them to devote themselves
3 solely to activities which ensure liberty for cities. Anyway, what need was there to worry about wealth in a society where the establishment of equal contributions to the messes and a uniform standard of living excluded the search for wealth in order to obtain luxury? They do not even need wealth for clothes, since, for them, adornment
4 is not rich fabrics but bodily health. Money is not even to be acquired to spend on the other members of one's mess; he made working physically to help one's companions more honourable than spending money to this end, showing that the former involves the use of char-
5 acter, the latter of wealth. He prevented the acquiring of money by dishonesty. First, he established a currency such that even ten minas could not be brought into the house without the knowledge of the master and servants—it would take up a lot of space, and need a
6 wagon to move it. There are also searches for gold and silver, and if any is found, the possessor is punished. Why, then, should anyone devote himself to making money when the pains of possessing it must outweigh the pleasure to be had from spending it?

VIII Everyone knows the outstanding obedience of the Spartans to their rulers and laws; in my view, however, Lycurgus did not even try to instil this discipline until he had secured agreement among the leading men of
2 the state. I deduce this from the fact that in other cities the most powerful citizens do not even wish to give the impression that they are afraid of the magistrates, thinking that this is illiberal, while in Sparta the leading citizens show the greatest respect for the magistrates, and pride themselves on being humble, and running rather than walking in answer to a summons. They think that if they set an example of exaggerated obedience the rest will follow; this has proved to be the case.

3 It is likely that these same people helped to establish the power of the Ephorate. They realised that obedience was of vital importance in the city, in the army and in the home, and they thought that the greater the power of the office, the more likely it was to over-awe the people.

4 Ephors have the right to inflict punishments at will, to require immediate payment of fines, to depose magistrates during their term of office, to imprison them, and even to put them on trial for their lives. Since they have so much power, they do not always allow office-holders to complete their year of office as they see fit, as is done in other cities, but, like tyrants or presidents of the games, they punish an offender as soon as the offence is

5 detected. Among many other excellent ways in which Lycurgus encouraged the citizens to obey the laws willingly, one of the finest seems to me the fact that he did not deliver his laws to the people before going to Delphi with the leading citizens, and asking the oracle whether it would be more desirable and better for Sparta to be governed under his proposed laws. Only when the reply was that it would be better in every way did he deliver his laws; thus he made it not merely illegal but sacrilegious to disobey laws sanctioned by Delphi.

IX   Another aspect of Lycurgus' institutions which may properly be a source of wonder is his establishment of the principle that a noble death is preferable to living in dishonour. Investigation shows that fewer of those who believe this are killed than of those who choose to retreat

2 from danger. In fact, one is more likely to avoid an early death through courage than cowardice, for courage is easier, more pleasant, more resourceful and stronger. Manifestly glory goes particularly with valour, for all

3 wish somehow to be the allies of the brave. It is proper not to omit the means by which Lycurgus achieved this; he made it clear that the reward for the brave would be

4 happiness, for the cowardly misery. In other cities the coward suffers nothing more than the stigma of cowardice—he goes to the same market-place as the brave man,

sits with him, and attends the same gymnasium if he wishes. In Sparta anyone would think it a disgrace to take a coward into his mess or be matched against him 5 in a wrestling bout. When teams are being selected for the *sphairai* contests, such a man is often not picked, and in the chorus he is relegated to the most ignominious position; he must give way to others in the street, and rise even for younger men when seated. He must keep the unmarried women of his family at home, and answer to them for the disadvantages his cowardice inflicts on them;* he must endure a house without a wife, and yet pay the penalty for being a bachelor. He must not go about the city looking cheerful, nor must he imitate those who are without reproach; if he does, he must 6 submit to a beating from his betters. When such disabilities are attendant on cowardice, I am not surprised that Spartans prefer death to such a deprived and disgraceful existence.

x The provision by which Lycurgus required men to practise virtue even into old age seems to me good. By placing selection for the *Gerousia* toward the very end of life he ensured that they would not neglect the virtues 2 of an upright life even in old age. The protection he offered to good men past their prime is also worthy of admiration; by putting the members of the *Gerousia* in charge of capital trials he made old age more honourable 3 than the strength of youth. The contest for the *Gerousia* is correctly regarded as the most important that a man can enter. Gymnastic contests are noble, but they depend on the body; selection for the *Gerousia* depends on nobility of character. Just as the character is more important than the body, so rivalries hinging on it are worth more effort than physical contests.

4 Another admirable feature of Lycurgus' institutions was based on his realisation that where the encouragement of virtue is left to individual initiative the result is not sufficient to promote the good of the state; he therefore

* Or: 'answer to them for the fact that they are unmarried'.

decreed that all citizens must practise all the virtues in public life. Just as individually those who practise virtue surpass those who disregard it, so it is reasonable that Sparta is outstanding above all cities in virtue because she is the only one where nobility is consciously
5 practised in public life. For is it not also noble that, where other cities punish a man for wronging someone, Lycurgus decreed no less severe penalties for a man who
6 openly did not live as nobly as possible? His principle, it seems, was that if someone enslaves people, deprives them of something or steals, then only those who are directly harmed are wronged, but that wickedness and cowardice are a betrayal of the whole city. It therefore seems to me right that they should receive the severest
7 punishment. He laid down an inflexible requirement to practise all political virtue. Those who carried out their legal duties were given an equal share in the life of the states. He did not take into account physical infirmity or poverty; if anyone shrank from fulfilling what was required of him, Lycurgus decreed that he should no
8 longer even be considered one of the *Homoioi*. It is obvious that these laws are very old, for Lycurgus is said to have lived at the time of the sons of Heracles. Old as they are, they are very strange to the other Greeks; it is a most extraordinary phenomenon that they all praise such practices, but no city is willing to imitate them.

XI   The aspects I have discussed up to now are blessings common to times of peace and war; I will now demonstrate how Lycurgus' arrangements are superior to those
2 of other states for military purposes. First, the Ephors proclaim the age-groups to be called up, listing cavalry and infantry, and then also craftsmen, with the result that the Spartans have a sound supply of everything which is available in the city while on campaign as well. All equipment that the army needs centrally is specified, to be produced on wagons or baggage animals; in this
3 way omissions are least likely to be overlooked. He devised the following costume for battle: red cloaks,

86

thinking that this was least effeminate and most warlike, and bronze shields since they are quickest to polish and slow to tarnish. He also allowed those who were grown up to wear their hair long, on the basis that they would thus appear taller, more noble, and more terrifying.

4 Having equipped them in this way, he divided infantry and cavalry into six regiments. Each infantry regiment has one commanding officer, four company commanders, eight section officers and sixteen junior officers. At the word of command, each regiment forms

5 up in platoons two,* three or six abreast. The prevalent impression that Spartan formation under arms is extremely complicated is the opposite of the truth; the front rank man in the Spartan formation is in command,

6 and each file is self-sufficient.† The formation is so easy to understand that anyone who can recognise another man cannot go wrong, for some are designated to lead, others to follow. Deployments are ordered by the junior officers orally, acting as heralds, and the depth of the line of battle is established as they deploy. There is

7 nothing remotely difficult to learn in this. However, to fight on with whoever is at hand after the line has been disrupted is a secret not easily mastered except by those

8 trained under the system of Lycurgus. The Spartans also carry out with considerable ease manoeuvres which instructors in tactics think very difficult. When they are marching in column, obviously with every platoon following the one in front, if an enemy force appears in front of them, the word is passed to the junior officers to deploy to the left, and so down the column until the line is drawn up facing the enemy. If the enemy appears from the rear when the Spartans are in this formation, each file takes up reverse order so that the best men always

9 face the enemy. The fact that the leader thus finds himself on the left is not regarded as a disadvantage, but on occasions as a positive gain; should the enemy

* This number is missing from the text; two is the most likely restoration, though single file is possible.
† There is some doubt about the exact text here which renders the sense doubtful.

attempt an encircling movement, they would do so not on the unprotected side but on the shield side. If it seems right at any time or for any reason for the commander to have the right wing, they reverse the stations of the army by countermarching until the commander
10 is on the right wing and the rearguard on the left. If the enemy appear on the right flank while the Spartans are in column, they just swing each company to face them head on, like a trireme; thus the rear ranks occupy the right wing. They are no more disturbed by an enemy appearing on the left, but run forward,* or swing the companies to face them; this time the rear company will be on the left.

XII A word about the type of camp approved by Lycurgus. Because he realised that the corners of a square were useless, he used a circular camp except where a hill provided security, or there was a wall or river in the rear.
2 By day sentries were stationed by the arms dumps looking inwards, for they watch out for friends, not enemies. Cavalry keep watch for the enemy from points where they have as wide a view as possible to detect an enemy
3 approach. By night the Skiritai were assigned to the outposts around the main force, though now this duty may also be undertaken by mercenaries if there happen to be
4 any present. One must be quite clear that the rule that spears should always be carried has the same purpose as the banning of slaves from the arms dumps, and the fact that those who leave their posts for necessary purposes go only so far from their companions and their weapons as they must to avoid giving offence; the
5 common basis is safety. They change the sites of their camps frequently to harm the enemy and help their friends. It is laid down that all Spartans must take exercise all the while they are on campaign, with the result that they improve their own splendid physique and appear more dignified than other men. The exercise area and running track must not exceed in size the

* There is some doubt about the exact text here which renders the sense doubtful.

area covered by the camp so that no one may get far
6 from his arms. After exercise the senior officer present
has the order given to sit down; this is a form of inspection; after this comes the order to break their fast, and
to relieve the outposts quickly. There follow amusements
and a period of relaxation before the evening exercise.
7 The order is then given for the evening meal, and, after
singing a hymn to the gods to whom they have sacrificed
with good omens, to rest by their arms.

There is no cause for surprise in the length of my
account; it would be very difficult to find anything
meriting attention in military matters which the
Spartans have overlooked.

XIII   I will now describe the power and the honour which
Lycurgus decreed for the king on campaign. First, the
king and his entourage are maintained at public expense
when in the field. The regimental commanders eat with
the king, so that, since they are always present, they
may take a larger part in any necessary deliberations.
Three others of the *Homoioi* also eat with them and see
to their every need, so that nothing may distract them
from concentrating on matters connected with the war.
2 But I will go back to the beginning, to the moment when
the king leaves the city with the army. First, he sacrifices
in Sparta to Zeus the Leader and to the gods associated
with him. If the omens here are good, the fire-bearer
takes fire from the altar and leads the way to the frontiers
of the state. There the king sacrifices again to Zeus and
3 Athena; when the omens from both are good, then he
crosses the frontier. The fire from these sacrifices is
carried in front, and never put out, and sacrificial victims
of all sorts follow. Whenever the king sacrifices, he starts
the rites before dawn, wishing to obtain the favour of the
4 gods before the enemy. There are present at the sacrifice the regimental and the company commanders and
the section officers, the commanders of foreign detachments and of the baggage train, and any of the commanders of the detachments from individual cities who
5 wish to be present. Two of the Ephors are also present,

but take no part unless the king invites them to do so; needless to say, by watching each man's conduct they exercise a restraining hand on all. When the sacrifice is over, the king summons everyone and issues the orders for the day. Watching this, one might think that the other Greeks were amateurs in military matters, and the

6 Spartans the only true professionals. When the king is leading the army, if no enemy appear, nobody marches in front of him except the Skiritai and cavalry outriders. If they expect a battle, the king takes the first company of the first regiment and wheels to the right until he takes up his position between two regiments and two

7 regimental commanders. The senior member of the king's council arranges the necessary supporting troops. The council consists of the *Homoioi* who share the king's mess, prophets, doctors, *aulos*-players, the commanders of the army and any volunteers present. There is therefore no problem about making the necessary arrange-

8 ments, for nothing is unforeseen. Other Lycurgan provisions affecting battles seem to me useful: when a goat is sacrificed with the enemy already in sight, it is the custom that all the *aulos*-players present should play and all the Spartans wear garlands; all armour must be

9 polished. Young men are also permitted to go into battle with their hair oiled, looking cheerful and impressive. Words of encouragement are spoken by the junior officers, for not even a whole platoon can hear the words of the junior officer of the next platoon. The regimental commander is responsible for seeing that the process is

10 effectively carried out. When they decide that it is time to camp, the king is in charge, and indicates the site; however, he has no authority to despatch embassies, whether to friends or enemies. All are subject to the king's authority when they have any business to transact.

11 Lawsuits are referred by the king to the *Hellanodikai*, applications for money to the treasurers, and any booty which is brought in is handed over to the auctioneers. With this system, the king is left with no duties on campaign except those of a priest in the religious field and a general in human affairs.

xv* I would also like to describe the agreement which Lycurgus made between king and state. The royal authority at Sparta is the only one which remains to-day unchanged in its original form; investigation would show that all other constitutions have undergone modifications and are even now in the process of change.

2 He laid it down that the king should make all public sacrifices for the state because of his divine descent, and

3 should lead the army on any foreign campaign. He granted the king the choice parts of the sacrificial victims, and set aside enough land in many of the surrounding cities to ensure that he was not without adequate means,

4 and yet was not too rich. So that the kings should eat in public, he established a state *sussition* for them; he also honoured them with a double portion at meals, not so that they should eat twice as much but so that they should have the means of honouring anyone they

5 wished. He also gave them the right of choosing two companions each for their *sussition*, who are called *Puthioi*. They also received the right to take one pig from each litter, so that a king would never be without

6 victims should he need to consult the gods. A spring near their houses provides a plentiful supply of water; those without such an amenity will realise its manifold uses. Everyone stands when the king enters except Ephors

7 seated on their official thrones. Oaths are exchanged every month, the Ephors swearing on behalf of the city, the king for himself. The king swears to rule according to the established laws of the city, the city to maintain the royal authority unimpaired as long as the king keeps his

8 oath. Such are the honours the king receives in Sparta during his lifetime; they do not greatly exceed the position of a private citizen. Lycurgus did not wish to encourage a tyrannical attitude in the kings, nor to make

9 the people envy their power. The honours given to a king after death by Lycurgus' legislation are intended

---

* Chapter xiv appears to be an intrusion in its present position, and may well be a later addition to the main treatise; it is therefore printed at the end. For discussion, see the Introduction, and the Commentary on xiv.

to demonstrate that kings of Sparta are honoured not as men but as heroes.

*   *   *

XIV   If someone were to ask me whether I felt that the laws of Lycurgus still remained unchanged, I could not
2 confidently say yes. I know that in the past the Spartans preferred to stay in Sparta in moderate prosperity rather than expose themselves to the flattery and cor-
3 ruption involved in governing other cities. In the past they were afraid of being proved to have gold, but there are those now who even pride themselves on possessing
4 some. In the past the purpose of the expulsion of foreigners and the ban on foreign travel was to prevent citizens from being infected with idleness by foreigners; now I understand that the apparent leaders of the state are eager to govern foreign cities for the rest of their lives.
5 There was a time when they worked to be worthy to lead, but now they are far more interested in ruling than
6 in being worthy of their position. This is the reason why, whereas formerly the Greeks used to come to the Spartans and ask them for leadership against reputed wrongdoers, now many are encouraging each other to prevent
7 a revival of Spartan power. There is, however, no cause for surprise that such reproaches are being cast at them; they obviously do not obey either the gods or the laws of Lycurgus.

COMMENTARY

I,1–2 Sparta was certainly one of the most famous and powerful states of Greece at the time of writing, but one might well question the assertion that she had one of the smallest populations of all, though the exact size is a vexed question. Xenophon is clearly confining himself to the Spartiates; Herodotus gives a figure of 8000 adult males for the year 480 (vii,234), and this corresponds well with a field force of 5000 at Plataea; by the time of Mantinea (418), the figure has dropped to 3,072 on a slightly reduced call-up (Thucydides v,68,3); by 371, the field force of Sparta is said to have fallen to 700 (Xenophon, *History* vi,iv,15), implying a total of men of military age of about 1,200. These numbers may be compared with the effective fighting forces of Athens in 432–1; Thucydides (ii,13,6) lists 13,000 hoplites, and a further force of 16,000 reserves to man the walls and forts of Attica; the latter would have included those under training and some metics. On the other hand, there were many Greek cities notably smaller than Sparta; for example, Plataea's garrison during the siege at the beginning of the Peloponnesian War included 400 Plataeans (Thucydides ii,78,3); one can hardly believe that the Athenians had tolerated the evacuation of any able-bodied defenders before the siege started. Further, just as the Athenian figures are in a sense misleading in that they take no account of the large number of Athenians occupied in naval affairs, so the figures for Sparta do not include the forces of the *Perioikoi* nor the armed Helots who often formed a part of her army. The commonplace that Sparta was a small state may well have arisen from a combination of the fact that she was *relatively* small for a state with such an important position in the affairs of Greece, and the way in which the Spartiates were obviously and heavily outnumbered by the Helots and others who lived under their domination.

The steady decline in the size of the Spartan population can be ascribed to a large number of factors, but not least will have been economic pressure arising from the land tenure system (see below), and the fact that Sparta was a rigid and exclusive oligarchy—there was virtually no question of recruitment to their number from outside the charmed circle. Loss of life in the earthquake normally dated to about 465 was considerable, and had long-term effects. It is also likely that Xenophon thinks in terms of Spartiate numbers in the fourth century rather than the fifth.

On the other hand, in ascribing the success of Sparta to her system of training, Xenophon must be right; the whole of this work shows the way in which the young Spartans were brought up to be efficient members of what was undoubtedly the finest military machine the Greeks had yet produced.

On the position of Lycurgus, and the claim of 'originality', see the Introduction.

I,3-4 In beginning his discussion of the Spartan system with women in what he conceived as their only important role, as mothers of future Spartiates, Xenophon appears to have followed the lead of the Athenian oligarchic leader Critias, who wrote on the constitution of Sparta in verse and prose towards the end of the fifth century. In one of the surviving fragments of his works Critias says: 'I will begin with the birth of a man; how would one produce the best and strongest physique? If the father exercises energetically, eats well and tests his endurance to the limit, and the mother of the potential child is strong and takes exercise herself' (Diels-Kranz, II,88,32). Plutarch gives greater detail in his description of the exercise which the Spartan girls took: 'Lycurgus made the girls take exercise by running, wrestling and throwing the discus and javelin' (*Lycurgus* 14), and other sources add that Spartan girls learned to manage horses and drive carts. Again, the motive given is physical fitness for the bearing of children.

The contrast drawn in the text with 'other cities' no doubt applied to many other Greek states (though not to all*), but is aimed mainly at the upbringing of Athenian girls. The question of the position of women in Athens is much debated, and the present commentary is no place for a full analysis. The extreme on the one side alleged that they virtually never went out of doors unattended, and generally led a dull and extremely cloistered existence. This was questioned very strongly by Gomme,† who amassed much evidence which showed that there must at least have been considerably greater freedom for some women at certain times. It seems that Cimon's siter Elpinike (to take an upper class example) led a very free life, and common sense suggests that in the poorest families the women must frequently have left home on their own unaccompanied. There were many families without slaves, and while the women probably did not usually do the day-to-day buying of household necessities in the market-place, many did have market stalls at which they *sold* produce; it is difficult to believe that they were chaperoned. On the other hand, it seems that many Athenian girls led their lives in seclusion for much of the time before marriage, and were not much freer afterwards. The reason for the former is probably the high value put on virginity at marriage—hence the tight control and presence of chaperones; for the latter, we have the evidence of two court speeches where an advocate takes considerable pains to prove

---

* See for example Chios (Athenaeus XIII, 586c) and Elis (Pausanias V,16,2–6).

† 'The position of women in Athens in the fifth and fourth centuries', *C.Ph.*xx (1925) 1–25 = *Essays in Greek History and Literature* 89–115.

that a man's wife existed, which suggests strongly that she had been so little seen in public that the other side had been able to suggest that she did not exist.* In sum, it appears that Xenophon represents 'accepted' ideas and standards, as one might expect; he disapproved of (and disregarded) the greater freedom arrogated to themselves by the wealthy and aristocratic, and also the greater freedom forced on the lowest classes by economic pressures.

Granted that many women led a cloistered existence, it is not really surprising that many of their occupations were sedentary—there was hardly space for anything else, and not even the wealthiest houses had anything like the long galleries of stately homes in England, designed to make exercise practical within the house. Economic necessity reinforced the other pressures; a house had to be as nearly self-supporting as possible, and obvious tasks for the women were the spinning and weaving of cloth, and the making of clothes; these were in fact the normal occupations of most women in Greece for much of their time. For the poorest, the household routine would also have taken up a good deal of time, though in better-off families slaves undertook the heavier jobs. Xenophon himself elsewhere recommended that a wife should take some part in the general running of the household, and should mix flour and knead dough to get some exercise (*Oeconomicus*, x,11). Such occupations were a meagre substitute for the Spartan training, or for that matter, for the life of the peasant women, who, then as now, worked in the fields.

Whatever the modern reaction to the average life of Greek women or the Spartan deviation from the norm, Xenophon makes it clear that the reasons behind the Spartan system (and his approval of it) were not humanitarian; the motivation was purely eugenic, and the approach here, as in the section dealing with the begetting of children where the husband was incapable or unfit, was as totalitarian as any that has ever been proposed. Just as for military reasons Spartiates were relieved of the day-to-day problem of obtaining a living by the grant of a plot of land, so the women were relieved of menial work which could be done by slaves so that they could concentrate solely on their most important function—to produce healthy and acceptable children to serve the state.

The difference of diet stressed by Xenophon is given the same nominal motive, but is in all probability also connected with the amount of exercise the girls took. In the classical period the diet of most Greeks was poor by modern standards and relatively deficient in proteins; they ate meat only a few times a year after a major state sacrifice, though fish was more readily available. It is not likely that the Spartan girls' diet was noticeably superior in this respect, but at least they appear to have had a reasonable quantity of food. It is quite possible that Xenophon has exaggerated the contrast.

The freedom of life enjoyed by the Spartan girls and women was no

---

* See W. K. Lacey, *Family*, 168.

doubt of benefit to them, and certainly of practical value in a society where the men were away from home on service to the state even more than was the general rule elsewhere; at such times the women had to manage all the affairs of the household. However, they came in for some stinging criticism from other Greeks: Ibycus (sixth century BC) called Spartan girls 'thigh-showers', and Peleus in Euripides, *Andromache* 595–601 elaborates: 'No Spartan girl could lead a respectable life even if she wanted to; they leave their houses in loose dresses showing naked thighs, and race and wrestle with boys; intolerable behaviour. It is hardly surprising if Spartan women are not respectable.' Although Peleus goes on to discuss Helen as the classic case, the reference of the earlier diatribe is surely contemporary. Aristotle says that Spartan women 'live without restraint in respect of every sort of dissoluteness' (*Politics* 1269,b,22); Plutarch refers to 'the laxity of morals which *later* affected them' (*Moralia* 228 B; my italics), and elsewhere is clearly at pains to deny what he takes to be a common charge: 'Marriage was so regulated for physical and political reasons, and was so far removed from the immorality which was later attributed to Spartan women ...' (*Lycurgus* 15), and '(Lycurgus) freed (the girls) from all weakness and effeminacy of all sorts by making them, like boys, only wear one garment in processions. ... There was nothing disgraceful in the light clothing of the girls, for they were modest, and there was no outrageous behaviour; in fact, it produced simple ways, and a desire for health and beauty' (*Lycurgus* 14).

Spartan marriage customs were in some measure bound to produce such charges (see below) and prejudice was inevitable where behaviour differed so radically from that in the rest of Greece; one may compare the accusations levelled at the first women to take advantage of Ataturk's reforms in Turkey after the First World War, and the similar attitude of the older generations in many Moslem countries today to girls who, with government encouragement, are taking to Western styles of dress, even when these are, to European eyes, very conservative.

I,5–6 These sections continue the general theme of the paragraph, that Lycurgus' motive was eugenic. The provision that men and women should marry in their prime is in distinct contrast to the rest of Greece, where it was normal for men to be above thirty when they married, while their brides were often only about fourteen. Xenophon, speaking probably of Athens, comments on the fact that it is very unlikely that a man and wife will have anything in common as a basis for conversation (*Oeconomicus* III,12), and a factor in this must have been the wide disparity in their ages, as well as the girl's relative lack of education. There is some evidence to suggest that the normal age of marriage for a Spartiate was in his twenty-fifth year; for girls it is more difficult to be definite, but Xenophon and Plutarch suggest that they were fully mature. The eugenic reasoning advanced appears to be biologically sound only in that mothers who are too young tend to have smaller children and greater problems in childbirth. On the other hand, while infrequency of meeting may make conception marginally more likely, there is no evidence that it has any effect on the physique of the child. Similarly, the better diet and superior physical fitness of Spartan mothers would be likely to make childbirth easier and less dangerous, but will hardly have affected the children except during pregnancy.

The attribution of these marriage customs to Lycurgus is one of the more blatantly obvious anachronisms in the traditional account of Sparta. The common life of the men in the *sussitia* looks like a survival of an extremely primitive tribal arrangement, and the existence of similar institutions in Crete makes it likely that these customs antedate the arrival of the Dorians in Southern Greece. Again, Plutarch has a fuller description (*Lycurgus* 15): 'Women were carried off by force at their marriage, not when they were small and not ready for marriage, but when they were in their prime and fully grown. The woman who was called the bridesmaid received the bride, cut her hair short, and dressed her in a man's cloak and sandals, and laid her on a mattress alone in the dark. The bridegroom came, not drunk or feeble through excesses, but sober as always, after dining with his companions. He entered, untied her ceremonial belt and carried her to the bed. Then, after spending a short time with her, he left for his usual accommodation soberly, to sleep with the other young men. Such also was his way of life thereafter, spending the day and sleeping with his comrades, and only visiting his bride secretly and with circumspection, afraid of the shame if anyone in the household should hear him. His bride also joined in the planning to facilitate their clandestine meetings as opportunity offered. This was not just a brief period, but sometimes long enough for children to have been born before the father had seen his wife by the light of day. These meetings not only instilled self-restraint and control, but meant that children were likely to be begotten whenever they met, and there was always something new and fresh in their love; they were not sated or exhausted by unlimited association.' Here are relics of a society where marriage by capture was the rule, though it is only symbolic in Plutarch's account. Many of the rules governing early married life originate in a situation where a man's military commitments had to outweigh all else; it is not without significance that the Spartiates were allowed to set up house with their wives at the age of thirty, that is after ten years of fully effective military life. Similarly, the way in which husband and wife met suggests some sort of trial marriage which did not become fully valid until a child was born.* The dressing of the bride as a man is paralleled from Argos (another Dorian state), where the bride wore a false beard on her marriage night; there is probably some trace of primitive *rites de passage* here.

I,7–10   The provisions outlined in these sections are most unattractive to the modern reader, and Plutarch's similar description is an attempt

___
* On Spartan marriage, see Lacey, *Family*, 196ff, to which the above discussion is much indebted.

to defend them without much confidence that he will succeed (*Lycurgus* 15). The arguments advanced are eugenic, and, above all, based on the interest of the state; it is vital that there should be children, and that these children should be born of healthy stock. An idea traceable in some primitive societies is that the 'noble seed' of the great warrior must be utilised as widely as possible for the future benefit of the tribe, and some remains of this feeling may lie behind the controlled permissiveness at Sparta. The personal feelings of the individual must be totally subordinate to the needs of the community. Such arguments are at least comprehensible, if distasteful, in the context of historical Sparta's perilous man-power position. In contrast, the justification offered by Xenophon is very naïve; if the Spartans really felt as he suggests they did, this must surely have been the result of long habituation to the practices described, and a rationalisation of the strains involved, rather than the reason for introducing them. One feels that he is being as naïve as Plutarch is when he says that these measures 'freed marriage of the hollow and effeminate vice of jealousy, and kept it free of all irregularities' (*ib.*). It is notable, and typical of the attitude of most ancient Greek writers, that the feelings of the women involved are barely considered.

On points of detail: clearly some Spartans did not marry at the usual age, despite the penalties which this involved (see below), and others will have remarried; from these will come the older husbands with young wives. It is to be presumed that those who 'did not wish to live with a wife' must have been either widowers, since the disgrace of the unmarried was such that they can hardly have been acceptable partners for someone else's wife within the terms laid down in this passage, or those whose wives had behaved in some way disgracefully so as to disqualify them in their husband's eyes, although he did not wish to divorce them and remarry. In either case, it is likely that these extreme steps were usually only taken when the man did not have male offspring already.

As to the concluding sentence, it is open to doubt whether Xenophon has made his point, for the answer to the question is clearly meant to be that Spartans *were* outstanding. Their excellence could as well be attributed to the rejection of weakling children at birth and the rigorous efficiency and single-mindedness of their upbringing as to the stress on eugenics.

II,1 In switching to a discussion of education, Xenophon opens, as is his normal practice, with a contrast with non-Spartan practice, and here again it appears that he is considering Athens. He picks out the two features which offend him most: the entrusting of children to slaves at an impressionable age, and the physical pampering implicit in their clothes and diet. The *paidagogos* was a slave whose duty it was to supervise his charges' discipline, though inevitably he also had considerable general influence over them; however, there is no evidence of widespread harm resulting from this, and one must assume that parents took

some care in selecting a *paidagogos*. Pericles answers the criticism which
was widely levelled at Athens even in his day in philo-Laconian circles,
that her education was 'soft' in the funeral speech put into his mouth
by Thucydides (II,39,1): 'Their educational system imposes laborious
discipline from early years in their search for manly courage, while we
live in a more relaxed fashion; none the less, we meet equal dangers no
less effectively than they.' For a full description of the Athenian
educational system, see F. A. G. Beck, *Greek Education 450-350 BC*, 72-
146.

II,2-4 Xenophon omits one feature which might well be most
offensive to other Greeks, the inspection of children at birth and their
exposure if there was any suspicion of weakness. Exposure of infants
was accepted in Greece, but the motive is presumed to have been
economic, and it is more than likely that the average Greek would
have looked askance at the eugenic reasoning behind the Spartan
system; for details, see Plutarch, *Lycurgus* 16.

The Lycurgan *Paidonomos* was a senior citizen—in Xenophon's eyes
the exact opposite of the Athenian *paidagogos*, since he was a man of
proved excellence. Plutarch says: 'one of the respected leading men
was appointed *Paidonomos*, and the boys were organised in companies
under his direction, each under the most prudent and warlike of the
Eirens' (*Lycurgus* 17). One must assume that he took only a general
supervisory role in the organisation of the children, not a detailed part
in their education, because of the numbers involved. One imagines
that his job was not so dissimilar from that of the Headmaster of a
Comprehensive School, who, because of its very nature, cannot know
his pupils well, but is responsible for the general outline of their courses,
and also for the administration of the most serious punishments—
though, fortunately, we do not nowadays tolerate the floggings which
are implicit in the description here, and were more severe in Sparta
than was normal in the rest of Classical Greece; W. G. Forrest described
the Spartan system as 'increasingly brutal and brutalising training
schedules which passed for education'.* One is not totally surprised
that the result of the system 'is considerable obedience'—'respect' is
slightly more surprising, and is perhaps a tribute to the efficiency of the
'brain-washing' element in Spartan education.

Plutarch says more than Xenophon about clothing: it was not until
the twelfth year that the young Spartans had only one garment each,
and it is quite possible that the regulation about going barefoot was
not applied in winter until they were adult members of the *Krupteia*.
The arguments from agility, hardiness and sure-footedness advanced
in support of this practice might be reinforced by pointing out that the
Krupteia had to operate night and day with great stealth, and if the
members were used to going barefoot and not bothering about changes
of clothing this might increase their silence and efficiency. However,

* *A History of Sparta 950-192*, 52.

going barefoot was not confined to Spartans—vases show that it was normal for Greeks to exercise barefoot; it could be a positive disadvantage in battle for obvious reasons.

II,5–8 Xenophon now switches to a discussion of the life of the Spartan man, looking first at the age group referred to as 'Eirens'; Plutarch describes them as follows (*Lycurgus* 17): 'they call those who are already in their second year beyond the class of boys Eirens, and the oldest boys Melleirens. This Eiren, then, who is twenty, controls those under him in the practice battles, and has them as servants at table indoors; he orders the older ones to carry wood, the younger vegetables. They steal what they bring, some going to gardens, others slipping very subtly and cautiously into the men's *sussitia*. Anyone who is caught receives a severe beating for stealing carelessly and unskilfully.' Thus the Eirens were young men in their twentieth year and upwards, though it is not clear whether they remained in this 'class' for the whole of their twenties or only a part. Their main duties were military service of all kinds, supervising the younger members in the educational system, and controlling the Helots.

The whole section smacks of rationalisation; Xenophon (presumably drawing on commonly held views about Sparta which were more than likely believed by the Spartans themselves) produces fairly plausible arguments to justify the sparse fare at the common tables where the Spartans ate, but the reasons are much more likely to have been produced to explain an existing situation than to be causes for establishing such a system from the beginning. Sparta did not import on a large scale, and her food supply was probably adequate for subsistence and no more. Theft to alleviate the pangs of hunger was a standard part of the ancient traditions of Spartan education—Plutarch (*Lycurgus* 18), amongst others, preserves the story of the young Spartan who had stolen a fox-cub and concealed it under his garment, and, rather than reveal what he had done, allowed it to tear his guts out; obviously an improving tale about Spartan courage, but it is surely in order to ask why he should *steal* a fox—and who from!

II,9 The text of this section is obscure. Later there was a ceremony at Sparta which is first mentioned by Cicero (*Tusculans* II,34), whereby the young men (authorities differ about their exact age) were whipped in front of the altar, and those who endured for the longest time received great honours. Ollier (and others) rightly question the detailed authenticity of such a ceremony for classical Sparta when the first mention of it is found so late; Sparta used her 'quaint old customs' very much as 'tourist bait' in the Roman period, and it is more than likely that there were some half-understood revivals which were all the more savage because brutality was expected. If the ceremony were merely a test of endurance, why the cheeses? On the other hand, the theft of cheeses from the altar could have formed some part of a ceremony connected with Artemis as presiding over agriculture; if the stealing were central, the aim would presumably be agility, swiftness and coolness, and the object to receive as *few* blows as possible.* It looks as if Xenophon may hint at a partial survival of a primitive ceremony, which was later modified into the one described by Cicero, and combined it with some other ceremony involving agility; it is impossible to be sure. He may have been led to include the garbled version here by the combination of the references to stealing in the previous sections, and the general theme of toughness and endurance which runs through his whole description of Spartan education.

II,10–11   Finally Xenophon reverts at considerable length to the question of authority, and stresses the importance attached to arrangements which ensured that the boys throughout their whole training were never not under authority of some sort. This obsession with control, which Xenophon stresses to the exclusion of much interesting detail which he might have included about what Spartan children were taught, may reflect Xenophon's own interest in discipline, but it is also a comment on the whole Spartan system, which assumed that children were basically wild animals that needed training and controlling with great care in order to preserve useful wild instincts, while adapting them to the state's purposes.

II,12–14   The whole discussion of pederasty is clearly defensive, and very naïve. Such practices were widely accepted, though controlled, in Classical Greece, and may have formed an even more important part of life in a primitive tribal structure, where military needs dominating everyday life dictated that young men should grow up in an all-male society. Further, such bonds were useful in warfare, encouraging loyalty and comradeship. Xenophon's distinction between the spiritual and physical aspects of such attachments is interesting as an example of ingenious and ingenuous special pleading, but it is tempting to wonder how much even he expected to be believed.

To call chapter II a description of the 'educations of Sparta and of the other Greek states' is a travesty; Xenophon has given us an outline of what he regarded as the most important of those features of Spartan education which were geared to produce the qualities in which he claims, overtly or by implication, that Sparta excelled: obedience, respect and self-control. Simonides said 'They say that Sparta was called the man-tamer because its citizens were subservient to the laws ... as horses are broken right from the outset' (Plutarch, *Agesilaus*, 1, frag. 218 Bergk). While den Boer is broadly right in saying that 'children of genuine Spartans are regarded as the property of the state', one must beware of the tendency to regard this as unusual or to read back modern prejudices; the whole tenor of Pericles' funeral speech

---

* The whipping may have some parallel in the rites of the Lupercalia at Rome, and den Boer sees the theft of the cheeses as a survival of a puberty rite in the course of which the young men attained full manhood by seizing the cheeses, and acceptance as warriors by demonstrating their hardihood.

in Thucydides is similar—the individual is subservient to the needs of the city. The difference in Sparta is one of degree, not of basic outlook.

Some of the omissions in Xenophon's account emerge later; for example, they had some musical training because it had practical application in war time (see below on XIII,6–11). On literacy, Plutarch said 'their letters they learnt only for practical purposes' (*Lycurgus* 16), and the traditional Greek belief about Spartan anti-literacy is summed up, probably about 400 BC, in a curious philosophical rag-bag called the *Dissoi Logoi* (II,10; Diels-Kranz II,90,2,10). 'The Spartans think it is a good thing for children not to pursue musical and literary studies, the Ionians that it is disgraceful for them not to have a good knowledge of the whole field.' Sparta was not quite the cultural desert which this implies. Ceremonies connected with the worship of Artemis Orthia imply at least some form of literary competition, though not necessarily any form of originality in the entrants; perhaps Homer and the Spartan poets were known at least. Further, there was singing and dancing; see (e.g.) Aristophanes, *Lysistrata* 1296ff.

Xenophon, then, has concentrated exclusively on the aspect of Spartan education which was summarised by Plutarch immediately after the passage quoted above: 'The whole of the rest of their training is designed to produce obedience, fortitude in distress and victory in battle.'

III Xenophon approves of the Spartan approach of keeping 'teen-agers' as busy as possible to exclude time for other, less desirable occupations. In this he claims that Sparta is again the opposite of the rest of Greece, and seems to be describing a much exaggerated parody of the extremely 'hearty' Public School of the 1920s. Such a full-time educational system was only practical, of course, in a society where the state took financial responsibility for maintaining the children, for in the rest of Greece most children of this age were contributing to the family income. In Athens, for example, only those boys wealthy enough not to have to work seem to have spent their 'teens' in further education like the Spartans, though it was not state-controlled or organised, and the objectives were totally different. Secondly, the Spartan system could only work in a rigidly authoritarian society; in any other, the boys would revolt against an arrangement designed 'for them to have as little free time as possible' (§2). A small point worthy of note à propos of III,3 is that the heirs-apparent of the kings were exempt from the *Agoge*; Plutarch points out that Agesilaus was unusual in that he had been through the full training since he was not heir-apparent in his youth. The simplest explanation of this is that the Spartans did not wish to risk the possibility of their future kings performing poorly. Alternatively, the Spartans perhaps regarded qualities other than those instilled by the *Agoge* as more important for their rulers; they may have realised that the stress on obedience was not an ideal training for a future king.

The modesty of the Spartans was proverbial (§4–5), but the logic of the comparison between men and women which Xenophon makes does not bear a moment's scrutiny. One suspects that he was led to draw this conclusion because, while the Spartan men were notably more modest than the average Greek, the women *appeared* to be much less so because of the greater freedom of their lives. The whole passage is a rhetorical exaggeration.

The last sentence is a passing hint at the fact that the adolescents were from time to time admitted to the adult *sussitia* for the main meal, a process which was regarded as part of their education: 'Boys also used to attend the *sussitia* regularly, as if they were going to schools of self-control. They used to listen to the political discussions, and watch the examples of gentlemanly behaviour; they got used to humour and jesting without ribaldry, and learnt to take a joke without being offended' (Plutarch, *Lycurgus* 12).

IV,1–6 It was natural and essential that Lycurgus should take particular care of those who had just reached manhood, not merely for the obvious reason given, true as this was, but also because it was from this group that the Eirens were drawn who controlled in detail the education of the next generation of Spartiates. Thus it would matter not merely that the individual Eirens chosen for this job should be outstanding, but also that the whole group should be seen to stand for the virtues which the Spartan state held to be most important; this necessity sprang from the right and duty of all Spartiates to take a hand in the upbringing of the children (VI,1). Naturally also, in such a male-orientated and authoritarian society, the 'teenagers' would admire and imitate those who were a little older than themselves. There is a further element involved in this spirit of competition which Xenophon saw as central at this stage: the Spartan education as outlined up to now must have killed initiative and personal ambition—its main aim appears to have been to produce a uniform body of highly disciplined robots. Again, Plutarch: 'overall, Lycurgus trained the citizens neither to wish nor to be able to live as individuals. Like bees, they were always to be integrated with the state, swarming round their leader, almost beside themselves in their eagerness and rivalry to belong wholly to the state.' (*Lycurgus* 25) By providing a motive for individual self-improvement at a late stage in the educational process, Lycurgus encouraged them to develop beyond the universal minimum which had been achieved by their earlier training.

The group of 300 picked by the *Hippagretai* (apparently officials whose sole job was to select and manage these three groups of 100 men) were the élite of the young Spartan army, and formed the bodyguard of the king on campaign (cf. Thucydides V,72,4), and were sometimes mounted, hence their title of 'knights'. The picture of rival groups fighting whenever they met is hardly attractive, but perhaps comprehensible if the primary objective was to prove one's physical strength; despite the right of any passer-by to separate the contestants, ill-feeling must have been generated, and this cannot have helped the unity which Xenophon claims was generated by the system in national crises. Élite units within modern armies are sometimes similarly unpopular. Some have connected this passage with the *sphairomachia* of IX,5, which is probably to be interpreted as some form of boxing rather than a ball game, the name deriving from boxing gloves shaped like modern ones, as opposed to the thongs with which Greek boxers normally bound their hands; however, such an assumption would lead to the deduction that the whole of the 20–30 age group wore, or at least carried their gloves whenever they were out, which is surely too ludicrous to be conceivable. It is implicit in this passage that the membership of the group of 300 could change in the course of the ten years, and one is at liberty to doubt whether the rivalry was as pure and admirable as Xenophon implies. It is also likely that it led to a good deal of suspicion, hypocrisy and jealousy; the opposite is stressed in Pericles' funeral speech, and may be a conscious contrast: 'We not only have freedom in public life, but we do not indulge in anger and suspicion towards our neighbours in private if he does as he likes; we do not even put on disapproving looks, which, although harmless, are hurtful' (Thucydides II,37,2).

IV,7 That the 'other Greeks' did not require their senior citizens to keep fit in centrally organised programs is merely an extension of the normal freedom of approach to adult life which they adopted. A reasonable sense of self-preservation must have made them keep moderately fit: they knew they would in all likelihood have to take part in hoplite battles involving considerable exertion, and that their survival depended on their ability to 'last the course'. In point of fact, many Athenians did go to the gymnasia every day before dinner (Xenophon, *Symposium* I,7). That hunting was a major part of an adult Spartan's way of life not only arose from the terrain which surrounded Sparta, where they had within their own territory extensive and good hunting areas, but is also another example of the survival of the values of a fairly primitive community. Xenophon, himself a 'country gentleman', was interested in hunting, and a treatise on the subject survives which may at least be based on his own ideas; it is interesting that in it the author defends hunting against those who attack it as a waste of time (*on Hunting* XII,10f).

V,1–6 Xenophon has now described some aspects of the Spartan educational system up to the age of thirty, at which point the Spartiate was entitled to some relaxation of rigid discipline; he could, for example, set up house with his wife. It is important to be clear that Xenophon's account is selective, confined to the aspects which the author wishes to emphasise in contrast to the systems of other Greek states, those which he believes contribute most to the outstanding position of Sparta; witness the rhetorical questions with which he concludes each section.

In turning to a general discussion of Spartan life, Xenophon starts, not unnaturally, with the feature which was most noticeably different from the Greek norm, the communal life in *sussitia*. The nearest equivalent is a modern army mess, but the parallel is not close. All Spartiates had to eat the main meal of the day in their *sussition* until they were sixty, and between the ages of twenty and thirty had to spend the night with their companions also. Membership of a *sussition* was an essential prerequisite of full citizenship, and election at the age of twenty was dependent on satisfactory completion of the *Agoge*, physical fitness and acceptance by the members; one negative vote barred election. How membership was decided is uncertain; it may either have been a matter of being invited to join a certain group (or putting oneself up for it), or the *sussitia* may have had some territorial basis linked to land tenure. Whichever is correct, one cannot imagine that there was any significant wastage due to 'black-balling' because of the chronic shortage of manpower. It is perhaps marginally more likely that membership was not tied to land tenure because it appears from Plutarch (*Lycurgus* 12) that each *sussition* usually had about fifteen members; any territorial basis would be likely to lead in time to numerical disparity.

Xenophon again suggests that the institutions described were established with social motives, whereas they must surely have been survivals of a traditional way of life, which were probably later tightened up and systematised. From them may well have sprung *as results* the aspects of life which are here claimed as *motives* for the institution of the system. The military value of *sussitia* was universally recognised, and commented on as early as Herodotus (1,65); the mixing of age groups was a reflection of the army organisation (see below), and is paralleled in the modern army mess. Now, as then, the mixing of age groups may bring shared experience and some degree of restraint as well. The recounting of noble deeds (§ 6) is reminiscent of Achilles signing of the 'famous deeds of heroes' (Homer *Iliad* ix,189), and in a wider field is typical of any similar gathering of military men off duty.

The *sussitia* drew monthly contributions from each member. Plutarch gives the following figures: a bushel of barley, eight *choes* (about three and a half imperial gallons) of wine, five minas of cheese (either five or seven lb. approximately, depending on the standard used by Xenophon), two and a half minas of figs, and a small sum of money for meat and delicacies (*Lycurgus* 12). Dicaearchus, a historian of the fourth century quoted by Athenaeus (iv,141c), gives figures which are a half as much again for barley and wine, indefinite for cheese and figs, and 'around some ten Aeginetan obols' for meat. Assuming the figures to be somewhere in the right region, they do not represent a princely diet, and it is not surprising that Spartan food had a poor reputation in Greece, nor that they found it necessary to supplement their basic provisions by hunting. Plutarch tells how a king of Pontus bought a Spartan cook in order to have some of their famous *zomos*; when he tasted it, he was disgusted, and the cook's answer implied that it could only be appreciated after the rigours of a Spartan day (*Lycurgus* 12).*

The restrictions on drink refer to drinking parties, which normally followed dinner; in the rest of Greece, the toasts were announced and the wine passed round so that each should drain his cup to it in turn. It is this practice which Lycurgus is said to have banned, since it meant that individuals did not have control over the strength of what they drank (Greeks normally drank their wine diluted with water), nor over how much they drank, since they were expected to respond to the general toasts. Lycurgus' provisions were widely noticed in the ancient world.

A verse fragment of Critias preserves a contrast between Spartan drinking parties and others (Diels, II,88,6,9ff): 'such drinking (referring to non-Spartan parties) frees the tongue and leads to disgraceful stories, and weakens the body; dark mist sits in the eyes, and forgetfulness rots the memory, and the mind is befuddled. Servants cease to be obedient, and ruinous expense falls on the household. Spartan young men drink enough to bring joyful hope to the mind of all, and friendship and restrained gaiety to their conversation. Such drinking is good for the body, good for the mind, and not harmful to the purse; it is well suited for love and for sleep, the threshold of weariness, and also for Health, the sweetest of divinities to men, and for Self-control, the sister of Piety. . . . The drinking of too many healths brings momentary pleasure but enduring pain. The Spartan way brings food and drink enough for thinking and working, but no excess; they have no day set aside for over-indulgence and drunkenness.' The excesses that often accompanied drinking parties are illustrated on a wide range of vases; one may naturally question the uniform sobriety with which the Spartans were credited—there was no check on what those over thirty did after they had gone home—but the whole Spartan system encouraged self-control. Xenophon realised that the theoretical ideal of equality of wealth was not a practical reality (see below), but, leaving this aside for the moment, it is probable that the *sussitia* did have many of the effects claimed for them; in particular, they would undoubtedly have fostered the comradely spirit which springs up in any similar military órganisation, and would to that extent have been useful in the Spartan system. Equally, there was presumably a sound educational effect, as claimed, if the *sussition* was well conducted, though absence of 'wickedness and foul talk' would depend very much on individual members. Restraint on excessive spending are more likely to have come from the various provisions and customs which restricted public display, discussed below.

V,7–9 Sections 7 and 8 have something of the ring of afterthoughts

---

* A slightly different version of the story is given elsewhere by Plutarch (*Moralia* 236 F). It is not clear exactly what *zomos* was; A. H. M. Jones describes it as 'a peculiarly nauseous haggis', and Plutarch implies that it was made of blood, salt and vinegar, possibly with meat added. (*Moralia* 128 C).

to the main point. The matter of walking home at night only applied to those over thirty, since the others would be required to sleep where they were, and Xenophon's wording raises various other questions. The requirement to walk without a torch may make sense in preserving a soldier's night vision, but suggests dire possibilities if Aristophanes' description of the filth in the streets is anything to go by—as it presumably is in the absence of main drainage in Greek towns (*Wasps* 248,259). The phrase 'they must walk during the night as they do by day' is obscure: is one to take it as meaning with downcast eyes and without speech, with their hands within their cloaks (III,4)? This could pose certain problems even if they were sober.

The relation of diet to exercise is fairly obvious (assuming the interpretation of the corrupt sentence to be approximately accurate), but adds little, and one might have expected the point at the end of §3. Doubtless few would have quarrelled with the conclusion about Spartan physical health in §9 although it is somewhat exaggerated for effect, but it would have followed better from a full discussion of the training undertaken in the gymnasia. There is no clear indication why Spartan exercise was so much superior to that of other Greeks, though Ollier sees a possible hint in Xenophon's *Symposium*, II,17f with 1,7, where it may be implied that there was some particular form of dance which was Spartan and particularly well designed to develop all parts of the body.

VI,1-3 The exaggeration is manifest, not least in the last section; it is incredible that Sparta should have reached such a communistic-cum-utopian state that all goods were treated as common, and nobody minded if his neighbour helped himself at need. On the other hand, when one recognises the subjugation of the individual to the needs of the state which was normal in Greece, and reached its height in the Spartan tradition, it is possible to see this happening at times of crisis. Similarly, it is more credible to see the exercise of authority over another's children as being the exception rather than the rule. Yet here again, the necessity is more likely to have arisen at Sparta than elsewhere: they placed great stress on the training of boys by men, and yet the adults were so often absent on public service. There is practical sense behind the institution, but the moral value is presumably, as usual, deduced by Xenophon rather than the motive for introduction.

VI,4-5 The danger of being caught out late must have been pa,-ticularly relevant to the Spartan situation with the greater range of territory which could be covered and the difficulty of some of the terrain; it is noteworthy that the only reason which was normally accepted for absence from the evening meal in the *sussition* was that a man had been benighted while hunting. The exact nature of the caches of food referred to here is obscure, but it must be assumed that they were left in known spots for such an emergency, and regularly replenished; they presumably consisted of dried vegetables or some similar food which would last reasonably well. The accepted translation of this passage which implies that well equipped parties left behind what remained after they had eaten is scarcely tenable; there must have been more pattern than this, or the system would have been virtually useless.

The concluding sentence of the chapter implies that the arrangements of the *sussitia* and the provisions for hunting expeditions managed to level out inequalities of wealth in the society to an acceptable degree. Aristotle is definite that this was not so; there were Spartans who were so poor that they could not raise their contributions to their *sussition* without which they were expelled, and lost their status as full citizens (*Politics* 1271 a 30ff), while others were very well off. Xenophon's rose-coloured spectacles are in evidence again.

VII If a system such as that at Sparta was to work effectively, it was essential that those who were to concentrate solely on military affairs had an assured source of income which would not be affected by their prolonged absence. Such a system would inevitably preclude normal competition for wealth; as Xenophon notes, the Spartiates were required to give their attention to other matters. Implicit behind this chapter is the thorny question of the 'lot' or parcel of land which it is said every Spartiate received, and from which he derived his necessary fixed income. If one could accept the evidence of Plutarch and other very late writers at face value, there would be no problem; unfortunately, as with so much relating to Lycurgus and early Sparta, the earlier the authority, the less clear the evidence. Xenophon says nothing of a Lycurgan land distribution or of a system of lots for every Spartiate, and Aristotle knew nothing of Lycurgan land reforms. Whatever be the exact truth in this vexed matter (which is not central to this chapter), it is certain that each Spartan had somehow a minimum land holding from which he derived income. In extreme cases his income was so low that he found it difficult to maintain his contributions to his *sussition* and keep up a family.

The 'Lycurgan' equality which is implicit in this chapter is certainly far from the truth at any period of Spartan history on which we have any information, and may always have been theoretical rather than real. At least some proportion of the land was the personal property of the family which held it, rather than state land allocated to them, and such land could be given away or left by will. Therefore, if a family only had daughters, the land would pass with them into families where the men already had holdings of their own; the inevitable result was inequalities of wealth which would increase with the passage of time. Aristotle says of his own day: 'Almost two-fifths of the whole country belongs to women because there are many heiresses and dowries are large' (*Politics* 1270 a 23).* Note that at Sparta women could own property, while at Athens they could not.

* Plato, *Republic* VIII,547 c 6–548 c 7, forms an instructive critical picture, which, for all its ostensibly theoretical nature, may plausibly be related to Sparta of the period.

Lycurgus cannot be credited with the decision to retain the primitive iron currency referred to in §5; no other currency was known in Greece until well after his death, whichever of the possible periods one accepts for his life. The owning of precious metals was restricted in some way in Classical Sparta, and the restriction was at least partly successful since writers so often ascribe many of the evils which later overtook her to its breakdown. Therefore, despite the implausible motives given, Xenophon must be on the right lines in his analysis. However, the ban on coinage was not total. The money contributions to the *sussitia* may have been made in the local iron currency, but visitors to Sparta presumably paid for accommodation and daily necessities in coin, and Spartan embassies abroad must have needed some money in coin to pay expenses; this may have been officially minted for the purpose. The Spartans offered the Messenians 'large sums of money' as a reward for smuggling food to Sphacteria in 425 (Thucydides IV,26,5). Then there are the vast fines imposed on some offenders, for example Agis II, fined 100,000 drachmae (Thucydides V,63,2), and Pleistoanax 15 talents, which is 90,000 drachmae (Ephorus; Jacoby, *F Gr H* II,70 F 193); there are other instances from the fourth century. Such fines may have been intended to force a man into exile rather than to be paid, but suggest at least the possibility of payment, whether in land, precious metal or coin. Perhaps the kings were exempt from the general prohibition on possessing precious metal; cf. below on xv. Further, it is never suggested that Spartiate families were totally self-sufficient; they had to acquire at least some of the necessities of life which they did not produce. Probably Sparta avoided coining money of her own for general use until late—the earliest extant Spartan coins date from about 300 BC —but enough coin found its way in from other states for some of their everyday purposes, and this circulated. The restriction on the acquiring of wealth, and therefore by extension on the regular use of coinage, only applies, of course, to the Spartiates; the *Perioikoi*, who often lived by trade and were vital to the existence of Sparta, used money as all other Greeks.

The rejection of commercial enterprise, necessary as it may have been to the military position of Sparta, probably did more harm than any other single factor to her cultural life, since it is a truism that all cultural pursuits are ultimately financed from the surplus of income over the expenditure needed for bare minimum survival; such a surplus was unlikely to appear without trade in ancient Greece.

VIII The logic of this chapter is not one of historical sequence; Xenophon is discussing the famous Spartan obedience, which leads him first to consider how Lycurgus secured the agreement of the people, though he disregards opposition which Plutarch says his measures met on their first introduction (*Lycurgus* 3 and 5); cf. below on xv. Then, although the powers he discusses are of much later origin, as he himself realised, he turns to the Ephors as clear examples of the obedience of Spartans even when holding magistracies; finally, he reverts to what he regards as Lycurgus' master stroke in securing obedience.

Like the last, this chapter raises problems of dating. First, it is not remotely likely that the whole of the *Eunomia* was brought in at one time, and it is therefore difficult to decide when the supposed consultation of the Delphic oracle took place. A document called the Great Rhetra is preserved in Plutarch, *Lycurgus* 6 (cf. Tyrtaeus frag. 3 Bergk), which is traditionally Lycurgan and sanctioned by Apollo, but must surely be dated to the seventh century, and probably not early in it either. Many of the other provisions, especially those which Xenophon has been discussing in the previous chapters, and which are therefore presumably referred to here, must be much earlier. However, it is not plausible to suggest that any legislator would have thought it worth while to get his proposals approved by Delphi much before 725, when the oracle first began to emerge as a political force. Delphic approval for one provision may have been extended in popular tradition to the whole system, much of which had been in existence for a long time in the late seventh century. The oracle may have been consulted about then in connection with a tightening up of the Spartan system which appears to have taken place then. It is worth noting that the approval of Delphi would have carried a good deal more weight with an average Greek than we might suppose from a modern standpoint; however, it is unlikely that even Delphic approval could have carried through reforms which were not basically acceptable to the Spartans and seen to be necessary.

The date of the institution of the Ephors is another insoluble conundrum. They held a position of power by the sixth century, and it is tempting to link this authority with the name of Chilon, who was Ephor in 556–5; however, Ephors probably existed well before this. By the fifth century their powers were very considerable, and Xenophon only touches on those which are germane to his theme. A frequently used analogy to the position of the Ephors is that of the Tribunes at Rome, but Tribunes had not the real powers of the Ephors, who also accompanied the kings on campaign after the beginning of the fifth century. Further, in many ways Ephors look like representatives of the aristocracy curbing the royal power; cf. xv,7.

The possibility of deposing magistrates in the course of their year of office was far from unique; as Xenophon well knew, all magistrates had to have their conduct approved once a month at Athens (to take only one example), and any complaint could lead to prosecution and deposition; equally, Athenian magistrates could be impeached at any time of the year for a sufficiently serious offence. The difference was that the Ephors apparently acted on their own authority (therefore 'like tyrants'), whereas at Athens or elsewhere a court decision was required. Xenophon's desire for the telling contrast has led him to obscure the precise point of difference.

IX It would indeed be a 'source of wonder' if one man had been able to establish the Spartan principle of bravery and their preference for death to dishonour. Such is the code of primitive, aristocratic and war-like societies, and it is not surprising to find such values elevated to the level of the greatest of virtues at Sparta. The Spartan scale of values was perhaps best expressed at an early date by Tyrtaeus, who, despite an anti-Spartan tradition that he was a lame Athenian summoned to Sparta to bolster morale at a time of difficulty during the second Messenian War of about 640–20, was probably himself a Spartan, and held command in the war:

'I would not remember nor include in my song any man for swiftness of foot or wrestling skill, not even if he had the strength and stature of the Cyclops and ran more swiftly than the north wind from Thrace, nor yet if he were more handsome than Tithonus or wealthier than Midas or Cinyras, nor again if he were more royal than Pelops the son of Tantalus or more sweet-tongued than Adrastus, nor even if he had every virtue other than might in war. A man is not good in war unless he has the courage to look on blood and slaughter and stand face to face with his foe and strike. This is virtue, this is the best and finest prize for a young man to win among men. It is a blessing common to the city and the whole people when a man stands firm in the front rank with determination, utterly forgetting the disgrace of flight, protected by his courage and endurance, steeling his neighbour by his words; this man is good in war. Swiftly he routs the savage ranks of the enemy, eagerly he stems the tide of battle. He who falls in the front rank and loses his dear life brings glory to his country, his people and his father; wounded many times in front through shield and breastplate, he is mourned by old and young alike, and the whole city grieves with bitter longing. His tomb, his children and his line are marked out among men; never will his glory and his fame perish; although he is in the tomb, he achieves immortality, for mighty Ares slew him at his moment of glory as he stood and fought for his children and his land. If he escapes the black fate of death and upholds the proud boast of his spear in victory, young and old alike honour him, and great are his joys before he dies; as he grows old he is outstanding among the citizens, and none would willingly deprive him of his honour or his rights; all yield place to him, the young, his contemporaries and his elders. This is the peak of virtue to which each should now aspire, never relaxing in war' (Diehl[3] 1,i,9).

The opposite point of view was expressed much more succinctly (and arguably more gracefully) at about the same time or a little earlier by Archilochus of Paros: 'Some Thracian now glories in the shield I dropped by a bush; there was nothing wrong with it, but I had no choice—and I saved my life. What do I care for that shield? To hell with it! I can get just as good a one again' (Diehl[3] 1,iii,6). Plutarch (*Moralia* 239 B) records a story that as soon as Archilochus arrived in Sparta he was expelled for having written this epigram.

Whatever the truth of the story about Archilochus, it is surely true that not all Spartans naturally shared Tyrtaeus' approach to war, and this supposition is borne out by Xenophon and other sources, which list detailed penalties for those guilty of cowardice; even Spartans needed more than abstract ideals to encourage them to live up to the very high standards expected of them. In fact, if a Spartan deserted in the face of the enemy, the least penalty was to lose his citizenship; the penalties referred to here must therefore be for lesser forms of cowardice —it was not enough merely to do the minimum.

The whole discussion of penalties is obscure and rather unsatisfactory. The statement that cowards in other Greek cities suffer very little is demonstrably false, another rhetorical exaggeration designed to heighten the contrast. In Athens cowardice was a specific charge; those found guilty suffered partial loss of citizen rights, including exclusion from the market-place and state sacrifices—and here again for an offence less than actual desertion in the face of the enemy. Granted the military orientation of Spartan society, exclusion from the *sussitia* and social ostracism are penalties which are only to be expected; the others mentioned are less easy. The *sphairai* contests have already been noticed in passing in IV,6. For long, scholars held that this was a form of ball game, but it seems more likely that it was a type of boxing match, particularly since the 'game' is said to be the nearest possible simulation of war. Obviously the branded coward could not be included in the group of 300 outstanding young men picked by the *Hippagretai*; it is not surprising that cowards were also left out of the less formal *sphairai* contests if they were some form of para-military exercise.

Plutarch (*Lycurgus* 21) refers to three choruses of differing age groups whose function was to sing of deeds of bravery, past, present and future; it is not surprising that the cowards did not play a major role, here, though Xenophon refers not merely to them, but to a wider field, including dancing. The reference to unmarried women is again presumably a matter of social ostracism, though this ostracism extended not merely to a coward's daughters but also to other girls whose guardian he might be. Spartans were unwilling to marry into such a family—for eugenic reasons? It is not surprising that it was difficult for a coward to find a wife, but the implication of this passage appears to be that a branded coward's wife might leave him, and despite this he would be subject to the penalties inflicted on bachelors. Plutarch describes the disabilities of the unmarried Spartiates (*Lycurgus* 15): 'They were excluded from watching the boys and girls at exercise. During the winter the magistrates ordered them to walk around the market-place without cloaks, and as they walked they had to sing a song against themselves stating the justice of their punishment for disobeying the laws; they were also deprived of the respect and service which the young showed to their elders.' Xenophon calls this *atimia*; while the primary meaning is 'disgrace' in this context, it is also used as the term for partial or total loss of citizen rights. Marriage was regarded as part of a man's duty to the state, and it was normal for the proposers of ideal constitutions, such as Plato, to include penalties for men not married by a certain age, usually the mid-thirties.

The final sentence is more of a comment on Xenophon than on Sparta.

X Xenophon here ends his discussion of the Spartan educational system, with all its pervasive and life-long control of what a man did; it has something of the feel of '1984' with 'every man's neighbour' taking the place of 'Big Brother'. The whole tone, particularly in §§4–7 is more theoretical, almost philosophical, than that of the previous nine chapters. He gives his approval to the core of Lycurgus' provisions, recognising their severity, but arguing their justice; finally he points to their antiquity, for him yet another proof of virtue. 'All praise' them is at least an exaggeration; the truth is betrayed by the remainder of Xenophon's concluding sentence.

On matters of detail, see the Introduction on the date of Lycurgus and on the *Homoioi*. The *Gerousia* was the main advisory council in Sparta, consisting of the kings and twenty-eight members who were all over the age of sixty. The method of election to this body is yet another 'primitive' survival, described in detail by Plutarch, *Lycurgus* 26. In brief, the candidates appeared before the assembly of Spartiates, who shouted their approval of each one. Men locked in a building near by where they could not see the Assembly, and therefore could not see which candidate appeared when, judged the loudness of each shout; the loudest won. Members of the Gerousia had a position of very great honour and probably considerable influence in day-to-day, informal discussions, though their political power 'on paper' was not very great. Xenophon approves, without apparently considering the dangers of a governing council many of whom must have been approaching senility, and the repressive effect its existence must have had on younger men with good ideas. Aristotle (*Politics* 1270 b 36–1271 a 13) is well aware of the disadvantages, and describes the method of election (not unjustifiably) as 'childish'.

XI The main aim, one might almost say the only aim, of the Lycurgan system was to produce the best possible military machine; it is therefore natural that Xenophon should turn now to a more detailed discussion of the Spartan army. He starts, as he did with the life of a Spartiate, from the very beginning, and it is interesting to see that the tradition on which he draws does not go back to a period earlier than that at which the Ephors established themselves as powerful magistrates; it cannot have been before the mid-sixth century at the earliest that they had control of the mobilisation of the army, and it is more likely to have been later. Similarly, the division of the army into regiments (*morai* §4) appears to have been a fairly recent innovation. Almost all Xenophon's military description relates to the Spartan army as he knew it himself in the early fourth century. He is presumably drawing on his extensive experience of fighting with Spartans, particularly in Asia Minor under Thibron and Dercylidas in 399–7, and under Agesilaus, to whom he became greatly devoted, in 396–4. For all this, there are numerous small details which cannot be made to tally with our knowledge of the actual Spartan field army of the period. This is the basis of one of Chrimes' main attacks on the authenticity of the work, but it seems more likely that here, as elsewhere, Xenophon sacrifices detailed precision to a generalised and idealised picture designed to support his main thesis of the excellence of Sparta.

XI,2–3 It is difficult to judge how much superior the Spartan supporting forces were to those of the other Greeks. Xenophon was an experienced soldier, and his remarks in this section therefore merit great respect; note, however, that he merely comments on the efficiency of the system without specifically claiming superiority over others, although the properly organised baggage train *sounds* more efficient than the average administration of such things in Greece. Naturally, the artisans taken on campaign would have been *Perioikoi* or Helots; such occupations were not for the *Homoioi*. Despite the 300 so-called cavalry enlisted under the *Hippagretai*, Sparta did not have a regular cavalry force until 424; before this date the cavalry were a despised and unimportant arm of the forces, raised and equipped *ad hoc* for a particular job.

The red cloaks appear to have been worn in battle not merely because it was a colour which women in Greece did not wear, but also because blood would show up less on them if the soldiers were wounded (Aristotle, *Constitution of Sparta* fr. 86 = Müller *FHG* ii, p. 130; Plutarch, *Moralia* 238 F). It is perhaps also relevant that red appears to have been associated throughout primitive Greece with amulets and other similar magical devices to ward off harm. Red cloaks are not exclusively Spartan. There are records of whole armies so dressed, of which only small sections were actually Spartans; had they been deliberately equipped in the Spartan fashion to produce a psychological effect on their enemies? The mention of bronze shields is more difficult in that they were standard throughout Greece at the time; it is possible that the Spartans had only recently abandoned the larger, leather shield of antiquity. If this were so, the comment would be explicable, even if grossly anachronistic, since Xenophon would be giving a reason for their adoption, and also incidentally commenting on Spartan turn-out —one can easily believe that they took more pride in the polish of their shields than the average Greek.

A fragment of Plato the comedian comments mockingly on the Spartans' long hair in wartime (Kock, 1,124); presumably it was archaic. To wear it was a considerable relaxation of the normal restrictions for those under thirty, as is shown by the passage in Plutarch where the bride has her hair cut short so that she shall look like a young man (see above on 1,5–6).

XI,4–6 The division of the army into units is a subject on which ancient authorities conflict; in translating I have deliberately selected words to represent the various grades of officer and divisions of the army which carry as little overtone as possible from the modern world. Preconceptions should be totally eliminated from the reader's mind if possible, because in Sparta, as elsewhere in the ancient world, the whole officer structure and arrangement in tactical units was so different that terms are not transferable. The important aspect is that Sparta had a standard and highly organised officer structure, a feature missing from almost all contemporary Greek armies, who lacked more than anything the skill and steadiness in command best seen in the Roman centurion. Because of their command structure, the Spartans were able to carry out certain fairly basic manoeuvres on the battle-field which were beyond other Greek forces; normally, once a Greek army was committed there was little the general could do except join the ranks and hope to inspire those immediately around him by his example.

By Xenophon's day the *Perioikoi* were probably brigaded with the Spartiates in the hoplite army; he does not point this out because it would have been out of key with the whole passage which is dealing in wide generalisations, and to mention the essential contribution of the *Perioikoi* to the Spartan army would have lessened the impact of the picture he is painting. The exact numbers in each unit, and the total for the army are matters of deep controversy beyond the scope of this commentary; Thucydides (v,68,3) gives a slightly different picture. For a full discussion, see Gomme, Andrewes and Dover, *Commentary* Vol. IV, 110–7, and Wade-Gery, *Essays in Greek History*, 71ff.

XI,7–10 The superior discipline of Spartan forces contributed enormously to their success, not least because of their steadiness (§7). For his security the Greek hoplite depended on the protection offered to his exposed right side by his neighbour's shield; thus any casualty or disruption of the line was potentially dangerous, and real discipline and automatic reactions were essential. The various manoeuvres mentioned in these sections are largely self-explanatory, though they must have depended on a detailed chain of command and precise reaction, for there is no question that Xenophon understates the difficulty of executing them in the face of the enemy. He was probably led to do so by the practical professional's contempt for the theorists (the 'instructors in tactics' of §8). When an enemy appeared in the rear the Spartans took up reverse order because the lines were normally drawn up with the most experienced men at the front; if they had not reversed their positions, the least experienced would have gone into battle in the front rank, and thus born the brunt of the fighting. The commander of a Greek army was normally stationed on the right, as was the commander of each individual unit in the line; this gave him greater control over the tendency of the hoplite to edge to the right to get more protection from his neighbour's shield. The claim that there is no disadvantage in having the commander on the left must assume the discipline of the Spartan army which would have minimised this tendency. The point about encircling is obscure; an attempt by the enemy to encircle the commander personally (rather than the whole formation) is probably meant, and, if so, then one can understand the benefit of having the shield on the outside.

XII It is surprising to find Xenophon even mentioning the shape of the Spartan camp, since Greek armies did not normally fortify their camps heavily, regarding them as places to be abandoned, not defended, if the enemy approached; the whole Greek fighting technique was geared to set-piece battles in the open. The reason for Xenophon's description may be a desire to give a context to his description of life inside the camp; he is the only authority for a circular camp.

The postings of sentries by day and by night show not merely military sense, but also that even on campaign the Spartans did not trust the Helots and other non-Spartans who accompanied them; this can be the only deduction from the central storage and guarding of arms, and one must assume that the arms dumps were guarded by night as well as by day, unless §7 is to be read as implying that all arms were drawn by their owners each night before they went to sleep. It is perhaps less than likely that the Helots would all be left armed during the night if such security precautions were taken during the day.

The Skiritai came from the northern end of Spartan territory, and were a hardy mountain people. It seems probable, though it is nowhere specifically stated, that they were light-armed specialists; cf. XIII,6. Mercenaries were first used by the Spartans in the course of the Peloponnesian War (Thucydides III,109,2), and became a regular feature of the Spartan army, as of those of all other Greek states, in the fourth century. The tone of §4 is again defensive; probably many Greeks mocked the Spartans for their excessive caution even within their own camps, but again the passage is useful evidence of their attitude and position.

The daily routine in the camp is much what one would expect of Spartans, though a little more relaxed than their way of life in peacetime; such relaxation on campaign was unique in Greece (Plutarch, *Lycurgus* 22). Their efficiency and organisation contrast vividly with the laissez-faire apparent in the accounts of the encampments of some other Greek armies, for example that described in Demosthenes, *Against Conon*, 3f. To stress the piety of the Spartans in camp would be only natural for Xenophon, who throughout his life showed more than ordinary respect towards the traditional Greek religion.

XIII By a natural transition Xenophon now moves to a brief discussion of the kings; not merely were they in themselves a unique survival in Greece proper, but they commanded the army. It is with the latter aspect of their position that he is concerned, not with a general discussion of their role in the Spartan constitution. Xenophon assumes throughout that only one king was present on a campaign. The rule that only one king should accompany an army was established after the fiasco of Demaretus' disagreement with Cleomenes in 506, thus reversing earlier practice (Herodotus v,75). Xenophon reflects the situation of his own day.

XIII,1–5 It was normal for the king to be maintained at public expense at all times (Herodotus vi,57), and Xenophon presumably comments because not merely he, but also his council were publicly maintained on campaign. The membership of the council is specified in §7; the most important members were the six regimental commanders. The list is not in order of importance; Xenophon appears to have listed first those who were almost always present—hence the high position of the *aulos*-players—and then those whose duties would often prevent their presence at meals. The 'volunteers' might be anyone invited, and in all probability it was in this capacity that Xenophon himself was a member of the entourage of Agesilaus.

The detailed description of sacrifices and the great importance attached to them are in tune with Xenophon's own interests, but are neither surprising nor a piece of archaism. One of the king's main functions was as an intermediary between men and gods; cf. xiii,11. Modern readers tend to be misled by the 'advanced' and 'rationalist' tone of a few Athenian writers into thinking that official religion was not of any great importance in classical Greece; the reverse is true, as can be seen from a mass of evidence, not least the impiety trials in Athens towards the end of the fifth century. For the particular point of sacrifices at the border being taken seriously, see (e.g.) Thucydides v, 54,2. Quite incidentally, Xenophon shows up an important distinction: whereas in Sparta itself the Ephors had at least as much constitutional authority as the kings, on campaigns the authority of the king was much greater despite the restriction noted in §10 below—an exact parallel to the greatly increased power of a Roman magistrate in the field.

The sacrifice offered to Zeus the Leader is not merely a sacrifice to the father of the gods, but also to a god who was specifically a war god, under a name traditional at Sparta. 'The gods associated with him' are probably the Dioskouroi, Castor and Pollux, since they, and particularly Castor, were the tutelary war-gods of Sparta. Athena was associated with Zeus in at least one Spartan cult; the sacrifice mentioned by Xenophon was probably offered to her in her role as a tutelary divinity of Sparta called Athena of the Brazen House. To preserve the fire from a particular sacrifice for use on subsequent occasions was not solely a Spartan custom; such fire was regarded as peculiarly sacred and pure.

The hour of the day-to-day sacrifices is a little unusual; it was normal to sacrifice to the Olympian gods early in the day, but not as early as this. Xenophon's explanation, that the Spartans intended to preempt the favour of the gods before the enemy held their sacrifice, is possible, but it smacks of his personal combination of piety and practical utility, and may be his own guess at the explanation of an ancient custom. The list of those present at the sacrifice requires no comment except for the 'commanders of foreign detachments'. They may be the

commanders of contingents from the Peloponnesian League, or of
detachments of *Perioikoi*, although he does not use the normal term for
the latter, and at the period referred to the *Perioikoi* were fully integrated in the Spartan army; it seems more likely that he is referring to
Spartiates assigned to command mercenary troops.

XIII,6–11 The fluent efficiency of the Spartan command structure
was apparent *en passant* in §§1 and 5 — irrelevant and trivial matters are
not allowed to distract the commander-in-chief, and once decisions
are taken they are transmitted smoothly; cf. Thucydides v,66,3f. A
similar theme runs through the rest of the chapter: the whole process is
thorough and efficient because the arrangements have already been
made, and each man knows his duties.

Before a battle, the king is said to take the *agema* of the first regiment.
It is possible (though unlikely) that this just means 'takes command of';
it may alternatively be that the *agema* is a division of the regiment.
However, Ollier has suggested attractively that, since the word came
later to mean the royal bodyguard in the Macedonian army, *agema*,
like other technical terms, was borrowed by the Macedonians from
Sparta, and therefore the reference here is to a similar special corps,
consisting of the 300 cavalry who were responsible for the king's safety.
The translation 'the first company' is intended to give something of an
'élitist' feel without prejudicing the issue. The king's position towards
the right wing was relatively well protected and secure, and from it he
could exercise as much control as was practicable over the actual battle
line. He was in no position to control the reserves, and Xenophon notes
that this was the responsibility of the senior member of the king's
council, who was presumably the senior regimental commander. It is
symptomatic of the lack of sophistication of a hoplite battle that it was
not felt necessary for the commander-in-chief to have personal control
of the disposition of the reserves, nor, apparently, of where and when to
commit them.

In §§8–9 Xenophon digresses to describe certain ceremonies at the
beginning of an actual battle. The sacrifice of a year-old male goat,
presumably to Artemis Agrotera, was a form of sympathetic magic
designed to ensure that the same fate overtook their enemies. The
musicians played the *aulos*, an instrument whose basic principle was not
unlike that of our oboe, and their presence was designed to enhance the
dignity of the occasion, and, combined with the dress of the army, was
presumably intended to have an effect on the morale of the enemy. A
noteworthy feature of a Spartan battle line was that it advanced in an
organised and controlled way to the music of the *aulos*. Their soldiers
had enough confidence and skill to do without the initial advantage
which most Greek armies sought from the impact of as fast a charge as
a hoplite could achieve, and they did not rely on shouting to encourage
each other as they went into battle.

The discussion of 'words of encouragement' (§9) is extremely obscure.
Perhaps Xenophon refers to the period immediately before the two

sides actually met when general exhortations would be inaudible
because of the *auloi* and general din. Even if this is so, it is suprising that
the members of a single platoon, about thirty-two men, probably in
four columns eight deep, could not hear their commanding officer;
perhaps the whole process has been 'telescoped', and the point at
issue is that the commander of the *next* platoon could not hear, and
therefore the message had to be passed from the man on the nearest
corner of the neighbouring platoon.

Xenophon returns in §§10–11 to the main theme of the chapter, the
position of a king on campaign, and ends with some fairly random
notes, together with an analysis of how he was relieved of unnecessary
duties. The special officers mentioned handled some of the more
delicate matters about which disputes might arise, particularly between
the Spartiates and their allies. The functions of the king remain purely
military and religious, which is not meant in any way to detract from
his position, but rather to emphasize its dignity: all that really mattered
at the time was entrusted to him.

XV   After ascribing all the excellent aspects of the *Eunomia* to Lycurgus,
the book not unnaturally concludes with a chapter on the method by
which he ensured acceptance of his reforms. Despite the tendency of
classical Sparta to ascribe almost everything to Lycurgus, nobody ever
suggested that he was responsible for the double kingship; it was rightly
recognised as being of much earlier origin. It was therefore necessary
to posit some process whereby reform was accepted, and men realised
that this reform involved some curtailment of the powers of the kings.
Xenophon does not descend to the sort of folk-tales purveyed by
Plutarch, who claims to have details of the strife which was the prelude
to the reforms, and even to be able to give a significant number of
names of those involved (*Lycurgus* 3 and 5), but concentrates on the
firmer ground of the position which was established for the kings,
implying that a reasonable compromise was reached. Accepted throughout the chapter is the belief, already mentioned in the Introduction,
that the Spartan constitution remained unchanged from the time of
Lycurgus until after the classical period; this is absurd, whatever the
date assumed for Lycurgus, but does reflect the truth that Sparta
received a stable constitution relatively early, and retained it for a long
period with surprisingly little modification and an almost total lack of
the violent change endemic in Greek politics. Chapter xv is the nearest
the whole work comes to discussing the constitution in the modern
sense, but there is no attempt at an exhaustive analysis. To take but
two obvious examples, there is no discussion of the power to initiate
legislation nor of the exact relative positions of kings and Ephors. Yet
again, Xenophon is concerned with the actual situation rather than
historical sequence or detailed precision. One point could be misleading: §§6–7 might be read as implying that Ephors were instituted, or
more likely already important, at the time of Lycurgus; that this was
not so is clear, and Xenophon himself implied as much in viii,3.

The *Education of Cyrus* betrays in Xenophon a tendency to favour royalty, and he gives his preference full rein here. He restates the essence of the king's position: the leader of the state in matters of religion and war. This is, no doubt, a primitive survival, and the privileges which went with the position, and are listed here, were equally antique; the 'grant' by Lycurgus must in reality represent a moment of constitutional change when the kings were allowed to *retain* their ancestral privileges. On one point Xenophon is wide of the mark: Plato said: 'One must be quite sure that they (the Spartans) are the wealthiest of the Greeks in gold and silver, and the king is the wealthiest of them; the largest share of this income belongs to the kings, and the royal tribute which the Spartans pay to them is not insignificant' (*Alcibiades* I, 123 a–b). Despite all this income, the kings lived at public expense. There is no question that there were differentials of wealth, and that the 'inner group' of families were better off than most Spartiates; Xenophon's own discussion of the lending of hunting dogs (VI,3) demonstrates that differences existed. Within the inner group, it would not be surprising if the two royal families were the most wealthy; they owned a considerable amount of land, and had large incomes and profitable privileges, including receiving the skins of sacrificial victims, mentioned here. Perhaps Xenophon is judging by the way of life of Agesilaus, which was notably modest.

The remaining details included by Xenophon are tantalisingly brief and disjointed, but together paint a picture of the high status of the king in society, while at the same time showing that he was not totally exempt from the ordinary duties of a Spartiate. The obligation of eating in the *sussitia* may have been waived relatively often, but it was there in theory, and it is recorded that Agis II was prevented from disregarding it when he returned from a successful foreign campaign (Plutarch, *Lycurgus* 12); equally, the king's arrival did not interrupt an Ephor engaged on public business. The exchange of oaths was a mark of the constitutional restraints on the king, and presumably dates from the time of their imposition. There was nothing unique about this *type* of oath being taken regularly by various organs of government in a Greek state.

Having chosen to focus so much attention on the regal aspect of the Spartan constitution, Xenophon tones down the unbalanced effect by his final remarks on the kings when alive, and perhaps it is not implausible to see the influence of Agesilaus here; if there was any question of the work being published, a king who wished to achieve his aims in Sparta by being modest could not have had his position jeopardised by Xenophon's fondness for royalty; their close association was too well known. The temporary lowering of the grandiose tone is more than compensated for by the stress laid on the semi-divine honours rendered to the kings after death; they included widespread and compulsory mourning, representatives to attend the funeral from all over Laconia, and the suspension of public business; the details are given by Herodotus (VI,58).

XIV It is impossible to conceive that this chapter was originally designed to stand between XIII and XV as the manuscripts transmit it; its tone is altogether different, it refers to Sparta in decline, and is manifestly condemnatory, while the whole of the rest of the work is laudatory, and rather uncritically so. Assuming that XIV is genuine, which seems likely since a forger would hardly have inserted such a manifestly different piece so ineptly, one must fall back on some theory such as that propounded in the Introduction which assumes that Xenophon had written, but not 'published' the work fairly early in his life, and that XIV is a 'postscript' attempting to analyse briefly the cause of Sparta's later downfall.

Xenophon is by no means the only source for the fact that Spartans, once removed from the restraints inherent in life in Sparta, tended to fall away from 'Lycurgan' standards; Pausanias and Lysander were flagrant examples, and there were many more. In the years immediately following 404 many Spartans had to go abroad, and even live abroad for long periods to administer Sparta's newly won dominion in Greece; worse, many of them were sent out as Harmosts, a position which made them virtual tyrant of a city; what could be more different from the restraints of everyday life at home? Equally, Sparta's position dictated that she must admit many more foreigners to Sparta itself, and therefore the ancient practice of expelling foreigners fell even more into abeyance. The practice was never rigid, but in times of tension had provided a way by which the leaders of the state could and did prevent the ordinary Spartiate from being exposed to seditious ideas; compare the story of Archilochus, above. At the time when XIV was written it was apparently these very leaders of the state who were most corrupted—perhaps understandably so if they had in any case been the wealthier members of society. The tragedy of the change is epitomised for Xenophon by the fact that, whereas formerly the Greeks in general looked to Sparta for moral leadership, now they were banding together to prevent a revival of her power. He can only comfort himself with the assertion that the fault lay not with the *Eunomia* which he admired so much, but with the men who rejected all that it stood for. However, such a disastrous collapse calls into question the whole of a system which cannot instil into those brought up under it sufficient strength of character and devotion to their professed ideals to stand up to any prolonged exposure to standards different from their own.

SELECT BIBLIOGRAPHY

1 ANCIENT SOURCES

(a) The *Politeia of the Spartans*:

The present translation has been based on *Xenophontis Opera Omnia*, Vol. v; *Opuscula*, edited by E. C. Marchant, (Oxford, Oxford University Press, 1920) and also Marchant's edition in the Loeb Classical Library, *Xenophon* Vol. vii, *Scripta Minora*, (London, Heinemann, and Cambridge, Mass., Harvard University Press, 1925) and *Xenophontis Opuscula*, edited by G. Pierleoni, (Rome, Acad. dei Lyncei, 1954). There is no adequate commentary in English; the standard work is *Xénophon, La République des Lacédémoniens*, text, translation and commentary by F. Ollier, (Lyon, Bosc, 1934) a thorough and intelligent analysis to which I owe a good deal. I have also consulted *Jenofonte, La Republica de los Lacedemonios*, edited by M. R. Gomez, revised by M. F. Galiano, (Madrid, Instituto de Estudios Politicos, 1957) (in Spanish). K. M. T. Chrimes, *The Respublica Lacedaemonorium ascribed to Xenophon*, (Manchester, Manchester University Press, 1947) is ingenious, though I disagree with many of the conclusions reached there.

(b) Other works:

Plutarch's *Life of Lycurgus* is a mine of information, some reliable, some wildly anachronistic; other Plutarch lives of Spartans also contain useful material, but *Moralia* 208 B–242 B (*Sayings of Spartans, Ancient Customs of the Spartans* and *Sayings of Spartan Women*) must be treated with great caution. All are available in the Loeb Classical Library, *Lives*, edited by Bernadotte Perrin, xi Vols, 1914–26, *Moralia*, ed. F. C. Babbitt, Vol. iii, 1931. For modern discussions of Plutarch, see: C. P. Jones, *Plutarch and Rome*, (Oxford, Clarendon Press, 1971) and D. A. Russell, *Plutarch*, (London, Duckworth, 1973).

Other information in classical authors tends to be scattered; some of the more obvious passages are referred to in the commentary. The majority of these works are available in Loeb or Penguin translations; for others, references are given to the standard collections. The ancient sources behind much of our knowledge of Sparta are fully listed in A. H. M. Jones, *Sparta*, (Oxford, Blackwell, 1967); this is much the most valuable aspect of this book.

2 GENERAL WORKS ON SPARTA

On Sparta in general, see W. G. Forrest, *A History of Sparta 950–192 BC*, (London, Hutchinson; New York, Norton, 1968); Paul Cartledge, *Sparta and Lakonia* (London and Boston, Routledge & Kegan Paul, 1979); L. F. Fitzhardinge, *The Spartans* (London, Thames and Hudson, 1980); mention may also be made of H. Mitchell, *Sparta*, (Cambridge, Cambridge University Press, 1952 (paperback edition 1964).) Three excellent constitutional essays on Sparta by A. Andrewes, A. H. M. Jones and F. W. Walbank are to be found in *Ancient Society and Institutions, Studies presented to Victor Ehrenberg*, (Oxford, Blackwell, 1966), pp. 1–20; 165–75; 303–12; compare the chapter on Sparta in A. Andrewes, *The Greek Tyrants*, (London, Hutchinson's University Library, 1956). Three important articles are: W. G. Forrest, 'The Lycourgan Reform', *Phoenix* XVII (1963), 157–79; Chester G. Starr, 'The Credibility of Early Spartan History', *Historia* XIV (1965), 257–72; M. I. Finley, 'Sparta', in *Problèmes de la Guerre en Grèce ancienne*, edited by J. P. Vernant, (Paris, Mouton, 1968) 143–160 (in English).

3 OTHER WORKS

Interesting material on Sparta and her influence may be found in E. Rawson, *The Spartan Tradition in European Thought*, (Oxford, Clarendon Press, 1969); E. N. Tiger-stedt, *The Legend of Sparta in Classical Antiquity*, (Stockholm, Almqvist & Wiksell) Vol. I, 1965. W. den Boer, *Laconian Studies*, (Amsterdam, N-Holland Publishing Company, 1954) centres his analysis in Part III on an anthropological approach, which on occasions leads to curious history; however, there are some thought-provoking ideas.

On the subject of education, the following books all contain useful analyses of Sparta in particular, and also of the systems of other Greek states: W. Jaeger, *Paideia* (trans, G. Highett), (4th edition, Oxford, Blackwell, 3 vols, 1954–61); F. A. G. Beck, *Greek Education, 450–350 BC*, (London, Methuen, 1964); H. I. Marrou, *A History of Education in Antiquity* (trans. George Lamb), (London, Sheed and Ward, 1956). On the family in general, and in particular on the problems of Spartan family life (if one may use the term at all), see W. K. Lacey, *The Family in Classical Greece*, (London, Thames and Hudson, 1968, cited as *Family*). Finally, a great deal of excellent material and detailed critical discussion can be found by an intelligent use of the indices of A. W. Gomme, A. Andrewes, K. J. Dover, *A Historical Commentary on Thucydides*, (Oxford, Clarendon Press, 5 vols, 1945–81).

The Boeotian Constitution

INTRODUCTION

The extremely brief outline of the constitution of Boeotia translated here is excerpted from a longer fragment of a history of Greece which apparently took up the story where Thucydides broke off. It was discovered in two extensive sections of papyrus in Egypt in 1906 and 1934; despite ingenious speculation, the identity of the author remains unknown, though it is likely that he was one of a number of writers whose names we know from other sources, though their works have not survived in manuscript form. Within a passage dealing with the history of the years 396–5 in great detail and with considerable skill, the outline of the Boeotian constitution forms a digression designed to provide necessary background to the history being discussed; it must have been written after 386 because that was the date of the alteration of the Boeotian constitution here described as in the past ('at that time' xi,2); internal evidence suggests a date certainly before 346, and probably before 356.

The interest—and vital importance—of this brief excerpt from a fragmentary work is that it is the only surviving account of a Greek oligarchy. Aristotle gives a lot of information on the theory of oligarchy, and sometimes gives illustrative examples, but here is the only practical, as opposed to theoretical, account of an example of the form of government under which many Greeks lived in classical times.

To understand the document, it is necessary to remember that Boeotia was a confederation of more or less autonomous cities under the general leadership of Thebes. Thebes was significantly the largest city, and no doubt usually much the most influential, but she did not control towns like Orchomenus and Tanagra. Towns in Attica like Marathon and Eleusis were integrated with Athens; the relationship was completely different. This confederation under the hegemony of Thebes was dissolved under the terms of the King's Peace in 386; it probably came into existence when Boeotia was liberated from Athenian control in 447. There is no evidence that the constitution outlined here was not in force for the whole of the period 446–386, though the status of individual cities altered, most notably that of Plataea after she fell to the Boeotians in 427.

THE BOEOTIAN CONSTITUTION

XI,2 The situation in Boeotia at that time was as follows: there were four *Boulai* then in each of the cities; not all the citizens were entitled to membership, but only those who owned a certain amount of property; each *Boule* in turn met before the main session, and held a preliminary discussion, after which they put proposals about the matters under consideration to the other three. Decisions

3 approved by all four became valid. Such was the form of local government in each town, but the affairs of Boeotia as a whole were handled as follows. All the population was divided into eleven wards, and each one provided one Boeotarch in the following way: the Thebans contributed four, two for the city and two for Plataea, Scolus, Erythrae and Scaphae together with the other territories which had formerly been politically united with those cities but were then subject to Thebes. The men of Orchomenus and Hysiae provided two, as did those of Thespiae together with Eutresis and Thisbae. Tanagra produced one, and another came from Haliartus Lebadaea and Coronea, and the last from Acraephia, Copae and Chaeronea; in the last two cases each of

4 the three cities provided the Boeotarch in turn.* The wards provided the magistrates in this way, and together with each Boeotarch they supplied sixty members of the central *Boule*, and paid their expenses themselves. Each had the duty of providing about 1000 hoplites and 100 cavalry. In general terms, in the same proportion as the

---

* For the locations of the places mentioned, see Map 2. Note that Hysiae is not the town of that name near Plataea, but a variant of the name of the town more normally called Hyettus on Lake Copaïs. Acraephia is spelt Acraephnium in the text, and other variants of the name are found.

distribution of magistrates were the benefits they received from the central treasury and the contributions they made to it, the jurors they supplied, and the extent of their share of everything in the state, good and bad. Such was the political organisation of the people as a whole; the *Boulai* and Assemblies of the Boeotians used to meet on the Cadmea.

COMMENTARY

The first section (XI,2 of the whole work) describes local government, Each city had a Council divided into four sections called *Boulai*, each of which discussed business before submitting it to the other three; a proposal had to be approved by all four before it was passed. Membership was not open to all, but only to those with a certain amount of property. The minimum qualification is unknown, but Pollux quotes Aristotle as his authority for a yield of forty-five Attic *medimnoi* (measures) as the minimum at Orchomenus; this may have been the general qualification for the whole of Boeotia. Exactly how much this figure represents is not certain, but it is not high. It has been suggested that the qualification was approximately the equivalent of hoplite status; thus a little under half the population would have had full rights. This suggestion is supported by the fact that at the battle of Delium there were rather more light-armed troops (the poorer men) than hoplites in the Boeotian forces (Thucydides IV,93,3). On the other hand, a yield of 45 medimnoi is remarkably low in the light of the Athenian qualification for hoplite status of 200; it seems more likely that the qualification for citizenship was lower than that for hoplite status. A further restriction is implicit in Aristotle when he says that active participation in the political life of Thebes was denied to anyone who had been involved in trade within the last ten years (*Politics* 1278 a 25) or menial labour (*Politics* 1321 a 29). This has been understood as implying that the property qualification had to be satisfied in land; however, it is by no means certain that the provision mentioned by Aristotle was in force at the time of the constitution of 446–386. It is reasonable to conclude that this was a widely based oligarchy. Even those not eligible for political rights are described as citizens; in other words, they had full civil rights except for active participation in politics, and could presumably obtain that right if they increased their property. There was probably also an age qualification for any form of office, as was normal throughout Greece, but this is not stated.

We do not know how many members there were in each of the *Boulai*, nor whether they were elected or chosen by lot. It is a reasonable conjecture that they were elected, as was normal in oligarchies, and one may guess that each *Boule* had a fairly large membership; the normal reason why a section of the legislative body met to hold a preliminary discussion was that the main body was too unwieldy to permit efficient drafting of legislation. Equally, the fact that the local councils did not delegate full authority to take decisions to one section is in accord both with the normal Greek suspicion of any form of delegation and also with the fact that most Greek oligarchies appear to have been as eager for equality as the democracies once they had taken the original step of limiting those entitled to take part. More surprising is the apparent implication that all four *Boulai* had to approve a measure. To give the right of veto to one quarter of a legislative body would be very cautious, and the text may rather imply approval by a majority in a meeting where all four sat together. It has been assumed plausibly that each *Boule* conducted the preliminary discussions for a quarter of the year; it may be that membership was for one year at a time, but there is no evidence either way, as equally there is nothing to indicate whether members could serve for a second and subsequent terms consecutively or there was a principle of rotation which ensured that all those eligible had been members before anyone sat for a second time. It is even conceivable that all those eligible took part; this is very unlikely since the individual local constitutions and the central administration of Boeotia are so similar that it is natural to assume that both were established after the same model—and in the latter case the four bodies were selected representatives, sixty from each ward.

The function of these city *Boulai* was strictly local government. Some have tried to suggest that the decisions of the central Boeotian council was subject to ratification by the local *Boulai*, but this seems unlikely, particularly in the field of foreign affairs; if the central authority did not decide this, it is hard to see what its function was, and it is equally hard to see how Boeotia could have pursued any foreign policy at all, let alone the consistent one she did adopt, if it had been subject to the veto of small constituent towns.

The author gives us in §3 the first detailed account of the arrangements lying behind the central government in Boeotia. There were ten sovereign states, Thebes, Orchomenus, Thespiae, Tanagra, Haliartus, Lebadaea, Coronea, Acraephia, Copae and Chaeronea; the status of the other towns mentioned is disputed, but was probably akin to that of the villages scattered through Attica; for the purposes of the central government they formed single units with the sovereign states to which they were linked, but preserved a significant measure of local autonomy. Citizenship was probably dual, that of the local town being held at the same time as that of the sovereign state they were attached to, though whether their independence went so far as to have their own local *Boulai* is unknown. There is nothing to disprove the extreme suggestion that they were totally independent and merely grouped with a larger place for the purposes of selecting a Boeotarch and members of the central *Boule*. This is perhaps unlikely, though there is no evidence that they were in the same state of subjection as Plataea and its attendant territory after 427. The composition of the eleven wards given is that of the early fourth century, the period being covered by the historian. It had not always been the same; Plataea stood totally aloof from the Boeotian Confederacy as an ally of Athens before 427, and it is probable that before 447 Thebes only had two Boeotarchs out of a total of nine. Thereafter, although Thebes 'contributed' four, Thucydides implies (IV,91) that there were only two *Theban* Boeotarchs at Delium in 424, which argues that the other two were somehow selected by Thebes, but were citizens of the subjected cities. Similarly, Chaeronea was subject to Orchomenus until after 424. The organisation reflected the current political situation in Boeotia, and changed with it.

A narrative piece from Thucydides is illuminating in considering how the constitution described in §§3–4 worked: 'When they got home, the Boeotians reported the proposals of the Spartans, and what the Argives whom they had met had said, to the Boeotarchs who were pleased and all the more enthusiastic. . . . Not long afterwards, ambassadors came from Argos with the proposals already discussed; the Boeotarchs approved their proposals and sent them away, promising to send ambassadors to Argos to discuss an alliance. Meanwhile, it was decided first by the Boeotarchs, the Corinthians, the Megarians and the ambassadors from Thrace to swear to help whoever needed aid. . . . Before the oaths were taken, the Boeotarchs reported the agreement to the four *Boulai* which have supreme power and recommended that oaths be exchanged with cities which were willing to enter into an arrangement for mutual assistance. The Boeotians in the *Boulai* did not accept the recommendation because they were afraid to cross the Spartans by making an alliance with the Corinthians, who had left the Spartan Alliance. For the Boeotarchs had not told them of what had transpired at Sparta, and that the Spartan Ephors Kleoboulos and Xenares and their friends had recommended them to become allies of the Argives and Corinthians first and then treat with the Spartans themselves. The Boeotarchs had supposed that the *Boule*, even without this information, would not vote against the proposals which they made to them in the preliminary discussion' (V,37,4–38,3 with omissions).

The Boeotarchs were clearly the senior magistrates of the Boeotian confederacy, and the Thucydides passage illustrates the amount they were prepared to do on their own initiative. The Spartan Ephors were attempting to push a policy through which might well not have been acceptable if it had been openly discussed in Sparta, and this entailed a certain amount of secrecy in the negotiations, and therefore less open discussion on both sides; even allowing for this, the Boeotarchs were attempting to initiate a major step in foreign policy without any consultation with the sovereign council until the last moment. Secondly, and equally important, they were confident that they could get their way with the *Boule*. Here is an excellent example of the dominance of the executive branch of government which the Athenians were at such pains to avoid.

Turning to the other side, the *Constitution* gives us the numbers of the members of the central *Boule*, 660, and Thucydides tells us that it functioned in the same way as the local councils, in four groups.* The reference to preliminary discussion suggests that one of the four groups here also met in advance to prepare material for the full meetings. This would mean that Boeotia had a central leadership permanently in session and consisting of the Boeotarchs and 165 *Boule* members. Whether the members of the *Boule* paid their own expenses or were financed for this by the ward they came from is not clear from the text. The normal oligarchic principle that nobody should receive any reward for public service is in favour of the former, while the phrasing of the actual Greek of the text is difficult to interpret this way, and inclines to the latter alternative. Either way, the implication of Thucydides that each section was on duty for a quarter of the year, while the other three attended only plenary sessions makes sense both from a practical point of view and also economically; to give up a quarter of a year's work is a severe enough burden, and if the members had effectively been on duty for a whole year it would have seriously limited the number of people who could have taken part. Such indications as we have suggest that Boeotia was not a very narrow oligarchy. Again, it is not clear how the sixty members from each ward were selected, nor how the 660 were allocated to the four divisions; it is implied that the division of wards, and therefore the allocation of members, as of Boeotarchs, was roughly proportional to population. This is a highly original arrangement, and surely a conscious improvement on earlier leagues; it is much fairer than the one city = one vote system used by Athens and Sparta.

Throughout, there is a built-in factor which favours the predominance of Thebes; after 427, not merely did they provide, or somehow control the selection of, four of the eleven Boeotarchs and 240 of the 660 members of the *Boule*, but the *Boule* met on the Cadmea, the citadel of Thebes. Thus there would be much less hardship for the Theban members in attending than for the others, and they would be much more likely to have a full attendance of their delegation. However, Thebes' representation probably reflected fairly her proportionately greater size and population.

The army was levied from the wards—another reason for thinking that they were more or less balanced for size—and commanded by the Boeotarchs. Thucydides (iv,91) implies that they took supreme command in turn, but we do not know how long for, and there are other passages which suggest the settlement of disputes within the eleven by a vote. The situation is closely parallel to the Athenian *strategoi*, where sometimes one man was given overall command, and on other occasions some or all would have equal authority, and therefore settle disputed decisions by voting. The size of the army accords well with the known numbers of Theban troops at various battles, though it must always be borne in mind that the author is only concerned with hop-

---

* Thucydides must be referring to the same body whether he talks of the *Boule*, thinking of the whole, or of *Boulai*, thinking of the four constituent sections.

lites (another argument for relating full citizenship to hoplite status). Thebes also had a significant force of light-armed troops, who were citizens below the minimum census for full rights. At Delium there were 10,000 of them, compared with 7,000 hoplites* and 1,000 cavalry. The rulers of Boeotia were apparently prepared to take a calculated risk in arming such a large number of those without full rights in the state. It is likely that at least some of them were discontented with their position, and probably had democratic leanings, particularly with the example of Athens so close; however, the risk appears to have been justified. Equally, the number of cavalry is higher than the normal Greek ratio at such battles; either there was a fuller levy, or the Boeotians had a stronger force than was generally the case; the latter is likely in view of the high number of Boeotian cavalry in the fourth century. One must deduce a fertile and prosperous countryside and a significant number of people wealthy enough to maintain horses, which was not the normal situation in Greece except in Thessaly. Perhaps the water-logged land around Lake Copaïs could feed horses and cattle, but could not be used for cereal crops.

Two points remain. First, there was some form of federal legal system, to which the jurors mentioned would have been sent. This is an interesting and advanced development, presumably designed to settle disputes between individual communities rather than local cases. Secondly, the author stresses that the burdens and benefits of the state were shared in the same proportion as representation in the central government. This was a normal principle, which may incidentally have served as some check on an area attempting to gain undue influence by getting too many representatives, but is important as illustrating again the interest in equality within the full citizen body which Greek oligarchs had every bit as much as the democrats. The dissatisfaction which had spread through the Boeotian confederacy by 386 probably arose not from any unfairness in the arrangements, nor from dislike of the position of Thebes, which was no more dominant than was justified by her size and the number of towns subject to her, but from a theoretical dislike of anything which interfered with a city's total autonomy. It is arguable that this centrifugal tendency contributed significantly to the undoing of Greece.

* This figure suggests the interesting speculation that Boeotia had adopted the Peloponnesian practice of sending a two-thirds mobilisation from every section except that invaded, which would provide its full strength.

SELECT BIBLIOGRAPHY

The Hellenica Oxyrhynchia (the title by which the historical fragment from which the *Boeotian Constitution* is drawn is usually referred to) was first published by B. P. Grenfell and A. S. Hunt in *Oxyrhynchus Papyri* v, (London, Egypt Exploration Fund, 1908), pp. 110–242; this publication includes text, translation and commentary. The most recent edition is that of V. Bartoletti (Leipzig, Teubner, 1959), which renumbers the chapters, XI appearing as XVI; I have used the better established numbering of the London edition. The fullest study and analytical commentary is that of I. A. F. Bruce, *An Historical Commentary on the 'Hellenica Oxyrhynchia'*, (Cambridge, Cambridge University Press, 1967), to which this discussion owes a great deal.

Apart from these works, a good discussion may be found in J. A. O. Larsen, *Representative Government in Greek and Roman History*, (Berkeley, University of California Press, 1955) ch. 2, particularly pp. 31–40, and the same author's 'The Boeotian Confederacy and Fifth Century Oligarchy' in T.A.P.A. 86 (1955), 40–50. Note also the fundamental discussion of P. Salmon, 'Les Districts Béotiens', *REA* 58 (1956), 51–70 (in French). See also R. J. Buck, *A History of Boeotia* (Edmonton, University of Alberta Press, 1979).

APPENDIX TO PART I

The following passage (Herodotus III,80–82) is different from the other works translated in the present volume in that it is purely theoretical. After the murder of the Magi by Darius and six other conspirators, Herodotus interrupts his narrative with this analysis of the three possible forms of government. It need hardly be said that not merely is the dialogue not historical, but also there was never in reality a chance of any form of government in Persia other than monarchy. It is impossible to fix the date of composition of the present passage accurately, but it probably falls in the period between about 450 and 430, which makes it the earliest extant specimen of Greek political theory. There seems little doubt that, for all Herodotus' protestations of genuineness at the beginning,* it is heavily influenced by Sophistic speculation of the period, and may even represent the gist of a well-known theoretical treatise.

80 When the disorder had died down and five days had passed, those who had revolted against the Magi met in conference, and speeches were made which some Greeks refuse to believe in, but made they were all the same. Otanes recommended the establishment of a democracy in Persia in the following words: 'It seems to me no longer right for one man among us to have supreme power, for monarchy is neither pleasant nor good. You saw how far Cambyses went in his outrageous behaviour, and you have suffered the same from the Magus. How could the rule of one man be a well-adjusted system when he can follow his whims and be answerable to nobody? The best of men given such power would change his attitude from the normal, for his present good fortune produces pride, and envy is inevitably a part of human nature. These two vices are the root of all wickedness, for excessive pride leads him to many outrageous deeds, and others spring from envy. A tyrannical† ruler ought to be without envy, for he has all

---

* Compare also Herodotus VI,43,3.

† 'Tyrannical' and 'tyrant' in Herodotus are primarily technical terms for one-man rule; the prejudicial overtones, though not absent, are significantly less than they are in later Greek writers and in the modern use of the word.

blessings; but his attitude to the citizens is the opposite of this, for he envies the best among them their survival, takes pleasure in the worst, and is the most ready to entertain slanderous accusations. It is impossible to please him; if you show him reasonable respect, he is angry because he does not receive extreme flattery; if someone fawns on him, he is angry at being flattered. The most serious aspects are these: he upsets established laws, outrages women and executes men without trial. Now, when the people hold power, first they enjoy the finest title of all, isonomy, equality before the law, and secondly avoid all this monarchical practice. Magistracies are filled by lot, the holders must answer for their conduct in office, and all decisions are referred to the people. It is my opinion, then, that we should abandon monarchy and put the people in power; in them is all good.'

81 Such was the opinion of Otanes, but Megabyzus recommended an oligarchy in the following terms: 'In that Otanes advocated the end of rule by one man I agree with him, but his recommendation of handing power over to the people is not the best solution; there is nothing more stupid and liable to excess than the senseless mob. It is utterly intolerable for men escaping the insolent violence of a tyrant to suffer the same at the hands of an uncontrolled mob. A tyrant at least acts with knowledge, but knowledge is beyond the capacity of the people. How could they have knowledge when they have never been taught and have no personal experience of anything which is fine? When they are involved in affairs, they thrust all before them senselessly like a river in flood. Let the enemies of the Persians rely on the people, but let us select a council of the best men, and invest them with power. We shall personally be members, and it is reasonable to assume that the best people will produce the best policy.'

82 Such was the opinion of Megabyzus; Darius was the third to express his opinion: 'I agree with what Megabyzus said about the masses, but I do not agree about oligarchy. With three forms of government to choose from, democracy, oligarchy and monarchy, if we assume that each is outstanding of its kind, I maintain that the last is far superior to the others. Nothing can be better than the one outstanding man; he would look after the masses irreproachably using his excellent judgement, and would be able to maintain maximum secrecy about measures against enemies. In an oligarchy, when many are aiming at distinction in public

life, violent personal feuds tend to appear; when each individual wishes to dominate and carry the day with his own policy, the result is intense feuds, which lead to sedition, and sedition leads to murder, which in its turn produces the rule of one man; this demonstrates the measure of the superiority of monarchy. With the people in power corruption is inevitable; corruption does not produce feuds, but strong bonds among the corrupt as they conspire to further their common aims. This situation continues until a champion of the people appears and puts a stop to it; the result is public respect, and this respect leads to his getting sole power— again a proof of the superiority of monarchy. In summary, where did we get our freedom from? Who gave it to us? The people, oligarchy, or monarchy? In my opinion, since we were freed by one man, we should preserve this constitution, and apart from that we should not change established laws which are good; it would be a recipe for disaster.'

PART II

The Constitution of Athens
by
ARISTOTLE

The Constitution of Athens

GLOSSARY

The following Greek words and technical terms are used in the text; references after the brief definition are to passages of the Commentary where the words are more fully discussed. Plurals are given in brackets.

Archon   One of nine magistrates at Athens; the Archon, sometimes called the Archon *Eponumos* ('who gave his name' to the year in which he held office) was at one stage the chief magistrate of the city; LV–LVI.

Boule (-ai)   The council which prepared material for consideration by the *Ekklesia* and supervised day-to-day administration; XLIIIff.

choregos (-oi)   The provider of a chorus; LVI.

deme   A subdivision of Attica; XXI.

dikasterion (-a)   The jury-courts, in which a juror was called *dikastes (-ai)*.

dokimasia   The investigation of the credentials of a magistrate before he took up office; LV.

eisphora (-ai)   Extraordinary capital levy.

Ekklesia   The assembly of adult male citizens; XLIII.

Ephebe   A young Athenian aged 18–20 undergoing military training; XLII.

Ephetai (plural)   Jurors in an archaic homicide court; LVII.

Epikleros (-oi)   A girl without brothers whose Father was dead; XLII.

eupatridai (plural)   The collective name for the old aristocracy of Attica.

euthuna (-ai; usually plural in the Classical period)   The investigation of an office-holder's conduct at the end of his term of office; LIV.

hektemoroi (plural)   Citizens under a form of bondage; II.

Heliaia   The Athenian *Ekklesia* sitting as a court; LXVIII.

Hellenotamiai   'Treasurers of the Greeks'; in effect, chief treasurers of the Delian League; XXX.

Hieromnemon   A recorder whose functions are not fully known.

hippeus (-eis)   'Cavalryman'; the name used for the second social class at Athens.

hoplite   A heavily-armed infantryman; they formed the backbone of Greek armies from the late seventh century onwards.

King Archon   A modern name for one of the three senior Archons; LVII.

kolakretai (plural)   Financial officials at an early date in Athens; VII.

kurbeis (plural)   Wooden plaques on which laws were inscribed; VII.

Liturgy   An item of public expenditure undertaken by an individual at Athens; XXVII.

metic   A resident alien; LVIII.

mina / mna   A measure of weight, also used for a sum of money.

naukraria (-ai)   An early division within the Athenian state whose chief officers were called *naukraroi*; VIII.

pelatai (plural)   Men in a situation analogous to that of the *hektemoroi*; II.

pentakosiomedimnos (-oi)   A member of the highest property class established by Solon; VII.

Polemarch   One of the three senior Archons; LVIII.

poletai (plural)   Financial officers; VII and XLVII.

proxenos (-oi)   The word for two different positions: (a) XLIII; (b) LIV and LVIII.

Prytany   A member of the committee of the *Boule*, or that committee; XLIIIf; prytany (small p) is used for their term of office.

seisachtheia   'Shedding of burdens'; Solon's cancellation of debts; VI.

strategos (-oi)   Literally 'general', but from the early fifth century the office at Athens had also much wider functions, and the ten *strategoi* were the nearest equivalent there was to a board of chief magistrates.

symmory   A group who jointly undertook a financial burden; LXI.

Thesmothetes (-ai)   One of the junior six of the nine Archons; LIX.

thetes (plural)   The lowest class at Athens.

trierarch   The commander of a trireme, the normal Greek warship.

trittus (-ues)   (a) An early division of the Athenian state; VIII.
(b) A unit created by Cleisthenes; XXI.

zeugites (-ai)   A member of the third of the four classes at Athens.

A few other technical terms have been used in the Commentary and defined on the spot.

INTRODUCTION

Aristotle was born in Stagirus in the Chalcidice in 384, but came to Athens while still a youth, and spent twenty years in Plato's Academy, first as a pupil and later working to a greater or lesser degree on his own. After the death of Plato and the election of Speusippus to head the Academy, Aristotle left Athens for a period, in the course of which he spent some time as the tutor of Alexander the Great; he returned to Athens in 335, and set up his own philosophical school in a grove sacred to Lycean Apollo and the Muses—hence the name Lyceum.* Here he stayed until 323, when he left under threat of prosecution because of a wave of anti-Macedonian feeling at the time of the death of Alexander the Great. He retired to Chalcis where he died the next year.

His writings are divided into three groups: popular works, many in dialogue form, which were published early in his career; collections of information and records; philosophical and scientific works. Of these categories, only the third was known (except through fragmentary quotations) until the *Constitution of Athens* was rediscovered at the end of the nineteenth century; the first group and the rest of the second remain lost.

The *Constitution of Athens* was one (perhaps the first) of a collection of memoranda on the constitutions of 158 states, most of which were Greek. The papyrus from which our text is drawn was acquired by the British Museum from an unknown site in Egypt; it consists of four rolls totalling eighteen feet eight inches in length. The Aristotle text is copied on the back of a set of accounts written in the first century AD, and was itself copied at least by the first quarter of the second century, and probably towards the end of the first. There are also two fragments of a papyrus codex in Berlin which contain parts of four chapters; they were copied in the fourth century AD. The opening of the work is missing, and was missing from the copy from which our papyrus was transcribed, for the copyist left a column blank at the beginning. The text appears to end very abruptly, but there is every indication that the copyist had reproduced all the text in front of him, and thought that he had reached the end of the work; see below on LXIX.

The collection of information on constitutions was probably made during Aristotle's second period in Athens, for he must have had the

---

* The philosophical school was referred to as the Peripatetic school from Aristotle's habit of walking up and down in a covered court while teaching.

assistance of a group of pupils in the compilation of so massive a body of information, particularly at a time when he was also writing other works as well as teaching. Some have denied that Aristotle himself wrote the surviving document, both on stylistic grounds and because there are significant differences of view between the present treatise and Aristotle's *Politics*. Granted the style is different, there are similarities as well, and the work is of a different type from anything else of his which survives. Further, the fact that others will have had a hand in compiling what we have may have some bearing on differences of view as well as those of style. The work was known in the ancient world and accepted as genuine then, and this conclusion seems correct; such differences as exist are attributable to the type of work and its intended audience.

It had been generally assumed that the collection of constitutions was made as a basis which Aristotle was to use for writing his *Politics*. However, the latest date mentioned in the *Politics* is 336, while the *Constitution of Athens* mentions the Archonship of Kephisophon (329/8); it does not note either the loss by Athens of control of Samos or Antipater's modification of the Athenian constitution, both of which occurred in 322. Thus the writing of the *Constitution of Athens* seems to have fallen in the period 328–322; consideration of the types of warships discussed suggests that XLVI,I at least may have been completed before 325/4; see below on XLVI,I. It is thus extremely unlikely that the *Constitution of Athens* as we have it was a preliminary study for the *Politics*, for it appears to have been written seven to ten years later. However, it is possible that the material was collected prior to the writing of the *Politics*, and put into its present shape at a later date.

The work falls into two sections. The first (chapters I–XLI) is a historical survey of the development of the constitution of Athens which is divided into eleven 'changes'; chapters XLII–LXIX describe the constitution of Aristotle's own day in four sections, the franchise (XLII), legislation (XLIII–XLV), administration (XLVI–LXII), and the judiciary (LXIII–LXIX). Both sections assume wide knowledge of technical terms, and some knowledge of constitutional practice in Athens. Some have doubted whether the work in its present form could have been intended for publication, but the grounds for doubt do not seem very convincing; Aristotle does not require anything like as much background knowledge of his reader as does (for example) Thucydides. More serious is the suggestion that the work contains some muddled sections and has not been properly revised — again this has led to suggestions that it was composed for private circulation and never fully revised for the public. There are difficulties however; to take two examples, the account of the tyranny of Peisistratus is not totally consistent (XIV–XVII), and the description of the selection of jurors is not a model of clarity (LXIII–LXV). Equally, there are surprising omissions, notably no description of the highly complicated procedure for modifying existing laws, which was set up after the fall of the Thirty and remained in force in Aristotle's own day; similarly, the list of cases brought before the *Thesmothetai* (LIX) is not complete. However, the form of the work suggests that it was intended for a wider public than the immediate circle of his pupils and associates, and the contents and omissions could well have been dictated by what Aristotle was particularly interested in at the time of composition. There are certainly faults in the book as we have it, but they are not sufficient reason either for rejecting Aristotelian authorship (that would be a very dangerous line of argument), or for denying that it could have been published.

Aristotle's sources for his own day posed no problems; he or his pupils could attend all the functions and ceremonies which he describes, at least as spectators, and in addition he would presumably have had access to the state archives. For the historical section he was in greater difficulty. He certainly knew and used Herodotus, Thucydides, Xenophon and a number of the local Attic historians, including Hellanicus and Androtion, whose works are now almost totally lost. He used and quoted extensively Solon's poetry, and also would have had at his disposal many documents from the past either preserved in archives or collected by his school. However, for anything before Solon, and for many events in the sixth century where evidence like Solon's poems did not exist, he would have had to rely on such information as had been culled by earlier writers and on tradition. How reliable such tradition was is a much debated point, and is important, for Herodotus and Thucydides probably relied on it too; it is doubtful whether they were significantly better off than Aristotle because they were writing a century or so earlier. This is not the place for a detailed discussion of this topic; suffice it to say that all information which purports to come from the period before the Persian Wars must be handled with caution, and the earlier it is, the more cautious one must be. The lack of precision of the information about the reforms of 487, and even about the earliest political activities of Pericles shows that the material preserved by tradition was not detailed or full.

A further source of confusion affected the material by the time Aristotle handled it: the political feuds of the end of the fifth century were marked by an attempt to return to the 'ancestral constitution', and there is no doubt that at least some of those who wished to abolish the radical democracy fathered some of their own political ideas on venerable names from Athenian history in the hope of making them more respectable and acceptable. Thus a flood of propaganda clouded the issue still further; cf. notes on IV and XXX below.

As a result of all these factors, the notes discussing the historical section of this work contain a fair amount of discussion of the reliability of what Aristotle tells us. Criticism must not be allowed to obscure the fact that the work is extremely valuable, and gives every appearance of having been constructed on the basis of a thoughtful analysis of the available information. It is itself a source of first-class importance, which is precisely why it is well worth while to attempt to clarify or correct points of detail where possible.

It is hoped that readers will be able to read the text in conjunction with the notes. I have not split the notes into minute sections, but written explanatory sections on each chapter; the text itself is worth reading as a work of historical and analytical literature, and the form of the notes is intended to make it possible to read them in reasonable-sized sections; it may thus take a little longer to find the discussion of a particular point, but immediate speed of reference has been sacrificed in order to avoid the scrappiness which would have inevitably resulted if each point had been taken separately in the order in which it was discussed by Aristotle. The index and cross references should enable those who wish to do so to check everything which is said on a particular point; on the other hand, I have not hesitated to repeat information on occasions to ensure the clarity of a particular discussion and avoid the need for excessive cross-reference. Perhaps, in conclusion, it should be stressed that Aristotle did not write a history of Athens; naturally, therefore, the notes do not attempt to do so either. Their aim is to give just so much of the history as is necessary for the understanding of the text, and to examine the points made there.

THE CONSTITUTION OF ATHENS

THE HISTORY OF THE CONSTITUTION

I ... the accuser being Myron before a jury selected by birth who had taken their oath over sacrificial victims. When it had been decided that sacrilege had been committed, the bodies of the guilty were disinterred and their families exiled in perpetuity. Epimenides of Crete purified the city on these terms.

II 2 After this there was an extended period of discord between the upper classes and the people. The constitution was in all respects oligarchic, in particular in that the poor, together with their wives and children, were the slaves of the rich; they were described as *pelatai* and *hektemoroi*, which referred to the terms on which they worked the fields of the rich. The whole land was under the control of a few men, and if the ordinary people did not pay their dues they and their children could be seized. Further, all loans were made on the security of the person of the debtor until the time of 3 Solon—he was the first champion of the people. The harshest and most resented aspect of the constitution for the mass of the people was this slavery, although they had other complaints, for they had virtually no share in any aspect of government.

III 2 The primitive constitution before the time of Draco, then, was as follows. Eligibility for office depended on birth and wealth, while tenure was at first for life and later for a period of ten years. The most powerful and earliest of the political offices were those of the King Archon, the Polemarch and the Archon. The first was that of the King, being traditional, while the office of

Polemarch was the first added to this because of the incompetence of some of the kings in war; it was in

3 this way that they sent for Ion in a crisis. The last of the three was that of the Archon. Most people say that it was established in the time of Medon, though some say it was under Acastus, arguing from the fact that the nine Archons swear to observe their oaths as was done under Acastus that it was at this time that the sons of Codrus surrendered the kingship in return for the powers granted to the Archon. Whichever of these alternatives is true, the difference of date is not great; that the Archonship was the last of the three offices is shown by the fact that the Archon does not control any of the traditional ceremonies as the King Archon and the Polemarch do, but only ceremonies which are later additions; hence the importance of the office is of recent

4 origin, arising from these later additions. The *Thesmothetai* were instituted at a much later date when offices were already annual; their function is to inscribe the laws and preserve them for the decision of disputes. Because of its late date, the office of the *Thesmothetai* is the only archonship which was never anything but

5 annual. Such, then was the chronological sequence of these offices. All nine Archons did not have the same official residences; the King Archon lived in the building now called the Boukoleion near the Prutaneion, evidence for which is the fact that the union and marriage of the wife of the King Archon with Dionysus even now takes place there. The Archon had the Prutaneion, while the Polemarch had the Epilukeion, a building formerly called the Polemarcheion, but renamed the Epilukeion when it was rebuilt and furnished by Epilukos as Polemarch; the *Thesmothetai* had the Thesmotheteion. Under Solon all the archons were brought together in the Thesmotheteion. The Archons had full power to decide cases themselves, not only to hold preliminary hearings as now. Such then was the position of the Archons.

6   The Council of the Areopagus had the duty of watching over the laws, and had wide-ranging and important

powers in the city since it punished and fined all offenders without appeal. Archons were chosen on the basis of birth and wealth qualifications, and they made up the Areopagus; this is the reason why this is the only office which is still held for life today.

IV The above is an outline of the first constitution. A short time after this, in the Archonship of Aristaichmos, Draco introduced his legislation; this constitution was as 2 follows. Political power had been handed over to those who provided their own armour. They chose the nine Archons and the Treasurers from those men who had an unencumbered property qualification of not less than ten minae; the lesser magistrates were chosen from those who armed themselves, while the *strategoi* and cavalry commanders had to show unencumbered property to the value of at least a hundred minae and legitimate children, by citizen wives, not less than ten years old. The Prytanies had to receive sureties for them, as also for the *strategoi* and cavalry commanders of the previous year until after their *euthuna*, the sureties being four citizens from the same class as the *strategoi* and cavalry com- 3 manders. There was a *Boule* of 401 members, selected by lot from the citizen body. All those over thirty years old cast lots for this and the other offices, and nobody could hold the same office twice until all those eligible had held it; then the allotment started again from the beginning. If a member of the *Boule* failed to attend a sitting of the *Boule* or *Ekklesia*, he was fined three drachmae if he was a *pentakosiomedimnos*, two if he was a *hippeus* and one if he was a *zeugites*. The Council of the 4 Areopagos was the guardian of the laws and supervised the magistrates to ensure that they acted legally. If a man were wronged, he could lay information before the 5 Areopagus specifying the law he relied on. Loans were made on the security of the person of the borrower, as noted above, and the land was under the control of a few men.

SOLON

v   In this political situation, when the majority were the
slaves of the few, the people opposed the leaders of the
2   state. When the strife was severe, and the opposition of
long standing, both sides agreed to give power to Solon
as mediator, and entrusted the state to him; at that time
he had written the poem which begins:

> Grief lies deep in my heart when I see the oldest
> of the Ionian states being murdered. . . .

In this poem he champions both sides against the other,
and argues their position, and then recommends an end
to the prevailing rivalry.

3   Solon was one of the leading men by birth and reputation, but 'middle class' in wealth and position; this is
agreed from other evidence, and Solon himself makes it
clear in the following poem, where he advises the rich
not to be greedy:

> Restrain in your breasts your mighty hearts; you
> have taken too much of the good things of life;
> satisfy your pride with what is moderate, for we
> shall not tolerate excess, nor will everything turn
> out as you wish.

He always attaches the over-all blame for the strife to
the rich; this is why he says at the opening of the poem
that he is afraid of their 'avarice and overbearing pride',
since this was the cause of the conflict.

vi   When he had taken power, Solon freed the people
both then and for the future by making loans on the
security of a person's freedom illegal; he passed laws,
and instituted a cancellation of debts both private and
public which men call the *seisachtheia*, for they shook off
2   their burdens. Some try to attack him in this context; it
happened that when Solon was about to introduce his
seisachtheia he told some of the leading citizens, and then
(according to the democratic version of the story) he
was outmanoeuvred by his friends, while those who wish
to blacken his reputation say that he was a party to

fraud. These men borrowed money and bought large areas of land; shortly afterwards, when debts were cancelled, they were rich. This is alleged to be the origin of those who later appeared to have been wealthy for 3 generations. However, the democratic account is more convincing. It is unlikely that Solon would have been so moderate and impartial in other respects, that, when he had it in his power to subject the other group and become tyrant of the city, he chose to incur the hostility of both sides, and preferred what was right and the salvation of the city to his own advantage, but yet would have sullied himself with such a trivial and 4 manifest fraud. That he had power to become tyrant is demonstrated by the perilous state of the city's affairs at the time; he himself mentions it frequently in his poems, and all other sources agree. One must therefore conclude that this charge is false.

VII Solon established a constitution and enacted other laws; the Athenians ceased to use Draco's code except for his homicide laws. Solon's laws were inscribed on *kurbeis* set up in the portico of the King Archon, and all swore to observe them. The nine Archons used to take their oath on the Stone, and undertook to set up a golden statue if they broke one of the laws; hence the oath which 2 they still take now. Solon made his laws binding for a hundred years and arranged the constitution in the 3 following way. He divided the people into four property classes according to wealth, as had been done before; the four classes were: *pentakosiomedimnoi, hippeis, zeugitai* and *thetes*. He distributed the major magistracies to be held by the *pentakosiomedimnoi, hippeis* and *zeugitai*, allotting the nine Archons, the Treasurers, the *poletai*, the Eleven and the *kolakretai* to various classes in accordance with their property qualification. The *Thetes* received only the right to sit in the *Ekklesia* and the 4 *dikasteria*. The property qualification for a *pentakosiomedimnos* was a minimum yearly return from his own property of 500 measures, dry or liquid. The *hippeis* had a minimum of 300, and some say that the class was also restricted to those able to maintain a horse; they deduce this from early dedications, for there is a statue of Diphilos on the Acropolis with the following inscription:

> Anthemion, the son of Diphilos, made this dedication to the gods, having risen from the *thetes* to the class of the *hippeis*.

A horse stands by, showing the connection between the *hippeis* and being able to maintain a horse. None the less, it is more plausible that this class should have been defined by measures of produce like the *pentakosiomedimnoi*. The minimum qualification for the *zeugitai* was 200 measures, wet and dry combined, while the remainder of the population formed the *thetes* and were not entitled to hold office. This is why even now, when they are about to cast lots for a magistracy and a man is asked what his class is, nobody would say that he was one of the *thetes*.

VIII Magistracies were selected by lot from a group previously elected by each tribe. For the nine Archons, each tribe made a preliminary selection of ten men, and they cast lots among them; this is the origin of the practice which survives today by which each tribe picks ten men by lot, and then lots are cast again among them.* Evidence that Solon instituted selection by lot in accordance with property classes is the law about the Treasurers which is still in force; this lays down that the Treasurers shall be 2 selected by lot from the *pentakosiomedimnoi*. These were Solon's provisions about the nine Archons. In early times, the Areopagus had summoned the candidates and selected the man it judged suitable for each office itself 3 and installed him for the year. Solon retained the four tribes which already existed and the four tribal Kings; within each tribe there were three *trittues* and twelve *naukrariai*. The officers in charge of the *naukrariai* were called *naukraroi*, and they controlled contributions and expenditure; this is why many of the laws of Solon which

* Although in Aristotle's day there were then ten tribes (as instituted by Cleisthenes) in place of the four of Solon's time.

are no longer in force contain the phrases 'the *naukraroi* shall collect' and 'shall be spent from the funds of the

4 *naukrariai'*. Solon instituted a *Boule* of 400 members, 100 from each tribe, and he gave the Areopagus the duty of watching over the laws, analogous to its earlier position of guardian of the constitution. It had extensive supervisory powers over the important aspects of political life, and punished wrongdoers with full powers to inflict fines or other penalties; fines were deposited in the treasury, and there was no obligation to state the reason for the fine. The Areopagus tried those who conspired to overthrow the constitution under a law of impeachment which Solon introduced.

5 Solon realised that the city was often split by factional disputes but some citizens were content because of idleness to accept whatever the outcome might be; he therefore produced a specific law against them, laying down that anyone who did not choose one side or the other in such a dispute should lose his citizen rights.

IX The magistracies were reformed in this way. The following seem to be the three most popular features of Solon's constitution: first and most important, that nobody might borrow money on the security of anyone's freedom; secondly, that anyone might seek redress on behalf of those who were wronged; thirdly, the feature which is said to have contributed most to the strength of the democracy, the right of appeal to the *dikasterion*, for when the people have the right to vote in the courts they

2 control the constitution. The fact that the laws have not been drafted simply or clearly, but are like the provisions controlling inheritances and heirs, inevitably leads to disputes; hence the courts have to decide everything, public and private. Some think that Solon made his laws obscure deliberately to give the people the power of decision. This is not likely; the obscurity arises rather from the impossibility of including the best solution for every instance in a general provision. It is not right to judge his intentions from what happens now but by analogy with the rest of his provisions.

x   Those were the democratic aspects of his legislation; before introducing his laws, he carried out the cancellation of debts, and after that the increase of the measures,

2   weights and coinage. For it was under Solon that the measures were made larger than the Pheidonian standard, and the mina, which formerly had a weight of seventy drachmae was increased to the hundred it now contains. The old coin was the two-drachma piece. He established weights for coinage purposes in which the talent was divided into sixty-three minae, and the three added minae were divided proportionately for the stater and the other weights.

xi   After the reform of the constitution which has been described above, Solon was annoyed by people approaching him criticising some parts of his legislation and questioning others. He did not wish to make alterations or to incur unpopularity while in Athens, and so went abroad to Egypt for trading purposes and also to see the country, saying he would not return for ten years; he said it was not right for him to stay to interpret the laws but that everyone should follow them as they were

2   drafted. He had incurred the hostility of many of the leading men because of the cancellation of debts, and both sides had changed their attitude to him because his legislation had been different from what they had expected. The common people had expected him to redivide all property, while the wealthy had expected him to restore them to their traditional position, or at most only to make minor alterations to it. Solon had resisted them both, and, when he could have made himself tyrant by joining whichever side he chose, had preferred to be hated by both while saving his country and giving it the best constitution possible.

xii   That this was Solon's attitude is agreed by all authorities, and he himself comments on it in his poems in the following terms:

    To the people I gave as much privilege* as was

   * Plutarch, in quoting this poem (*Solon* 18), gives 'power' not 'privilege'.

sufficient for them, neither reducing nor exceeding
what was their due. Those who had power and were
enviable for their wealth I took good care not to
injure. I stood casting my strong shield around both
parties, and allowed neither to triumph unjustly.

2 In another passage he describes how the ordinary people
should be handled:

The people will follow their leaders best if they are
neither too free nor too much restrained, for excess
produces insolent behaviour when great wealth falls
to men who lack sound judgement.

3 In another passage he discusses those who wish for a
redistribution of land:

They came to plunder with hopes of riches, and each
of them expected to find great wealth; they thought
that although I spoke soothingly I would reveal
stern determination. Their expectation was vain,
and now they are angry and look askance at me like
an enemy. This is wrong, for with the gods I carried
out what I said, and did nothing else foolishly; it
does not please me to act with the violence of a
tyrant nor to give equal shares of our rich country to
worthless and noble alike.

4 He discusses the cancellation of debts and those who had
previously been enslaved but were freed through the
seisachtheia in the following passage:

Which of my aims did I abandon unattained, the
aims for which I had assembled the people? My
witness to this before the judgement of the future will
be the great mother of the Olympian gods, dark
Earth; I took up the markers fixed in many places—
previously she was enslaved, but now is free. Many I
brought back to Athens, their divinely founded city,
who had been sold abroad, one unjustly, another
justly, and others who had fled under compulsion of
debt,* men who no longer spoke the Attic tongue, so
wide had their wanderings been. Those at home,
suffering here the outrages of slavery and trembling

* The word translated 'debt' is doubtful; see Commentary on this
passage.

at the whims of their masters, I freed. This I achieved
by the might of law, combining force and justice; I
carried it out as I promised. I drafted ordinances
equally for bad and good, with upright justice for
each. Another man holding the spur that I held, a
man of evil counsel and greed, would not have
restrained the people. Had I been willing to indulge
the enemies of the people or do to them what the
people wished to do, the city would have lost many
men. That is why I set up a strong defence all round,
turning like a wolf at bay among the hounds.

5 Again, of the later attacks of both parties he says
reproachfully:

If I must express my reproach of the people in clear
terms, they would never otherwise even have
dreamed of what they now possess. The greater and
more powerful also should praise me and make me
their friend,

for, he says, if anyone else had held his position,
he would not have restrained the people nor checked
them before they squeezed all the cream from the
milk. But I stood, as it were in no man's land, a
barrier between them.

XIII   For these reasons, then, Solon went abroad. When he
had left, the city was still very disturbed; four years
passed peacefully, but in the fifth year after his Archonship they did not appoint an Archon because of the
dissension, and four years later the same thing happened
2 again for the same reason. After the same interval,
Damasias was chosen Archon, and retained the position
for two years and two months until he was forcibly
removed from office. Then the Athenians decided
because of the civil strife to choose ten Archons, five from
the *Eupatridai*, three from the men of the country and
two from the artisans; they held office the year after
Damasias. This demonstrates the great power of the
Archon, for the strife clearly always centred round this
3 office. In general, the Athenians lived in a state of con-
tinual turmoil in internal affairs, some finding the cause

and reason for dissent in the cancellation of debts, which
had reduced them to poverty, some being angered by
the great change in the constitution, and some motivated
4 by private feuds. There were three groups. The first was
that of the Shore; their leader was Megacles the son of
Alcmeon, and they favoured a middle-of-the-road policy.
The second group was that of the Plain; their aim was
oligarchy, and their leader Lycurgus. The third group
was that of the Uplands; they were led by Peisistratus,
5 and he seemed to be the most democratic leader. This
faction had been joined by those who had lost money
when the debts were cancelled because they were
impoverished, and those who were not of pure Athenian
descent because of anxiety about their position. Evidence
of this is the fact that after the abolition of the tyranny
the Athenians revised the lists of citizens on the grounds
that many were exercising citizen rights who were not
entitled to them. Each group took its name from the
area in which it farmed.

PEISISTRATUS

XIV   Peisistratus had the reputation of being a strong
supporter of the people and had distinguished himself
in the war against Megara; he wounded himself, and
persuaded the people that his political opponents had
done it, with the result that they voted him a bodyguard
on the proposal of Aristion. With the assistance of these
'club-bearers' he rose against the people and seized the
Acropolis in the thirty-second year after the legislation
2 of Solon, which was the Archonship of Komeas. It is said
that when Peisistratus asked for the bodyguard, Solon
opposed him, claiming to be wiser than some and braver
than others; he said he was wiser than those who did not
realise that Peisistratus was aiming at tyranny, and
braver than those who kept silent although they knew it.
When he failed to persuade his hearers, he placed his
arms in front of his door, saying that he had done all he
could to help his country—he was already a very old
man—and insisted that the other citizens should do the
3 same. Solon's appeal fell on deaf ears, and Peisistratus

seized power, and ran the state more like a private citizen than a tyrant. However, when the tyranny had not yet had time to take root the groups led by Megacles and Lycurgus combined to expel him in the Archonship of Hegesias, which was the sixth year after he first took

4 power. In the twelfth year after this Megacles was hard pressed by dissensions, and opened negotiations with Peisistratus; having agreed that Peisistratus would marry his daughter, he brought him back by a primitive and very simple trick. Having spread a rumour that Athena was bringing Peisistratus back home, he found a tall beautiful woman called Phye, whom Herodotus says came from Paiania, but others say was a Thracian flower girl from Kollytos, dressed her as Athena, and brought her into the city with Peisistratus. Peisistratus rode on a chariot with the woman beside him, and the inhabitants fell to the ground and accepted him with awe.

xv Peisistratus returned to Athens for the first time in this way. He was expelled for a second time in about the seventh year after his return; he did not keep his position for a long time, but, being afraid of both groups because he did not wish to treat Megacles' daughter as his wife,

2 retired abroad. First he joined in the foundation of a place called Rhaecelus near the Thermaic Gulf, and then moved to the area around Mt. Pangaeus. He grew wealthy there and hired mercenaries, and so came to Eretria and made his first attempt to recover the tyranny by force in the eleventh year after his expulsion. He received wide support, and in particular that of the Thebans, Lygdamis of Naxos, and the *hippeis* who con-

3 trolled affairs in Eretria. After winning the battle of Pallene, he took Athens, disarmed the people, and established his tyranny on a firm basis. He also took

4 Naxos and established Lygdamis as tyrant. He disarmed the Athenians in the following way. During a review of the people in full armour at the Theseum, he began to address the crowd, and spoke for a short while. When they said that they could not hear him, he told them to

come up to the gate of the Acropolis where he would be more audible. While he continued his speech, a group who had been specially detailed for the purpose collected the people's weapons and locked them in the buildings of the Theseum, near by; when they had finished, they 5 signalled to Peisistratus. When he had concluded his speech, he told the crowd not to be surprised or alarmed by what had happened to their weapons; they should go home and look after their private affairs—he would take care of the state.

XVI   That, then, was how Peisistratus' tyranny was first established, and those were the vicissitudes it passed 2 through. As noted above, Peisistratus ran the state moderately, and constitutionally rather than as a tyrant. He was benevolent, mild and forgiving to those who did wrong, and moreover he advanced money to the bankrupt to further their work so that they could make a 3 living as farmers. He had two motives for doing this; he did not want them in the city, but scattered in the country, and if they had enough to live on, and were busy with their own affairs, they would neither want to meddle with affairs of state nor have the time to do so. 4 The working of the land increased his revenues, for he 5 took a ten per cent tax on produce. He also had the same motive for establishing the magistrates of the demes and for travelling round the country frequently, inspecting and settling disputes: it made it unnecessary for the people to come into the city and neglect their work. 6 It was on one of these circuits that there occurred the incident of the farmer on Mt. Hymettus and the land later called 'tax-exempt'. Peisistratus saw someone working an area that was all stones, and, being surprised, told his attendant to ask what the land produced. 'Aches and pains,' the farmer replied; 'Peisistratus ought to take his ten per cent of the aches and pains too.' The man made the reply not knowing that he was speaking to Peisistratus, while the latter was delighted at his frankness and industriousness, and exempted him from all taxation.

7 Peisistratus did not in general impose any heavy burdens on the people during his rule, but always preserved peace abroad and at home, with the result that it was often said that his reign was a golden age—for when his sons later took over his position their rule was much more

8 severe. The most important facet of all those discussed was that he was naturally inclined to support the common people and was benevolent. It was his aim to govern in accordance with the laws, and not to claim any superior position for himself. He was once summoned for murder before the Areopagus; he appeared in person to make his defence, but his accuser panicked and failed to

9 put in an appearance. This is why he remained in power for a long time, and when expelled recovered his position easily. He was supported by the majority of both nobles and the common people; he attracted the former by his association with them, and the latter by the assistance he gave them in their personal affairs; he was liked by

10 both. Athenian laws about tyranny were mild at the time, and in particular the law about the establishment of a tyrant, which ran as follows: 'This is the law and traditional practice of the Athenians; any man who attempts to establish, or aids in the establishment of, a tyranny shall lose his citizenship together with his family.'

XVII Peisistratus, then, grew old in office, and fell ill and died in the Archonship of Philoneos, having lived for thirty-three years since he first set himself up as tyrant, and having ruled for nineteen of those years; for the

2 remainder he was in exile. From the dates it is manifestly absurd to suggest, as some do, that Peisistratus was loved by Solon, and was general in the war against Megara for possession of Salamis; their ages make it impossible if one calculates each man's life and the date of his death.

3 After Peisistratus' death, his sons ruled, and conducted affairs in the same way. He had two sons by his citizen wife, Hippias and Hipparchus, and two by his Argive wife, Iophon and Hegesistratos, who was also called Thet-

4 talos. Peisistratus had married Timonassa, the daughter

of an Argive from Argos called Gorgilos; she had previously been married to Archinos, the Ambraciot, who
was of the family of the Cypselids. This was the origin
of Peisistratus' friendship with Argos; Hegesistratos
brought 1,000 men to fight with him at Pallene. Some
say that Peisistratus married her during his first exile,
others while he was in power.

XVIII   Their position and age meant that the state was run
by Hipparchus and Hippias; Hippias was the older, a
natural politician and a wise man, and he presided over
the government. Hipparchus was fond of amusements,
and interested in love affairs and the arts—he was the
man who sent for Anacreon and Simonides and their
2 associates and the other poets. Thettalos was much
younger, and violent and outrageous in his behaviour,
which was the cause of all their troubles. He fell in love
with Harmodius, and when his love was not returned,
far from restraining his anger, he gave vent to it viciously;
finally, when Harmodius' sister was to carry a basket in
the procession at the Panathenaia, he stopped her, and
insulted Harmodius as effeminate. Hence Harmodius
and Aristogeiton were provoked to their plot, in which
3 many took part. At the time of the Panathenaia, when
they were watching for Hippias on the Acropolis (for it
so happened that he was receiving the procession while
Hipparchus despatched it), they saw one of the conspirators greet Hippias in a friendly way. They thought
that they were betrayed. Wishing to achieve something
before they were arrested, they went down into the city,
and, not waiting for their fellow conspirators, killed
Hipparchus as he was organising the procession by the
4 Leokoreion; thus they spoiled the whole attempt. Harmodius was killed immediately by the guards, but
Aristogeiton was captured later, and tortured for a long
time. Under torture he accused many nobles who were
friends of the tyrants of complicity. At first enquiries
had been unable to find any trace of the plot, for the
story that Hippias had disarmed those in the procession
and searched them for daggers is not true, for they did

not carry weapons in the procession at that time—it was
5 a later innovation of the democracy. The democrats say
that Aristogeiton accused the friends of the tyrants
deliberately in order to involve them in impiety and
weaken their faction if they killed their friends who were
innocent; others say that he was not making it up, but
6 did reveal those who were in the plot. Finally, when,
despite all his efforts, death eluded him, he promised that
he would implicate many others; having persuaded
Hippias to give him his hand as a pledge, he reviled him
for giving his hand to the murderer of his brother. This
angered Hippias so much that his fury overcame him,
and he drew his dagger and killed him.

XIX   After this the tyranny became much more severe; in
avenging his brother, Hippias had killed or exiled many
2 people, and was distrusted and hated by all. About three
years after the death of Hipparchus, Hippias tried to
fortify Munichia because of his unpopularity in the city
of Athens; he intended to move his residence there, but
while this was going on he was expelled by Cleomenes,
the Spartan king, because the Spartans were repeatedly
receiving oracles instructing them to end the tyranny at
3 Athens. The reason was this. The Athenian exiles, who
were led by the Alcmeonids, could not bring about their
return unaided; a number of attempts failed. One of
these unsuccessful attempts involved the fortification of
Leipsudrion, a point below Mt. Parnes; there they were
joined by some supporters from the city, but the place
was besieged and taken by the tyrants. This was the
origin of the well-known drinking song about the disaster
which ran:

> Alas, Leipsudrion, betrayer of friends, what heroes
> you destroyed, men brave in battle and of noble
> blood; then they showed the quality of their families.

4   Having failed, then, in all other attempts, the Alcmeonids contracted to rebuild the temple at Delphi, and
in this way they obtained plenty of money to secure the
support of the Spartans. Whenever the Spartans consulted the oracle, the priestess instructed them to free

Athens; finally she persuaded them, although they had ties of hospitality with the Peisistratids.* The Spartans were swayed no less by the friendship between the
5 Peisistratids and the Argives. First, they sent Anchimolos with an army by sea. He was defeated and killed because Kineas the Thessalian came to the help of the Athenians with a thousand cavalry. The Spartans were angered by this, and sent their king, Cleomenes, with a larger force by land; he defeated an attempt by the Thessalian cavalry to prevent his entry into Attica, shut up Hippias inside the so-called Pelargic wall, and be-
6 seiged him with Athenian help. While he was conducting the siege, it happened that the sons of the Peisistratids were captured as they attempted to slip out of the city secretly. After their capture, the Peisistratids agreed, in return for the children's safety, to hand over the Acropolis and leave with their own property within a period of five days. This was in the Archonship of Harpaktides when they had held the tyranny for about seventeen years after the death of their father; the whole period including their father's reign had lasted forty-nine years.

CLEISTHENES

xx   After the fall of the tyranny, there was a struggle between Isagoras the son of Teisander, who was a supporter of the tyrants, and Cleisthenes, who was of the family of the Alcmeonids. When Cleisthenes lost power in the political clubs, he won the support of the people
2 by promising them control of the state. The power of Isagoras waned in turn, and he called in Cleomenes again, for he had ties of friendship with him. He persuaded him to 'expel the curse', for the Alcmeonids were
3 thought to be amongst those accursed. Cleisthenes retired into exile, and Cleomenes arrived with a few men and expelled seven hundred Athenian families as being under the curse. Having done this, he tried to dissolve the *Boule* and to put Isagoras and three hundred of his

* A collective name for the sons (and descendants) of Peisistratus.

friends in control of the city. The *Boule* resisted and the people gathered; the supporters of Cleomenes and Isagoras fled to the Acropolis. The people surrounded them and besieged them for two days; on the third they let Cleomenes and all those with him go under a truce, and

4 recalled Cleisthenes and the other exiles. The people had taken control of affairs, and Cleisthenes was their leader and champion of the people, for the Alcmeonids had been the group probably most responsible for the expulsion of the tyrants and had stirred up trouble for

5 them for much of the time. Even before the Alcmeonids, Kedon had attacked the tyrants, and therefore his name also figures in the drinking songs:

> Pour a draught also for Kedon, boy, and do not
> forget him, if it is right to pour wine for brave men.

XXI   The people trusted Cleisthenes for these reasons. At that time, as their leader, in the fourth year after the overthrow of the tyranny which was the Archonship of

2 Isagoras, he first divided all the citizens into ten tribes instead of the earlier four, with the aim of mixing them together so that more might share control of the state. From this arose the saying 'No investigation of tribes' as an answer to those wishing to inquire into ancestry.

3 Then he established a *Boule* of 500 instead of 400, fifty from each tribe; previously there had been 100 from each. His purpose in not splitting the people into twelve tribes was to avoid dividing them according to the *trittues* which already existed; there were twelve *trittues* in the four old tribes, and the result would not have been a

4 mixing. He divided Attica into thirty sections, using the demes as the basic unit; ten of the sections were in the city area, ten around the coast and ten inland. He called these sections *trittues*, and placed three into each tribe by lot, one from each geographical area. He made fellow demesmen of those living in each deme so that they would not reveal the new citizens by using a man's father's name, but would use his deme in addressing him. Hence the Athenians use their demes as part of

5 their names. He set up demarchs with the same functions

as the previous *naukraroi*, for the demes took the place of the *naukrariai*. Some of the demes he named after their position, others after their founders, for not all were still 6 connected with a particular locality. He left the citizens free to belong to clan groups, and phratries, and hold priesthoods in the traditional way. He gave the tribes ten eponymous heroes selected by the Delphic oracle from a preliminary list of a hundred.

XXII These changes made the constitution much more democratic than it had been under Solon. A contributory factor was that Solon's laws had fallen into disuse under the tyranny, and Cleisthenes replaced them with others with the aim of winning the people's support; these 2 included the law about ostracism. It was in the fifth year after this constitution was established in the Archonship of Hermokreon, that they formulated the oath which the *Boule* of 500 still take today. At that time they selected the *strategoi* by tribes, one from each; the Polemarch was 3 the overall commander of the army. Eleven years later, in the Archonship of Phainippos, the Athenians won the battle of Marathon. This made the democracy so confident that after a further two years had passed they first used the law of ostracism; it had been passed from a suspicion of those in power, because Peisistratus had started as leader of the people and *strategos*, and become 4 tyrant. The first to be ostracised was one of his relations, Hipparchus, the son of Charmus, of Kollytos; it was the desire to expel him which was the primary motive of Cleisthenes in proposing the law. With the customary forbearance of the democracy, the people had allowed the friends of the tyrants to continue to live in Athens with the exception of those who had committed crimes in the civil disorders; their leader and champion was 5 Hipparchus. In the year immediately following, the Archonship of Telesinos, they cast lots for the nine Archons by tribes from the five hundred previously elected by the demesmen; this first happened then after the tyranny; all their predecessors were elected. In the same year, Megacles, the son of Hippocrates, from

6 Alopeke was ostracised. For three years they ostracised
the friends of the tyrants, the original purpose of ostracism, but in the fourth year they also removed anyone
else who seemed to be too powerful. The first man to be
ostracised who was not connected with the tyranny was
Xanthippus, the son of Ariphron.

7 Two years later, in the Archonship of Nikodemos,
when the mines at Maroneia were discovered and the city
had a surplus of one hundred talents from their exploitation, some recommended that the money should be distributed to the people. Themistocles prevented this; he
did not say for what he would use the money, but recommended that a talent should be lent to each of the
hundred wealthiest Athenians. If the people approved
of what it was spent on, the expenditure should be borne
by the state; if not, they should recover the money from
those who had borrowed it. The proposal was approved
on these terms, and he had a hundred triremes built, one
by each man. This was the fleet in which they fought the
barbarians at Salamis. Aristides, the son of Lysimachus,
was ostracised at this time.

8   Three years later, in the Archonship of Hupsichides,
because of Xerxes' expedition, they recalled all those
who had been ostracised; for the future they decreed that
those who had been ostracised should not live nearer to
Athens than Geraistus or Scyllaeum under penalty of
losing their citizenship for good.

THE AREOPAGUS

XXIII   Up to this point the city went on growing and developing its democracy by gradual stages, but after the Persian wars the Areopagus became strong again and
ran the city, not because it was voted the position
but because it had been responsible for the battle of
Salamis. When the *strategoi* did not know how to
handle the situation, and ordered each man to see to his
own safety, the Areopagus provided each person with
2 eight drachmae and embarked them in the ships. For
this reason the Athenians respected the Areopagus,
and were well governed at this time. At the time they

paid attention to military training, were respected by the Greeks, and took the hegemony at sea despite the Spartans.

3 The champions of the people at this period were Aristides the son of Lysimachus and Themistocles the son of Neocles, the latter with the reputation of being an expert in military matters, the former a clever politician and an outstandingly just man; therefore they employed the one as a general and the other as a political adviser.

4 These two men worked together over the rebuilding of the walls of Athens despite their differences, but Aristides was the instigator of the defection of the Ionians from the Spartan alliance, when he seized the opportunity offered by the disgrace of the Spartans caused by the behaviour

5 of Pausanias. Hence he was the man who assessed the first list of contributions to be paid by the cities two years after the battle of Salamis, in the Archonship of Timosthenes. He also gave the oath to the Ionians 'to have the same enemies and friends', in the ratification of which they dropped the lumps of iron into the sea.

XXIV Athens' confidence increased and she built up a significant financial reserve; Aristides recommended them to seize the hegemony and to live in the city rather than the countryside; there would be a livelihood for all, some on expeditions, others on garrison duty, and others in government; in this way they would hold

2 the hegemony. The people agreed, took control, and treated their allies more tyrannically except for the peoples of Chios, Lesbos and Samos; they used them as guards of the empire, and so allowed them to retain their own constitutions and such possessions as they had.

3 The result was also affluence for the masses, as Aristides had suggested. More than twenty thousand men earned their living as a result of the tribute, the taxation and the money the empire brought in. There were six thousand *dikastai*, sixteen hundred archers, and twelve hundred cavalry, and five hundred members of the

Boule. There were five hundred guards in the docks and fifty others on the Acropolis; offices in the city occupied up to seven hundred men, and up to seven hundred were employed abroad. In addition to them, when later they were at war, there were two thousand five hundred hoplites and twenty guard ships and other ships to carry the tribute employing two thousand men selected by lot. There were also those maintained by the state at the Prutaneion or as orphans, and the guards of the prison. All these people were paid from public funds.

EPHIALTES

xxv   The people were supported in this way. For about seventeen years after the Persian wars the constitution remained the same under the guidance of the Areopagus, although it was gradually deteriorating. Then, with the increase of the power of the masses, Ephialtes the son of Sophonides became champion of the people; he had a reputation for incorruptibility and justice in public life. He launched an attack on the
2 Areopagus. First, he removed many of its members on charges of administrative misconduct. Then, in the Archonship of Konon, he stripped it of all its additional powers including the guardianship of the constitution; he distributed them among the *Boule*, the *Ekklesia* and
3 the *dikasteria*. He was aided in the reforms by Themistocles, who was a member of the Areopagus, but was facing a charge of treason with Persia. Because Themistocles wanted the Areopagus to be ruined, he told Ephialtes that they were intending to arrest him, and told the Areopagus that he would lay information against certain persons who were plotting to overthrow the constitution. Then he took a group selected by the Areopagus to the place where Ephialtes was, ostensibly to show them a meeting of the conspirators, and talked with them seriously. Ephialtes was so alarmed when he saw this that he took refuge at an altar dressed in a suppliant's
4 single garment. Everyone was amazed at what happened, and there followed a meeting of the *Boule* at which

Ephialtes and Themistocles made accusations against the members of the Areopagus. They repeated these accusations before the *Ekklesia* until they succeeded in depriving them of their power. ...* Ephialtes also died shortly afterwards, murdered by Aristodikos of Tanagra.

XXVI The Areopagus lost its supervisory powers in this way. In the years which followed, the enthusiasm of the demagogues led to an increasing absence of control in political life. It happened that at this time the better citizens were without a leader, for their principal spokesman, Cimon the son of Miltiades, was rather young and had only recently entered public life, and in addition to this the majority of them had perished in war.† Military service at that period depended on the citizen rolls, and the *strategoi* in charge were militarily inexperienced but respected for the achievements of their ancestors; the result was that two or three thousand of the men on any expedition were killed, and the better men from both the upper classes and the mass of the 2 people were decimated. In their administration the Athenians did not pay the same amount of attention to the laws as they had done in earlier periods; they made no innovation affecting the selection of the nine Archons, except that in the sixth year after the death of Ephialtes they decided to admit *zeugitai* to the preliminary selection of those from whom the nine Archons would be selected by lot. The first member of this class to be Archon was Mnesitheides; all previous Archons had been *hippeis* or *pentakosiomedimnoi*, while the *zeugitai* had held only the ordinary offices, unless any of the legal restrictions had 3 been disregarded. Four years later, in the Archonship of Lusikrates, the thirty justices were re-established who 4 were known as the magistrates of the demes. Two years

---

* A surprising *kai* ('and' or 'also') preserved in the papyrus suggests that a clause or sentence is missing; it may have contained an account of the death of Themistocles.

† The historical order of events is very confused here; see the Commentary.

later, in the Archonship of Antidotos, because of the large size of the citizen body, it was enacted, on the proposal of Pericles, that those whose parents were not both citizens should not themselves be citizens.

XXVII   After this, Pericles became one of the leaders of the people, first becoming famous when he was a young man and prosecuted Cimon at his *euthuna* as *strategos*. With Pericles, the state became still more democratic; he deprived the Areopagus of some of its powers and turned the state particularly towards naval power, with the result that the masses had the courage to take more into 2 their own hands in all fields of government. Forty-eight years after the battle of Salamis, in the Archonship of Puthodoros, the Peloponnesian War broke out; during this the citizens were shut up inside the city walls, and grew accustomed to earn their living by military service, and decided, partly consciously and partly through the force of circumstances, to run the state themselves. 3 Pericles introduced pay for those serving in the *dikasteria* as a political move to counter the effects of Cimon's wealth. Cimon possessed a kingly fortune, and not merely performed his public liturgies magnificently but also maintained many of the members of his deme, for any member of the deme of Lakiadai who wished could come to him every day and receive adequate maintenance, and all his estates were unfenced so that anyone who wished could help himself to the fruit. 4 Pericles' wealth was not adequate to match such liberality, and Damonides of Oia, who was thought to have suggested most of Pericles' measures, and was later ostracised for this very reason, suggested to him that since he could not match Cimon in private resources, he should give the people what was their own; Pericles accepted his advice, and arranged pay for the *dikastai*. Some say that the quality of *dikastai* declined, since it was always the ordinary people rather than the more respectable who took care to ensure that their names 5 were included in the ballot for places on the juries. This was also the beginning of corruption of the *dikastai*, the first instance being Anytus after he was *strategos* at Pylos; he had been accused over the loss of Pylos, but bribed the court and was acquitted.

XXVIII Throughout the period of Pericles' ascendancy the state was run reasonably well, but after his death there was a marked decline. It was then that the people first got a leader who was not approved by the respectable citizens; before this the leaders had always come from this
2 class. The first leader of the people was Solon, and he was followed by Peisistratus, both of them aristocrats of good family. After the fall of the tyranny there was Cleisthenes, an Alcmeonid, and he had no opponent after the expulsion of Isagoras and his supporters. Then Xanthippus was the leader of the people and Miltiades leader of the aristocrats; then came Themistocles and Aristides. After them, Ephialtes led the people and Cimon the wealthier classes; then Pericles led the people while Thucydides, a relative by marriage of Cimon, led
3 the other group. After the death of Pericles, Nicias, who died in Sicily, was the leader of the upper classes, while Cleon the son of Cleainetus led the people. The latter appears to have corrupted the people more than anyone else by his violence; he was the first to shout when addressing the people, he used abusive language, and addressed the *Ekklesia* with his garments tucked up when it was customary to speak properly dressed. After them, Theramenes the son of Hagnon was leader of the other group, while the leader of the people was Cleophon the lyre-maker who introduced the two-obol payment. This was paid for some time and then was abolished by Kallikrates of Paiania; he first promised to add a third obol to the distribution. Both these last two politicians were later condemned to death, for, even if the people are deceived for a while, they tend later to hate those who have induced them to follow an unsuitable course of
4 action. After Cleophon there was an unbroken series of demagogues whose main aim was to be outrageous and please the people with no thought for anything but the present.

5   The best leaders in Athens after the early period seem to have been Nicias, Thucydides and Theramenes. Almost everyone agrees that Nicias and Thucydides were not only true gentlemen and good politicians, but also that they looked after the city like fathers. There is some dispute about Theramenes because he happened to live at a time of political turmoil. If one avoids a superficial judgement, he does not appear to have destroyed all constitutions, as hostile assessments suggest, but to have supported all so long as they did nothing illegal; he was capable of taking part in politics under all forms of government—the mark of a good citizen—but refused to support and hated regimes which disregarded the law.

THE FOUR HUNDRED

XXIX   To resume, as long as the fortunes of war were reasonably evenly balanced, the democracy was preserved, but when after the disaster in Sicily the Spartan side gained a considerable advantage because of their alliance with the king of Persia, the Athenians were forced to change their democracy into the regime of the Four Hundred. Melobios delivered the speech introducing the resolution, and Puthodoros of the deme Anaphlustos drafted the motion. The decisive consideration in winning over the majority of the people was the belief that the king of Persia would be more likely to make a military alliance with them if their government was

2 oligarchic. The decree of Puthodoros ran as follows: the people should choose another twenty men from those over forty years of age to join the emergency committee of ten already in existence; they should take an oath to formulate such measures as were in the best interests of the state, and should make proposals for its safety; anybody else was at liberty to make proposals so that

3 they might select the best of all the suggestions. Kleitophon added a rider to the proposal of Puthodoros, to the effect that those chosen should search out the traditional laws passed by Cleisthenes when he established the democracy, in order that they might assist their delibera-

tions; the reasoning was that Cleisthenes' constitution was not democratic but similar to that of Solon.

4 The first proposal of the committee when selected was that it should be obligatory for the Prytanies to put to the vote all proposals which related to the safety of the state; then they suspended the statute of indictment for illegal proposals and all impeachments and summonses so that any Athenian who wished could make proposals about what was being discussed. If anyone punished, summonsed or brought before a court anyone for doing so, he should immediately be indicted and brought before the *strategoi*, and they should hand him over to the Eleven for execution.

5 After these preliminaries, they laid down the following principles: all money accruing to the state was to be spent on the war and nothing else; nobody was to receive pay for any office for the duration of the war except the nine Archons and the Prytanies of the period, who should receive three obols each per day. The rest of the administration for the duration of the war should be put in the hands of those Athenians best qualified in person and property to serve the state, up to a total of not less than five thousand. They should have the power to make treaties with whomsoever they wished. The people should elect ten men from each tribe over forty years old who should in their turn select the five thousand under an oath taken on unblemished sacrificial victims.

xxx These were the proposals which the chosen committee put forward. When they had been passed, the Five Thousand chose a hundred of their own members to draw up the constitution. The proposals which were
2 drafted and put forward by them ran as follows. The *Boule* is to consist of men over thirty years of age on a yearly basis without pay. From their number should come the *strategoi*, the nine Archons, the *hieromnemon*, the commanders of the tribal hoplite and cavalry units, the cavalry commanders and the commanders of garrisons, as also the ten Treasurers of the treasury of Athena and the other gods, the twenty *Hellenotamiai*, who were also

to take charge of all the other sacred funds, ten in charge of sacrifices and ten overseers. All these officials should be chosen from a larger group elected from the *Boule* in office at the time. All other offices should be filled by lot by men not members of the *Boule*; the *Hellenotamiai* who actually handled the finances should not sit in the *Boule*.

3 Four *Boulai* should be established for the future from the specified age group, and one section, selected by lot, should act as the *Boule*; the other citizens should be allocated among the sections. The hundred on the drafting committee should divide themselves and the others as equally as possible into four sections, cast lots between the sections, and the term of office of a *Boule*

4 should be one year. The members of the *Boule* were to take whatever decisions seemed best to them both to ensure the preservation of Athens' financial resources and their use for necessary purposes, and in other fields. If they wished to discuss a matter with a wider group, each member could call in an associate of his own choosing from the same age-group. The *Boule* should meet once every five days unless more frequent meetings were

5 felt to be necessary. The nine Archons were to handle the drawing of lots for the *Boule*, while five men selected by lot from the *Boule* should count votes, and one man should be selected by lot from them each day to put motions to the vote. The five selected by lot should also cast lots among those who wished to address the *Boule* in the following order of precedence: first priests, second heralds, third embassies, fourth any other persons. The *strategoi* should have the right of addressing the *Boule* on matters of war without having to draw lots for prece-

6 dence. A member of the *Boule* who failed to attend at the Bouleuterion at the appointed time was to be fined a drachma per day's absence unless he had obtained permission to be away from the *Boule*.

XXXI They drafted the above constitution for the future, and put forward the following interim proposals. There should be a *Boule* of four hundred according to tradition, forty from each tribe to be chosen from a group previously elected by their fellow tribesmen from those over thirty years old. The *Boule* was to appoint the office-holders and draft the oath which they were to take, and take such measures as seemed beneficial about the laws, the 2 *euthunai* and other matters. They were to observe such laws as might be passed in the constitutional field, and might not change them or enact others. The *strategoi* for the moment were to be selected from all the Five Thousand; when the *Boule* had been established and had held an inspection in full armour, it was to select ten men as *strategoi* and a clerk for them, and those selected were to hold office for the following year with full powers, and 3 consult the *Boule* if they needed to. They were to choose one cavalry commander and ten commanders of the tribal cavalry units; in the future the *Boule* were to choose these officers according to the proposals. Neither they nor anyone else might hold any other office more than once except for membership of the *Boule* or being a *strategos*. For the future, the hundred men are to allot the Four Hundred among the four sections so that they may take part when the citizens join the rest in membership of the *Boule*.*

XXXII The hundred men chosen by the Five Thousand drafted these proposals. When they were enacted by the main body under the presidency of Aristomachos, the *Boule* of the year of Kallias' Archonship was dissolved on the fourteenth day of Thargelion before finishing its year of office, and the Four Hundred took office on the twenty-second of the same month. The democratically selected *Boule* for the next year ought to have taken office 2 on the fourteenth of Skirophorion. So the oligarchy was established in the Archonship of Kallias, about a hundred years after the expulsion of the tyrants; the main instigators of it were Peisander, Antiphon and Theramenes, who were well born and had the reputation of being out- 3 standing in intelligence and judgement. When this consitution was established, the Five Thousand were only nominally chosen; the Four Hundred, together with the

* The sentence is obscure, and may be corrupt.

ten *strategoi* with full powers, entered the Bouleuterion
and ruled the city. They sent a proposal of peace to the
Spartans on the basis that each side should retain what
it held. When the Spartans refused unless Athens surrendered her maritime power, they abandoned the
proposal.

XXXIII The constitution of the Four Hundred lasted about
four months, and Mnasilochos of their number was
Archon for two months in the Archonship of Theo-
pompos, who was Archon for the remaining ten months.
When the Athenians were defeated in the sea battle near
Eretria and the whole of Euboea revolted except for
Oreus, they were more incensed by the disaster than any
previous defeat, for Euboea was of more service to them
than Attica at the time; they therefore overthrew the
Four Hundred, and handed over the conduct of affairs
to the Five Thousand who provided their own armour,
passing a decree that there should be no pay for office.
2 Those most responsible for the overthrow were Aristo-
krates and Theramenes; they did not agree with what
was being done by the Four Hundred, for they decided
everything themselves, and referred nothing to the Five
Thousand. The constitution at this time appears to have
been a good one, for they were at war, and power
belonged to those who provided their own armour.

DEMOCRACY RESTORED

XXXIV The people shortly overthrew the Five Thousand. In
the seventh year after the overthrow of the Four Hundred, which was the Archonship of Kallias from Angele,
the battle at Arginusae was fought. Thereafter, first the
ten *strategoi* who won the battle were all condemned by
a single vote, although some had not been present at the
battle and others had been rescued by other ships; the
people had been misled by those who were enraged by
what had happened. Then, when the Spartans were
willing to surrender Decelea and make peace on the
basis of the status quo, some were in favour, but the
people rejected the proposal; they were deceived by

Cleophon who came into the *Ekklesia* drunk and wearing his breastplate, and prevented peace being made. He said he would not permit it unless the Spartans

2 surrendered all the cities they had taken. Their mistake was brought home to them shortly afterwards; in the next year, the Archonship of Alexias, they lost the battle of Aegospotami, as a result of which Lysander became master of the city and established the Thirty in the

3 following way. The peace terms specified that the Athenians should be governed by their ancestral constitution; on this basis the democrats tried to preserve the democracy, while the nobles who belonged to the political clubs and the exiles who had returned after the peace wanted an oligarchy. Those who did not belong to any political club, but in other respects seemed outstanding citizens, aimed at establishing the ancestral constitution; among them were Archinos, Anytus, Kleitophon, Phormisios and many others, and their leader was Theramenes. Lysander sided with the oligarchs, overawed the people, and forced them to vote an oligarchy into power on the proposal of Dracontides of Aphidna.

THE THIRTY AND THE TEN

XXXV   So the Thirty were established in the Archonship of Puthodoros. When they had secured their power in the city, they disregarded the proposals which had been passed about the constitution except for appointing five hundred members of the *Boule* and the other magistrates from a group previously elected from the thousand,* and choosing ten colleagues to govern the Peiraeus, eleven guards for the prison and three hundred whip-bearers as their attendants; in this way they controlled the city.

2 At first they behaved with restraint towards the citizens, and pretended to be aiming at the ancestral constitution; they took down from the Areopagus the laws of Ephialtes and Archestratos about the members of that body, repealed disputed laws of Solon, and abolished the power of the *dikastai*; they claimed to be correcting the

---

* Perhaps corrupt; see Commentary.

constitution and removing ambiguities. For example, they made it legal for a man to leave his property to anyone he wished without restraint, abolishing the irritating provisos 'unless he be of unsound mind, incapacitated by age, or under the influence of a woman'; their aim was to eliminate opportunities for informers.

3 They made other similar reforms. They carried these measures at an early stage, and they got rid of the informers and the wicked mischief-makers who flattered the people to their disadvantage. The people were delighted, thinking they made these changes for the best of motives.

4 When the Thirty had tightened their grip on the city, there was no type of citizen they did not attack. They killed those remarkable for wealth, family or reputation, aiming to remove any potential threat and to lay their hands on their property. After a short time they had killed no less than fifteen hundred men.

xxxvi The city was being undermined in this way, and Theramenes was angry at what was happening; he urged the Thirty to stop behaving so outrageously, and to give the best citizens a share in government. They opposed him at first, but when stories of Theramenes' proposals leaked out, and the people supported him, they were afraid that he might become the people's champion and overthrow their regime; they therefore compiled a list of three thousand citizens who were to receive a share

2 in the government. Theramenes attacked this move too, firstly because in aiming to share power with the respectable element they restricted it to three thousand as if virtue were restricted to a body of this size, and secondly on the grounds that they were attempting two totally conflicting things, to base their regime on force and yet create a regime weaker than those it ruled. The Thirty disregarded these criticisms, but postponed publication of the list of the Three Thousand for a long time, and kept the names of those who had been chosen secret; when they did decide to publish it, they cut out some who had been included and included others who had not been on the original list.

XXXVII   When it was already winter, the Thirty led a military expedition against Thrasybulus and the exiles who had seized Phyle, and were defeated; they therefore decided to disarm the citizens and kill Theramenes. This they achieved by laying two laws before the *Boule* and ordering their approval. The first gave the Thirty full power to execute any citizen whose name was not included on the list of the Three Thousand. The second deprived of all rights under the present constitution anyone who had taken part in the destruction of the fort at Eëtioneia or had acted in any way in opposition to the Four Hundred who had established the previous oligarchy. Theramenes had done both, with the result that when the laws were passed he lost his citizen rights, and the Thirty had the

2   power to execute him. After Theramenes had been executed, they disarmed all except the Three Thousand, and the savagery and wickedness of their regime increased considerably. They sent an embassy to Sparta which specified charges against Theramenes and asked for help; the Spartans sent Kallibios as harmost, and about seven hundred men who garrisoned the Acropolis.

XXXVIII   The exiles from Phyle then seized Munichia, and defeated an attempt by the Thirty and their adherents to dislodge them. The men from the city returned after the battle, met in the Agora the next day, and deposed the Thirty and elected ten citizens with full powers to bring the war to an end. After taking office, they did nothing to further the purpose for which they had been chosen, but sent to Sparta for help and to borrow money.

2   Those who had full citizen rights were angry at this, and the Ten were afraid that they might be overthrown; therefore, with the aim of terrifying the people (in which they were successful), they seized one of the most outstanding citizens, called Demaretos, and executed him. The result was that they had firm control of affairs with the backing of Kallibios and the Spartan garrison and also that of a number of the Athenian *hippeis*, for some of them were particularly keen that the exiles from Phyle should not return to Athens.

DEMOCRACY FINALLY RESTORED

3   The group which held the Peiraeus and Munichia
gradually gained the upper hand in the war as the whole
people went over to their side, and so the men in the city
deposed the Ten who had first been elected, and chose
another ten men with the reputation of being outstanding
citizens; it was under them that the reconciliation was
arranged and the democracy returned, and they worked
enthusiastically to this end. Their main leaders were
Rhinon of Paiania and Phaullos of Acherdos; they were
negotiating with the men in the Peiraeus before Pausanias arrived, and after he had come joined in supporting
4   the return of the exiles. The peace and the end of the
hostilities was brought about by Pausanias, the Spartan
king and the ten mediators who later came from Sparta
at his request. Rhinon and his friends were commended
for their goodwill towards the democracy, and, although
they had taken office under an oligarchy, they underwent their *euthuna* under a democracy; however, nobody
brought a single complaint against them—neither the
men who had stayed in the city nor those who had
returned from the Peiraeus. On the contrary, because
of what he had done Rhinon was immediately elected
strategos.

XXXIX   The reconciliation was brought about in the Archonship of Eukleides on the following terms. Those of the
Athenians who had remained in the city and wished to
leave should live in Eleusis, where they should retain full
citizen rights, have complete self-government and enjoy
2   their incomes. The temple was to be common to both
sides, under the traditional control of the Kerukes and
the Eumolpidai. Those living at Eleusis were not allowed
to visit the city of Athens, nor were those living in Athens
allowed to visit Eleusis, with the exception for both sides
of the celebration of the Mysteries. The people at Eleusis
were to contribute to a defence fund from their revenues
3   like the other Athenians. If any of those leaving the city
took over a house at Eleusis, they were to do it with the

agreement of the owner; if agreement proved impossible, each was to select three assessors, and the owner was to accept the price they fixed. Any inhabitants of Eleusis acceptable to the new settlers were to live with them
4 there. Those wishing to move out to Eleusis had to register within ten days of the swearing of the reconciliation oaths if they were in the city at the time, and move out within twenty; those abroad at the time had the same periods from the moment when they returned to
5 Athens. Nobody living at Eleusis could hold any office in the city of Athens until he had been registered as having moved his residence back to the city. Homicide trials in cases where someone had killed or wounded a person with his own hands were to be conducted in
6 accordance with traditional practice. There was to be a total amnesty covering everyone except the Thirty, the Ten*, the Eleven and the governors of the Peiraeus; even they were to be immune from prosecution once they had submitted to the *euthuna*. The *euthuna* for the governors of the Peiraeus was to be held before the citizens of the Peiraeus, while those who had held office in the city were to appear before citizens with taxable property there. On this basis those who wished to could leave the city. Each side was to repay separately the money which it had borrowed for the war.

XL   After the conclusion of a settlement along these lines, those who had fought with the Thirty were afraid, and many intended to move out of the city, but put off registration until the last moment, as men always do. Archinos saw the number involved, and cancelled the remaining days for registration because he wished to keep them in the city; many were compelled to remain, much against their will until they recovered their con-
2 fidence. This was a sound move by Archinos, as was his later indictment of Thrasybulus for illegal proposals

---

* The text does not make clear which of the boards of ten discussed in xxxviii is referred to; see Commentary.

when the latter tried to give citizenship to all who had
had a part in the return from the Peiraeus although some
were manifestly slaves. A third good move was when he
seized one of the returned exiles who was attempting to
disregard the amnesty, brought him before the *Boule*,
and persuaded them to execute him without trial. He
argued that their actions would show whether they
intended to preserve the democracy and stand by their
oaths: if they let the man go, they would encourage
others, while if they executed him, they would establish
an example for all. This is just what happened, for after
his execution nobody ever again tried to flout the
3 amnesty. The Athenians appear to have handled their
affairs, both private and public, as well and with as much
statesmanship as any people ever have shown in a
similar situation. They not only refused to entertain any
charges based on previous events, but they also repaid
as a state the money which the Thirty had borrowed from
the Spartans for the war, although the agreement had
specified that the men of the city and those of the Peiraeus should repay their debts separately; they felt that
this ought to be the first step in restoring unity and con-
cord in the state. In other states the democrats, far from
making contributions themselves in similar circum-
4 stances, redistribute the land. Athens was reunited with
Eleusis in the third year after the oligarchs moved there,
in the Archonship of Xenainetos.

XLI   That final reconciliation happened subsequently.
When the people regained power they established the
constitution which is still in force, in the Archonship of
Puthodoros. . . .* It was just that the people should take
control because they had secured their return by their
2 own efforts. This was the eleventh change of constitution. The first was the modification of the original constitution when Ion and those with him came to Athens;
it was then that the Athenians were first divided into
the four tribes and established the tribe kings. The
second change, the first after this which had the status of

* There must be something missing here; see Commentary.

a constitution, was under Theseus, and moved the state a little away from absolute monarchy. After this came the constitution of the time of Draco, under which the Athenians first had written laws. The third change after the period of dissension came under Solon; it sowed the seeds of democracy. The fourth was the tyranny under Peisistratus. The fifth, after the fall of the tyranny, was the constitution of Cleisthenes, which was more democratic than that of Solon. The sixth came after the Persian wars, when the Areopagus had over-all control. For the seventh, which followed this one, Aristides showed the way, but Ephialtes brought it to completion by depriving the Areopagus of power. Under this constitution the city made innumerable mistakes under the guidance of the demagogues because of their control of the sea. The eighth was the establishment of the Four Hundred, while the ninth followed it with the return of the democracy. The tenth was the tyranny of the Thirty and the Ten. The eleventh came after the return from Phyle and the Peiraeus; it has lasted to the present day with ever-increasing power being assumed by the people. They have made themselves supreme in all fields; they run everything by decrees of the *Ekklesia* and by decisions of the *dikasteria* in which the people are supreme. For the judicial powers of the *Boule* have passed to the people, which seems a correct development, for a small number are more open to corruption by bribery or favours than a large.

3   At first the Athenians declined to institute pay for attendance at the *Ekklesia*. When attendance was poor, and the Prytanies had tried many devices to encourage citizens to come so that the people might ratify proposals by their vote, payment of one obol was instituted as a first move on the proposal of Agurrhios; Herakleides of Clazomenae, who was called 'the king', raised it to two obols, and Agurrhios made it three.

THE PRESENT CONSTITUTION

XLII   The constitution of the present day is as follows. Full citizenship belongs to men both of whose parents were citizens, and they are inscribed on the list with their fellow demesmen when they are eighteen years old. When they are being registered, the members of the deme vote under oath first on whether they appear to have reached the legal age, and if they do not, they are returned to the status of children, and secondly on whether a man is free and born as the laws prescribe. If they decide that he is not free, he appeals to the *dikasterion*, while the demesmen select five of their number as accusers; if it is decided that he has no right to be registered as a citizen, the city sells him into slavery, but if he wins his case, the demesmen are required to

2 register him. Then the *Boule* reviews those who have been registered, and if it is decided that a man is younger than eighteen, the demesmen who registered him are fined. When the Ephebes have been approved, their fathers meet by tribes and choose under oath three members of the tribe over forty years old whom they consider best and most suitable to take charge of the Ephebes, and from them the people elect one for each tribe as guardian, and they elect a controller from the

3 rest of the citizen body for all of them. These men take the Ephebes, and after visiting the temples they go to the Peiraeus and take up guard duties, some at Munichia and others at Akte. The people also elect two trainers for them, and two men to teach them to fight in armour, and to use the bow, the javelin and the catapult. The guardians receive a drachma each for their maintenance, and the Ephebes four obols. Each guardian receives the allowances for the members of his tribe and buys what is necessary for them all centrally (for they live together by tribes), and takes care of everything else for them.

4 This is how they spend the first year of their training. At the beginning of the second, at a meeting of the *Ekklesia* held in the theatre, they demonstrate to the people their knowledge of warfare, and receive a shield and spear from the city. For the year thereafter they patrol the

5 countryside and man the guard posts. For their two years service they wear the military cloak, and are exempt from all duties. They cannot prosecute or be

prosecuted so that there may be no reason for their leaving their post; the only exception is to deal with matters of inheritance or an *epikleros*, or to take up a priesthood hereditary in a man's family. After this two years, they join the main citizen body.

XLIII   That is how citizens are registered and Ephebes trained. The holders of all routine offices in the state are selected by lot except for the treasurer of the military funds, the controllers of the Theoric Fund and the supervisor of the water supply. These are elected, and hold office from one Panathenaic festival to the next. All military officials are also elected.

2   The *Boule* of 500 members is selected by lot, 50 from each tribe. Each tribe acts as Prytany in an order decided by lot, the first four for thirty-six days each, the last six for thirty-five, for they work by a lunar year.

3   The Prytanies eat together in the Tholos at the city's expense, and summon meetings of the *Boule* and *Ekklesia*; the *Boule* meets every day except for holidays, the *Ekklesia* four times in every prytany. They publish the

4   agenda and place for each meeting of the *Boule*, and also draw up the agenda for the *Ekklesia*. In each prytany the *Ekklesia* meets for one plenary session, in which there must be a vote on whether all office-holders have performed their duties well; there must also be discussions of the corn supply and the safety of Attica; those who wish to bring impeachments do so at this meeting, lists of confiscated property are read out, and also claims to inheritances and to marry *epikleroi*, so that nobody

5   may be ignorant of any unclaimed estates. In the sixth prytany, in addition to the business already discussed, they put to the vote the question of whether an ostracism should be held, and hear accusations against informers, whether Athenians or metics (with a limit of three of each), and allegations against anyone who has

6   failed to fulfil an undertaking made to the city. The second meeting must hear petitioners, and anyone who wishes may appear as a suppliant on any subject he chooses, private or public, and address the people on it.

The other two meetings deal with other matters, amongst which the law prescribes the consideration of three motions about sacred matters, three concerning heralds and embassies, and three about secular matters. On occasions they also consider matters without a preliminary vote. Heralds and ambassadors report to the Prytanies first, and despatches are delivered to them.

XLIV One man is picked as chairman of the Prytanies by lot, and holds office for a night and a day; he cannot preside for longer, nor can the same man serve twice. He holds the keys of the sanctuaries where the treasure and the public records are kept; he holds the city's seal, and must remain in the Tholos with one third of the Prytanies

2 selected by him. When the Prytanies summon a meeting of the *Boule* or *Ekklesia*, he casts lots for nine chairmen, one from each tribe except the one supplying the Prytany; he casts lots again among the nine for the man who will actually preside, and he hands over the agenda

3 to them. The nine take over, and are responsible for good order, put forward topics for discussion, assess the voting, and control everything else. They also have the right to adjourn the meeting. An individual may not preside at a meeting more than once in a year, nor be one of the nine chairmen more than once in each prytany.

4 They elect *strategoi*, cavalry commanders and other military officers in the *Ekklesia* in accordance with the will of the people; the elections are held on the first meeting after the sixth prytany when the omens are favourable. There must also be a preliminary resolution to hold the elections.

XLV In former times the *Boule* had powers of punishment by fine, imprisonment or execution. Once when the *Boule* had handed Lusimachos over to the public executioner and he was already sitting waiting for the sentence to be carried out, Eumelides of Alopeke saved him, saying that no citizen ought to be executed without a vote of the *dikasterion*. When the *dikasterion* heard the case, Lusimachos was acquitted and was nicknamed 'the man who escaped the rod'. The people deprived the *Boule* of all powers of fine, imprisonment or execution, and passed a law that if the *Boule* condemned a man or punished him, the *Thesmothetai* were to bring the condemnations or punishments before the *dikasterion* and their decision should be final.

2 The *Boule* conducts the investigations into the conduct of the great majority of the magistrates, particularly those who handle money; their decision is not final, but subject to appeal to the *dikasterion*. Private citizens too can bring a charge of acting illegally against any office-holder they wish; he has a right of appeal to the *dikaster-*
3 *ion* if condemned by the *Boule*. It also considers the credentials of the following year's *Boule* and of the nine Archons; in the past, their decision was final, but now there is a right of appeal to the *dikasterion* for those disqualified.

4 In these matters, then, the *Boule* does not have the final decision, but it holds a preliminary discussion on everything that is to come before the people, nor can the people vote on anything that has not been previously discussed by them and put on the agenda by the Prytanies. Anyone who violates this law is liable to a prosecution for an illegal proposal.

XLVI The *Boule* is in charge of the completed triremes, the tackle stores and the ship sheds, and builds new triremes or quadriremes, whichever the people vote to construct, and tackle and ship sheds for them, but the people elect the naval architects for the ships. If the *Boule* do not hand them over to the new *Boule* completed, they cannot receive the usual reward, for they receive the reward under the next *Boule*. The triremes are constructed under the supervision of a board of ten members of the *Boule*.
2 The *Boule* inspects all public buildings, and if it decides that someone has committed an offence, it reports him to the people, and hands him over to the *dikasterion* if they find him guilty.

XLVII   The *Boule* also joins the other magistrates in most areas of the administration. First, there are ten Treasurers of Athena, one picked by lot from each tribe; in accordance with Solon's law (which is still in force) they must be *pentakosiomedimnoi*, but the man picked by lot holds office even if he is very poor. These officers take over in front of the *Boule* the image of Athena and the Victories, and the other ceremonial equipment and the money.

2   Then there are the ten *poletai* picked by lot, one from each tribe. They let out all the public contracts, sell the right to work the mines, and let the rights of collecting taxes with the treasurer of military affairs and those in charge of the Theoric Fund; this is done in front of the *Boule*. They confirm the position of anyone elected by the *Boule*, and matters concerning mining leases which have been sold, both those where rights of exploitation have been sold for a period of three years and those where special agreements cover a period of ten years. They sell the property of those exiled by the Areopagus and of other exiles before the *Boule*, and the nine Archons confirm the transaction. They list on whitened boards taxes sold for a period of a year with the name of the buyer

3   and the price. They hand the boards over to the *Boule*. They list separately on ten boards those who have to pay their instalments every prytany, on three boards those who have to pay three times a year, and on a separate list those who pay once a year in the ninth prytany. They also list the properties and houses confiscated and sold in the *dikasterion*, for they are responsible for their sale. The price of a house must be paid in five years, of land in ten; these payments are made in the ninth prytany.

4   The King Archon produces a list of the leases of the sacred estates on whitened boards; they are leased for a period of ten years, and the rent is payable in the ninth prytany. For this reason a great deal of money is collected

5   in this prytany. Lists of the payments due are deposited with the *Boule*, and the state secretary keeps them; when a payment is due, he takes from the pigeon holes the list of those whose payments are due on this particular day, and whose entry must be cancelled after payment,

and hands it over to the Receivers; the other lists are stored separately so that nothing may be prematurely cancelled.

XLVIII   There are ten Receivers, one picked by lot per tribe; they take the lists, and in front of the *Boule* in its chamber erase the record of the money that has been paid, and return the records to the state secretary. If anyone fails to pay an instalment, his name is recorded there, and he has to pay double the arrears under penalty of imprisonment. The *Boule* has the legal right to exact the money 2 or imprison the defaulter. On one day they receive all the payments and divide the money among the magistrates, and on the next they bring a record of their actions on a board and read it out in the chamber. They also pose the question in the *Boule* whether anyone knows of any malpractice by a magistrate or a private citizen in the division; if anyone is suspected, there is a vote on the case.

3   The members of the *Boule* select ten of their number by lot as auditors to check the accounts of the magistrates 4 every prytany. They also select by lot one man from each tribe for the *euthuna* and two assistants for each of them. They are required to sit each market-day* by the statue of the eponymous hero of their tribe, and if anyone wishes to bring a charge, whether of public misdemeanour or private malfeasance, against any of those who have undergone the *euthuna* in the *dikasterion* within three days of that hearing, he records on a whitened board the names of the accuser and the defendant, the charge, and the fine which he considers suitable, and 5 hands it to the representative of his tribe. The latter takes it and reads it, and if he considers the charge justified, he hands a private suit to the deme justices who prepare cases for the relevant tribe for the courts, while if it is a public offence, he reports the matter to the *Thesmothetai*. If the *Thesmothetai* take it over, they reopen the examination

---

* The word translated as 'market-day' may not be the correct restoration of a damaged part of the papyrus, but no convincing alternative has yet been suggested.

of this man before the *dikasterion*, and the decision of the jury is final.

XLIX   The *Boule* also reviews the horses, and if a man appears to have a good horse but to be maintaining it badly, deprives him of his maintenance allowance. Horses which cannot keep up, or will not remain in line but run away, are branded with a wheel on the jaw, and are disqualified. They also review the mounted skirmishers to find who seem to be suitable for this, and anyone they vote against loses his horse. They also review the infantry attached to the cavalry, and anyone voted

2   against loses his pay. The cavalry are enrolled by a board of ten elected by the people for this purpose; the names of those enrolled are handed to the cavalry commanders and the commanders of the tribal cavalry units who receive the list and bring it before the *Boule*. They open the sealed document in which the names of the cavalrymen are listed, and erase the names of those previously enrolled who swear that they are prevented by physical disability from serving as cavalry. Then they call those newly enrolled, and if anyone swears that he is physically or financially incapable of serving, they dismiss him. Those who do not take this oath are subject to a vote by the *Boule* as to their suitability for cavalry service; if they are approved, they are enrolled, if not they are dismissed.

3   The *Boule* used to take decisions about the models and the robe, but this is now done by a *dikasterion* selected by lot, for it was felt that the *Boule* was swayed by personal feelings. The *Boule* joins the treasurer of military affairs in supervising the making of the statues of Victory and the prizes for the Panathenaia.

4   The *Boule* also reviews the incapable; for there is a law that anyone with property of less than three minae who suffers from a physical disability which prevents his undertaking any employment should come before the *Boule*, and if his claim is approved he should receive two obols a day subsistence from public funds. There is a treasurer selected by lot to handle this.

5   The *Boule* also cooperates with the other magistrates in most of what they do.

L   Those then are the areas of administration handled by the *Boule*.

A board of ten are also selected by lot to take care of the sanctuaries; they are given thirty minae by the Receivers, and repair the temples most in need of
2 attention. There are ten city commissioners, of whom five hold office in the Peiraeus and five in the city itself. They see that the girls who play the flute, the harp or the lyre are not hired for more than two drachmae; if more than one man wishes to hire the same performer, they cast lots, and allocate her to the winner. They ensure that the dung collectors do not deposit dung within ten stades of the walls, and see that no building either obstructs or has balconies overhanging the streets; they also prevent the construction of waste pipes with outfalls from above into the street, or windows with shutters opening into the road. With assistants provided by the state, they remove the corpses of those who die in the streets.

LI   Ten superintendents of the markets are selected by lot, five for the Peiraeus and five for the city. They are required by law to supervise goods for sale to ensure that
2 merchandise is pure and unadulterated. Ten inspectors of weights and measures are similarly selected, five for the city and five for the Peiraeus to ensure that honest
3 weights and measures are used by those who are selling. There used to be ten commissioners in charge of the corn supply, picked by lot, of whom five were allocated to the Peiraeus and five to the city, but there are now twenty for the city and fifteen for the Peiraeus. They ensure first that there is no sharp practice in the selling of unground corn in the market, secondly that the millers should sell their barley flour at a price corresponding to that of unmilled barley, and thirdly that the bakers should sell loaves at a price corresponding to the price of wheat, and containing the full weight which the

commissioners have laid down as the law requires them
4 to do. They also pick by lot ten commissioners of trade
to supervise trading and ensure that two-thirds of the
corn imported is brought to the city.

LII   The Eleven whose duty it is to take care of prisoners
are selected by lot. They execute thieves, kidnappers and
brigands who confess their guilt, while if they deny the
charge, they bring them before the *dikasterion*, and if they
are acquitted let them go, and if not put them to death
after their trial. They report to the *dikasterion* land and
houses listed as belonging to the city, and hand over to
the *poletai* any that is judged to be public property. It
is also part of their duties to bring summary indictments
before the *dikasterion*, though the *Thesmothetai* also introduce some similar indictments.
2   Five men are picked by lot to introduce cases where
proceedings may be instituted every month, each of
whom covers two tribes. Cases falling in this category
include failure to pay a dowry which is owed, failure to
repay a loan made at an interest of a drachma per mina,
or a loan of capital made to finance the opening of a business in the market; prosecutions for assault, cases involving friendly loans, cooperative ventures, slaves, animals,
3   trierarchies and banking matters. These officials introduce
and handle 'monthly' cases of these classes, while the
Receivers handle cases involving tax-farming, with the
power to make a final decision in cases up to ten drachmae; they refer the remaining 'monthly' cases to the
dikasterion for settlement.

LIII   The Forty are picked by lot, four from each tribe, and
other suits are brought before them. They used to be a
board of thirty, and travel round the demes to try cases,
but after the tyranny of the Thirty their numbers were
2   increased to forty. They can make the final decision in
cases involving up to ten drachmae, but anything above
that they hand over to the Arbitrators. These officials
then take the case, and if they cannot bring about a
settlement, give a decision; if the decision satisfies both

sides and they accept it, the case is ended. If one party appeals to the *dikasterion*, the Arbitrators place the depositions, the challenges and the relevant laws in boxes, one for each side in the case, seal the boxes, add the decision of the Arbitrator written on a tablet, and hand everything over to the four members of the Forty who handle

3 the cases of the tribe of the defendant. They take them over, and bring the case before the *dikasterion*, cases of less than 1,000 drachmae before a jury of 201 members, those over 1,000 before 401 jurors. At the hearing it is forbidden to use laws, challenges or depositions other than those used in front of the Arbitrator and sealed in

4 the boxes. The Arbitrators are men in their sixtieth year; their age is known from the Archons and the eponymous heroes. There are ten eponymous heroes for the tribes, and forty-two for the age-groups; the Ephebes' names are recorded together with the Archon under whom they were enrolled and the eponymous hero of the previous year's Arbitrators; this used to be done on whitened boards, but they now use a bronze plaque which is set up in front of the chamber of the *Boule* by

5 the statues of the eponymous heroes. The Forty take the list under the name of the last of the eponymous heroes, and allot to those on the list the cases for arbitration and cast lots to decide which each will decide. The man selected is required to arbitrate as directed, for the law provides that if any man fails to serve as an Arbitrator when his age-group is performing this duty he shall lose his citizen rights, unless he happens to hold public office that year or to be abroad; only these categories are exempt.

6 Information can be laid before the Arbitrators as a body if anyone is wronged by an individual Arbitrator, and the penalty laid down by law for anyone condemned under this procedure is loss of citizen rights;

7 there is a right of appeal. They also use the names of the eponymous heroes for military service; when they send an age-group on campaign, they publish a notice saying that the groups from one Archon and eponymous hero to another are called up for service.

LIV   The following offices are also filled by lot: five commissioners of roads, whose duty it is to employ the slaves
2 provided by the city to repair the roads. Ten Auditors
and ten assistants for them, to whom all those who have
held public office must submit their accounts; this is the
only body which audits the accounts of those subject to
the *euthuna* and submits the results to the *dikasterion.* If
they detect anyone who has been guilty of embezzlement, the jury condemns him for theft of public money,
and he is sentenced to pay ten times the amount stolen;
if they demonstrate that anyone has taken bribes and
the jury convicts him, they assess the size of the bribe,
and again he pays ten times this amount. If they con-
demn him for maladministration, they assess the amount,
and this is what he pays as long as he pays up before the
ninth prytany; if not, the sum is doubled. Fines of ten
times the amount involved in the offence are not
doubled.

3   They cast lots for the officer called Clerk to the
Prytanies, who is in charge of the documents, keeps the
decrees which have been passed, checks the transcrip-
tion of everything else, and attends meetings of the
Boule. In earlier days this official was elected, and they
used to elect the most famous and reliable men; their
names are recorded on the inscribed texts of alliances,
and grants of *proxenia* and citizenship; now they are
4 selected by lot. They also pick another man by lot to
look after laws; he attends the *Boule* and also checks all
5 transcriptions. The people elect the clerk whose duty it
is to read out documents in the *Ekklesia* and *Boule,* and
this is his only duty.

6   Ten sacred officials are elected who are called 'those
in charge of expiation'; they make sacrifices ordered by
oracles, and if good omens are required they see to it
7 with the prophets. Another ten religious officials are
selected by lot, called 'those in charge of annual rites';
they offer certain sacrifices and are in charge of all four-
yearly festibals except for the Panathenaia. The four-
yearly festivals are: 1. the mission to Delos (which is also
celebrated every six years); 2. the Brauronia; 3. the

Heracleia; 4. the Eleusinia; 5. the Panathenaia; none
of these festivals occurs in the same place. The Hephaistia
was added to the group in the Archonship of Kephisophon.

8 They appoint by lot an Archon for Salamis and a
demarch for the Peiraeus; they celebrate the Dionysia in
each place, and appoint the *choregoi*. In Salamis the name
of the Archon is recorded.

LV The holders of the above offices are selected by lot,
and their duties are those listed above. As to the so-called
nine Archons, I have already described their original
ways of appointment; to-day, six *Thesmothetai* and their
secretary and also the Archon, the King Archon and the
Polemarch are appointed by lot from each tribe in
2 rotation. Their qualifications for office are checked first
in the *Boule* of 500, except for the secretary, whose
qualifications are checked only in the *dikasterion* as
happens for other office holders—for all officials,
whether selected by lot or elected, have their qualifications checked before they take up office; the nine
Archons have to go before both the *Boule* and the
dikasterion. In the past a man who was disqualified by
the *Boule* could not hold office, but now there is an appeal
to the *dikasterion*, and the final decision is taken there.
3 When they are checking qualifications, they ask first:
'Who is your father, and what is your deme? Who was
your father's father, and who was your mother, and her
father and his deme?' Then they ask whether the
candidate is enrolled in a cult of Apollo Patroos and Zeus
Herkeios, and where the shrines are, then whether he
has family tombs and where they are; whether he treats
his parents well, pays his taxes, and has gone on campaign when required. When these questions have been
asked, the candidate is required to call witnesses to his
4 answers. When he has produced the witnesses, the question is put: 'Does anyone wish to bring any charge
against this man?' If an accuser appears, the accusation
and defence are heard, and then the matter is put to the
vote by a show of hands in the *Boule* or a ballot if the

hearing is in the *dikasterion*. If no one wishes to bring an accusation, the vote is held immediately. In former times, only one ceremonial vote was cast,* but now everyone is required to vote on candidates, so that if a criminal has managed get rid of all his accusers it is still in the power

5 of the jurors to disqualify him. After this investigation, the candidates go to the stone on which are the parts of the sacrificial victim, and standing on it they swear to administer their office justly and in accordance with the laws, and not to take bribes in connection with their office, and if they do, to dedicate a golden statue. At this stone also the Arbitrators give their decisions on oath and witnesses swear† to their depositions. After taking the oath the candidates go to the Acropolis, and repeat the same oath there; after that they take up their office.

LVI   The Archon, the King Archon and the Polemarch each have two assessors of their own choice, and these men have their credentials checked in the *dikasterion* before they take up their positions, and are subject to the *euthuna* in respect of their tenure.

2   As soon as the Archon takes up office, he proclaims that every man shall hold and control until the end of the year such property as he held before he took office.

3   Then he appoints for the tragedians three *choregoi* who are the richest of all the Athenians; formerly he appointed five for the comedians, but now the tribes provide for them. Then he receives the *choregoi* appointed by the tribes, those for the men's and the boys' choruses and the comedies at the Dionysia, and for the men's and boys' choruses at the Thargelia; those for the Dionysia are each provided by one tribe, but two tribes combine for the Thargelia, each of the tribes serving in turn. The Archon then arranges exchanges of property, and presents any claims for exemption which may arise if a man claims

---

* That is, where no charge was brought, a single, formal vote of acquittal was all that was required.

† See note on this translation in the Commentary.

either to have performed this liturgy before, or to be exempt on the grounds of having performed another liturgy after which his period of exemption has not yet passed, or not to be of the required age—for the *choregos* of the boys' chorus must be over forty years old. The Archon also appoints *choregoi* for Delos, and a chief of the sacred embassy to take the young people on the
4 thirty-oared vessel. He is also in charge of the procession to Asclepius when the initiated hold a vigil, and the procession at the Great Dionysia. In arranging the latter he is aided by ten assistants who used to be elected by the people and meet the cost of the procession out of their own pockets, but now are picked by lot, one from each tribe, and receive a hundred minae for their expenses.
5 The Archon also organises the processions at the Thargelia and to Zeus Soter; he organises the contests at the Dionysia and the Thargelia. These are the festivals which
6 he organises. Some civil and criminal proceedings come before the Archon; he holds a preliminary hearing, and then introduces them into the *dikasterion*. They include cases of illtreating parents, in which the prosecutor is immune from penalty; accusations of offences against orphans, which are brought against the guardians, and of offences against *epikleroi*, which are brought against the guardians and the people living with the *epikleroi*; accusations of mismanaging the estate of an orphan, which are also brought against the guardians; charges of insanity where it is alleged that a man is wasting his substance because he is of unsound mind, and requests for the appointment of officials to divide up property where a person is unwilling to share out what is held in common; requests to constitute or decide a wardship, for production in court, for enrolment as a guardian,
7 and claims to estates and *epikleroi*. He also looks after orphans, *epikleroi*, and widows who declare themselves pregnant after the death of their husbands. He has the power to fine offenders or bring them before the *dikasterion*. He rents out the houses of orphans and *epikleroi* until they are fourteen years old, and takes security for the leases; he exacts maintenance from

guardians who do not provide it for children in their care.

LVII These matters are the province of the Archon. The King Archon supervises the Mysteries together with assistants elected by the people, two of whom are elected from the whole citizen body, one from the family of the Eumolpidai, and one from the Kerukes. Secondly he has charge of the festival of Dionysus called the Lenaia, which involves a procession and contest. The King Archon and his assistants jointly arrange the procession, but the contest is in his hands alone. He also arranges all torch-races and virtually all the traditional sacrifices.

2 Cases of impiety come before him and disputes over priesthoods. He also decides all disputes about religious matters which arise between the clans or the priests; all cases of homicide come before him, and he it is who proclaims the exclusion of an individual from the things specified in the laws.

3 Charges of murder or wounding where a man deliberately kills or injures someone are heard before the Areopagus, as are cases of poisoning which result in death, and cases of arson; these are the only cases decided by that body. Charges of unintentional homicide, conspiracy to kill, and the killing of a slave, metic or foreigner are heard by the Court of the Palladion. Where a man admits to having killed someone but claims that his action was lawful, as for example if he caught an adulterer in the act, or killed unwittingly in war or in the course of the games, the case is heard in the Delphinion. If a man has retired into exile in a situation where reconciliation is possible and is then accused of killing or wounding someone, his case is heard in the

4 court of Phreatto, and he pleads his case from a boat anchored near the shore. Except for cases brought before the Areopagus, all these cases are tried by *Ephetai* selected by lot; the case is brought before the court by the King Archon, and the hearing is held in a sacred area out of doors; during the case the King Archon does not wear his crown. At all other times the defendant is excluded from all sanctuaries, and is even barred by law

from the Agora, but for the trial he enters the sacred area and makes his defence. When the offender is not known, the proceedings are held against 'the guilty party'. The King Archon and the Tribal Kings also proceed against inanimate objects and animals.

LVIII   The Polemarch makes the sacrifices to Artemis the huntress and to Enualios, and arranges the funeral games in honour of those who have fallen in war, and makes the
2   offerings to Harmodius and Aristogeiton. He hears only private suits which involve metics, tax-exempt metics and *proxenoi*; it is his duty to take them and divide them into ten groups, and to assign by lot one group to each of the ten tribes, and the jurors of the tribe must then bring
3   them before the Arbitrators. The Polemarch himself introduces cases where a man is accused of disregarding his patron or not having one, and also cases involving inheritance and *epikleroi* of the metics; in other respects, the Polemarch performs for the metics the same duties as the Archon performs for citizens.

LIX   The *Thesmothetai* are responsible first for announcing the days on which the *dikasteria* will sit, and then for allotting the magistrates to the courts; the latter bring
2   cases to court as the *Thesmothetai* direct. They bring impeachments before the *Ekklesia*, and they introduce motions for the deposition of magistrates and all accusations brought in the *Ekklesia*, indictments for illegal proposals and accusations of having proposed laws against the interests of the state, indictments against the chairmen or president, and the *euthunai* of the *strategoi*.
3   They hear cases where the prosecutor has to make a deposit, including charges of wrongly claiming citizen rights, or using bribery to this end, which arises when a man uses bribery to escape a charge of wrongly claiming to be a citizen, charges of malicious prosecution, bribery, false entry in the lists of state debtors, falsely witnessing a summons, failure to erase the name of a debtor who has paid, non-registration of a debtor, and adultery.
4   They also introduce the investigations into the credentials of all candidates for office, the appeals of those

whose registration has been refused by their demes, and
5 condemnations sent for confirmation by the *Boule*. They
also introduce private suits involving trade or the mines,
and cases where a slave is accused of slandering a free
man. They allocate courts to the magistrates by lot for
6 public and private suits. They validate international
agreements and introduce cases arising under them, and
also charges of bearing false witness in the Areopagus.
7 The selection of the jurors by lot is done by all the
nine Archons together with the secretary of the *Thesmothetai*, each handling his own tribe.

LX Such then is the position of the nine Archons.

Ten commissioners are also selected by lot to run the
games, one from each tribe. When they have passed the
preliminary examination, they hold office for four years,
and they organise the procession at the Panathenaia, the
musical contest, the athletics and the horse races, and
they arrange the making of Athena's robe and the vases
for prizes in conjunction with the *Boule*; they also give
2 olive oil to the athletes. This oil comes from the sacred
olives, and the Archon collects three-quarters of a pint
per tree from the owners of the land in which they grow.
In the past the city used to sell the fruit, and if anyone
dug up or cut down one of the sacred olives, he was tried
before the Areopagus and the penalty for those found
guilty was death. Ever since the owner of the land has
paid the contribution of oil, the law has remained in
force, but the penalty has been allowed to lapse. The oil
is now levied as a tax on the property, not collected from
3 the trees themselves. The Archon collects the oil due in
his year of office, and hands it over to the Treasurers for
storage on the Acropolis; he is not allowed to take his
seat in the Areopagus until he has handed over the full
amount to the stewards. At other times the stewards keep
the oil on the Acropolis, but at the time of the Panathenaia they measure it out to the commissioners of the
games, who give it to the winning contestants. The prizes
for those who win the musical contests are of silver and
gold, for those who win the contests in manliness, shields,

but for those who win the athletic events and the horse races, olive oil.

LXI   All military offices are also filled by election. There are ten *strategoi*, who once were elected one from each tribe, but are now elected from the whole people. They are allocated by show of hands, one to the hoplites, to command on any expedition, and one to patrol Attica and to fight any enemy who invades the country; two are stationed in the Peiraeus, one in Munichia and one in Akte—their duty is to guard the Peiraeus; one is in charge of the symmories, and enrols the trierarchs, arranges any exchanges of property for them, and introduces cases where there are disputes to the *dikasteria*; the remainder are despatched to deal with any

2   situation that may arise. There is a vote in every prytany on their conduct of their office, and if the people vote against a man, he is tried in the *dikasterion*, and if condemned, the jury assesses the appropriate penalty or fine, while if he is acquitted he resumes his position. When in command of troops, they have the power to imprison anyone for insubordination, to discharge him, and to impose a fine, though this last is not usual.

3   Also elected are ten regimental commanders, one for each tribe; they lead their fellow tribesmen, and

4   appoint the subordinate officers. Two cavalry commanders are also elected from the whole citizen body; they lead the cavalry, divided into two units of five tribes each. They have the same authority over their men as the *strategoi* have over the hoplites, and are likewise

5   subject to a monthly vote on their conduct. They also elect ten tribal commanders, one per tribe, to command the cavalry just as the regimental commanders command

6   the hoplites. They elect a cavalry commander for Lemnos

7   to command the cavalry there, and a steward for the 'Paralos' and another for the 'Ammonis'.

LXII   The magistrates chosen by lot were formerly divided into two groups, those who, with the nine Archons, were selected from whole tribes, and those who were selected from the demes in the Theseum. However, when corruption affected the choices of the demes, the selection of the latter officers was transferred to the whole tribe also, except that members of the *Boule* and the guards are still selected by demes.

2 The citizens receive the following fees for public services: at ordinary meetings of the *Ekklesia* a drachma, but nine obols for the plenary session; jurors receive three obols, while members of the *Boule* receive five, and the Prytanies a sixth for their maintenance. The nine Archons receive four obols each for maintenance and have a herald and *aulos*-player to maintain, and the Archon of Salamis gets a drachma a day. The commissioners of the games receive their meals in the Prytaneion in the month of Hecatombaion during the Panathenaia, starting from the fourth day of the month. The sacred commissioners to Delos receive a drachma a day from Delos, and the officers sent out to Samos, Scyros, Lemnos or Imbros receive money for maintenance.

3 Military offices may be held repeatedly, but no other office may be held more than once, except that a man may sit in the *Boule* twice.

LXIII The allocation of *dikastai* to the *dikasteria* is conducted by the nine Archons for their respective tribes, and the secretary of the *Thesmothetai* handles the tenth tribe.

2 There are ten entrances into the *dikasteria*, one for each tribe, twenty allotment machines, two for each tribe, one hundred boxes, ten for each tribe, and other boxes into which are thrown the tickets of the *dikastai* who have been successful in the ballot. There are two urns by the entrance to each court, and staves equal to the number of *dikastai* required; the same number of ballot balls are thrown into the urns as there are staves, and the balls have letters written on them starting with the eleventh of the alphabet, *Λ*, the number of letters corresponding

3 with the number of courts to be filled. Those over thirty years of age may sit as *dikastai* as long as they are not public debtors and have not lost their citizen rights. If a

man who is disqualified sits, information is laid against him and he is brought before the *dikasterion*; if he is found guilty, the jury assess whatever penalty or fine seems to them appropriate, and if it is a fine, he must be imprisoned until he has paid the previous debt on the grounds of which he was indicted and the additional

4 fine imposed by the *dikasterion*. Each *dikastes* has a ticket of boxwood with his name, his father's name and his deme written on it, together with one of the first ten letters of the alphabet, those up to K; the *dikastai* of each tribe are divided into ten roughly equal sections under

5 the ten letters. The *Thesmothetes* draw lots for the letters which are to be placed by each court, and his servant puts the relevant letter up in each case.

LXIV The ten boxes stand in front of the entrance for each tribe, and the letters up to K are inscribed on them. When the *dikastai* throw their tickets into the box which has the same letter on it as is on their ticket, the servant shakes the boxes and the *Thesmothetes* draws one ticket

2 from each. The man drawn is called the ticket-inserter, and inserts the tickets from the box into the column over which is the same letter as there is on the box. This man is selected by lot to prevent malpractice if the same man should always make the draw. There are five columns of

3 slots in each allotment machine. When the Archon has put the cubes into the machines, he draws lots for each tribe according to the allotment machines. The cubes are bronze, some white, some black; he puts in as many white cubes as *dikastai* are needed, one per five columns, and black cubes in the same proportion. When the Archon takes out the cubes, the herald calls the men who have been selected; the ticket-inserter is included in their

4 number. When a man has been called, he steps forward and draws a ball from the urns, and holds it out with the letter upwards, and shows it first to the presiding Archon. The Archon then puts the man's ticket into the box on which is the letter which is on the ball, so that he shall go to the court which he has drawn by lot, not the one he wishes to sit in, and it may not be possible for anyone to

5 arrange to have the jury he wishes. There are beside the

Archon as many boxes as there are courts to be manned, each with the letter on it which has been allocated to the relevant court,

LXV   When the *dikastes* has shown his ball to the servant, he goes inside the inner door. The servant gives him a staff of the same colour as that of the court whose letter was the same as the one on his ball, so that he is compelled to sit in the court to which he has been allotted. If he goes into a different court, the colour of the staff gives him

2 away, for a colour is painted on the lintel of the entrance of each court. He takes his staff and goes into the court whose colour corresponds to his staff and whose letter is the same as that on his ball, and when he enters he receives an official token from the man selected by lot

3 to distribute them. The *dikastai* then take their seats with their ball and staff having got into court in the manner described above. The ticket-inserters return their tickets

4 to those who have been unsuccessful in the ballot. The public servants from each tribe hand over the boxes of each tribe, one for each court, in which are the names of the members of each tribe who are sitting in each court. They hand them over to those who have been selected by lot to return them to the *dikastai* in each court, so that they may summon them by using their tickets, and so give them their pay. There are five of these officials.*

LXVI   When all the courts have their requisite juries, two allotment machines are set up in the first court, with bronze cubes on which are the colours of the courts and other cubes on which the names of the Archons are written. Two *Thesmothetai* picked by lot separately put the cubes in the machines, one putting the colours into one machine, the other the names of the Archons into the other. The herald announces whichever magistrate is picked first as allocated to the court which is drawn first, and the second to the second, and so on, so that no magistrate may know where he is to preside but each will preside over the one he draws by lot.

* The number is missing in the text; cf. LXVI,3 and Commentary.

2   When the *dikastai* have arrived and been allocated to their courts, the presiding magistrate in each court draws one ticket from each box, so that he has ten, one from each tribe, and puts these tickets into an empty box, and draws five of these, and of the five drawn one supervises the water clock and the other four the voting, so that nobody may interfere either with the man in charge of the clock or those in charge of the voting, and there

3   may be no chicanery in these matters. The remaining five of the ten drawn receive instructions detailing how and where the jury will receive their pay in the court itself; this is done separately by tribes after they have fulfilled their duties, so that they may receive it in small groups and not cause trouble because there are a lot of people crowded together.

LXVII   After these preparations, they call the cases. If they are dealing with private cases, they call four, one from each of the categories defined by law, and the litigants take an oath to speak to the point; when they deal with public cases, they summon the litigants, but deal with only one case.

2   There are water clocks with narrow tubes attached; they pour the prescribed amount of water into them, and this decides the length of time allowed for the speeches. They allow ten measures for cases involving over 5,000 drachmae, with three measures for the supporting speech, seven measures for those up to 5,000, with two for the supporting speech, and five and two for those under 1,000; six measures are allowed for the deciding of disputed claims, and second speeches are not allowed.

3   The man in charge of the water clock cuts off the flow of water when the clerk is going to read out a decree, law, piece of evidence or contract. If, however, parts of the day's hearing have been allocated to each side, then he does not cut it off, but an equal period of time is allowed

4   to the prosecutor and the defendant. The standard of division is the length of the day in the month of Poseideon

. . . . . .

The following section of the papyrus is so badly mutilated that the text cannot be reconstructed; the only section of which something may be made is:

... The day is divided into proportionate parts ... for contests where the penalty laid down on conviction is imprisonment, death, exile, loss of citizen rights or confiscation of property. ...

There follows a further mutilated section of papyrus.

LXVIII The majority of the juries are of five hundred members ... but when it is necessary for public suits to have a jury
2 of 1,000, two juries are combined in the *Heliaia*. The votes are cast with tokens of bronze which have a pipe through the middle, half of them pierced and half blocked. At the conclusion of the speeches, those chosen to supervise the voting give each member of the jury two tokens, one pierced and one blocked, showing them clearly to the litigants so that the jury do not receive either two pierced tokens or two blocked ones. Then the designated official takes the staffs, in return for which each *dikastes* when he casts his vote receives a bronze tag with the number three on it, for when he hands it in he receives three obols; this is to ensure that all vote, for no one can receive a tag without voting.
3 There are two containers in the court, one of bronze and one of wood; they can be taken apart so that nobody can introduce votes into them fraudulently before the voting begins. The *dikastai* cast their votes in them, the bronze container counting while the wooden is for the vote which is not used. The bronze one has a lid with a hole in it through which only one token can pass, so that
4 the same man may not insert two tokens into it. When the jury are about to vote, the herald first asks whether the contestants wish to protest at any of the evidence, for protests cannot be lodged after voting has commenced. Then he makes a second announcement: 'The pierced token for the first speaker, the solid for the second.' The *dikastes* takes the tokens from the stand, holding the pipe

in the token so that he does not show the litigants which is pierced and which is not; he places the token that counts in the bronze container, and the other in the wooden one.

LXIX   When the voting is complete, the servants take the container which counts and pour out the contents on to a reckoning frame which has as many holes in it as there are votes so that it may be easy to add up the tokens which count, both the pierced and solid ones. Those selected by lot for the task count them up on the board, separating the solid from the pierced, and the herald announces the number of votes cast, the pierced for the prosecutor and the solid for the defendant. Whichever gets more votes wins, while if the votes are equal the

2   verdict goes to the defendant. If it is necessary, they then assess a penalty by voting in the same way; for this the *dikastai* return their tags and take back their staffs. Each side is allowed half a measure of water for their speeches at this stage. When the *dikastai* have fulfilled their duties as required by law, they take their fees in the part of the building assigned to them.

COMMENTARY

I The surviving papyrus copy of the *Constitution of Athens* is not complete (see Introduction); an epitome of the lost early chapters is printed in the Appendix. The first preserved sentences contain the end of a discussion of the conspiracy of Cylon and its aftermath. Cylon, an Olympic victor in 640, had attempted to seize power in Athens, and when the coup failed had escaped; some of his supporters took refuge as suppliants at an altar, but were tempted away with an offer of safe conduct and then executed. Megacles, of the family of the Alcmeonids, was responsible, and his action brought pollution on the state and his family.

The date of Cylon's conspiracy is not known. While he must have been a young man to win a running race at Olympia in 640, he cannot have been very young when he tried to win the tyranny; in the present passage Aristotle implies that all those who were responsible for the sacrilege were dead at the time of the purification of the city and Myron's accusation, which argues that some considerable time had elapsed after Cylon's attempt. We know that the coup was attempted in an Olympic year, and the most plausible date for it is 632; tradition associates the purification of the city by Epimenides with the archonship of Solon (594/3), suggesting that it may have taken place in 595/4. This sequence of dates is possible, though it implies that the Alcmeonids were rehabilitated fairly fast, for they were influential in Athens in the 560s, immediately before the tyranny of Peisistratus. It is alternately possible that the purification and the resultant expulsion of the Alcmeonids took place towards the end of the Peisistratid tyranny, when we know that the Alcmeonids were in exile; their guilt, which is normally referred to as the 'curse of the Alcmeonids', was certainly a live issue towards the end of the sixth century since Isagoras used it in 508 against Cleisthenes (xx,2–3). There may even have been two attacks on the Alcmeonids. The main ancient sources describing the Cylon affair are: Herodotus, v,71; Thucydides 1,126 (a polemical answer deliberately correcting Herodotus on some points); Plutarch, *Solon* 12.

There is nothing inherently implausible in a trial after those guilty had died. Often plague or natural disaster led to a search for any possible pollution which might explain it; when one was found, appropriate action was taken, which included the disinterring and removal of the bodies of guilty parties who had died in the meantime.

II 'After this' means after the Cylon affair, not after the purification. Any attempt at reconstructing the economic or social conditions prevailing at Athens before the time of Solon is extremely problematical; one is virtually reduced to deduction from what Solon himself did (in so far as *that* can be reconstructed) and analogies from the development of other states; however, we are probably not significantly worse off than Aristotle was in this respect, with the proviso that he had access to a greater body of Solon's writing than we have, and had the benefit of sundry reconstructions made by earlier Greek writers on the subject which are now lost. While they probably knew more than we do about Solon's legal code, it is not likely that they had authentic texts of his constitutional provisions. In the last decade of the fifth century a concerted effort was made to establish the details of Solon's legislation, and the evidence suggests that this was successful only in the legal field.

That Athens at this period could reasonably be described as oligarchic cannot be doubted. Power was in the hands of property owners, and active participation in politics was probably restricted to a small proportion of the citizen body; a larger group may have sat as some form of assembly to vote on major issues, though it is unlikely that they conducted any real discussion on them. Equally, the economic situation was oppressive. Most of those who farmed probably had small plots, and therefore would be badly hit by a single poor harvest; eventually many fell into a form of subjection or slavery through debt. This much is clear from Solon's ban on lending money on the security of the person of the borrower or of members of his family, and it must be this economic power to which Aristotle refers when he says that 'the whole land was under the control of a few men' (II,2).

Aristotle here speaks of both those who were slaves and those who were *hektemoroi*, 'sixth-parters'. The exact position of the *hektemoroi* is not known, but one can be reasonably sure that they worked land under some form of tenure which entailed their surrendering one sixth of the produce to an over-lord, and may have encroached on their freedom in other ways, notably on their freedom to move from their place of residence. The *pelatai* were dependents who were required to pay certain dues to their masters; compare Plato *Euthyphro* 4 c, where the status is referred to *en passant* as if there were no problem in understanding it. Much later, Dionysius of Halicarnassus and Plutarch used the word to translate the Latin word *clientes*, but one need not assume that the parallel was close, nor that they really understood the status of the *pelatai*. It appears that the *hektemoroi* were perhaps in a particular form of the bond status which affected the *pelatai*, and that the latter term could cover a wider range of differing statuses. Neither group is identical with those enslaved for debt, though it is specifically said that if the *pelatai* defaulted on their payments, they and their families were liable to be seized and sold as slaves. It is probable that much of the slavery for debt at such a relatively primitive stage of the development of the society was primarily aimed at securing the services of the debtor and his family in lieu of payment rather than recovering the loan on which he had defaulted by realising a man's 'cash value'. Whether the bondage which resulted from failure to pay money due was for life or for a limited period corresponding to the debt is unknown.

That there was discontent at the time is not surprising. Economic problems must have been accentuated by the increase in the size of the population; that Solon banned the export of cereals indicates a chronic shortage at home (as well as the fact that higher prices could be obtained by selling abroad despite the costs of transport). Political discontent would have sprung from this, and probably existed higher up the social scale as well. Generally those who defended the state demanded a major say in its government (cf. Aristotle, *Politics* 1321 a 5–14); the introduction of hoplite warfare into Greece in the seventh century had meant a radical change in fighting methods, since success in battle now depended on a very much larger group of people than before. These hoplites were probably asking for a share of power, and may have been joined by the merchants. In a number of states a similar situation was resolved by the establishment of a tyranny; in Athens Solon sought a less radical solution. 'Champion of the people' was a convenient phrase coined in the fifth century to describe an influential politician, not an official position.

III At this point Aristotle looks back to the earlier institutions of Athens to provide a background to the succession of constitutional changes to be discussed in the coming chapters. Presumably he had mentioned the kings of Athens, or at least Theseus and one or two others, in the lost opening. One of the earlier products of the awakened interest in the early history of Attica which marked the second half of the fifth century were complete lists of Archons and kings. The lists were constructed on the basis of tradition, and as we have them are manifestly unreliable in the early sections. To give one example, a period of seventy years (752/1–683/2) is postulated when the Archon, having ceased to hold office for life, held it for ten years; a ten-year Archonship is intrinsically not very plausible, and it is even less likely that if it did exist, all Archons lived for their full ten years — it would be remarkable if, as the lists suggest, no holder had died in office. In all probability, a traditional date for the end of the monarchy (perhaps 1066) was accepted, and because the known names of Archons were inadequate to cover the years available, the ten year archonship was used to 'stretch' the available names over the required period.

This is not to say that some of what Aristotle records is not plausible and probably well founded. The early origin of the Polemarch, a commander-in-chief to substitute for an incompetent monarch, is most likely, and it is equally likely that a second Archon was added early to relieve the king in other functions. Whether this was the Archon who was later called the Archon *Eponumos* is another matter. Aristotle's phrasing about the King is obscure here; in calling his office 'first' and 'traditional' he *may* be referring to the Archonship, but may just as well be referring to the actual position of king which would naturally be described in this way. It is unlikely that there should have been a 'King Archon'* while there was still a king, while it is very probable that when the kingship was abolished the Archon who took his place took over his functions. In other words, Aristotle's very proper attempt to use the evidence and deduce from the lack of religious functions of the Archon *Eponumos* that he was the last to be created should be turned upside down: the Archon *Eponumos* would not have had any religious functions as long as the monarchy existed precisely because those functions were the king's prerogative. When the kingship was abolished an Archon was needed to take his place, and naturally took over his religious functions; because of the conservatism of Greeks about things religious he also took the title of King Archon because it was felt that in some ways the most important function of the king was as an intermediary between gods and men, and that his name set him apart as particularly capable of performing the function. The Archon (as the Archon *Eponumos* is usually called) was in charge of religious ceremonies of later origin, probably postdating the monarchy; it was not these 'later additions' (§3) which made the Archonship great, but its political power; cf. Thucydides 1,126,8. It may be asked why the Archon and not the King Archon presided and became the senior magistrate. Any answer must be hypothetical, but a reasonable guess may be that as a senior counsellor of the king before the abolition of the monarchy he had always been a leading citizen, and so, on the abolition of the monarchy, naturally became the senior magistrate in preference to the newly established King Archon.

'*Thesmothetai*' was the official title of the other six magistrates, who together with the three Archons already discussed formed the board normally referred to as the 'nine Archons'. Their later origin accords well with their largely legal duties; in a primitive society, there is no need for a large number of courts, and therefore for a number of magistrates to preside over them. At the end of §5 Aristotle correctly records their changed status from that of judges in the early period to presidents over preliminary hearings under the developed democracy (see below on XLV and LIX). The Areopagus was a council consisting of ex-Archons, and may have even elected the Archons at an early stage (VIII,2). Its composition on a basis of wealth and birth, with life membership, makes it a very typical early aristocratic advisory council, such as the primitive Senate at Rome. In the historical period it does not appear to have had significant political functions, but it is probable that, again like the Senate, it acted as an advisory council to the Archons after the abolition of the monarchy, and, further, was a council whose advice it was difficult to disregard; thus it could have been very influential without leaving any trace of actual, concrete political functions for later writers to record. Its political influence would have faded into the background

---

* 'King Archon' is a convenient modern phrase; the Athenians referred simply to 'the King'.

with Solon's reforms, and even more so under the Tyranny, and this would explain the absence of any popular memory of this aspect of its early duties. What *was* remembered was its general supervisory powers over the lives and morals of the citizens. Again, this was a normal function of an aristocratic council, though the extent of the power varied; in Rome it was largely delegated to the Censors. How much such power was constitutionally established and how much simply 'assumed' is probably too sophisticated a question to ask of a primitive period when constitutions were ill-defined and a matter of tradition, not written law. The censorial power survived, at least in a modified form, until 462/1 (see below on xxv). Life tenure was never abolished; it was a most undemocratic feature, but when the Areopagus was stripped of all real power it retained the traditional basis of membership. It survived for a very long time as an élitist body; an interesting letter of the Emperor Marcus Aurelius in the second century AD has been recently published: only the sons of freedmen, not freedmen themselves are to be eligible for membership of the Areopagus, although freedmen are admitted to the *Boule*.

For what we know of the buildings referred to in §5 see *The Athenian Agora; a Guide*, published by the American School of Classical Studies at Athens (3rd ed. 1976), with further bibliography. The 'marriage' of the wife of the King Archon to Dionysus was a symbolic ceremony celebrated each year in the course of the festival of the Anthesteria.

IV Chapter II looks like a prelude to a description of Solon's legislation; then chapter III digresses into a historical discussion of the origins and development of the Archonship. Now Aristotle returns not to the constitution of Solon but to the situation at the time of Draco's legislation, traditionally 621. There is a recapitulation of the various stages of the development of the Athenian constitution in XLI which is at odds with the implication of this passage in that it does not include Draco as one of the eleven stages stated to have been discussed—or if it does, the previous stage cannot be included; for further discussion see below on XLI. Further, Aristotle states clearly elsewhere (*Politics* 1274 b 15) that Draco made laws (a penal code) 'for an already existing constitution'.

Von Fritz and Kapp (pp. 8ff) have revived an old suggestion of P. Meyer,* and argue that there is nothing in III–IV which shows conclusively that Aristotle meant that Draco was the author of a new constitution, although this is the traditional interpretation. The chapters can, according to them, be as easily read as the description of the existing state of an aristocratic society of a period of which Draco was 'the most representative figure'. This is hard to accept; the traditional view did not become traditional for nothing, and is certainly the easiest way of understanding the text. Nevertheless, it is just possible to take the passage in the way in which they suggest; if one does, Aristotle has been guilty of extreme obscurity.

* *Des Aristoteles Politik und die* Athenaion Politeia, 31–44.

Whether Aristotle believed that Draco altered the constitution or not, the account which he gives leads to the inescapable conclusion that what he describes bears very little relation to any actual early constitution of Athens in the later seventh century. To be sure, some of the statements he makes were probably true of the period, notably the giving of some share in political power to the hoplite class (§2) and the method of election of Archons. As to the hoplites, note the pluperfect tense, 'had been handed over'; perhaps this change, a normal step in the development of a Greek state, was thought of as having occurred before the time of Draco. Alternatively, the text could be read as implying that it was the first of his measures. Either way, they are likely to have received some form of franchise before Solon's time, and the fact is equally likely to have been forgotten in the shadow of his even more sweeping reforms. It is worth remembering that hoplite status was the qualification for full citizenship revived by the moderate oligarchs in 411.

Many details in IV, however, must be later, including the following: the relative unimportance of the Archons compared with the *strategoi*— the latter had to satisfy ten times as high a property qualification; the stipulation that the *strategoi* had to have legitimate offspring over ten years old; the very existence of the *Boule* (its existence has been questioned even in Solon's provisions), and even more the fact that it had four hundred *and one* members; the selection of the *Boule* by lot, and the rotation of membership; the position of the *Ekklesia*; finally the august supervisory role of the Areopagus, which was very much the position which the less extreme democratic theorists of the later fifth century thought it ought to hold, but far less powerful than the position which it probably did hold. All these provisions smack of the speculations of the last quarter of the fifth century, a time when many felt that the extreme democracy had failed, and they should look for something better in the past to which they could return in order to save the situation. A significant number of features imply a fourth- rather than fifth-century date for the construction of the document, in particular the number of members of the *Boule*; it seems that even juries in the fifth century tended to be of round numbers, despite the potential inconvenience inherent in that, while the *Boule* had to be a multiple of ten to ensure equal representation of all tribes. Equally, the provisions about securities until a man had passed through the *euthuna* (see below on XLIII and LIV,2) and the requirement that *strategoi* must have legitimate sons are both typical of fourth- rather than fifth-century thinking.*
Finally, the whole chapter is suspiciously similar to the moderate proposals of 411/10; cf. XXX,3 with Commentary, and Thucydides VIII,86ff.

In summary, there seems little doubt that Aristotle had access to 'information' which was not what it claimed to be. There is nothing very surprising in the ascription of the constitution to Draco. The moderate oligarchs believed that the Athenian constitution had once

* For a full discussion, see A. Fuks, *The Ancestral Constitution, passim.*

been better than it was under the extreme democracy, and attempted to reconstruct the past on the basis of flimsy or non-existent evidence. The more unscrupulous among them attempted to lend their own proposals added respectability and persuasiveness by passing them off as the work of revered figures from earlier days; Draco, who was famous for a body of stern but just criminal law, was an obvious candidate. It is impossible to be sure when the version which Aristotle reproduces was first put together; the last twenty years of the fifth century are the likely period, but there are also probable fourth-century features, notably those singled out above.

In the absence of reliable authorities on the early period it is quite possible that Aristotle accepted the 'constitution' as genuine; it has some plausible parts. Whether he regarded it as a change made by Draco or as the existing situation at the time when Draco passed his penal code cannot be determined; on this question hangs the interpretation of the 'legislation' of §1 — whether it was criminal or constitutional.

Detailed discussion of §§2–5 will be reserved for the discussion of xxx, for the ideas clearly fit with those of the reformers of 411/10, but a few points may be dealt with now. The identity of the Prytanies mentioned is unknown; they cannot be the fifty members who formed a committee of the Cleisthenic *Boule*, and there are considerable difficulties about identifying them with the 'Prytanies of the *naukraroi*' mentioned by Herodotus (v,71) in connection with the Cylon affair; it is just possible that the word was (or was later thought to be) an early title for the Archons. The principle of rotation, which ensured that all those eligible held office once before anyone had a second term, is a more sophisticated idea than would be likely in the seventh century; it was a typical device used to secure equality within a restricted group in a moderate oligarchy. Fines for non-attendance prove that Aristotle did not think the *Boule* was paid; loss of pay is the equivalent of a fine in that case. The fines themselves are stated in money terms, which must be an anachronism in the days of Draco, since Solon, at a later date, still based his division of classes on produce; see below on vii, where the terms used for the classes are also discussed.

The final sentence returns to some of the major grievances which led up to the Solonian reforms, and picks up the thread very closely from the end of ii. It is possible that iii and iv were added later or substituted for earlier material; in particular, iv,1–4 may have ousted another discussion of Draco. Even if the material is later, it may still be by Aristotle, not fully harmonised with its context; signs indicate that the work was not carefully revised for publication; see the Introduction. Alternatively, iii–iv may have been added by one of Aristotle's pupils employed on collecting the *Constitutions*.

SOLON

V Aristotle opens the eight chapters in which he discusses Solon's legislation with a recapitulation and expansion of his earlier assessment of the causes for discontent in Attica. Here, as elsewhere in the discussion, he bases a good deal of his account on Solon's poetry—a use of sources which inspires confidence in what he has to say. The fact that Solon chose verse as the medium for what amounts to a series of pamphlets justifying his political actions is not surprising in the context of his day. At that time prose literature did not exist; secondly, there is an oracular quality about some of the things he says, and verse was the normal medium for such pronouncements; thirdly, verse is easier to remember than prose, and Solon certainly intended his ideas to circulate orally from man to man. The use of verse for political propaganda was common throughout the ancient world, and a large number of epigrams survive, mainly from Roman days, which contain material which would today appear either as newspaper comment, 'letters to the editor', or on Radio and Television discussion programs. By writing verse, a politician ensured wide circulation for his ideas.

The rising tide of discontent in Athens is well demonstrated by the measures taken by Solon as well as the statements of Aristotle and others. Here is, incidentally, another reason for doubting that Draco did more than codify the law: the traditional date for Solon's Archonship is 594/3, and the necessity for what he did after a period of less than thirty years, combined with the tradition that the political troubles were of long standing, must at least cast doubt on the effectiveness of any supposed measures of Draco. Such social discontent often led to the establishment of a tyranny in Greek states: a champion of the people gained support in order to right injustices, and then either was willingly granted power or kept it by force. That Solon attempted a different way out suggests that the crisis was not yet extreme nor the demand for a tyranny too widespread, and indicates that the nobles were prepared to make concessions in an attempt to preserve something of their position. In other states, for example Corinth, the establishment of a tyranny had been accompanied by the expulsion of the former ruling group; cf. Solon's comment, xii,4. Solon himself must have been a member of the ruling group in order to qualify for the Archonship, though §3 suggests that he did not regard himself as one of the inner group. Aristotle describes him as one of the *mesoi*, translated here as 'middle class'; this term must not be read in a modern sense, but as implying that he was only moderately wealthy and influential.

Aristotle is quite clear that Solon's legislation was a compromise—he worked for and against both parties. However, he blamed the rich for the troubles of the state. The situation may not have been as extreme as that outlined in the opening sentence; there must have been a proportion of the population who were neither wealthy nor virtually slaves. However, as suggested on ii,2, above, the number of people in some form of bondage was probably increasing, and it is equally likely that discontent had risen sharply both through greater political awareness and because those who were debt bondsmen could not take advantage of the opportunities offered by trade or emigration since they were tied to the land.

VI   The first group of measures discussed are economic. In all probability Solon also enacted them first, since it was essential to liberate the debt bondsmen before anything could be done to build a stable society. The *seisachtheia* is presented as a cancellation of debts, as also in Plutarch *Solon* 15, but covered also other kinds of obligation, such as those of the *hektemoroi*. Some modern scholars have questioned a cancellation of debt on the grounds that it would have caused too much havoc in a community in which trade was already developing significantly. They follow Androtion, the fourth-century writer of a history of Attica, as quoted by Plutarch (*Solon* 15): 'Some writers, of whom Androtion was one, say that the poor were relieved not by a cancellation of debts, but by a moderation of interest rates . . .' Androtion is a slightly earlier authority than Aristotle; however, Plutarch himself rejects his interpretation, and supports the rejection by quoting Solon's own lines about uprooting the stones which indicated that land was encumbered. Exactly what encumbrage the stones indicated is uncertain, but the most plausible suggestion is that they were a sign of the liability of the *hektemoroi*. The uprooting of the stones must be conclusive; they could hardly be removed if the liability still existed. The only way to reconcile the accounts of Androtion and Aristotle is to suggest that Solon cut interest rates so severely that this, combined with his supposed currency reforms (see below on x), enabled debtors to pay off their debts immediately. This explanation is much more complicated than the account accepted by Aristotle, and implies a delicacy and sophistication of economic thinking which is unlikely at such an early period. If these liabilities were abolished, it is hard to see how other forms of debt (which were presumably only a small proportion of the total) could have been excluded.* Equally, Solon not only banned loans on the security of the person of the creditor or his family for the future, but also attempted to remedy as much as he could of the harm caused by the practice in the past: 'He says that of the citizens sold for debt he brought some back from abroad "no longer speaking Attic Greek because of their long wanderings; those who were under the yoke of slavery in Attica" he says he made free' (Plutarch *Solon* 15, quoting Solon, frag. 24,11ff; cf. below XII, 4).

Aristotle follows a pro-Solonian source in rejecting the story that Solon either made a personal profit from the *seisachtheia*, or at least connived at some friends doing so; the allegation must have come from an anti-Solonian source. The rejection is probably right, as is the argument that such profiteering was out of character, and pointless when he could have made himself tyrant. The story looks like a fabrication from the period of political controversies at the end of the fifth century when both sides, while looking for early precedents for the changes they wished to introduce, probably also attempted to blacken

---

* In Androtion's day, Solon was admired by the oligarchs as well as the democrats, and his account of the *seisachtheia* probably represents an attempt to clear Solon of the charge of having cancelled debts—an action utterly repugnant to the wealthy.

the chosen 'heroes' of the opposition. The story is repeated and again denied by Plutarch (*Solon* 15), Plutarch includes the added detail that Solon himself was a creditor to the tune of five talents, and was among the first to cancel the debt under the law. The story may well be apocryphal, but if it is not, it may be taken as confirmation that all debts were included, not merely mortgages on land.

VII Aristotle makes only a passing reference to the legal enactments of Solon, as opposed to his constitutional and economic measures—they were not strictly relevant to his subject. Draco's legal code had probably been an improvement on the previous state of affairs in that it was, in all likelihood, the first codification of the laws, as the Twelve Tables were at Rome. Such a codification was a necessary step in the development of a state in that while the law remained unwritten the ordinary litigant was at the mercy of the 'memory' of the presiding magistrate, who was normally a noble; codification at least removed one potential source of abuse. On the other hand it is generally agreed in our sources that Draco's code was extremely severe; it was said that the laws were written not in ink but in blood (Plutarch, *Solon* 17).

We do not know exactly which laws Solon changed, nor what he put in their place—a particularly unfortunate omission in our sources. Centuries later, fragments of the inscribed copies of Solon's laws were seen by Plutarch (*Solon* 25) and he quotes one of them (*ib.* 19); in all probability a full text was preserved in Aristotle's day on the *kurbeis* (inscribed wooden pillars) he mentions here. The ancient tradition says that Solon's laws were published on these *kurbeis*; actual publication is likely, since, if Draco had produced a published legal code, it is hardly likely that Solon's legislation was not similarly published. We do not know what happened to them in the Persian sack of Athens (480–79); if they were on wood, they may have been carried away to Salamis or Troezen, but they may have remained in the city, perhaps on the Acropolis, which a small section of the population believed would not fall (Herodotus VIII,51). If they stayed in the city they were presumably destroyed. However, even if they were destroyed, they were such an essential part of the basis of Athenian life that it is likely that a reasonably accurate text could be restored from memory when the city was reoccupied. The restored democracy of 410 ordered Solon's laws to be collected and inscribed definitively; our accounts imply that the work was successfully completed.

The oath to observe Solon's legislation taken by all is mentioned also by Plutarch (*Solon* 25); the stone on which the magistrates took the oath was tentatively identified in the Agora excavations in 1970, being found exactly where Aristotle states just outside the newly identified Stoa of the King Archon. The golden statues have caused a great deal of dispute; what exactly is meant still remains uncertain, but the general intention is clearly a heavily deterrent penalty, effectively a large fine; cf. LV,5. The period of a hundred years during which the laws were not to be changed is echoed by Plutarch, but apparently

contradicted by Herodotus (1,29): 'Solon came to Sardis, having legis-
lated for the Athenians at their request; he had gone abroad for ten
years nominally to see the sights, but really to avoid being forced to
change any of the laws he had made, for the Athenians could not do so:
they were bound by solemn oaths to observe whatever laws Solon laid
down for ten years.' Possibly the hundred year period is correct, but ten
is much more plausible, since it would give a reasonable testing period
for the new arrangements without suggesting that the Athenians bound
themselves to observe whatever Solon decided for the whole of their
lifetime and beyond.

The four property classes are listed by Aristotle in §3, and then
defined in §4. In all probability the names of the second, third and
fourth classes were already in existence, and Solon may have done little
more than formalise and redefine the qualifications for membership.
The important change of nomenclature in the first class, from *eupatridai*,
nobles, to *pentakosiomedimnoi*, a purely property-based qualification,
indicates that, whereas up to then birth as well as wealth had been an
essential prerequisite for membership of the highest class, and therefore
for any real share in political power, the basis was now solely wealth,
defined in terms of annual produce of dry goods (corn) or wet (olive
oil or wine). This change means that Aristotle must be wrong (§3)
when he implies that all four classes existed before Solon; the mistake
might possibly have arisen if the names had been connected with the
supposed constitution of Draco referred to in IV.

This much is certain; what the changes imply is more debatable.
Solon's classification is expressed in terms of agricultural produce, as
one would expect at a period before the introduction of coinage as a
normal basis for the exchange of goods. However, the analogy of other
Greek states suggests that the pressures which led to Solon's appointment would have sprung in part from the discontent of a group who
were reasonably well off but debarred by birth from an active share
in politics. On the face of it, the switch to a timocracy implicit in the
change of name of the top class, so that membership depends solely on
income, would solve the problem. However, the fact that income is
considered solely in terms of agricultural produce raises the thorny
problem of whether land was alienable or not. It has been widely
assumed that it was not, and this view has given rise to considerable
problems in the attempt to discover exactly what Solon's reforms were
intended to achieve. However, such flimsy evidence as there is tends to
suggest that land was alienable, as was other property, although in
practice alienation was probably a rare event. A passage in the *Iliad*
(XIV,119–24) refers to the father of Diomedes moving to Argos, where
he acquired land and other property; Odysseus promised to give
Eumaeus a house and land (*Odyssey* XIV,61–4); alienability of land was
accepted in the world portrayed by Homer and Hesiod. Evidence for
the early classical period is lacking except for a number of negative
provisions restricting, or in some cases excluding, alienation; there
seems little point in these provisions unless the possibility of alienation

existed. Thus it seems that Solon's change in the definition of the property classes opened the way to a share in political life to some who had hitherto been excluded. There was probably considerable social pressure which made alienation rare, not least the strong feeling that the property of the family group was held in trust for the whole group by the head of the family, and should therefore be preserved intact if possible. It may well therefore have been difficult for those who were wealthy but owned no land to find land which they could acquire in order to qualify under the new provisions.*

Whatever the immediate effect, there is little doubt that the spread of money under Peisistratus meant that before the last quarter of the sixth century the basis of the classes was at least partly monetary, and that therefore the way into a full share in political life was open to all, however they reached the qualifying property standard.

To attempt to give any modern equivalent for the various property qualifications for the classes would be extremely difficult;† suffice it to say that the wealthy must have been the small minority in Solon's day, while in the later fifth century there is some indication that a little over half of the population were of the census of the *zeugitai* or above. There is no doubt that Aristotle is right to reject the explanation of the qualification of the *hippeis* based on horses; the class was almost certainly in existence before Solon, and at that time membership probably did depend on a man being able to maintain a horse or horses at his own expense. The statue referred to in the inscription quoted was to Anthemion; Aristotle has misinterpreted the Greek genitive giving the name of Athemion's father as defining the name of the man portrayed. The horse is clearly symbolic, and does not upset the argument supporting a produce basis for the class.

'The major magistracies' (§3) in fact include all the positions which are normally called magistracies in discussions of the Ancient World; there is some doubt about the reading here, and the sentence is not precise on details. The nine Archons came from the top two classes, and the *zeugitai* were not formally admitted until the middle of the fifth century (xxvi,2); the *thetes* never were, though in practice later, as Aristotle notes right at the end of the chapter, nobody was refused solely on the grounds of his property class as long as he did not actually say he was one of the *thetes*; this relaxation is presumably to be dated some time in the second half of the fifth century under the radical democracy. At the time of Solon's legislation the Archonship was still the most important office in the state, and it is hardly surprising that it was not open to all. The Treasurers (of Athena) were always selected

---

* For the arguments for alienability of land, see M. I. Finley, 'Alienability of Land in Ancient Greece', *Eirene*, 7 (1968), 25–32. If the arguments for the possibility of alienation are accepted, they remove the necessity for complicated analyses which attempt to show that Solon was trying to do, such as C. Hignett, *A History of the Athenian Constitution*, 99ff, and N. G. L. Hammond, 'Land Tenure in Athens and Solon's *Seisachtheia*', *JHS* 71 (1961) 76–98.

† See A. French, *The Growth of the Athenian Economy*, 19ff.

from the top class (VIII,1) on the grounds that their wealth was some guarantee against embezzlement. The other offices were divided among the *hippeis* and *zeugitai*; the *poletai* supervised taxation and public contracts, and sold confiscated property (cf. XLVII); the Eleven supervised the state prison (cf. LII), and the *kolakretai* held a very ancient office with financial duties which were changed from time to time; they may originally have had some connection with the distribution made after a sacrifice. They do not appear after 411.

The common people probably in fact sat in the *Ekklesia* even before Solon, but their position may have been precarious, and it may not have met often. Solon appears to have confirmed their right to membership, and it is a likely assumption that after his time the *Ekklesia* was regularly consulted on important questions; they probably took the final decision, though it is doubtful if even at this time they had more than the right of voting for or against a proposal. The mention of *dikasteria* here probably refers to the *Ekklesia* sitting as a court to review decision and sentence in the most important cases; the wording of IX,1 shows that the form of hearing was that of an appeal from the decision of a magistrate. The complex fifth- and fourth-century system of *dikasteria* ultimately developed out of this step, but was a far cry from it; in the sixth century cases were still decided by the magistrates and the Areopagus. None the less, the innovation was rightly regarded as ultimately a cornerstone of democracy; cf. IX,1 and Plutarch, *Solon* 18.

VIII The alleged selection of Archons by lot under Solon must be considered in conjunction with XXII,5 and LV,1. The first of these two passages states that in 487/6 (the Archonship of Telesinos) 'they cast lots for the nine Archons by tribes from the five hundred previously elected by the demesmen; this first happened then after the tyranny; all their predecessors were elected.' LV,1 explains how nine of the ten tribes produced the Archons, and the tenth their clerk; thus there was a post for each tribe. According to the *Constitution of Athens* the selection of the Archons by lot was a feature of the constitution of Solon, but this contradicts the statement that they were elected, which Aristotle makes twice in the *Politics* (1273 b 40, 1274 a 16). Because Aristotle here accepts selection by lot under Solon, he has to assume that the practice had lapsed under the tyranny—hence the phrasing of XXII,5 (quoted above) about the change in 487/6. Selection of as many office holders as possible by lot was a feature of radical democracy, the purpose being to produce real equality of opportunity between all candidates; any form of election might well produce a higher level of competence, but introduced an element of aristocracy in the Greek sense, the selection of the *best* people. Selection by lot is not in tune with the apparent drift of Solon's legislation; he was clearly aiming at a compromise which preserved a significantly oligarchic element while giving the people enough to appease their immediate grievances. However, the tradition that the casting of lots had some part in the selection of Archons under Solon was accepted by at least some of the fourth-century historians of Attica.

The use of lot is attested at an early date (e.g. Homer, *Iliad* VII,161ff), where its purpose was to leave a decision to the will of the gods and to avoid responsibility for invidious decisions. Solon's reforms must have led to controversies in the course of elections, and it is possible that VIII,1 may be correct (and a deliberate correction by Aristotle of the views which he expressed in the *Politics*). It seems more likely that under Solon's constitution the Archons were elected, and the idea of an element of selection by lot arose in the course of the political theorising at the end of the fifth century; it may have sprung from the pre-conception that Solon was the 'father of democracy' combined with the known democratic nature of the use of the lot in selecting magistrates. It is perhaps worth noting the suggestion that Aristotle's detailed interest in the Archonship argues that he had access to a monograph on the subject.*

One may accept without hesitation the statement that in Solon's day the Treasurers—that is, the Treasurers of Athena, who were in charge of the main state treasury—came from the highest of the four property classes, but that there was an element of lot in their selection then as there was in the time of Aristotle is virtually unthinkable.

The next section (VIII,2–3) fills in some of the background to the reforms. The nominating power of the Areopagus 'in early times' is extreme; such unfettered control, if historical, must have belonged to a very early period of Athenian history. The tribal structure appears to be historical, and to be of very early origin. The *trittues* and *naukrariai* were apparently administrative subdivisions, but virtually nothing is known about them; Herodotus mentions the Prytanes of the *naukraroi* (V.71), but Thucydides apparently contradicts him (1,126,8). In the absence of the opening chapter(s) of the *Constitution of Athens*, which might possibly have cast some light on the subject, nothing useful can be said.

Hignett launched an all-out attack on the existence of a Solonic *Boule*, regarding it as a mistaken reading back of the Cleisthenic *Boule* into the time of Solon, with the numbers adjusted to harmonise with four tribes rather than ten.† The substance of his attack rests on the following points: first, it is unlikely that the Athenians were politically mature enough to handle such a constitutional innovation; secondly, there is very little for the *Boule* to do in the constitution of Solon as described by Aristotle and Plutarch; thirdly, there is very little evidence about the supposed *Boule* at all. The first point, however, begs the question of what it did do, about which we know nothing. Secondly, it must be remembered that it is the details of constitutional practice about which Aristotle is least sure, and therefore presumably about which there was the least reliable information available; one might reasonably expect the *existence* of such a council to be remembered, but its functions forgotten. Further, if the *Ekklesia* had a more regular part in decision-making, there was presumably need, then as later, to prepare matters

---

* On the Archonship, see further XXII,5 with Commentary.
† *A History of the Athenian Constitution*, 92ff.

for its agenda; there is no suggestion that the Areopagus did this, yet this is exactly what Plutarch (*Solon* 19) says the *Boule* did do—though this again may be reading later practice back into the sixth century. Plutarch also says at one point (*Solon* 19) that Solon 'established' the council of the Areopagus; this is manifestly wrong (as Plutarch himself showed; *ib*.) but may conceivably cover a renaming of that council: until the new *Boule* was established, the Areopagus would have been called simply 'the *Boule*' ('the council'), since it was the only council in the state, while thereafter there was need of differentiation— hence the new name. Finally, Plutarch says (*ib*.) that Solon wished the state 'to be moored to two councils like anchors, supposing that the city would be less tossed by storms, and the people more tranquil'. The suggestion that some lines of Solon lie behind this is attractive. Hignett points out that it is surprising that Plutarch did not actually quote him; but, to take a parallel case, Plutarch, *Solon*, 15,1 is surely based on something Solon wrote, although it is not a verbatim quotation. Some sort of restraint on the people was needed after the reforms, and the Areopagus could hardly be relied on to give the new order a fair chance since it consisted of *eupatridai* who were life members. A detailed analysis of all the arguments on this thorny problem is beyond the scope of the present commentary; the safest conclusion seems to be to accept the ancient authority for the existence of a Solonic *Boule*, while remembering that there are grounds for doubt. To accept its existence does not imply that there is any certainty about its functions or the basis of membership. It may have been intended to preclude 'snap' meetings of the *Ekklesia* if it had a probouleutic role, and it may have also been designed to counterbalance the influence of the Areopagus, whose members had life tenure, and would at any rate immediately after Solon's reforms have been virtually all old aristocrats.

The general position of the Areopagus outlined in §4 is very much what one would expect for an aristocratic council; perhaps most interesting and informative is that Solon was prepared to leave it so much unchecked power; cf. on xxv below. The functions ascribed to it do not in any way overlap with the preparatory work which may have belonged to the Solonic *Boule*; the latter would have been the innovation, the Areopagus the stabilising factor preserved from the previous constitution. The law mentioned in §5 is described by Plutarch as 'peculiar and unexpected'; he says that the motive was to prevent indifference or apathy. Surprising it certainly is, but since it is a legal provision rather than a constitutional matter, it was probably included in the published body of Solon's law, and is therefore more likely to be genuine than if it had been a constitutional change.

IX In his *Politics* Aristotle stresses that Solon gave the ordinary people the necessary *minimum* of power, while Plutarch (*Solon* 18) stresses the importance of the right of access to courts; both were vital in the powers and preservation of the later democracy, not least because anyone might now attempt to get any wrong righted in court, and because the

magistrates were now ultimately accountable to the people; cf. Aristotle *Politics* 1273 b 41, 1274 a 16. It is in this sense that Aristotle rightly
calls them the 'most popular features'; what he does not mean to imply
is that Solon's constitution was a democracy, as is made quite clear by
the quotation from Solon's own poetry at xii,1. The banning of loans
on the security of the person was popular in that it preserved the
citizen's liberty; to us it would seem an essential prerequisite for
democracy rather than an actual democratic feature.

The remainder of the chapter is taken up with stating and refuting a
misrepresentation of Solon's purpose which probably sprang from
oligarchic circles; it is recorded similarly, and similarly rejected, by
Plutarch (*Solon* 17); again, probably an echo of late fifth-century
controversy which was accepted by the historians of Attica.

X The changes in measures and weights described here have traditionally been explained as an attempt to bring Athens into line with
the standards used by Corinth, which was at the time the major trading
power of Greece, particularly in the wealthy and growing western
market. To assess exactly what Aristotle refers to, each 'increase' must
be taken separately.

The increase in measures refers to the fact that Athenian measures
were larger than those which Pheidon (of Argos) was supposed to have
instituted; this, then, was an absolute increase in their size. Turning to
the second 'increase', it is important to remember that the mina
and drachma were measures of weight before they were units of
money. Aristotle's account here could be taken as meaning that the
new mina contained 100 drachmae instead of 70, and that the drachma
remained constant. On the other hand, Androtion (preserved in
Plutarch *Solon* 15) says explicitly that Solon redivided the mina into
100 (smaller) drachmae instead of the earlier (larger) 70, and thus
the weight of the mina remained constant while that of the drachma
was reduced. Since Androtion is explicit, and Aristotle's account
can equally be understood this way, this interpretation is to be
preferred.

Turning to coinage, it is now generally believed that Solon cannot
have been responsible for any change because Athens did not mint
coins officially until the last quarter of the sixth century, and unofficially
minted coinage (of which some specimens survive) did not exist in
Solon's day in any significant quantity, if at all. There may well, of
course, have been a few coins in the city brought in by trade, but they
were a rarity and cannot have been widely used in commercial life, and
could not have been affected by any enactment of Solon because they
were not of Athenian origin. Whatever its date, the 'increase' referred
to by Aristotle is specifically related to the fact that the archaic unit of
coinage had been the didrachm, a two drachma piece; it appears
therefore to have been an increase in the face value of the coins issued,
for in the historical period (with one insignificant exception soon after
480) there was no Attic coin between the tetradrachm (four drachmae)

and the drachma.* The changes in weights referred to in the last sentence of §2 correspond to a decrease in the value of the mina by 5% for the purpose of minting coins; in other words, the cost of minting was offset by this reduction in value of the precious metal in the coins, and coins were no longer the strict equivalent in value of the same nominal weight of uncoined metal.

The changes affecting the coin standards must have taken place much later than Solon, at the earliest in the last half of the sixth century. There is, in fact, no compelling reason to accept any of these reforms as being Solonian; their inclusion in Aristotle's account merely proves the existence of a tradition in the fourth century that these 'increases' were made by Solon, a tradition which has been seen as 'a worthless aetiological invention, intended to explain the difference between the Aeginetan and Attic minae'. It is certainly difficult to produce a convincing explanation of what the reforms of measures and weights achieved or were aimed to achieve.†

Note that Aristotle separates the measures discussed in this chapter both from the 'democratic' reforms of the previous chapter and also from the cancellation of debts, which he places before Solon's main legislation. In this respect his account is superior to that preserved in Plutarch.

XI Solon pleased neither side, as often happens after a compromise; how much he achieved his extraordinary appointment by hinting to both sides that they would do well if he were given the power to bring in reforms must be a matter for pure speculation—as it must equally have been at the time when the first accounts of his reforms were written down in Athens. The tradition of his travels is widespread in the ancient sources; Herodotus (1,29–33) tells of a visit to Croesus while he was away from Athens. His motives were sensible: the Athenians had agreed to abide by his legislation for a period (on its length, see above on VII), and so, if they wished for change, presumably their only hope was to persuade Solon himself to advocate it. The best chance there was of achieving a lasting settlement lay in giving the new arrangements a reasonable trial period.

XII The concluding chapter of the description of Solon's reforms consists of a series of illustrative quotations from his own writings, covering much of what he did or was expected to do. They require little comment, but show clearly his moderate approach; his attitude to the people is very different from that of the fifth-century democracy. At the same time, it is inestimably valuable that Aristotle chose to sum the section up in Solon's own words rather than his own.

* This underlines how little coins had to do with everyday life; a tetradrachm would have covered the ordinary living costs of an Athenian family of four for perhaps eight days in the fifth century.

† On this very complex chapter, see M. H. Crawford, 'Solon's alleged reform of weights and measures', *Eirene* x, 1972, 5–8, with the works cited there.

The 'markers' in §4 are the stones which were placed on land to indicate that it was encumbered; their removal was symbolic of the *seisachtheia*. The Greek word translated as 'debt' has this meaning if it is χρείους; if it is χρειοῦς, as it may well be, the meaning is 'dire necessity'. The last few lines of this poem indicate that Solon believed that civil war was the only alternative to his compromise.

XIII The outbreak of strife followed fast on Solon's departure, underlining the basic weakness in his economic measures, and perhaps indicating dissatisfaction with his political settlement. On the economic side, it was one thing to remedy wrongs such as enslavement for debt, and to cancel debts; it was another to solve the economic problems which had led to the crisis. Solon had done the first, but had done relatively little to help those whom he had freed from debt or bondage to make an adequate living. There is little doubt that many of the poorer citizens had hoped for a full-scale redistribution of land. One may deduce from the fact that the bulk of Athenians in the fifth century were peasants, and the total absence of any reference to redistribution of land under the tyranny which must show that no redistribution took place then, that when Solon removed the 'markers' on the land, the men who were farming it received it as their own, free of the obligations represented by their previous status as *hektemoroi*. This was not a redistribution in the full sense, and many farmers must have been subject to the same economic stresses which led to their becoming *hektemoroi* earlier. After Solon, however, they must have also been in difficulties because it must have been harder to borrow, both from lack of security to pledge against the debt, and because lenders would have been very cautious after one cancellation of debts not to be caught by another. On the other side, while the upper classes must have been relieved that the land had not been redistributed, many who had suffered loss by the reforms were angry (XIII,5), and others did not like the widening of the political base of the city. It would have been miraculous if Solon's reforms had been more than a temporary palliative since they did not deal with long-term problems, adequate as they were as an immediate relief measure. That Damasias should have attempted to make himself tyrant—the only plausible explanation of his retaining the position of Archon for two years and two months—argues that the discontent was strong, and that for a period he was able to muster considerable support; years with no Archon elected indicate the same sort of tension. Aristotle rightly stresses the importance of the Archonship because of the strong contrast with the later fifth and fourth centuries, when the holder had become little more than a figurehead with purely formal duties.

The chronology of the period is highly obscure. The problem starts with the date of Solon's reforms. It was assumed above that they coincided with the date of his Archonship; there are two points here. First, his Archonship is normally dated 594/3, though it may have been 592/1; the second date is not well supported, and would be disregarded were it not for the fact that it would make some of Aristotle's later chronology (e.g. XIV,1) a little easier to disentangle. However, this is not a sufficient reason for abandoning it; 594/3 deserves as much confidence as we can place in most dates as early as this.

The second question is radical: did Solon produce the reforms in the year of his archonship? There is no intrinsic reason why he should have done; it is clear that he held an unusual position, and did not depend solely on the powers of an Archon. It might be argued that the Athenians would not have entrusted such sweeping powers to a young and untried man; they would be much more likely to pick a fairly senior ex-Archon of proven ability. Hignett* has tried on this basis to date Solon's reforms to the 570s, arguing that the disorder described in the *Constitution of Athens* makes much more sense as a prelude to them rather than a sequel. Some of the people Solon is supposed to have met on his travels after his reforms were alive at a date much later than 593–84. A further factor is that Plutarch (*Solon* 14 and 16) says that there was an interval between the *seisachtheia*, passed in Solon's archonship, and the other legislation.

On this basis, it has been suggested that the *seisachtheia* belongs to 594/3 but the other reforms to 592/1; this accommodates the dating suggested by XIV,1, and is attractive in a way, but Hignett and others have shown that Plutarch is not to be relied on here, and that the unanimous tradition of the sources behind Apollodorus' chronology, and therefore the local historians of Attica, agreed on the year 594/3 and ascribed Solon's reforms to this year. This should be accepted tentatively, but entails either redating the archonship of Komeas (XIV,1) —unlikely—or assuming an error in the transmission of the date for Solon implicit in that passage; this is the probable solution, particularly in the light of the evidence which will be adduced below to show that there is significant confusion in Aristotle's chronology of Peisistratus, perhaps compounded by actual manuscript errors in the transmission of the text.

The improbability of some of the tales connected with Solon's travels need not detain us; such stories often gathered around famous names from the past and had no respect for chronology.

The dates referred to in XIII,1–2 may, then, have been as follows:

Solon leaves Athens ?593 (though perhaps one should date this later and divorce his travels from his legislation).

Anarchy 590/89
(in all probability an Archon was elected, but the election was later held void because of irregularities)

Anarchy 586/5 (ditto)
Damasias Archon 582/1; 581/0; two months of 580/79

In XIII,4–5 Aristotle divides the Athenians at that time into three parties with conflicting aims. The 'Shore' is said to have followed a

* *A History of the Athenian Constitution*, 316–21.

'middle of the road' policy; it is a reasonable conjecture that they supported the Solonian position, and were therefore in favour of the status quo. This is the most reasonable interpretation of 'middle' in Aristotle's context—the other parties wanted changes, one in a reactionary direction, the other towards more radical reforms. It is interesting to find an Alcmeonid leading them; whatever the date of their expulsion for the Cylon affair, they were back now, and played an important if slightly erratic role in the succeeding decades. The 'Plain', the party of Lycurgus, was naturally oligarchic; they farmed the best land in Attica, and were probably among the wealthiest Athenians; they wished to abolish the more radical of Solon's measures. The 'Uplanders', led by Peisistratus, drew support from the poorer lands of Attica and the outlying districts (beyond the hills bounding the plain, not on top of them); no doubt many of them had gained from Solon's reforms, but many would have hoped for more, in particular some share of the richer land. In addition, Peisistratus assembled behind him all the discontented elements and those apprehensive of the dominance of one of the other two parties. On the later revision of citizen lists after the tyranny, see below on XXI.

PEISISTRATUS

XIV   The war against Megara, in which Peisistratus may well have been Polemarch, probably occurred about 565. Thereafter, having collected the main discontented groups behind him, Peisistratus used a not uncommon stratagem to obtain the tyranny; compare Dionysius I of Syracuse. Once he had his bodyguard, he was in a position to seize power. The date of this seizure was in all probability 561/0; accepting this date involves either emending 'thirty-second' to 'thirty-fourth' at the end of XIV,1 (not a hard change), or assuming that Aristotle made a mistake; since the latter is by no means impossible, I have translated the text unchanged. The suggestion that Solon took any part in the events is not likely, particularly if one accepts that his Archonship was thirty-four years earlier. He was known as the man whose reforms attempted to forestall the danger of tyranny in Athens and who had refused himself to take the opportunity of becoming tyrant. A story that he protested at Peisistratus' seizure of power was a very easy and likely invention.

The remaining half of the chapter brings us back to the problems of chronology. Aristotle's data represent the following sequence: tyranny seized 561/0; exiled 556/5; returns in league with Megacles 545/4; exiled 539/8 (XV,1)—and yet he did not rule for 'a long time' at this point; last return 528/7 (XV,2) after the battle of Pallene. He died in 527/6—and yet his last period of rule was said to be his longest. There is clearly something drastically wrong with this sequence. Even if one takes the 'twelfth year' of XIV,4 as being calculated from his first seizure of power, not his first exile, the return would be in 550, the second exile in 544, and the final return in 533, leaving only six years for his final period of rule. Finally, these figures cannot be reconciled with the stability implicit in xvi, or with xvii,1, where it is said that he lived for thirty-three years after the first seizure of power, and had ruled for nineteen years of the period. (Aristotle, *Politics* 1315 b 32, gives 17 years rule). Herodotus gives a different series of figures in which there are again inconsistencies.

There is no certainty that any truth at all lies behind the conflicting chronologies offered by the sources; if there is any basis of fact to them, the following tentative ideas may be suggested. There is no compelling reason to question the date of Peisistratus' first seizure of power, and there is agreement that Hippias, his son, was expelled in 511/10. The period of thirty-six years given by Herodotus (v,65) almost certainly refers to the period of uninterrupted rule by Peisistratus and his sons, and therefore suggests that Peisistratus's final return from exile was in 546/5. These dates have enough basis to be accepted cautiously; any further suggestions must be hypothetical, though it is probably a fair guess that the return engineered by Megacles did not last long; it is unlikely to have taken Megacles seven years to discover that Peisistratus was not treating his daughter as a true wife, and Aristotle himself says that Peisistratus did not rule 'for a long time' on this occasion.*

Two important points should be noticed. First, Peisistratus was not a tyrant in the modern sense of the word, but in the Greek sense—a ruler who was not a member of a hereditary dynasty. Throughout his period of power it appears that Peisistratus was outwardly an ordinary private citizen, though he had the threat of military force to fall back on, and must have discreetly controlled the election of Archons, and through them legislation. Secondly, it was not until Peisistratus had won the tyranny in an effective and clear-cut way by the battle of Pallene that he was secure in his position. Thus the other factions must have been significant and capable of organising effective opposition. Accepting the tradition that Peisistratus was the champion of the oppressed and did a good deal to improve their lot, we may deduce that the old aristocratic and wealthy families could still count on solid support from many of their retainers to back them in political action. This deduction will be supported, and will be important, in the discussion of the conflict surrounding Cleisthenes' reforms.

The story of Phye (cf. Herod. 1,60) is an excellent one, but whether it is to be taken literally is another matter; however, it is by no means impossible, and its sheer audacity perhaps lends it some credibility.

XV The opening of the chapter is over-compressed. Peisistratus was afraid of *both* groups because the one was already hostile, and he lost the support of Megacles and his followers because of his treatment of his daughter.

This chapter shows two important developments. First, Athens was

* Further investigation of this topic is almost as conjectural as it is complicated; those wishing to pursue the matter are referred to the standard histories and their bibliographies, and Rhodes, 191-9.

now for the first time looking overseas; she had not taken part in the main waves of Greek colonisation in the eighth and seventh centuries, probably because Attica was large and fertile enough to support the population, but Peisistratus extended her influence to Rhaecelus and the valley of the river Strymon, and also Mt. Pangaeum. The region was potentially wealthy; Mt. Pangaeum had extensive precious metal deposits, and the whole area was heavily forested, and later produced abundant timber. The immediate attraction for Peisistratus was as a source from which to finance his return to Athens, and Herodotus relates the later stability of the tyranny in part to this source of wealth. Peisistratus then built up allies among oligarchic states, hired mercenaries and obtained the support of Lygdamis, an adventurer hoping to get control of Naxos, and in this way returned with a strong army with which he recovered power. Henceforth he was firmly in the saddle, backed by allies and money, and with hostages being held for him by Lygdamis, whom he had installed as tyrant of Naxos. To disarm the people was a natural action for one in his position, but whether the story of how he did it, plausible as it is, is apocryphal or not cannot be determined, cf. below on xviii.

XVI Athenian tradition looked back to Peisistratus' reign as a golden age (§7), and Aristotle reflects the general attitude. There is little doubt that for the great majority of Athenians Peisistratus brought just the combination of stability and reform which was needed at this point in their history. Very few were exiled; only the most inveterate opponents retired, perhaps in many cases of their own free will. It is even doubtful whether their land was confiscated, since at least some members of families who had opposed the tyranny later returned and held the Archonship, notably the Philaids Cimon and his son Miltiades (Archon 524/3) and Cleisthenes the Alcmeonid (Archon 525/4); they must have been able to meet the property qualification in order to hold office. Peisistratus presumably followed the practice which Thucydides ascribes to Hippias (vi,54,6) of ensuring that the right people held the Archonship; this would also ensure a reasonably benevolent Areopagus since Archons automatically became members of that body. Otherwise, the constitution of Solon continued unchanged as far as we know; a period of stability in which two generations could get used to greater responsibility in government probably contributed significantly to the political maturity of the Athenians, which in its turn enabled them to adopt and put into practice immediately the more far-reaching reforms of Cleisthenes. In describing Peisistratus as ruling 'constitutionally rather than as a tyrant' Aristotle uses the word 'tyrant' in the fourth-century sense. Peisistratus interfered as little as possible with the existing political machine; he superimposed his own power on it, and kept it running, just as the Romans changed as little as possible of the previously established local government in new provinces. He was perhaps fortunate that Solon had already substantially restructured it.

Peisistratus's economic measures (§§2–4) remedied the troubles which had led first to Solon's extraordinary appointment and then to his own rise to power. Granted that his precarious position in the first few years argues that the crisis was not as pressing as in some other states, none the less a good deal needed doing. The encouragement of agriculture benefited in particular those who had originally supported his rise, for they were the farmers with the poorer lands, and therefore those who needed assistance to put their farms in working order. No doubt both motives ascribed to his generosity in this respect are valid inferences, but there is little doubt that the second (to ensure that the people had enough to live on) was the more important. It is surprising that Aristotle does not mention Peisistratus' buildings in this context (cf. Aristotle *Politics* 1313 b 20ff), particularly the temple of Olympian Zeus below the Acropolis which was such a huge undertaking that it was not finally completed until 700 years later under Hadrian. Such grandiose public works have an element of propaganda, but they also provide some jobs; Julius Caesar's building program in Rome is an obvious parallel. No doubt the increased revenue which resulted from greater prosperity was welcome to Peisistratus (and must have helped to pay for the building), but neither that nor keeping the people too busy to have time to think of sedition are key considerations; apart from righting political wrongs, a tyrant keeps his people happy above all by providing them with an adequate income and a stable economic situation so that they can recognise that they are better off than they were before.

The magistrates of the demes were an admirable institution which brought justice to the people; the trouble involved in the journey to Athens, on top of the uncertainty inherent in any lawsuit, must have been a considerable deterrent to those suffering minor injustices. The system was abolished after Peisistratus, but revived again in 453 (xxvi,3). It was all part of his concern with the welfare of ordinary people, particularly the country-dwellers, which Aristotle is at pains to illustrate here by mentioning his travels and including the 'improving' anecdote about the farmer on Hymettus, of which the moral is: 'a good tyrant is human and just'; compare the story that he was even willing to answer a summons in a court of law—though the fact that his accuser lost his nerve may be as informative as the fact that Peisistratus was prepared to attend. For the rule of his sons (xvi,7), see below on XVIII–XIX.

The whole drift of this chapter contradicts the impression given by Aristotle's chronological data that the tyranny was insecure and that there was significant opposition—'he remained in power for a long time, and when expelled recovered his position easily' (xvi,9). The fairness of his rule combined with the restraint which apparently allowed the nobles to retain their lands (which could be later used as the equivalent of hostages) were wise decisions.

In §10, the law against tyranny is said to be mild; in the fifth century the penalty for attempting to overthrow the democracy was death and confiscation of property. It appears that Aristotle was misled by the later meaning of *atimia* ('loss of citizenship'); in the sixth century a man sentenced to *atimia* was an outlaw who could be killed with impunity.

XVII The chronology has been discussed above (see on XIV), and Aristotle must be right to reject the alleged connection between Solon and Peisistratus. Border wars with Megara must have been frequent occurrences, and the error presumably arose because the one in which Peisistratus was involved was confused in folk memory with the more important occasion in the 590s when Athens fought Megara for Salamis.

The marriages of Peisistratus are complex, and it is more than probable that he married his Argive wife Timonassa bigamously. Both Aristotle and Herodotus (v,94) imply that the marriage to Timonassa was not a legal marriage, but they may well be reading back into the sixth century later attitudes; there are parallels for bigamy as at least tolerated in the earlier period. Hippias and Hipparchus, the sons of his Athenian wife (whose name is unknown) were much older than Thettalos, one of the sons of Timonassa (XVIII,2), which argues that he married her before Timonassa, whom he married not long after his first seizure of the tyranny. Hippias and Hipparchus were at least in their teens at the time of the marriage with Megacles' daughter (Herodotus I,61). Note that Thettalos was clearly a separate person, not another name for Hegesistratos (§3); see Gomme, Andrewes, Dover on Thucydides VI,55,1 (*Commentary* IV,333).

XVIII The story of the end of the tyranny (XVIII-XIX) was obviously of great importance to the Athenians, and it is given at length by Aristotle. He seems to have combined two accounts which to some extent conflict: one appears to have given all the credit to Harmodius and Aristogeiton, the young aristocrats who killed Hipparchus, while the other stressed the part of the Alcmeonids in bringing about Spartan intervention and the final expulsion of Hippias. That there was conflict is shown by the polemical tone of Thucydides' digression on the subject (VI,54–59); he is specifically aiming to correct erroneous impressions, notably that Hipparchus was the ruler. Herodotus (v,55) agrees with Thucydides, and one must assume that a contrary version was current in the fifth century, probably adopted by Hellanicus, and that this provoked Thucydides' contradiction. It may have originated with propaganda aimed at devaluing the efforts of the Alcmeonids, which drew from the fact that Hipparchus was killed, not Hippias, the superficially plausible deduction that he had been the tyrant; thus the glory for 'ending' the tyranny could be ascribed to the Tyrannicides if one was prepared to overlook the significant point that the tyranny did not *in fact* end until three years later, or to redate the death of Hipparchus and disregard the last three years of the rule of Hippias, as was done by the compiler of the *Marmor Parium*, a third-century chronological inscription. Aristotle is the first extant source to mention the compromise version that the brothers ruled together (XVIII,I), but even he is clear that Hippias was the older and the more serious, and the whole tenor of his account suggests that Hippias had the real power.* However the key fact, which for obvious reasons was played down in Athenian traditions, was that it was not the Athenians, but the Spartans who (of all people) overthrew the tyranny of Athens.

The general outlines of the story of the conspiracy are the same here as they are in Herodotus and Thucydides, but details vary. Thucydides states specifically that the rejected lover was Hipparchus, not Thettalos (VI,54,3), that there were few conspirators (VI,56,3), and also that they selected the Panathenaia for the attempt expressly because that festival was one of the few occasions on which the citizens were allowed to carry arms (VI,56,2). On the first point there is no means of knowing the truth; on the second, Aristotle's version is supported by reference to a later change of practice, but this is not totally convincing since the law might have modified the existing custom rather than reversing a total ban on the carrying of arms. Aristotle may, none the less, be right to reject the story of the disarming of the procession and the search for daggers, for it looks suspiciously like a doublet of the story of how Peisistratus disarmed the people in 545 (XV,4). The earlier story is the more probable, and could well have been repeated in the sources as a plausible piece of embroidery attached to a not unlikely search for hidden weapons on the second occasion. The fact that they were searching for daggers casts some doubts on Thucydides' account, for if they had selected the Panathenaia as being an occasion on which they could legitimately be armed, why bother to carry hidden weapons?

The story of the fate of Aristogeiton after the murder of Hipparchus cannot be confirmed or denied; the involvement of Hippias in his actual death is perhaps suspicious, and some have gone so far as to deny the whole story as a later fabrication. Finally, the implied criticism of Hipparchus (§1) is perhaps an anachronism. The contrast between one serious and one frivolous brother is a cliché, and to base the criticism on the fact that Hipparchus brought poets to Athens is out of tune with the general policy of the tyranny, one of whose glories had been to encourage the arts. None of these points casts doubt on the main thread of our story, but it should be remembered that the basic unanimity of our sources is not as cogent as it appears at first sight, for it shows only that there was a generally accepted version current some seventy-five years after the event.

On small points, basket-bearers were a normal part of many religious processions, and were usually the daughters of distinguished families; compare Aristophanes, *Lysistrata* 646 and Theocritus II,66. The Parthenon frieze represents the Panathenaic procession; see, for example, the British Museum's *An Historical Guide to the Sculptures of the Parthenon*, 22ff. The Leokoreion was a memorial to the three daughters of Leos, situated in the Kerameikos, near the Agora.

---

* For detailed discussion, see Gomme, Andrewes, Dover, *Commentary* IV, 317–29.

XIX   Aristotle agrees with Herodotus (v,62) and Thucydides (vi,59,2)
that the death of Hipparchus led to increased severity in the rule of
Hippias, and one must assume that the present passage is intended to be
a more precise account than the general (and contradictory) remarks at
xvi,7 and xvii,3. In the deterioration into what we should call tyranny,
the Peisistratids followed the pattern normal for Greek tyrannies;
hardly any 'dynasties' survived the second generation.

The story of the expulsion of Hippias is told in greater detail in
Herodotus v,62-5, an account which Aristotle appears to be following.
Herodotus vi,123 says that the Alcmeonids were in exile throughout the
tyranny, and 'Peisistratids' at v,62,2 *may* also include Peisistratus himself. However, this cannot be right; assuming, as seems likely, that the
Cleisthenes who was Archon in 525/4 was the later reformer, the Alcmeonids must have been exiled at some date after his Archonship. It is
said that they led the exiles, and there is no indication that Cleisthenes
had deserted his family and become a supporter of Hippias; if he had, it
would be quite remarkable to find him so influential in Athens so soon
after the expulsion of the tyrants. Philochorus (Jacoby, *F.Gr.H.* iii B
328 F 115) says that it was the sons of Peisistratus, not Peisistratus himself, who exiled them; it is tempting to relate their exile to the aftermath of the murder of Hipparchus.

Little is known of the attempt centred on Leipsudrion, though the
disaster probably explains the switch from military action to diplomatic
pressure by the opponents of Hippias. From the fact that the first
Spartan attempt to unseat the tyrants was made in 512/11, only two
years after the plot of Harmodius and Aristogeiton, and the clear
implication of the authorities that it took some time for Delphic pressure to produce action in Sparta, one must date the Leipsudrion attack
very soon after the plot, perhaps in 513. The sequence in which the
stories appear in the sources is against putting Leipsudrion before the
plot. The place itself has been identified with a ruined fort on a ridge
running down from Mt. Parnes; hence the emendation adopted in
the text—the papyrus has 'over Mt. Parnes'. An Alcmeonid attempt to
return by force shortly after their exile is plausible, though there is too
much hypothesis in the reconstruction of the chronology for certainty.

The rebuilding of the temple at Delphi, as so many other aspects of
the history of the period, featured in both pro- and anti-Alcmeonid
sources. The Alcmeonids undertook the contract to rebuild the temple
after it had been destroyed by fire in about 548; subscriptions had been
invited from as far away as Egypt (Herodotus ii,180). Herodotus (v,62)
emphasised Alcmeonid generosity, noting that, having contracted to
build in ordinary stone, they built the façade in Parian marble at their
own expense. In the hostile propaganda they are represented as having
made a large profit out of the contract. Herodotus is probably right; it
is not surprising to find Aristotle accepting the anti-Alcmeonid (and
therefore broadly anti-democratic) version; to make an undue profit is
a curious way to attempt to win the support of the authorities at Delphi,
and slender evidence suggests anyway that the Alcmeonids got their

wealth from the east. The only conceivable way of reconciling the two stories is suggested by a contract for building a temple on Delos (*BCH* xiv,389); the contractors were to receive a half of the price on signing the contract, and another four-tenths when they had completed half the work. The theory has been put forward that the Alcmeonids misused the funds they received for building the temple in order to finance their attempt against Hippias, and then added the marble façade as a sort of *amende honorable* after 510, when they had recovered their lands and were comfortably in a position to repay the money they had misapplied. It is known from the Philochorus fragment referred to above that the temple was not completed until after 510. However, the suggested way of reconciling the two stories is a desperate solution, and it is more likely that there is no relation between them.

The Delphic authorities gathered information highly efficiently, and probably gained their reputation for prescience as much because they used this information well as for any other reason. Their knowledge gave them the ability to predict political moves with a greater likelihood of success and often to support the side which came out on top. The oracles advocating action against Hippias accorded well with what was by then the general policy of Sparta, to support oligarchies in the states where she had influence and to discourage tyrannies in so far as she could. The Delphic authorities therefore knew that their advice was likely to be acted upon. The Argives were traditionally enemies of Sparta, and the Peisistratid alliance with them would certainly have contributed to Sparta's decision. Argos had been severely defeated at the battle of Thyrea in 546, but must have been recovering by 515–10, for Sparta had to fight her again shortly after 500 at Sepeia.

Athens had an intermittent and not very effective alliance with Thessaly, an area which was more backward than much of Greece, and still under a loose, feudal type of constitution. Cavalry was the strong point of the Thessalian army, and this explains their success against Anchimolus, who made the mistake of attempting to land in the only area suitable for the use of horses in Attica in the face of the most experienced Greek cavalry force.

Cleomenes was much more successful than Anchimolos, and shut Hippias up on the Acropolis. The Pelargic Wall (not Pelasgic, as it has sometimes been incorrectly emended) was a vital part of the early defences at the north-west end of the Acropolis; it is described as 'nine gated', which implies nine layers of defence within each other, not nine separate entrances in the wall. It was probably destroyed by the Persians; the area was an open space in the later fifth century. The fortifications were very strong, and there is no reason to think that Hippias could not have held out for a long time but for the unfortunate accident of the children's capture. Herodotus (v,65) is probably Aristotle's source when he talks of 'children of the Peisistratids' rather than the 'children of Hippias', as Thucydides (vi,55,1). Similarly, in the prelude to the Marathon campaign, Thucydides concentrates on Hippias alone, while Herodotus again talks of the Peisistratids. That Hippias was in a fairly strong position even after the children had become hostages of the enemy is underlined by the fact that he and his family were given five days to collect their goods, and were allowed to take their private property out of Attica. They retired to Sigeum near the Hellespont, which remained in their hands until 490 at least.

Hippias was expelled in 511/10. Assuming that Aristotle's dates were calculated exclusively, seventeen years from the death of Peisistratus is accurate, but 'forty-nine years earlier' gives us 560/59, a year later than the probable date for Peisistratus' first accession. The dates and figures given cannot be reconciled exactly, but the discrepancies are not so great that one is forced to abandon the pattern he gives us. While it is not surprising that there was some doubt by Aristotle's day about dates so long ago, it *is* perhaps a little surprising to find the scientific and very precise Aristotle not being consistent with himself. This may well be an indication that the book was not fully revised before publication.

CLEISTHENES

XX The two leading contenders for power after the expulsion of the Peisistratids must have made their mark during the later years of the tyranny; Cleisthenes had probably been Archon fifteen years earlier, and it is a reasonable hypothesis that he played a leading part in the events of 511/10. Isagoras is called a 'supporter of the tyrants', but if this had been true he could hardly have been influential so soon after 510. Aristotle has schematised the divisions in the state into two groups, the 'enemies of the tyrants' who had led the exiles, and the 'friends of the tyrants' who had stayed in Athens and acquiesced in their rule. It is much more likely that the divisions among those influential in the years immediately after 510 fell within the group which had opposed the Peisistratids at least in the last few years of their rule.

It is interesting that Peisistratus became tyrant with the support of the poor, and returned after his first exile with the backing of the Alcmeonids, while the latter were instrumental in securing the expulsion of Hippias. It appears from Isagoras' proposals (below) that he was a reactionary who hoped to turn the clock back to a pre-Solonian constitution. The Alcmeonids have been frequently accused of political time-serving, but it appears from the above sequences that they followed broadly the same policy in the 550s as they did forty years later; Hippias had become more reactionary (see XIX,I).

Secondly, it is important to realise that Aristotle does *not* say that Cleisthenes was at this stage in favour of a democracy or anything like it, and Herodotus states positively that he was not (v,69,2). The struggle is said to have been waged in 'the political clubs'. These clubs were intermittently active in Athenian history, and later became centres for oligarchic discussion and planning, particularly against the radical democracy. It appears that the start of the battle between Isagoras and Cleisthenes was a struggle for power between two oligarchic faction leaders. The Spartans traditionally favoured constitutional government against tyranny; the Solonian constitution, in which the essence of power was concentrated in the hands of the relatively well off, would have satisfied them. Isagoras apparently wished to narrow the group holding power. Cleisthenes introduced the proposals which led to democracy as a counter move when he had lost the tactical battle to Isagoras—'he won the support of the people by promising them control of the state'. In other words, the move which led directly to the Athenian democracy (and all that that implied for the future of political thought and practice) arose as an *ad hoc* attempt to retain power in a faction fight between two oligarchs. However, once the move was made, the working out of the complicated system eventually implemented involved a great deal of careful and precise thinking.

Isagoras retorted by calling on Cleomenes to interfere again, and used the 'curse of the Alcmeonids' (see above on I) as an excuse. Cleisthenes did not wait for the outcome, but retired into exile before Cleomenes arrived. The 700 families forced to join him were presumably his political adherents—indicating wide support if there were so many who were significant enough to exile. The constitution proposed by Isagoras was a very narrow oligarchy with a ruling body of only 300. We do not know which *Boule* Isagoras and Cleomenes attempted to dissolve; some have held that it was the *Boule* of Solon, others the Areopagus. The former may have been won over to support Cleisthenes; if it had a probouleutic function, it could have been a significant factor. The latter was venerable, and perhaps naturally predisposed to support an oligarchy; however, effective opposition could perhaps most easily have come from a council of ex-Archons, most at least passive supporters of the tyranny (see above on XVI).

Cleomenes must have underestimated the problem, for he was caught with too small a force to control the situation when the Athenians rose against him and Isagoras—provoked we may guess at least as much by the second presence of foreign troops in Athens within four years as by Isagoras' proposals. All the events of this period are covered by Herodotus v,66–72 (intermingled with some fantasy linking Cleisthenes with his maternal grandfather, the tyrant of Sicyon); Aristotle appears to depend on the same source as Herodotus, or to be using him directly, for the strictly historical, as opposed to constitutional, part of the account. Herodotus adds that all the Athenians who joined Isagoras on the Acropolis were executed; only Isagoras was allowed to leave with Cleomenes and his men (v,74,1). Cleisthenes returned as 'champion of the people' (see above on II).

Nothing is known of Kedon beyond what is said here, and the text does not make it clear whether he was an Alcmeonid or not; his attempt may well have been one of those referred to in XIX,3.

XXI A summary of the political organisation adopted by Cleisthenes is necessary for the understanding of Aristotle's account and for any attempt to decide what Cleisthenes' purpose may have been. The basic unit chosen for political life was the deme; these small local units of widely varying size were already in existence throughout rural Attica, and were not unlike English parishes. The City, i.e. Athens and the Peiraeus, had to be similarly divided by Cleisthenes, for there demes did not exist previously. Under the Cleisthenic system there were perhaps about 170 demes in all; they had assemblies and officers, and were responsible for local government in their area. At the other end of the scale, Cleisthenes abandoned the four traditional Ionian tribes as politically active units. This much at least is clear: he wanted to make a complete break from old political divisions and loyalties.

In order to relate the demes to the ten new 'tribes' which he created, he established thirty intermediate divisions which he called *trittues*, which were not, as Aristotle points out, identical with the earlier twelve units with the same name. The *trittues* were divided on a geographical basis into three groups of ten; these three groups bear no relation to the old political divisions of the sixth century.* Since every tribe was to be composed of one *trittus* from each of the geographical divisions, and all tribes were to be of approximately the same size, the *trittues* had to be as nearly as possible numerically balanced. This is the most ingenious part of Cleisthenes' system, for the *trittues* formed an 'equalising bridge' between the numerically immensely disparate demes and the tribes. By allotting a different number of demes to each *trittus*—the sources suggest that the number might range from one to seven—he arrived at a balance. Having thus equalised the numbers, the *trittues* were divided between the tribes, one from each of the three geographical divisions forming a tribe. The change to ten tribes was accompanied by a change in the *Boule*: its numbers were raised to 500, fifty from each tribe. Why he selected ten tribes rather than another number is not clear, for Aristotle is wrong in saying that he could not have had twelve because of the previously existing *trittues*; there was nothing to prevent the creation of twelve totally new divisions. Trimmed of the manifestly fanciful parallels, the account of Herodotus (v,66–72) corresponds closely with that of Aristotle.

The main motive for the reform stressed by Aristotle is protection of new citizens. Just as Peisistratus had earlier championed those who felt their position in danger (XIII,5, presumably referring to those given citizenship by Solon), so Cleisthenes is said to have rallied behind him those whose citizenship was questioned by the narrow oligarchs. Perhaps a significant number had acquired citizenship under the tyranny in ways which would not be recognised as valid under a strict interpretation of traditional rules; how many may have been threatened is unknown. It must be remembered that it was rare until after the fourth century for a Greek born in one city to become a citizen of another; there was no process parallel to the naturalisation procedures available in most modern states. Foreigners were usually welcome to live in a city, but remained aliens subject to legal and tax disabilities; thus the

---

* For a detailed discussion, see J. S. Traill, *The Political Organisation of Attica*, *Hesperia*, Suppl. XIV (1975).

more conservative elements might, if they got power, annul as illegal grants made by a Solon or a Peisistratus. Aristotle states (XIII,5) that the citizen lists were revised, but this is difficult in the light of the statement that those who were likely to be (or had been) disfranchised are said to have supported Cleisthenes; it is hard to see how they could have done so if they had actually lost their citizenship. They could conceivably have rioted, but the implication is that they had a hand in his recall, which is a political action carried out by citizens. It is remotely possible, though most unlikely, that the revision had been carried out but not put into effect.

Turning to a different aspect of the same problem, until the reform of Cleisthenes it was normal for Athenians to identify themselves by their name and their father's name since a single name was not enough for identification. It is alleged that in this way the newly-arrived citizens would betray their origin immediately, whereas by substituting identification by name and deme Cleisthenes made them indistinguishable from long-established families. Granted that all citizens became officially indistinguishable for political purposes once they had been registered only by name and deme of residence in 508, it is a misunderstanding of the way Athens worked to suggest that the real situation was materially altered; most people knew a lot about many of their fellow citizens, and such a change of official procedure would have done nothing to affect knowledge of a man's family and origin. Patronymics were still widely used (e.g. LXIII,4), and by the end of the fifth century were normally given as well as the name of a man's deme. In addition, the old clans and phratries, membership of which had been an essential prerequisite for citizenship, and which were not open to new arrivals, continued to exist as religious entities even after the reform. Little had really changed for the moment, though it is arguable that in the long term the change did contribute towards producing a homogeneous society.

The real effect of the change lay not in the question of names but in the fact that henceforth the deme was central to political life. The deme assembly was the microcosm of the government of the city as a whole, and the deme was the starting-point for anyone who wished to hold any office in the city; for example, members of the *Boule* and some other officials were originally selected at deme level (LXII,1). As a basic unit for political life, the deme was much smaller and radically different from those used before; thus the reform cut across and broke up old alliances and power blocks. Membership of a deme was hereditary from the date of the reform and original registration. To us in our highly mobile society, this might suggest that political units would shortly be totally divorced from the geographical areas in which people lived; that this is not so is shown by the fact that local government remained in the hands of the deme assembly and its officers—nothing could be more absurd than local government by people who do not live in the area. No doubt some families moved, particularly into the city, but it cannot have been a large proportion of the population.

Further, if Aristotle is right that Cleisthenes placed *trittues* in tribes by lot, this is a most important point. It has sometimes been said that Cleisthenes by-passed the old tribes in order to break the power of the leading aristocrats over their 'retainers', and in particular to destroy the old situation where geographical areas tended to work as single units in politics; compare the political divisions at the time of the rise of Peisistratus. Had this been so, he would surely have planned the distribution of the *trittues* among the tribes to ensure that contiguous areas did not fall in the same tribe, not left it to chance. The exact boundaries of the trittues are not all known, but there are at least three cases where two adjacent *trittues* are in the same tribe. It has further been suggested that the distribution of *trittues* in tribes favoured the Alcmeonids by preserving their areas of influence undisrupted. It is impossible to be sure how important geography was since a *trittus* was primarily a centre of population rather than a precisely defined geographical area, nor can one say that the distribution adopted could not have been the result of the drawing of lots. However, the statistical probability of achieving the distribution adopted by casting lots is low, and it may be that the allocation was 'rigged'. If lots were in fact not cast, one must assume either that Cleisthenes arranged the whole thing under cover of a supposed casting of lots to conceal what he was doing, or that the use of the lot was a later addition to the story derived from sources which supposed that the 'founder of democracy' must have used that highly democratic procedure in reorganising the basic units of political life. In any case, the effect, and probably the purpose, of the reform was to reduce the influence of large geographical units and some previous allegiances in politics, but this was achieved more through the use of the demes than through the *trittues*.

Turning to the detailed effects of the reform, the ten new tribes were not merely the units from which the *Boule* was formed, and hence basic to what now became the most important of the organs of democratic government, but it later became normal for the nine Archons to come one from each of the tribes, for one of the *strategoi* to be a member of each tribe (initially, though not later in the fifth century), and there is evidence that tribal allocation was the basis of a number of the administrative boards which were later set up under the democracy—it may be guessed that most boards of ten or a multiple of ten contained an equal number of representatives of each tribe. The army was similarly divided into ten tribal regiments under tribal commanders. The demes each sent members to the *Boule*, their representation being proportional to their population; we know that in the fourth century Acharnae sent twenty-two members while Halimous sent three; many demes were even smaller. The *trittues*, on the other hand, played only a small part in every-day organisation. Their most important function was that the fleet appears to have been organised on a *trittus* basis with *trittus* commanders; Plato (*Republic* 475a) implies the existence of *trittus* officers also in the army.

Having superseded the old organisation for governmental purposes—

hence the point that Aristotle makes that the old *naukrariai* lost their powers—Cleisthenes made the statesman–like decision not to abolish the old order altogether. In particular, the old clans, phratries and tribes continued to fulfil their religious functions (§6). In this way he avoided offending religious and sentimental susceptibilities while depriving the old structure of all political power. Similarly, he submitted to Delphi the choice of heroes from whom the new tribes would take their names, and of whom they would maintain a cult. Thus, by implication he invoked the blessing of the oracle on the new dispensation. Some of the demes were named after the founders of the villages which were their nuclei; in other cases he used geographical names, apparently because the founder of the deme was no longer associated with the area; §5 is not very clear, but this seems to be the best way to take the ambiguous 'not all', since to refer it to demes would be very surprising as they were by definition geographical areas.

It is doubtful exactly when the reforms outlined above were proposed and enacted, but detailed implementation must have taken a long period because of the complexity of the administration involved; it may well have taken more than the year. The sequence in Aristotle is clear: Isagoras gets the better of Cleisthenes in a power struggle; Cleisthenes enlists the support of the people, and Isagoras' power wanes; Isagoras invokes Cleomenes, and Cleisthenes and his supporters go into exile; Isagoras and Cleomenes are expelled, and Cleisthenes returns; the constitutional reforms are then described. Herodotus agrees in general, but outlines the reform of the tribal structure before the expulsion of Cleisthenes. Cleisthenes' reforms cannot have been worked out, even as proposals, overnight, yet they were an answer to the rising power of Isagoras. It therefore seems more than likely that Cleisthenes realised he had to strengthen his position before the election of Isagoras as Archon, and so began to move in this direction; it does not seem probable that he published the proposals much before the election of the Archons, for it would be difficult to account for Isagoras' election contrasted with the popularity of Cleisthenes so soon afterwards if the people had had time to appreciate the latter's proposals. Equally, it seems unlikely that Cleisthenes would have been able to bring such changes into law while Isagoras was actually in office, granted the probable powers of the Archon at the time. On the other hand, it seems reasonable to suppose that the knowledge of what he proposed had something to do with what must have been a massive public reaction against Isagoras and Cleomenes, leading to their expulsion. There is no necessary reason to suppose that the reforms had been *passed*, as opposed to proposed, before Isagoras called in Cleomenes (despite the contrary implication of Herodotus v,69–70), and the order of the events as told in Aristotle is against this; Isagoras would have been sensitive to swings of public sentiment as well as Cleisthenes, and taken precautions accordingly.

Any suggested sequence of events must be speculative, but the most likely appears to be that Cleisthenes lost his power struggle with Isagoras before the latter became Archon, perhaps in 509, and therefore altered his whole political stance; his proposals did not become public knowledge until about the time of the election of Isagoras, who called in Cleomenes after taking up office, or at the earliest very shortly before he did so, because his presence in the Archon lists shows that he not merely started his year of office, but was not ejected very early in it—otherwise a different Archon would probably have replaced him in the list. Thereafter he was expelled, and Cleisthenes initiated the promised program of reforms. The objection that after the expulsion of Cleomenes Athens' position was so seriously threatened by the hostility of other states that she could not possibly have dared to implement such a radical reorganisation, which involved the army as well as the political structure of the state, has little force. First, we do not know how much the change to the army structure really meant in practical terms, apart from the reorganisation of the men into ten tribal regiments instead of four, nor do we know when it was implemented; as suggested above, not everything could have been done at once. Secondly, and far more decisive, if, as has been suggested, Cleisthenes received his support on the basis of a program of reform, he was in no position to pull back after the expulsion of his opponents and his own triumphant return. Whatever the threats from abroad, he had to carry through what he had promised to do.

XXII Cleisthenes' reforms were a great step *towards* democracy, yet Plutarch calls the result an 'aristocracy' (*Cimon* 15); the distinction is important. The people had a far greater say in the running of affairs, but the major officers of state were still elected, not selected by lot, and this for the Greek theorists was aristocracy, not democracy; cf. xxix,3. The statement that Solon's laws had fallen into disuse is contrary to the suggestion that the state continued much as before under the Peisistratids (see above on xvi); it is possible that in the last few years Hippias took more power than Peisistratus had done because of the threats to his position, and it may be a memory of this which lies behind Aristotle's remark.

The ascription of the law of ostracism to Cleisthenes has been much discussed. First, the facts such as they are. After the ascription, Aristotle gives a list of some of the early victims, starting with Hipparchus, one of the relatives of Peisistratus; this ostracism took place in 487, although it is said that he was the main object against whom Cleisthenes introduced the law. The ostracisms immediately following Hipparchus are said to have been aimed at the supporters of tyranny (§§5–7). A fragment of Androtion preserved by Harpocration runs: '(Hipparchus the son of Charmus) was related to the tyrant Peisistratus, and the first to be ostracised; the law of ostracism was then first laid down because of suspicion of the supporters of Peisistratus, because the latter had obtained the tyranny as a popular leader and general.' (Jacoby *F.Gr.H.* III B 324 F6). This fragment apparently contradicts the tradition preserved in Aristotle by dating the institution of ostracism twenty years later than he does. However, the text of Aristotle and that of Androtion as represented by Harpocration are so similar in many respects that it seems likely that Aristotle drew his information from the passage of Androtion which Harpocration excerpted. Further, the Harpocration quotation contains a very awkward piece of phraseology (translated above: 'was then first laid down'), and it seems that the selector of Harpocration's text abbreviated the text of Androtion carelessly so that the first occasion of the use of ostracism appeared as the date of its institution. Thus there is no conflict between Aristotle and Androtion: according to them, ostracism was introduced by Cleisthenes and first used against Hipparchus in 487.

Many scholars have held that it is almost impossible that Cleisthenes should have forged a weapon such as ostracism, and then that it should not have been used for twenty years. There are various possible explanations. The mechanism of ostracism itself, for which see Plutarch, *Aristides* 7 and a very clear summary in *OCD*², demanded a preliminary vote each year on whether the people wished an ostracism to be held at all (XLIII,5); if the vote was positive, there had to be a minimum of 6,000 votes cast at the actual ostracism for it to be valid. (An extreme interpretation demands that 6,000 votes should be cast against one 'candidate', but this seems an impossibly high requirement in the light of evidence for the size of attendances at the *Ekklesia*.) It is therefore possible either that the *Ekklesia* voted against the holding of an ostracism at all each year between the institution of the system and 488/7, or that if one was held not sufficient votes were cast for it to be valid. A third, ingenious suggestion is that Aristotle's information on the early history of ostracism depends on the decree of recall passed just before the Salamis campaign (§8); since those ostracised more than three years before Hipparchus would have served their ten years abroad and returned in the normal course of things, their names would thus not have been preserved.

There are objections to all these theories except the first. It is unlikely that the decree of recall would have specified the names of individuals, although there is no real doubt that Aristotle's information on the early victims of ostracism is based on documentary evidence of some sort. Desperately sparse as our evidence is for the politics and leading statesmen of Athens in the period 507–488, it would be remarkable if no memory whatever had survived of uses of the statute before Hipparchus.* As to the suggestion that earlier, indecisive ostracisms had been held, there is no theoretical reason why it should not be true, but it is remarkable that such archaeological evidence as we have confirms that 487 was the year of the first ostracism. About 11,000 *ostraka* (the fragments of pottery on which names were written in order to cast votes in the ostracism) have been found, mainly in the Agora and its surrounds and the Kerameikos. All of those apparently to be dated in the period before 480 can very plausibly be related to the ostracisms listed by

---

* The suggestion in Aelian, *Var. Hist.* XIII,24, that Cleisthenes himself was the first victim of ostracism has correctly been rejected.

Aristotle. This confirms the suggestion that there were no actual ostracisms before Hipparchus, and argues that there were no abortive attempts either.

We are left, then, with the alternative of accepting at face value Aristotle's statement that ostracism was introduced by Cleisthenes, and therefore with the necessity of accepting a period of twenty years in which the statute was not used. Two possible hypotheses may be suggested to explain the gap. Ostracism may have been devised by Cleisthenes to preclude any repetition of the dangerous rivalry between himself and Isagoras; if so, the period of disuse is explicable since such knowledge as we have of the history of the period between Cleisthenes and Marathon does not suggest that there were conflicts or crises which would naturally provoke the holding of an ostracism. Alternatively ostracism may have been part of the 'package' announced by Cleisthenes before the invasion of Cleomenes, designed to use Cleisthenes' popular support to eliminate Isagoras; after Isagoras had been expelled, it was not used. Its disuse in the next twenty years would again be comprehensible. Either of these hypotheses offers a sound motive for the introduction of ostracism, and the twenty years in which it was not used is not on this basis as implausible as has often been suggested.*

If the above argument is accepted, Aristotle's account needs modification only in the motive alleged for the introduction of the measure; it is not plausible to suggest that there was significant support in Athens for the return of the tyrants after Cleisthenes' reforms had been 'published'. On the other hand, if Hipparchus, a well-known member of the family of the Peisistratids, was the first victim of ostracism, what could be more natural than for later commentators to deduce (wrongly) that the measure had originally been designed against those aspiring to tyranny?

The known ostracisms before 480 were as follows: Hipparchus in 487; Megacles 486; a third 'friend of the tyrants' 485 (possibly Hippocrates, or Kallias the son of Kratios, who is attacked as 'a Persian' on twelve surviving *ostraka*; cf. §6); Xanthippus 484; Aristides 482. All those ostracised were recalled in 481/0 except Hipparchus who stayed abroad, probably in Persia. Those ostracised included three supporters of the Peisistratids, and one or two Alcmeonids; further, Xanthippus was connected with the Alcmeonids through his wife Agariste. The loyalty of the Peisistratids was naturally suspect during the period of the Persian Wars, and even if one rejects the highly dubious story of the flashing of the shield at Marathon (Herodotus VI,115, 121–5), there is here confirmatory evidence that the people of Athens regarded the Alcmeonids with suspicion. It is not altogether surprising to see them being ostracised after the leaders of the pro-tyranny faction. It is worth noting that the theory which sees ostracism as a method of deciding between opposing policies within the democracy and avoiding conflict at times of national stress has no support in the sources. This may well

* For the detailed arguments behind the above discussion of ostracism, see Rudi Thomsen, *The Origin of Ostracism*, Copenhagen, Gyldendal, 1972.

have been one of its effects at times, but is a sophisticated concept and unlikely to have been a motive for its introduction.

Throughout the period Themistocles and Aristides were champions of the people (XXIII,3). It is probable that until 483/2 they worked together at least when the question of ostracism was raised, and there is no reason why their cooperation should not have been general. The Hyperbolus fiasco (?416) demonstrates the dangers inherent in a system of ostracism unless it is properly 'managed'.

The residence limits for those ostracised after the initial years are given in §8; the 'not' in the translation is missing in the papyrus of the *Constitution of Athens*, but the correction is likely. Where we can be sure of the residence of those ostracised after 481 they lived outside the stated limits, e.g. Themistocles at Argos (Thucydides 1,135,3). Before this, Aristides, for example, had retired only to Aegina (Ps. Demosthenes *against Aristogeiton* ii,6). Geraistus was the south-eastern point of Euboea, and Scyllaeum the eastern point of the Argolid. If the 'not' were not inserted, the text would suggest a provision aimed to keep the ostracised out of contact with the Persians.

The Archonship of Hermocreon must be the year 501/0 because it was eleven years before Marathon (§3), not 504/3 as implied in §2; Dionysius of Halicarnassus confirms this by giving a different Archon for 504/3 (Akestorides; *Roman Antiquities* v,37).

The institution of the Bouleutic oath and the election of *strategoi* by tribes are corollaries of the Cleisthenic reforms. Either they were further democratic reforms whose authorship is unknown, or the date of their actual introduction confirms that a significant period was necessary to put the Cleisthenic system into full effect. The former is perhaps more likely, both since seven years seems an over-long time to wait to implement the election of a *strategos* from each tribe if it had been included in Cleisthenes' 'package', and because Aristotle switches from talking of Cleisthenes as author to the Athenians—'they' in §2.* The position over the oath taken by members of the *Boule* is the less definite of the two, for Aristotle is discussing the oath taken in his own day. There is nothing to prove that it was the first oath of the *Boule*—it may have been a modification of an original formula; there must surely have been an oath as soon as Cleisthenes established his *Boule*. Details of the oath can be reconstructed from a number of sources; it included provisions requiring the members to advise in accordance with the laws, to recommend the best course for the city, to denounce any unsuitable person who had been chosen by lot for the *Boule*, and not to imprison any Athenian who put up three guarantors of the same property class as himself unless he had been detected in a conspiracy to betray the city or subvert the democracy, or was a tax-farmer or his surety or collector who had defaulted on payment. The last provision (quoted by Demosthenes, *against Timocrates*, 144), argues that the oath was not totally unchanged in his own day, for it appears that the *Boule* lost all powers

* On the *strategoi* see further below on LXI.

of imprisonment in the reforms of 462/1; however, it may well have been substantially the same.

The switch to selection of Archons by lot from a group previously elected by the tribes took place in 487/6, and is a logical step in the development towards democracy; the confidence inspired by the success at Marathon probably had something to do with the introduction of the reform. However, §5 does not agree exactly with VIII,1, where the same system is ascribed to Solon. The conflict on numbers (VIII,1 says they were selected from ten previously elected by each tribe) may be explained in the way advocated by von Fritz/Kapp: 500 were selected by the demes, fifty for each tribe, and they were then reduced to ten for each tribe by tribal selection. The 100 who resulted would all be taken together for the final casting of lots. This is ingenious, but '500' is probably a manuscript corruption. Either way, there is no indication that at this early date the clerk to the nine Archons was selected at the same time, thus producing ten offices divided among the ten tribes, nor that there was any mechanism to ensure that there was not more than one Archon from one tribe.

Aristotle is, however, probably right in saying here that the Archonship was filled by election until 487/6; (see above on VIII). At any rate, the tyrants would have had to abolish sortition; elections can be easily 'controlled', but casting of lots is more difficult. Thucydides (VI,54,6) shows that the Peisistratids decided who was to hold the Archonship, though the wording need not imply that elections were suspended.

An inevitable result of Archonship with an element of lot in the selection process must have been a diminution of the standing of the Archons. The Athenians believed in the lot as an equaliser of everyone's chances in as wide a field as possible in politics, but always recognised that there were certain fields where expertise was vital, and in them they always used election, not lot. Aristotle is therefore right to insist (against Herodotus VI,109) that the Polemarch remained the elected commander-in-chief until 487/6. Thereafter one may presume that the Polemarch's authority was much less, in common with the other Archons, and it is no surprise to find the *strategoi* emerging as effectively the chief magistrates in Athens shortly after this.

The mines at Maroneia were a part of the area of Laurium; the Athenians drew significant income from mining the silver deposits there. The intention of 'some' to distribute the windfall to the people (cf. Herodotus VII,144) displays a simple-minded approach to economics; it arose from the idea that the property of the state was also the corporate property of the individual citizens, which in its turn sprang from the equation of the city with the body of the citizens. There is no trace here of the concept of building up a reserve fund comparable to that accumulated by Pericles in the period before the Peloponnesian War; indeed, economic forethought was very rare in the ancient world, the normal approach being to wait for a necessary item of expenditure to arise and then to decide how to finance it.

Herodotus (VII,144) says that 200 ships were built, not 100, and that

Themistocles used persuasion, not trickery; whichever is correct, the building of the ships was stressed by many writers in the ancient world as being a turning-point in Athenian history because it diverted her attention to the sea, and ultimately produced the situation where the fleet was the most important section of the Athenian armed forces; this had a direct bearing on the establishment of the radical democracy. Themistocles has perhaps as good a claim as Cleisthenes to be the father of the fully developed Athenian democracy, though it is doubtful whether either foresaw what their actions would lead to ultimately. If Themistocles got his fleet built by a form of trickery, this is a significant point; such action would have been virtually unthinkable sixty years later.

THE AREOPAGUS

XXIII The alleged ascendancy of the Areopagus is very reminiscent of the actual position of power stemming from prestige enjoyed by the Senate at Rome for a generation after the Second Punic War. Aristotle (§2) approves wholeheartedly, and his views are typical of those in the fourth century who disapproved of the radical democracy; notable among works stemming from this attitude is the *Areopagiticus* of Isocrates. The danger was that the theorists tended to read back into early history the political situation which they would like to have seen in their own day in Athens. It may be that the *strategoi* lost their nerve before Salamis and the Areopagus took over, but it is a surprising suggestion since Themistocles was one of them; loss of nerve was hardly a characteristic of his long political career.* On the other hand, if there were a vacuum to be filled, the Areopagus was the obvious body to step in, for the element of sortition had only entered the selection of Archons in the last seven years, and the members were therefore almost all in the body because they had been elected to the highest office in the state; one may guess that the great majority of mature Athenians of talent were members. However, the supposed rise of the Areopagus reverses the trend towards a more democratic control of affairs; an actual increase of power is particularly unlikely, as opposed to a pause in the development of the democracy, for it would be a reversion to a more primitive form of constitution. The Areopagus is said to have done exactly what the fourth-century theorists wished it could have done in their own day; this is suspicious, as is the vagueness of any information about the *political* functions of the Areopagus at any period. If that body had had any real power after 480, it may in practice have sprung from their right to hear impeachments, but it is surprising that we have virtually no idea of how their supposed power was actually exercised. Such arguments cannot prove anything, but they are enough to oblige us to treat Aristotle's bland statement with caution.

Athens took the naval hegemony (a word meaning 'leadership' and

* There is also the piquant implication that Themistocles lost his nerve as a *strategos*, but kept it as a member of the Areopagus.

usually used to imply the willing agreement of those who are being led)
as a result of a free vote both of the Ionians who had joined the Greek
effort against the Persians and of those who had been liberated thereafter. It was only later that Athens converted this hegemony into an
empire; cf. Thucydides 1,95,1. Whether it was really against the will of
the Spartans is another matter; they were by tradition averse to adven-
tures far from home, and had a good deal of trouble on their hands in
the Peloponnese; Athens had probably joined the Peloponnesian
League in 510 and there was no reason to suspect her of hostile intent at
this juncture, nor was there any question that Sparta was militarily by
far the most powerful state in Greece; Athens could not apparently pose
a threat to her position. Equally, the Spartans probably regretted what
they had done within a very few years; Diodorus Siculus (xi,50) records
a debate at Sparta, perhaps to be dated as early as 477, where the proposal to go to war with Athens in order to recover the hegemony of the
Greek League (i.e. the Delian League) was nearly carried. It was one
thing for Themistocles to trick them into allowing the rebuilding of the
walls of Athens; it was quite different when Athens appeared to be
reaching a position approaching parity with them.

Note that both Themistocles and Aristides are described as leaders of
the people; Aristotle is surely right here, rather than Plutarch who calls
Aristides an aristocrat (*Aristides* 2). Plutarch had presumably been misled by the apparent schematisation of fifth-century history in the sources,
which tended to produce one radical and one moderate leader at each
period. The suggested distinction between their talents (§3) is not
acceptable; each showed great ability in both politics and war. Indeed,
it is only the point about one being outstanding in justice which has led
to the translation offered, for linguistically the Greek could equally be
taken the other way round. There may be some corruption in the text.
Everything points to Aristides as a close collaborator with Themistocles
in the period up to the former's ostracism. Thereafter they worked
together in the immediate crisis of Salamis, but the fact that Themistocles was not a *strategos* for 479, while Aristides was not only a *strategos*,
but also one of the leaders in the organisation of the Delian League (cf.
Thucydides 1,96) shows that Themistocles' star was waning. By 478/7
(the year of the organisation of the League, §5) Cimon was coming to
the fore, and shortly afterwards stole the limelight from Aristides by his
astute handling of a problem over booty at Byzantium.

A final point which Aristotle makes is of vital importance; the form of
oath which involved casting red-hot lumps of iron into the sea implied
that the treaty was to last until the iron should float, that is for ever; cf.
Plutarch *Aristides* 25. When the allies later demanded the right to
secede they were going back on their original oath.

For the history alluded to in the chapter, see Herodotus viii,3;
Thucydides 1,95–97; Plutarch, *Aristides* 23–25 and *Cimon* 6–7.

XXIV Aristotle summarises as recommendations by Aristides and
resultant changes many of the constitutional developments of the fifth

century, some of which did not occur until well after Aristides' death
(c467). The tone of the chapter is disapproving, and an aristocratic or
oligarchic source may perhaps lie behind it; at all events, Aristides is
represented as responsible for much which was anathema to the con-
servatives, and there is a radical difference from the main line of the
story given by Plutarch, who represents Aristides as a conservative, and
contrasts his stance with that of Themistocles. Even Plutarch is forced
to admit that some democratic reforms were instigated by Aristides
(*Aristides* 22 and 25); Aristotle's account appears preferable to that of
Plutarch.

For the people to move from the country into the town would make
the democracy 'worse' in Aristotle's eyes, for he thought that the best
democracy was that in which the people lived by working the land
(*Politics* 1318 b 9ff; 1292 b 41ff). For the people to have real control
over everyday decisions it was necessary for them to be able to get to the
Ekklesia easily and whenever necessary, which was not always com-
patible with agriculture.

The transition from Delian League to Athenian Empire (described as
'to seize the hegemony') was gradual and almost inevitable. From the
start Athens was much more powerful than the individual member
states, and naturally (and by their wish) undertook the leadership. Her
influence grew as the custom of commuting service in the League fleet
to cash payment of tribute spread—it benefited both sides, at least in
the short term. Aristotle passes over the intermediate stages of this
gradual process, merely noting that three states retained some measure
of independence (though Samos was less free after the revolt of 441/0);
cf. Thucydides 1,99. They remained independent and on the whole
loyal (witness the behaviour of Samos in 405/4), and Aristotle's comment is cynical in implication. In any case, there is little doubt that the
subjection of the allies was hardly the original aim of Aristides, and it is
very doubtful whether it became even unacknowledged Athenian
policy until some time after he had ceased to be influential.

Aristotle then implies that the Athenians moved into the city so that
they could live off the income from the empire. This charge has been
levelled at the Athenian democracy in the form of the generalisation
'radical democracy was parasitic on the empire'. The charge has a
certain superficial attractiveness, but is not fully justified; in the fourth
century all the paid offices involved in running the fifth-century democracy continued to exist and receive pay at least at the same rate as in
the fifth century, and pay for attendance at the *Ekklesia* was added;
even without the empire Athens could finance all this. This is not to say
that Athens did not benefit financially as well as in other ways from the
empire; manifestly she did, not least in that there was enough money
coming in which was surplus to normal requirements to finance such
expenditure as the Acropolis building program. In the same way, the
existence of the empire meant the maintenance of a larger fleet, and also
involved certain jobs which were filled by Athenians which would not
have been necessary without the empire. Therefore the Athenians in

fact profited, but this is very different from saying or implying that the radical democracy depended on the empire for its very existence. Compare the note on the *Constitution of the Athenians*, 1,16 above.

Aristotle says that more than 20,000 people made their living from the empire. He lists 15,750 positions, but if one adds 4,000 for the guard of twenty ships (the normal complement of a trireme was 200), and allows for the unspecified number of people covered by the last sentence, the total and the sub-units tally. Different categories are mixed indiscriminately. It is quite probable that being a guard was a full-time occupation, and one could therefore reasonably expect to make a living wage; however, it has been calculated that jurors were very unlikely to make anything like as much. 'Pay' for them was not introduced until the time of Pericles (XXVII,3), and they then received two obols a day. This was in itself probably adequate as compensation for loss of earnings *for the one day*; however, not by any means all 6,000 jurors were needed on any particular day, and there were many public holidays when the courts did not sit at all; cf. below on LXIII–LXV. If a man had always been lucky enough to be picked in the ballot for jury places (below on LXIII–LXV), it is just conceivable that he could have received enough for bare subsistence as a bachelor; it is inconceivable that a family could have lived this way. Two points are implicit here: first Aristotle (or his source) has made the most of the figures to the detriment of the image of the democracy—it was not always wartime, not all jurymen sat all the time, and not all state officials were on duty all the time. The exaggeration is manifest. Secondly, the above analysis exposes the basic theory behind state 'pay' at Athens: 'pay' is a misnomer—it was compensation for the fact that while on state duty a man could not earn his living as usual. In order to make it possible for all who wished to take part in the running of the state there had to be some system whereby the poorer citizens would not go hungry if they gave up some of their working time; otherwise economic factors would have turned the state into a timocracy in fact (if not in name), for a man's participation in politics would have been limited by the length of time for which he could afford not to earn. The 'pay' system was highly democratic, but rested firmly on the presupposition that everyone was self-supporting independent of the state.

Of the individual groups mentioned, the 6,000 jurymen were the nominal role, 600 for each tribe. The bowmen must have been citizens not the Scythian bowmen who acted as a sort of police force; the latter were publicly owned slaves. The number of bowmen, as of cavalry, appears to be drawn from Thucydides' listing of the nominal muster-role of Athenian forces at the beginning of the Peloponnesian War (II,13,8); they would have been active only in wartime, and then not all of them. In the case of the cavalry, Aristotle seems to have taken the basic figure without noticing the distinction between 1,000 who were citizens and 200 horse archers who were Scythian slaves. Pay for the *Boule* was probably a feature of the reforms of 462/1 and the years immediately afterwards; by the late fourth century it was five obols a day, which was, and had to be, adequate for a family. Guards on the dockyards are not mentioned elsewhere, and may have been needed in any numbers only in time of war; Thucydides gives a general figure for the guarding of the walls of Athens and the Peiraeus and the area of Munichia (II,13,7). The functions of the guards on the Acropolis are not known; however, an inscription (IGi² 44 = Hill, *Sources*, B 45) records three archers to prevent runaway slaves and other undesirables reaching a certain place on the Acropolis where they could take sanctuary; also, one imagines that the main treasury was not left unguarded.

That there should have been the same number of state officials abroad as at home would be a remarkable coincidence; it is probable that the repetition of '700' is a manuscript error which has ousted some other figure. The figures are uncheckable, but 700 for those abroad seems very high, even allowing for the fact that Athens from time to time sent out commissions, for instance to supervise cities which had just been reduced after a revolt, e.g. Erythrae, Meiggs/Lewis 40. Cleruchies were subject to Athens, and officials visited them from time to time; the 'overseers' mocked in Aristophanes (*Birds* 1022ff) would have been included here; cf. Ps. Xenophon *Constitution of the Athenians* 1,18. The figure of 2,500 hoplites bears no relation to known numbers in particular battles; conceivably it represents Athens' peace-time needs at home and in the Empire, but this can only be a guess.

The ships mentioned total thirty (twenty guard ships and ten for the tribute); the standing fleet in peace time was sixty, and again it is difficult to reconcile the numbers; possibly Aristotle knew of some practice whereby normally only half the standing fleet was actually away from Athens at a time. However, this is pure hypothesis, and in any case the crews of all sixty were presumably paid for the eight months they were in commission; training would have occupied the time when they were not on foreign missions. Ten ships are unlikely to have been fully employed with the tribute, especially as it was the duty of the allies to deliver it themselves at the Great Dionysia each year. It has been attractively suggested that a minute change in the Greek makes these ships responsible for the 'guards' mentioned in LXII,1; they were presumably used to garrison temporary trouble spots, and transport would have been necessary. If this conjecture is right, there may in fact have been more than ten ships in this group; the figure ten is merely deduced from the known complement of a trireme, while troop-carrying ships would probably have had smaller crews to leave more space for the troops. The twenty ships would have been fully occupied patrolling the Aegean, and not least securing communications for vital grain imports, notably from the Black Sea. It is worth remembering that Athens kept the Aegean reasonably free of pirates for the duration of her empire.

The Prutaneion performed some of the functions of a town hall. A few people were honoured by the state for notable services by the privilege of free meals there (cf. Plato, *Apology* 36 d); however, they were a small group, and their privilege was hardly a substitute for an income. Orphans of those killed on active service were maintained by the state until they had grown up; thereafter they made their own living like everyone else. The inclusion of jailors shows that they cannot have been included in the 700 state officials in the city mentioned above. The whole section smacks of propagandist special pleading; it is of more use as an indication of areas in which some payment could be expected from the state at some time than as an indication of how many people received compensation for loss of earnings in any one year, let alone how many lived off money derived from the allies.

EPHIALTES

XXV The opening sentence requires no comment after the analysis of xxiv. Aristotle now switches from later developments back to the years immediately after Plataea. The phrase 'about seventeen years' has caused unnecessary problems because editors have counted (inclusively) back from 462/1, the year of Ephialtes' actual reforms. Counting exclusively there is no problem; if Aristotle were reckoning inclusively, he could as easily have been thinking of the time when Ephialtes first made an impact; 463/2 is, if anything, rather late for this. The statement that the constitution was 'gradually deteriorating', is the first note of criticism; Aristotle spoke of both Solon and Cleisthenes with approval, for he did not regard their constitutions as unacceptable, despite his aversion to real democracy; cf. xxix, 3.

The attack on the Areopagus made by Ephialtes, aided by Pericles, was the next major step forward in the development of the full democracy in Athens. The Areopagus was an obvious target, both because its members held office for life, which was the antithesis of democratic principles, and because the element of chance in their selection by lot must over a period of twenty-five years have somewhat changed the type of member; instead of being leading politicians, they would have been men of reasonable competence but not necessarily first class. Attacks on individual members for misusing their position were an obvious preliminary to an all-out attack on the institution itself, since the powers which the democrats aimed to remove were the general supervision of morals and 'watchdog role', and perhaps the right to hear impeachments (see above on xxiii); in a democracy such powers, if they existed at all, should belong to the people as a whole, not to a council of life members for which only the upper two property classes were eligible. There is no reason to question the traditional reputation of Ephialtes and Pericles for incorruptibility; it would have stood them in particularly good stead in this campaign. There is no doubt that Aristotle exaggerates the 'supervision' which the Areopagus had exercised, and it is probable that the powers which it is said to have recently acquired were in fact its since very early days (cf. viii, 4), even if it had originally started as a murder court. An allegation that its powers were usurped and not traditional would help the general campaign, and must have come from the opponents of the Areopagus.

The exact nature of Ephialtes' reforms is not stated by our sources, but we may deduce it from what other bodies are said to do from now on. The supervision of magistrates, the investigation of their eligibility before their year of office, and approval of their accounts afterwards were now divided between the *Boule* and the *dikasteria*; all other jurisdiction was handed over to the *dikasteria* with the exception of murder, assault and arson (LVII,3), and some forms of sacrilege including damage to the sacred olives (LX,2). The supervisory powers lapsed, and henceforth the *Ekklesia* was subject only to self-imposed limitations.

The story of the participation in these reforms of Themistocles must be apocryphal. He was ostracised in the later 470s, perhaps 472/1 (cf. Thucydides I,135), and was probably dead by 462. Cimon inclined to the side of the moderates, and it is not totally surprising that a story appeared connecting Themistocles, who was seen as the champion of the radicals, with the last major reforms leading to full democracy. The details of the story are a fine piece of fiction, recalling Themistocles' famous resourcefulness, and also having something of an echo of the way in which Peisistratus first got the tyranny. There is no stylistic reason for supposing the passage to be an interpolation by a later hand as some have suggested; it appears that Aristotle had got the story from some otherwise unknown source; it is remarkable that it is not even recorded in Plutarch, who quotes Aristotle for the murder of Ephialtes (*Pericles* 10), and one must assume that Plutarch had reason to reject it.

The murder of Ephialtes before the end of 462/1 indicates the tension of the time; political murders were very rare in Athens.* The only thing one may reasonably deduce is that the assassin was suborned by Athenian politicians, presumably by supporters either of Cimon (who had been ostracised just before) or of a still more conservative policy. Even Plutarch (*Pericles* 10) rejects the absurd story that Pericles was behind the murder.

XXVI Yet again, this chapter and the next raise problems of chronology. Aristotle passes from the statement that the Areopagus lost its power to a discussion of increasing disorder and disruption stemming from the increased power of the demagogic leaders of the people; then he says that 'at this time' Cimon was 'rather young', and therefore the 'better' people lacked leadership. Since Cimon was exiled in the year of the reform of the Areopagus, one is left with the choice of supposing either that the whole description refers only to a very short time, or that something more radical is wrong. If the former is the case, Aristotle is surely at least guilty of being misleading, and there is the added problem that it is difficult to see how, by any stretch of the imagination, Cimon can be described as 'rather young' in 462/1. He had had a prominent if subordinate position at Sestos and Byzantium in 478/7, sixteen years before, and was apparently in command the year afterwards. Even if Aristotle could be referring to a period of only a few months, the adjective 'rather young' must be wrong. The increased power of popular leaders fits well with the period immediately before

---

* Evidence suggests further that they were only employed by the oligarchs.

and during the attacks on the Areopagus, and could also presumably apply to the period before Cimon's actual ostracism. On the other hand, Cimon could hardly be said at this time to have 'only just entered politics'. The statement about casualties of those enlisted from the citizen roll fits better with the events after 461, since the slur on the commanders hardly suits a period when the experienced and skilful Cimon was in charge of operations on many occasions. In the later period Athens lost a large number of men in widely separated areas on operations at least some of which were not well handled. Aristotle is apparently either suggesting a general decline in the proportion of reliable citizens of all classes, or that fewer of the lower classes were killed because the 'better' men were more likely to stand their ground and so die. The Greek phrase translated 'the majority of them had perished' more naturally means 'the masses had perished', but this meaning is clearly unacceptable in the context, which demands a reference to the reason for the weakness of the position of the moderates. There must be some doubt about the soundness of the text here. Altogether, there are so many contradictions and obscurities in this section that it looks as if it was roughly compiled from a series of notes, and never sorted; efforts to make historical sense of it either tend to disregard some sections and be selective, or are forced to do violence to the Greek so that sense can be produced in a translation.

The reduced respect for the laws commented on in §2 is interesting, since one of the functions which the Areopagus lost in 462/1 was its duty to ensure that the laws were observed in day-to-day government. There was a procedure of indictment for making illegal proposals later in the century—the first known case occurred in about 415—but it is doubtful whether it existed as early as this, logical as it may seem to argue that the Athenians must have substituted some sort of check for the power which they had abolished; see below on XLV.

The *zeugitai* were admitted to the Archonship in 457, in which year Mnesitheides held office; cf. also above on VII. There is a slight curiosity here: one would have expected the first zeugite holder after, not in, the year of the reform; the actual reform was presumably enacted earlier. On the local magistrates, see above, XVI,5 with commentary and below LIII,I; they were reintroduced in 453/2, probably as a response to the general increase in the quantity and importance of litigation—it was felt to be a basic right to be able to go to law, and it would probably have been impossible to handle all cases in Athens, apart from the trouble of going to the city discussed above.

Pericles' citizenship law was introduced in 451; henceforth only children of parents who were themselves both Athenians could be accepted as citizens. That the law was not retrospective is proved by the fact that Cimon, whose mother was a Thracian princess, was *strategos* in 451/0. The stated motive of the law, 'because of the large size of the citizen body', cannot be accepted; it was not a measure of population control. The law was surely primarily directed against the aristocrats who married members of the aristocracy of other Greek cities or girls

from even farther afield—witness Cimon's mother. There may also
have been a protective element in that it encouraged ordinary Athenians to marry Athenian girls rather than foreigners; there must have
been a foreign element living in Athens, and the exotic has always had
a certain attraction. Further, the law aimed at restricting what the
Athenians rightly thought were the considerable privileges of citizenship to those they judged fully entitled to them. It is important to
remember that the law only laid down conditions for full citizenship.
There was no ban on liaisons, temporary or permanent, with noncitizens; the only stipulation was that any offspring could not be citizens. Ironically, Pericles himself lived for years with Aspasia, who was
not a citizen, and after the death of his children by his former (Athenian) wife, pleaded with the *Ekklesia* to give his sons by Aspasia citizenship; this was granted—most unusually.

XXVII Aristotle has switched his full attention to Pericles, and therefore reverts to the beginning of his known public career, his prosecution
of Cimon after the latter's return from the siege of Thasos in 463. Hence,
the opening words, 'after this', do not refer to the previous chapter, but
to the period of the domination of Cimon, which Aristotle characterised
as the period of control by the Areopagus (xxv,1). He had already made
it clear that Ephialtes was the prime mover of the reforms; it is no doubt
fair to give Pericles some of the credit, for the way in which he took over
from Ephialtes shows that he must have made his mark before 461, but
apparently the innovating and reforming ability belonged primarily to
Ephialtes. It is noteworthy that Ephialtes made sweeping changes,
while, brilliant as was Pericles' consolidation of the democratic position
in the long period when he was one of the leading statesmen, we cannot
certainly ascribe to him any radical change or innovation. Most of the
reforms were carried out either in 462/1 or shortly afterwards, and the
later changes were inevitable corollaries of what had already been done,
such as payment for service on juries and elsewhere in public life. The
citizenship law is a possible exception, but it is doubtful whether this
could fairly be described as a democratic innovation.

Here, as elsewhere, Aristotle connects the stress on sea power with the
increasing influence of the masses in government; cf. *Politicus* 1304 a 22;
1321 a 14. He does not offer a history of the period down to the Peloponnesian War, but concentrates on a few aspects. Increasing confidence on the part of the people is clear in their actions, though the
suggestion that the people decided to run the state themselves because
they were cooped up in Athens during the war and paid for their services is dubious. To have the final decision was to them their right, and
'pay' was merely a mechanism to allow them to exercise that right.

The reason given for Pericles' introduction of these payments must
be modified. It cannot have been an attempt to match Cimon's
liberality before the latter's ostracism, for they were not introduced
until after that, and when Cimon was ostracised there was nothing to
match. On the other hand, this passage suggests strongly that payment

for the *dikastai* was closely connected with the original reform. Stripping the Areopagus of so many powers must have led to a great increase of business in the *dikasteria*, and it may well have been necessary to provide some compensation for loss of earnings in order to get enough *dikastai* (jury service was not compulsory as it is today), apart from the fact that it was clearly democratic that as many as possible should be able to sit.*

The liturgies were a form of public service in Athens which fell only on the rich. Certain duties, such as maintaining triremes or providing choruses for festivals (LII,2 and LVI,3, with Commentary) were not financed by the state from general taxation but imposed on individuals who had to spend at least a fixed minimum sum; in the fifth century at least, they took pride in doing the job well, and often spent more than the stipulated minimum; see Lysias, *against a Charge of Taking Bribes*, 1–10. The system was in some ways similar to supertax, but there was a radical difference of approach, which is implicit in Aristotle's approving comment on Cimon; it is not usual now to hear people boasting of the amount of tax they pay — or at any rate not in the same way as was customary in Athens. The exhortation to 'give the people what was their own' (§4) is a famous quotation preserved in a number of sources; it presupposes a degree of sophisticated political awareness.

Aristotle adopts the standard aristocratic approach to the effect of introducing payment in the *dikasteria*; it is doubtful whether it was damaging, and certain that ordinary courts whose juries were not open to all the common people would not have been tolerated under the radical democracy, whether the reason was a legal ban or only economic pressure. Anytus was one of the accusers of Socrates; he was accused over Pylos in 409, which argues a surprisingly long time for the *dikasteria* to have been free of corruption. In fact, the mechanics of jury selection, and also court procedure, made bribery extremely difficult (LXIIIff and Commentary); it may be therefore that it *was* extremely rare, which would make the Anytus case memorable, and therefore all the more likely that Aristotle is right to say this was the first case.

Plutarch (*Pericles* 4) mentions a Damon as an advisor of Pericles, and refers to this passage of Aristotle in mentioning Damonides (*ib.* 9), it is hard to know whether the two are to be identified, or whether there was a teacher Damon, son of Damonides (as on a surviving vote for ostracism), and Damonides a politician who advised Pericles. The former is perhaps the better explanation, although it is possible that two men were confused, and some attributes of the teacher were transferred to the politician.

XXVIII The opening sentence is very brief and muted praise for Pericles, whether one compares it with Thucydides' views or considers

---

* There was a tradition in the ancient world (cf. e.g. Plutarch *Cimon* 17) that Cimon returned from ostracism after only five years. This cannot be so, but it is possible that Aristotle had it in mind, and therefore dated the rivalry in generosity, and therefore the institution of payment for the juries, to the years immediately following 457/6. For the sequence of events compare Plutarch, *Pericles* 9.

his achievements. Aristotle looks at him from the aristocratic point of view as the last democratic leader who was even tolerable, and one suspects he was tolerable only because he was at least himself an aristocrat, and restrained the more extreme democrats. Aristotle notes that leadership now moves out of the hands of the 'better' people for the first time.

In the list of leaders of the people (§2) Aristotle includes those who championed the advancement of the democracy, and is not giving an unbroken sequence. He did not intend to imply that Cleisthenes was influential from 508 until Xanthippus took over; in fact, there is no evidence that he took any part in politics after 508/7, and some have plausibly associated his disappearance with a popular revulsion against the submission to Persia which appears to have been made (or at least attempted) under him. The enmity between the democrats and Miltiades is well documented, particularly his prosecution in 493, and condemnation in 490/89. Themistocles is presumably listed with Aristides to preserve the sequence of pairs, though Aristides is again correctly listed as a leader of the people, not of the aristocrats; in fact Themistocles was Archon (*Eponumos*) in 493, and was of the same political generation as Xanthippus, though Miltiades was probably older. The Thucydides mentioned here was, of course, the son of Melesias, a different man from the historian, though probably related to him.

The attacks on Cleon, Cleophon and Kallikrates echo the standard aristocratic prejudices against the demagogues. They may well be justified in that the new-style leaders were not 'gentlemen' in the way an aristocrat would understand the term. However, neither Aristotle nor Thucydides give them their due for their undoubted abilities, in particular in the field of finance; one should compare Pericles' record in financing the Peloponnesian War with that of Cleon or even Cleophon before one dismisses them as incompetent adventurers. Exactly what the offence of Cleon was in speaking 'with his garments tucked up' is not clear; perhaps the point is that he looked like a labourer at work. If so, it may have been a deliberate gesture, though one must not forget that these maligned demagogues came from what we should call the middle class, not the working class; both Cleon and Hyperbolus were quite comfortably off; Cleophon himself was the son of a *strategos* of 428 (Meiggs/Lewis, pp. 41f). Their offence in the eyes of the aristocrats was that they were, in the Victorian phrase, 'in trade'.

The two-obol payment was introduced by Cleophon immediately after the fall of the Oligarchy of 411/10, and is mentioned in an inscription of 410/9 (Meiggs/Lewis 84); its purpose is not clear, but it may have been a general payment for any public service, so widely defined that almost anyone could qualify; in that way it would in effect be a form of poor relief just at the time when the occupation of Deceleia would be beginning to cause real hardship. It certainly was not the payment which in the fourth century refunded to citizens the cost of attending the theatre. The Theoric Fund, from which the fourth-century distribution was paid, was a major evil which absorbed all surplus revenue and applied it to the entertainment of the people; Demosthenes continuously complained of the difficulty of financing a sensible foreign policy because of its stranglehold. It appears from the present passage that Kallikrates proposed to raise the two-obol payment to three obols which had the (odd) effect of abolishing it. The circumstances are unknown, as are those of his death. On the other hand, the death of Cleophon is well documented; he was executed on a trumped-up charge shortly before the fall of Athens in 404. It is, however, very doubtful whether the people were responsible for this, as Aristotle suggests at the end of the paragraph; he appears to be attempting to salvage something to their credit from the period. In §4 Aristotle condemns the popular leaders of the fourth century *en masse* without considering one of them worthy to be named; they were different in type and aims from the men of Pericles' day and before, but it is doubtful whether they were as bad as he implies. Aristotle's prejudices were against them as people because of their origins and as statesmen because they failed to restore the glories of the fifth century.

Of the men whom Aristotle chooses to praise as the outstanding leaders after the early period, Nicias and Thucydides were sound, fairly conservative, moderate democrats; they believed in friendship with Sparta, the moderation of Athenian imperialism, and a generally cautious and quietist approach. There is little question that they were basically out of tune with the prevailing spirit of Athens; they did not often manage to influence the course of events unless some set-back had temporarily dimmed the prestige of the radical leaders. They may have 'looked after the city like fathers' (a phrase which was incidentally also used of Pericles), but this was not what the people wanted; the aristocrats thought they 'knew best', but towards the end of the fifth century the Athenians were notable for being independent and determined to take the decisions themselves. Aristotle tries hard to defend Theramenes, but his inclusion looks as if it was designed to keep up the pairing of moderate and radical. He did not have the standing of the other two, nor was he influential for so long a period. He gives the impression of a rather unpleasant political time-server, as is suggested by his nickname, 'the buskin', a shoe that would fit either foot; even his final gesture against the Thirty was only made when all was lost, and can hardly counterbalance the rest of his record. Even if one were to accept Aristotle's judgement, and admit his sincerity as a moderate, one must still remember that (in Andrewes' words) 'he must bear much of the blame for the internal troubles which lamed Athens in the last phase of the war' (OCD²*s.v.*).

XXIX The analysis of leaders throughout the period took Aristotle ahead of his main account of political changes; he now returns to the aftermath of the Sicilian expedition (415–3), with the threat of Persian intervention and the moves leading to the establishment of the oligarchy of the Four Hundred. The hope of Persian aid for Athens may have been a contributory factor in the change of constitution, for which

Alcibiades was at least in part responsible (Thucydides VIII,53,1), but the main impetus came from deep dissatisfaction with the conduct of the war by the radical leaders in the *Ekklesia*, who appeared to be leading Athens from disaster to disaster. The change was made easier by the fact that the situation was analogous, though opposite, to that of 462; then the absence of Cimon with 4,000 hoplites at Sparta may have materially affected the balance of the *Ekklesia* to the advantage of the radicals, and so helped Ephialtes to get his reforms through; now such fleet as could be mustered was virtually permanently at sea attempting to preserve the fragments of the empire. The balance of the *Ekklesia* may again have been altered, this time in favour of the anti-democrats, although organised intimidation was the key factor which tipped the balance at Athens—note the firmly democratic line of the fleet at Samos. For the history of the period, see Thucydides VIII *passim*; the treaties between Sparta and the Persians are in VIII, 18, 37 and 58 ,the story of the oligarchic coups in VIII,65–98.

THE FOUR HUNDRED AND THE FIVE THOUSAND

Aristotle gives his account of the first oligarchic period in fifth-century Athens in three sections: the preliminaries, the proposals, and the actual rule of the Four Hundred, with the period of the Five Thousand virtually passed over in silence as an appendix, although it lasted longer than the rule of the Four Hundred. He gives no indications of the places where meetings were held and his account does not raise the chronological problems implicit in Thucydides or in any attempt to combine the two accounts. It must be remembered always that Aristotle is writing a work on the constitution, not a full history.

The first move towards an oligarchy was taken very soon after the failure in Sicily; a board of ten senior statesmen, including the poet Sophocles, were appointed to act in a supervisory role in the crisis (Thucydides VIII,1,3). According to Aristotle, they formed the nucleus around which the commission of thirty was formed, and the latter produced the constitutional proposals; Thucydides (VIII,67) ascribes the proposals to a board of ten Commissioners, but Androtion and Philochorus both confirm that the ten were members of the thirty. Probably there is a simple contradiction here, although Thucydides may have had access to a source which suggested that an inner body of ten within the thirty had the real power. The whole period was a reign of terror in Athens, and Thucydides shows that many of the ordinary citizens had very little idea of what was happening. He was himself abroad at the time, and did not return for some years, by which time later events would probably have blurred the detailed memories of those involved. Aristotle did not write until about eighty years after the event. von Fritz/Kapp suggest that the Athenian archive was so developed by 412/11 that copies of all documents and proposals would have been kept there, but it is a sweeping thesis, and it also disregards the *prima facie* plausible possibility that the restored democracy would have destroyed at least those of the documents which had not actually become law. Even if the documents were preserved, they would not necessarily have shown who were the real instigators of particular measures. Somehow the main lines of the proposals were preserved, but it would be rash to suppose that Aristotle made his reconstruction on the basis of first-hand documentary evidence; he could have got much, though not all, of what he says from Thucydides; his other sources need not have been official.

The proposal of Puthodoros set the matter in motion; the rider of Kleitophon reflects propaganda of the period as well as being important in itself. Aristotle uses the standard formula for introducing an amendment in the *Ekklesia* to preface the rider. By saying of Cleisthenes 'when he established the democracy', Kleitophon reflects the moderate point of view, that the Cleisthenic democracy was the true democracy, not the later, more radical constitution. The final part of §3 may be a comment by Aristotle which reflects his own judgement, but to describe Cleisthenes' constitution as 'similar to that of Solon' is over-simplified, as the preceding accounts in the *Constitution of Athens* have shown. He may be giving what he believed to be Kleitophon's own views. Herodotus (VI,131,1) regarded Cleisthenes as the founder of Athenian democracy, and Thucydides gave the slogan of the reformers of 411/10 as 'not to have the same form of democracy' (VIII,53,1). Plutarch (*Cimon* 15) said that Ephialtes was a radical who upset the 'traditional laws', meaning the aristocracy in the Greek sense (cf. *Pericles* 3); his source was conservative in outlook. The investigation of earlier laws continued after the fall of the oligarchy. It is because it was undertaken at such a period of political turmoil that some of our information about the earlier history of the Athenian constitution is of dubious reliability and appears to reflect later propaganda rather than what actually happened. What was 'discovered' in the late fifth century became the accepted canon.

The suspension of constitutional safeguards was an essential preliminary to any revision of the constitution because the indictment for illegal proposals could be used against any resolution proposing a change in the basic structure of the democracy. Aristotle gives details, while Thucydides just includes the bare facts (VIII,67). The provision that offenders were to be handed over to the *strategoi* not the *dikasteria* suggests some form of martial law; it would not have been acceptable under ordinary democratic legal procedures. The general abolition of pay except for compensation at a very low rate for those on full-time duty (Prytanies) or with expensive ceremonial obligations (Archons) is the obvious step for a moderate reform. In this way the government is effectively open only to those who have enough money to devote time to it without endangering their livelihood. The limitation of active political rights to 'those best qualified in person and property to serve the state up to a total of not less than five thousand' represents, in effect restriction of these rights to those of hoplite status. There is an interesting contrast with Thucydides, who says (VIII,65,3) that the maximum number was 5,000. Aristotle's figure is confirmed by a speech which has been preserved among the works of Lysias, and was probably written in 410/9, which records that Polustratos, appointed to produce a list of the 5,000, included 9,000 on the list (*for Polustratos* 13). If the figure 9,000 is correct, the difference between Aristotle and Thucydides may represent two different stages in the development of the constitutional proposals. Either the first stage is represented by Aristotle, and had a propaganda motive to reassure the Athenians that the proposed oligarchy was not really narrow and exclusive, while Thucydides is nearer to what the instigators hoped to put into effect—a much narrower and more easily controlled group, or the reverse is true, and the oligarchs were forced to concede a wider group to conciliate doubters. The power to conclude treaties was no doubt included specifically to allow the oligarchs a free hand in negotiations with Sparta, but is implicit in their whole take-over of government.

The body of 100 chosen by the ten tribes were those charged with the enrolment of the 5,000. They began work only just before the Four Hundred fell; one of them was the Polustratos mentioned above.

XXX From the preliminary moves Aristotle turns to the actual drafting of the constitution. It is noteworthy that it is said that the proposals were ratified by the Five Thousand, although we know that body was not yet important (xxxii,3 and Thucydides viii,93,2). Thucydides (viii,67,2) says that the meeting of the *Ekklesia* at which the ratification took place was held at Colonus, outside the city walls of Athens. With the Spartans occupying Deceleia, perhaps only those who could afford to arm themselves could risk going to the meeting, and they would have to go in a large and organised body; this factor may have limited attendance to the hoplites.* As noted above, the hoplites were virtually synonymous with the Five Thousand in the minds of at least one section of the oligarchs, and this is presumably why the state-ment accepted by Aristotle could be made. One may deduce that Aristotle's source for xxx and xxxi believed the Five Thousand to have been established at an early stage; this is almost certainly wrong, but the impression may stem from propaganda moves at the Colonus meeting.

The remainder of the chapter describes a constitution drawn up 'for the future' (xxxi,1); the body of 100 responsible for drafting were selected at the meeting of the *Ekklesia* which also passed the preliminary suspension of the indictment for illegal proposals. It is legitimate to presume that the 100 men were carefully selected, and that the real drafting was largely done by a much smaller inner group. It is possible that this group of 100 overlapped to a significant extent with the body of ten from each tribe mentioned at the end of xxix, but the two are not identical, at any rate in theory.

The *Boule* was to be made up of men who were over thirty years of

---

* One would like to know what pretext was used to procure a meeting of the *Ekklesia* at Colonus rather than in the city.

age and members of the Five Thousand. In §3 a rotation among four sections, each called a *Boule*, is envisaged for the future; only one section was to be active each year. This is reminiscent of the constitution of Boeotia described by the Oxyrhynchus historian (see above, Part I), and was probably modelled on it. Naturally, members of the *Boule* were not paid. The magistrates of the state were *ex officio* members, selected from the active section of the Five Thousand. About 100 magistrates are mentioned in §2, and it therefore seems likely that the preliminary elections took place for each office in turn. If the drafters anticipated a vote at which would be presented a single slate of candidates successful in preliminary elections covering all posts, there would have been relatively few of those eligible who were not on the list as candidates for one post or another.

Of the less important offices mentioned, the *Hieromnemon* had recording duties, though exactly what they were is not known; the commanders of the tribal hoplite and cavalry units and the cavalry commanders are discussed below (LXI Commentary); the commanders of the garrison and the treasurers are self-explanatory, while the *Hellenotamiai* were treasurers of the tribute paid by the allies; their title ('Treasurers of the Greeks') was a survival from the original founding of the Delian League on a basis of something nearer equality, and was rooted in the old Greek league against the Persians. The number of *Hellenotamiai* was doubled at this time (Meiggs/Lewis, p. 258); this proposal at least was put into effect and the change was not reversed under the restored democracy. The commissioners in charge of sacrifices and the overseers were both groups of religious officials. All these positions were, of course, to be filled by election.

Nowhere does Aristotle or Thucydides give the size of the *Boule*; §5 suggests that there was an element of sortition in the allocation of members to each of the four divisions, as in the decision of the order in which they held office (§3) though an emendation to §5 eliminates the use of lot in the actual selection of members, and could be correct. Nowhere is it actually stated that there were 400 members in the *Boule*, though it may be implied in Thucydides VIII,93,2. The probabilities are heavily in favour of the proposition that the reformers were thinking in terms of a body of about this size, for this is the size which they selected for the preliminary *Boule* which took over at the time of the coup. Further, Solon's *Boule* was also of 400, which would be of at least symbolic importance to them; cf. xxxi,1. If they were thinking of 400, this cannot be made to tally with the suggestion that each *Boule* was a quarter of the Five Thousand, unless, as is just conceivable, they had in mind the phrase used by Thucydides 'up to five thousand', and were in fact planning for a very much lower figure. Here we come face to face with the root problem in all discussions of the sources on this topic. The whole oligarchy lasted for less than a year, during which period it underwent a number of modifications because of various pressures; at the same time, at least one theoretical 'blueprint for the future' was circulated. Chapter xxx is explicitly one of these plans, not an actual constitution which was put into practice. In all probability the plans had a large element of propaganda in them, and this may have been the main motive for their circulation. It is wrong, then, to expect that they will be fully analysed and worked out schemes with every detail complete. It is probable that such items as the exact size and composition of the *Boule* were not stated at the time of issue, and never subsequently decided because the plan was never put into practice. The 'Constitution of Draco' (above, IV) may be another such document from the period, though it appears to have some later additions or modifications; it is in many ways remarkably similar to the present plan. If Aristotle has seriously condensed his original source, this also may account for some of the obscurities.

Perhaps the most revolutionary feature of the plan as Aristotle describes it is that it apparently abandons the system of having two separate bodies, one to prepare legislation, and a larger one to take the final decision. There is no provision for a larger body to ratify the decisions of the *Boule* in office. This may be another example of excessive condensation, or perhaps the fact that members of the *Boule* could bring others of the Five Thousand to meetings (§4) was felt to be a sufficient way to involve those not in office in any year with the main decisions.* Why the *Hellenotamiai* who were handling the finances should be excluded is a mystery. The phrasing of the sentence also implies, interestingly, that not all were involved as active treasurers at the same time, but it is an odd provision to exclude the active ones from discussion and decision-making while admitting those who were not active; possibly there may be a corruption in the text.

There is no reason to suppose (with von Fritz/Kapp) that the hundred men mentioned in §1 as drafting the constitution were not the same as those in §3 who were to allocate citizens to the four divisions. The provisions for running the *Boule* are self-explanatory, and in any case theoretical; they tell us what was felt to be the right way of running such a body, not how one was actually run. The most interesting feature is the frequency of the use of the lot in deciding who should perform various functions. Again, we see the passion of the Greeks for equality, which is as strong within the restricted body of an oligarchy as it is in a democracy among the whole citizen body. The size of the fine for absence indicates the importance attached to proper performance of public duties, and is indicative of the fact that all members must have been reasonably well off.

XXXI The very vagueness of the phrase 'for the future' confirms the suggestion that the provisions outlined in xxx have a large element of propaganda in them; now Aristotle turns to the actual arrangements

---

* Conceivably, if the four *Boulai* were designed to be of 400 each, these 'associates' brought in were members of the Five Thousand not included in any of the four *Boulai*, but this seems unlikely since it would admit to decision-making those not included in the 'dormant' three-quarters of the *Boule*, although the latter were presumably thought of as more important than the ordinary members of the Five Thousand.

which were intended to cover at least the year 411/10; the reluctance with which the Four Hundred yielded to pressure to establish the Five Thousand argues that they had hoped to maintain these 'provisional' arrangements for a longer period.

According to Thucydides (VIII,67,3) the *Boule* of 400 was established by the following process: five 'presidents' were selected; they chose a hundred men, and each of the hundred picked three others to join him. This is a more precise statement than Aristotle's, and preferable not merely for that reason, but also because it is easier to see how the method described by Thucydides could be closely controlled by the leaders of the coup in order to ensure that the 'right' men were appointed. It may be that the added details recorded by Aristotle are correct; he says that the Four Hundred were selected from a previously picked body, and that the constitution of the group was balanced over all the tribes; such previous selection would give the 'Five Thousand' (or rather those who attended the *Ekklesia* meeting) the feeling that they had some say in the proceedings, while it was unlikely to lead to the exclusion of people regarded as vital by the conspirators; balancing membership among the tribes would satisfy the desire for equality within the oligarchic group. However, Aristotle omits the process by which the forty from each tribe were selected from 'the group previously elected'; another example of condensation, or of suppression in his source? von Fritz/Kapp regard the procedure as too cumbersome to be that used at the original establishment of the provisional Four Hundred (who, as they rightly point out, were selected in something of a hurry), and therefore advance the hypothesis that Aristotle preserves here also a document intended to pacify objections, embodying a 'somewhat less arbitrary' method of selecting the Four Hundred in future. This is not a necessary supposition. The process is not all that cumbersome, and could easily have been carried through in a day or two, particularly granted the possibility of coordination through the already highly organised oligarchic clubs. The fact that the old *Boule* and the *Ekklesia* went on meeting for a few days after the coup (Thucydides VIII,67–9) shows that the oligarchs did not have everything cut and dried immediately. The statement that the *Boule* of 400 was constituted 'according to tradition' probably means that it was believed to be an imitation of the *Boule* of Solon; the phrase was a normal propaganda expression to refer to his constitution.

The final provision of §1 effectively gives the new *Boule* full power to run the state. Constitutional reforms were to be observed (§2)—a virtual blank cheque for the inner group who would draft them. The appointment of *strategoi* could not even wait a day or two for the establishment of the *Boule*, for Athens was in the midst of a desperate crisis in the war; hence the provision of a temporary board of ten, to be superseded by those selected by the *Boule* as soon as possible. There is, of course, no necessary implication that the Five Thousand did not pick those wanted by the leaders, or that the *Boule* would necessarily make changes; what is reserved is the *right* to make changes, which means that a smaller group of oligarchs would be able to eliminate any undesirables if necessary. The *strategoi* so appointed were to have full powers for 411/10, and consult with the *Boule* where they needed to. This should be read in the light of the normal practice of the fifth century, whereby the appointment of *strategoi* 'with full powers' does not imply that they were something like military governors, but only that they were free to make their own military decisions without consulting the *Ekklesia* in a wider field than *strategoi* without the extra grant. The Five Thousand ('they' at the beginning of §3) also elected the next ranking officers for this occasion only to save time; thereafter they were to be elected 'according to the proposals', which may refer either to the document in xxx or to xxxi,2. Rotation of offices is decreed, as would be expected, with the obvious exception of *strategoi* (as under the democracy) and members of the *Boule* because there would not be enough men qualified if they could only hold office once, even if there were only 400 men at one time. Even under the democracy, a man was entitled to be a member of the *Boule* twice in his life, and with the strict equalisation of everyone's chances which prevailed there, the only logical deduction is that this provision was necessary to ensure that there were always at least 500 men willing and qualified to serve.

The final sentence of the chapter is either corrupt or very tortuous. The meaning may be that once the constitution described in xxx is brought into effect, the provisional *Boule* of 400 is to be allocated by the 100 men of xxx,3 to all four sections. They were presumably intended to be influential. Again, this is said to be 'for the future'—a phrase with an ominous ring to modern ears, when so many 'temporary' governments have somehow endured.

XXXII Aristotle now switches away from strictly constitutional analysis to actual events. There is no distinction in the text between the 'Five Thousand' and the 'main body' in the passing of the proposals and their ratification. Thucydides (viii,69,1) confirms that the establishment of the Four Hundred was ratified by the *Ekklesia* meeting at Colonus. The phrasing 'under the presidency of Aristomachos', without father's name or deme, is similar to the standard formula of inscriptions of the period. Aristomachos is otherwise unknown. Thargelion and Skirophorion are the last two months of the Athenian year, running from mid-May to mid-July approximately; the 'democratically selected *Boule*' would in the normal way have been chosen before the coup, and so could be referred to in the way it is here. Thucydides gives the details of the take-over of power in viii,69. The hiatus of eight days between the dissolution of the democratic *Boule* and the time when the Four Hundred took office was presumably covered because the Four Hundred had effective control although they had not as yet finalised and 'regularised' their position.

Aristotle sets the establishment of the Four Hundred in 411 (the end of the Archonship of Kallias) in the wide sweep of Athenian develop-

ment by referring back to the expulsion of the tyrants, as had Thucydides before him (VIII,68,4). For all the changes of the intervening
period, this was the first violent and total upset—a longer than average
period of stability in Greece. The three leading oligarchs are commended in glowing terms both by Thucydides and Aristotle, although
there is a sinister undertone to the passage of Thucydides on Antiphon.*
After the overthrow of the oligarchy, Antiphon was executed, Phrynichus had been assassinated, Peisander went into exile at Sparta, but
Theramenes had changed sides—his political opportunism is described
acidly by Lysias (*against Eratosthenes*, 66ff). He turns up again later as a
member of the Thirty in 404, as do Melobios and Kleitophon, who
were involved in the preliminaries of the coup of the Four Hundred
(XXIX,1 and 3); Mnasilochos (XXXIII,1) appears to have followed the
same course.

The final section states unambiguously that at the time the Four
Hundred took office the Five Thousand were only a possibility for the
future without any real existence, and also notes that the first move of
the oligarchs was an attempt to make peace on the basis of the status
quo; when the Spartans demanded the surrender of the naval empire,
they withdrew the proposal. Perhaps at this stage this was too much
even for them, though more probably their problem was that they
could not answer for the fleet at Samos, and the negotiations therefore
foundered. The Spartans were content to let Athens destroy herself for
a little longer before making a move. Here, as at the beginning of
XXXIII, Aristotle includes material not found in Thucydides.

XXXIII   The actual occasion of the fall of the Four Hundred was the
Spartan attack on Euboea described in Thucydides VIII,95. Euboea had
always been important for Athens as a source of food, and was doubly
so after 413, since the Spartan occupation of Deceleia had virtually
halted agriculture in Attica, and Athenian livestock had been transferred to the island. However, a contributory factor leading to their
overthrow after only four months was probably that they attempted to
retain power as a narrow oligarchy. At all events, Theramenes saw
which way things were moving for the second time, and joined the
agitation which led to the establishment of the Five Thousand (Thucydides VIII, 92). The title was not to be taken literally, for all those who
could supply arms for themselves (as hoplites) had full citizen rights;
there were many more than 5,000. In this respect, one may compare
the constitution ascribed to Draco in IV,1 and the constitution of
Boeotia in the Oxyrhynchus historian. Aristotle and Thucydides both
approve the compromise, reflecting their disapproval of radical democracy; Aristotle's words ring a little hollow after his warm praise for the
oligarchic extremists.

---

* VIII,68, where Phrynichus is also included among the leaders; his omission by
Aristotle is remarkable, particularly in view of the important part he plays in the
reference to these events at *Politics* 1305 b 27ff.

DEMOCRACY RESTORED

XXXIV The Five Thousand is not included by Aristotle in his list of the eleven changes of constitution at Athens, and he clearly regarded the overthrow of the Four Hundred as the change, and its successor as democracy. From this it follows that the actual constitution which succeeded the Four Hundred in 411 cannot have been identical with that described in xxx, though there were elements in common; otherwise Aristotle would surely have given details and included it as a twelfth change. Secondly, the transition from the Five Thousand to the full democracy was probably gradual. For some time before the Five Thousand had been working in full harmony with the fleet at Samos which had claimed to be the rightful Athenian democracy throughout the oligarchic usurpation.

Aristotle chooses to comment on only two events of the period between 410 and 404, the execution of the *strategoi* after Arginusae (406/5) and the refusal of Spartan peace terms shortly afterwards at the instigation of Cleophon. Both are no doubt selected as illustrations of the workings of the democracy, and are intended to be taken as typical. The Arginusae affair was certainly disgraceful, and the execution of the *strategoi* illegal in form, but Aristotle exaggerates, as also does Plato (*Apology* 32 b); only eight generals were present at the battle and indicted, and only the six who were injudicious enough to return to Athens were executed; cf. Xenophon, *History*, I,vi,27–vii,35. The peace terms are not mentioned by Xenophon, and are very similar to those which had been offered by Sparta after Cyzicus (410) and again rejected, probably on the urging of Cleophon. Cleophon was in favour of a vigorous war policy, but was clearly mistaken to reject the later proposals, and probably mistaken on the earlier occasion also; Aristotle accuses him of 'deceiving the people' (xxviii,3). He was very unpopular in some quarters (cf. *Frogs* 1504), and the breastplate might have been worn for protection, though it was more probably a theatrical gesture to discredit his opponents; compare Cicero at the time of the Catilinarian conspiracy. The cities whose surrender Cleophon demanded must presumably be those subject to Athens before the beginning of the war which had been captured by the Spartans or gone over to them.

The defeat of Athens inevitably involved a change of constitution, for the radical democracy had been consistently and implacably hostile to the Spartans. Again the phrase 'ancestral constitution' included by Aristotle in the treaty would have meant different things to different parties depending on their interpretation of earlier Athenian history. This was no doubt the reason for its use, for it would seem tolerable for the democrats, who would read it as implying the continuation of the essential elements of the democracy, while the Spartans were at liberty to interpret it in a far more oligarchic way, and so, once the peace had been accepted, enforce their will on a powerless city. The compulsory return of the exiles strengthened the oligarchic group, and was deliberate Spartan policy. The dispute is described by Diodorus (xiv,3,2–3), perhaps relying on Ephorus: 'The Athenians . . . made a treaty with the Spartans, which required them to take down their walls and revert to their ancestral constitution. They dismantled the walls, but did not agree about the constitution. Those aiming at an oligarchy said that the ancient organisation should be revived, according to which very few men had complete control; the majority of Athenians wanted a democracy and brought forward the constitution of their fathers and demonstrated that this was agreed to be a democracy.' Plutarch quotes the decree of the Ephors validating the actual peace, but, since it deals with the terms of surrender, perhaps naturally it contains no provision about the constitution (*Lysander* xiv); Xenophon also omits any mention of the constitution at this point (*History* ii,ii,20), though later he mentions the 'drafting of the ancestral constitution' in connexion with the appointment of the Thirty (ii,iii,2). Aristotle's statement is strong, though not decisive, evidence that there was at least some hint of a change of constitution in the originally negotiated terms.

Descriptions of the moves which led up to the overthrow of the democracy are conflicting. Lysias, in his speech *against Eratosthenes*, in attacking one of the Thirty, gives an account which is very hostile to Theramenes. He first describes how the extremists in the oligarchic clubs took control of the situation while the democracy was still nominally in control (§§43f); Critias figures largely here. Then in a long account (§§68–78) he describes the actions of Theramenes, implying that everything he did was designed to deceive and weaken the Athenians and ensure his own position. He went beyond the minimum terms demanded by the Spartans, and arranged the presence of Lysander at the decisive meeting of the *Ekklesia* to overawe any opposition. Significantly, Lysias claims the authority of Theramenes' own defence before the *Boule* for what he says. On the other hand, Diodorus (xiv,3,5–7) gives an account which is much more favourable to Theramenes, in which Lysander is the prime mover of the establishment of the Thirty, and Theramenes opposes him until threatened with execution. Aristotle appears to incline to the assessment of Lysias rather than that of Diodorus.

THE THIRTY AND THE TEN

XXXV Diodorus is the first surviving writer to use the term 'the Thirty Tyrants', which has become the accepted name for the group which took power in Athens in 404, although Aristotle describes their rule as 'tyranny' in xli,2; it is preferable to retain 'the Thirty', the term used by Xenophon, Aristotle and many other writers, omitting the word 'tyrants'. They are normally described as an extreme oligarchy, though they were in many ways more like a modern Latin-American military junta. According to Xenophon (*History* ii, iii, 2 and 11) they were appointed to draft the ancestral laws, but neglected to do so, and so retained supreme power. This is referred to obliquely by Aristotle in §1, but the phrase he uses might be read as implying that they should have done more than draft a constitution; if Aristotle had a tradition to this effect, it is now lost. The *Boule* of five hundred bears no relation to any previous *Boule*, for the history of the period shows that its functions were purely advisory, and it was no doubt designed to give the humbler supporters of the oligarchs a feeling of taking part in the government. The 'other magistrates' included the eight Archons in addition to Puthodoros; we do not know what other officials there were. Aristotle's text implies that (including the *Boule*) more than 500 appointments were made from a body selected from a larger group which itself numbered only 1,000; although there is no need to assume that the governors of the Peiraeus and the prison, let alone the 300 whip-bearers, came from this number, there may be something wrong with the text. The process of selection seems complicated if there were so few to choose from; perhaps one should read 'from the tribes' for 'from the thousand'. The governors of the Peiraeus and the prison were strong supporters of the Thirty—it is significant that they were among the few excluded from the general amnesty after the overthrow of the oligarchy (xxxix,6). The 'whip-bearers' were a gang of 'strong-arm men' used to enforce the will of the Thirty.

The removal of the laws concerning the Areopagus implies that the laws of Ephialtes curtailing its power were actually recorded there (cf. xxv,2), and their removal suggests that they were repealed and that the Areopagus may have recovered its old position, although this is not a necessary implication; the point is in any case theoretical since the Thirty allowed no exercise of power apart from their own.* Archestratos may have been a supporter of Ephialtes, though, if so, this passage is our only information about him; the name was not uncommon, and the reference could equally be to a later reformer. The laws of Solon which were abolished were probably those referred to in ix,2 above. Aristotle links the reform with the abolishing of the powers of the *dikastai*. He may mean that the *dikasteria* ceased to sit; however, one should probably take the reforms together, and read the latter provision as meaning that they abolished the right of the *dikastai* to interpret the law where it was not clear, particularly in view of the similarity of phrasing here and in ix,2. The example given at the end of §2 is the abolition of a provision which could obviously lead to litigation to decide, for example, whether a testator was in his right mind or not; however, this is not a matter of interpreting the law, but of judging the evidence. Litigation about inheritance was frequent and tiresome in Aristotle's own day; hence perhaps the example he selects, and his apparent approval of the measure. Excellent as it may be to reduce litigation, the frequency in modern legal codes of provisions similar to those which were suspended argues their necessity.†

* But see below on xlv.

† Note that the right to leave property outside the family existed only where there were no legitimate sons, and was subject to the claims of daughters and other male relatives in certain circumstances. This limitation presumably remained in force, but is not mentioned because Aristotle is discussing only provisions which caused disputes.

Informers were an inevitable result of the legal systems of both Greece and Rome. In neither was there any official comparable to the modern Public Prosecutor, and every case therefore had to be initiated by a private individual, cf. IX,I. Since there was an inherent risk in prosecuting because the decisions of juries were unpredictable and often rested on considerations other than a strict interpretation of the law and the facts, there had to be some sort of encouragement to people to undertake necessary but unpopular prosecutions—for example, those of politicians suspected of misappropriation of funds or misuse of their office. Prosecutions could be politically motivated, but it was usual for a leading politician not to take the risk involved; it was noted that Cleon was unusual in undertaking prosecutions himself, and in fact is said to have gained popularity by doing so. Hyperbolus also is said to have been fond of prosecuting (Scholiast on Aristophanes, *Acharnians* 846). Otherwise, encouragement to prosecutors was provided by the opportunity which a case gave to an aspiring young politician to make his mark, and also by provisions under which those successful received a reward. Inevitably, this in turn produced men willing to bring false charges in the hope of winning despite the facts. See further below on LIX. Such men were very unpopular, and the action of the Thirty in suppressing them was bound to meet with approval. It should be noted, however, that by suppressing them, the Thirty aimed not only to win popularity; they were also abolishing what they would have regarded as one of the worst vices of democracy. The figure of 1,500 murdered is probably the total for their period of rule, not, as Aristotle implies, only for a part of it.

XXXVI At this point the divisions in the ranks of the oligarchs come into the open. Theramenes may have always been inclined to a moderate form of oligarchy, something more akin to the Five Thousand he had supported before. Archinos and Kleitophon probably also supported this side; Archinos later went into exile and was a leader in the restoration of the democracy. The Thirty reacted with a typical delaying tactic comparable with the vague proposals about the Five Thousand propounded by the Four Hundred early in their period of power. It is a reasonable supposition that the Thirty never intended to bring the Three Thousand into any position of real power, even after they were eventually forced to publish the list. Theramenes returned to the attack on the basis that 3,000 was too few—the 'Five Thousand' he had supported may have numbered over 9,000 in fact—and on the basic premise that a government depending on force must be strong enough to govern. However, his attack was not immediately successful, and the Thirty retained their grip on the city. This whole chapter is very similar to Xenophon's account (*History* II,iii,15–20), though he implies that the Three Thousand were constituted without delay; both authors agree closely on Theramenes' views. Their difference on the narrative may indicate that Aristotle is not taking his account directly from

Xenophon, and that both authors had access to an account of what Theramenes actually said.

XXXVII The institution of the Thirty and their reign of terror had produced a large exodus of democrats who found refuge in the surrounding states, not least in Thebes. Although the Thebans had recently been so implacably hostile to Athens as to demand her total destruction when the peace of 404 was being discussed, they were now not merely horrified by the behaviour of the Thirty but also probably apprehensive of the enormous power of Sparta and the way she was using it. The exiles launched a daring attack on a remote fortress in north Attica called Phyle in January, 403. The failure of the Thirty in a counter-attack on the fort strengthened support for the insurgents, and probably in May they moved to Munichia and the Peiraeus (XXXVIII,1). In the interim Aristotle places the disarming of all the citizens except the Three Thousand, the execution of Theramenes and the introduction of a Spartan garrison on the Acropolis. This last move demonstrated the accuracy of Theramenes' assessment of the weakness of support for the Thirty. Xenophon, who was in Athens during the regime of the Thirty, dates the execution of Theramenes before the seizure of Phyle, and is to be followed here, and also in the suggestion that the Spartan garrison was introduced, and the people disarmed earlier. Xenophon's account of Theramenes' final speech and death (*History* II,iii,35–56) is a fine and dramatic piece of writing, interesting in the context of the hostility of the preceding account, and made all the more impressive by his statement that Critias struck Theramenes off the roll of the Three Thousand not in virtue of an enactment but solely by his power as leader of the Thirty. The violence on which the Thirty depended is admirably exemplified in the whole account. Theramenes' death resulted from an honourable stand, but can hardly be said to redeem his earlier career even if one does not accept fully the hostile view exemplified by Lysias, *against Eratosthenes* 67.

For the destruction of the fort at Eëtioneia and Theramenes' actions then, see Thucydides VIII,92,10; again Aristotle assumes that his audience knows what happened. One may connect the fact that the Thirty thought it necessary to explain the execution of Theramenes to the Spartans with the important part he had played in the peace negotiations of 404.

DEMOCRACY FINALLY RESTORED

XXXVIII The occupation of Munichia and its successful defence against the force sent by the Thirty led to the democrats occupying the Peiraeus; Critias had been killed in the attack on Munichia. The result was the deposition of the Thirty, and the substitution of a board of ten; they did not in fact 'bring the war to an end', but sent for Spartan help to reinforce the garrison on the Acropolis. Aristotle is alone in describing two successive boards of ten. If both are accepted, the first will have been some emergency group taking over from the

Thirty with aims similar to theirs, while the second will be the body of §3 who arranged the final reconciliation and the restoration of democracy. If there was in fact only one board of ten, it must have been a group of oligarchs who seized control after deposing the remnants of the Thirty. Certainty on this matter is impossible, but the evidence of Aristotle is not lightly to be disregarded.

By whatever means, a compromise was finally reached. Pausanias showed considerable statesmanship in effecting the reconciliation; he tacitly admitted that an oligarchy could be maintained in Athens only by force, and that this was neither desirable nor practicable without real support from a sizeable section of the population.

Xenophon's account of the sequence of events is superior to that of Aristotle; cf. *History* II,iv,1–39.

XXXIX The final reconciliation in 403 is dated in September by Plutarch. The settlement of the oligarchs and their supporters at Eleusis was the result of one of their last acts of tyranny (Xenophon, *History* II,iv,8–10); they had prepared the town as a retreat when they began to lose control of Athens, and had ejected or murdered a large number of the inhabitants—hence the superficially surprising provision in §3 which allowed only those citizens of Eleusis who then were acceptable to the oligarchs to stay in their own town. Eleusis was virtually independent of Athens until 401/0, when the surviving oligarchs were defeated and the town reunited with the rest of Attica; the leading oligarchs were murdered, the rest 'reconciled' (cf. XL,4 and Xenophon, *History* II,iv,43). The careful and detailed provisions about the temple and the priesthoods underline the importance of the Eleusinian Mysteries to all Athenians; the Kerukes and Eumolpidai were hereditary priests of the cult (cf. LVII,1).

The other details of the settlement as it affected Eleusis require no comment, but the whole document is remarkable for its good sense and equity. Only the core of the oligarchy—the Thirty, the Ten, the Eleven (the executioners) and the governors of the Peiraeus were excluded from the amnesty. The right of submitting to a *euthuna* was somewhat hollow; they were excluded from the amnesty for the crimes they had committed, and would have been putting their heads into a noose. The Ten referred to must be the first Ten if both boards are accepted (above, XXXVIII). In that case, presumably Rhinon went through the ordinary democratic *euthuna* (XXXVIII,4). If only one board is accepted, his position was all the more exceptional; he must have shifted from the oligarchic to the democratic side with great finesse.

XL Archinos is described as one of Thrasybulus' associates in restoring the democracy. Despite the lack of any condemnation here from Aristotle, his actions were not all admirable. His method of preventing too many people moving to Eleusis was illegal, but, as Aristotle says, he probably took the right decision; it prevented the secession of a large enough body to produce a real split in the state. What actual procedure be adopted is unknown; it must have been very abnormal. The democracy honoured the pledged amnesty, and as far as we know those who wished to go but did not do so were not legally victimised, however socially difficult their position may have been for a while.

The proposal of Thrasybulus to enfranchise those who had aided the return from the Peiraeus is a different matter. A scholiast gives fuller details: 'They trusted those who appeared to defend the laws. Archinos from Koile brought a charge for illegal proposal when the democracy was reestablished; Thrasybulus had proposed to grant citizenship to Lysias the Syracusan [the orator] because he had given five hundred shields to those fighting in Phyle and had hired three hundred mercenaries from Aegina. Archinos from Koile indicted him for an illegal proposal in that he had proposed a law when a *Boule* had not yet been constituted, and the jury condemned him for it. . . . Thrasybulus came forward in the discussion of the penalty, and said: "I judge myself worthy of death, for I did well by the Athenians, but they are ungrateful." The jury were ashamed, and fined him one drachma, but even so they did not make Lysias a citizen.' (Laurentian Scholion on Aeschines, *against Ctesiphon* 195). The story illustrates the difficulty of getting citizenship in a city other than one's own, for Lysias had not merely done the Athenians great services but had also lost his money, and his brother had been murdered by the Thirty; the action described here, together with the fact that Archinos blocked various proposals of crowns for those who had done good services in the return makes him seem somewhat less than magnanimous. His action in attacking someone for violating the amnesty was indeed right, for the only way of reestablishing the state after such a traumatic period was for the Athenians to turn their backs on the past, but it is legitimate to ask whether an illegal execution was the best way of reestablishing the rule of law; cf. XLV,1 with Commentary. At the same time, Archinos brought in a law to bar any actions brought in contravention of the settlement oaths (Isocrates, *against Callimachus* 2–3); clearly an influential man.

Lysias (*against Nicomachus* 22) suggests that the Athenians were in fact forced to refund the money borrowed by the oligarchs from Sparta. Despite this, Aristotle is right to praise the Athenian actions; one detects the note of surprise in what he writes—he did not normally find such virtue in democracies.

XLI After the anticipatory digression at the end of the previous chapter, Aristotle returns to his main theme. The apparent dating of the final establishment of democracy to the Archonship of Puthodoros is a year too early; the correct Archonship is given in XXXIX,1, and it seems that part of the sentence containing a reference to an event of the previous year is missing from the surviving text. The last sentence of §1 is again perhaps a slightly wry comment by Aristotle in view of his general opinion of democracy.

The stated total of eleven changes of constitution will work only if the constitution of Draco is not included; IV and XLI cannot be totally har-

monised. It has been noted above that there is every reason to reject the
content of IV on historical grounds, and perhaps reason to suspect that
it may have been an addition to the original text. The present passage
refers to 'the constitution of the time of Draco' and need not be read as
implying that there was any significant change in his day; Aristotle
mentions specifically only the passing of his 'laws'. The latter are
accepted as genuine, and the mention of his name here is probably
meant merely to place him in the chronological sequence; the existence
of the tradition which produced IV implies that he might have been
expected to feature in a list like the present one, and this may be why
Aristotle included him. The fact that he is included here in this way not
merely casts further doubt on the validity of IV but also makes it easier to
see how that chapter came to be included.

Of the other constitutions mentioned, those of Ion and Theseus were
discussed in the lost beginning of the papyrus; cf. the Appendix, p. 311.
Ion was the eponymous ancestor of the Ionians, and the four tribes at
Athens were supposed to be descended from his sons. None the less, the
Athenians believed that they were autochthonous, that is, that they had
always lived in Attica; yet Ion was a later arrival. They were trying to
maintain their claim to be autochthonous, of which they were very
proud, and reconcile it with their claim to be the hereditary leaders of
the Ionian Greeks. Theseus was traditionally responsible for making
Attica into one state. It is only after these two stages that we emerge
from the realms of myth into something which has a basis of historical
reality.

The other constitutions have been discussed in detail already.
Aristotle's slightly stilted comment on Aristides is a reference to the
development of the democracy after the Persian War; he quite rightly
not merely recognises that the change to Archonship by lot and the
other associated modifications of the constitution of Cleisthenes amount
to a new stage, which he calls 'the constitution after the Persian War',
but that there were changes between 478 and 462/1 which were significant enough to be worth mention although they do not merit the status
of a separate stage before Ephialtes. The radical democracy comes in
for some very harsh comment; the reader must decide how justified it is
in the light of the history of the period. The Five Thousand do not count
as a separate stage, again rightly, since they were more of a modification
which led directly to the restoration of democracy than a fully separate
constitution, however much Thucydides may have liked such a compromise. At the end of the enumeration of the constitutions, Aristotle
picks out the key characteristics of the constitution under which he
lived at Athens; the only redeeming feature appears to be that the
Athenians had devised a judicial system which was less easy to bribe
than some. His hostility is clearly implied, for all the admitted faults of
the democracy of the fourth century.

'Pay' for attendance in the *Ekklesia* was introduced about 400, though
the exact date is unknown; the fee was raised to three obols before 392
since it is referred to in Aristophanes, *Ekklesiazousai* 289–310; the way

in which it is mentioned may indicate that the sum had been recently raised. This last significant change before reaching the state of relative equilibrium which Aristotle describes as 'the present constitution' is indicative of the different spirit in Athens. Granted that in the fifth century meetings might be a hardship for dwellers in the country who were poor, nevertheless a sufficient number of people seem to have attended. After the restoration, the Athenians found that they could not get a reasonable attendance without some inducement; earlier men had been willing to make some sacrifice to perform their part in the government, but now this attitude had changed. The rapid rise from one to three obols is even more indicative; they were not prepared to accept a token, but only a sum which was reasonable compensation to a working man for the loss of a day's earnings.

Herakleides is an interesting exception to a general rule, for, as the text indicates, he was a native of Clazomenae, but was granted Athenian citizenship for his services in negotiations with the King of Persia (in 423 and afterwards); cf. Dittenberger, *Syll.* I³, 118.

THE ATHENIAN CONSTITUTION OF ARISTOTLE'S OWN DAY

Having described the historical development of the Athenian constitution, Aristotle turns to a detailed analysis of the various offices and institutions of his own day. The description is not fully applicable to the fifth-century democracy, but significant parts of it are, and they give us an invaluable insight into the details of government and administration which cannot emerge from the larger view of such historians as Thucydides and Xenophon. For them, the 'how' of political niceties is unimportant unless it had a direct bearing on the resultant action; we therefore get only a sporadic and fitful glimpse into procedure. Aristotle fills many of the gaps.

XLII Inclusion on the deme register was the basic proof of citizenship from the days of Cleisthenes, and enrolment took place before a man's fellow demesmen. Since 451/0 Pericles' citizenship law had required that both parents should be free and Athenian citizens, and the law had been reenacted after the fall of the oligarchy of 404/3. Nobody was admitted to full citizenship until he appeared to be eighteen; a man's age was the subject of investigation because there was no documentation of birth, and apparently many did not know their birthdays (cf. Plato *Lysis* 207 c). A man might produce evidence of the year of his presentation as an infant to the members of his father's phratry, or, if they could be found, witnesses to the Archonship in which he had been born. That disputes occurred shows that such evidence was not always available or decisive. That demesmen were fined for enrolling those who were judged to be under age (§2) will have ensured that they tried to avoid doing so.

There is no necessary contradiction between this passage and Aristophanes *Wasps* 578, where it is said that it is the privilege of the *dikastai* to decide on the maturity of the young men (and they much enjoyed their duty!); this would refer to the decision of disputed cases. Aristotle is, however, the only authority to assign the approval of the decision of the deme council on this to the *Boule*. The combination of passages implies that there was an appeal also from a decision that a man was too young; it would be surprisingly out of tune with normal Athenian practice if a relatively small body like the deme council could take such a decision without appeal being possible. If this deduction is correct, Aristotle's phrasing is less clear than it might be. Once enrolled in a deme, a man was officially of the age indicated by his enrolment class, and this dictated his military service and also when he would be eligible for positions like membership of the *Boule* which were restricted to those over thirty. Equally, the deme lists were used for selecting men to perform liturgies, to pay capital levies (*eisphorai*), and for other purposes.

An accusation that a man was not free born was serious. The Greek for 'free' probably implied also the possibility of acceptance as a full member of the community; a man could be rejected either for being of slave parentage or for being a foreigner. A man who failed to be enrolled on a deme list for one of these reasons was sold into slavery; the penalty was fitting for the son of slaves, who was a slave unless specifically freed. It is probably this class which Aristotle has in mind; to treat the sons of foreigners this way would have been unjust, particularly as they could not have been legally responsible for starting what the *dikasteria* had judged to be a fraudulent attempt to obtain citizenship.* Rhodes (499ff) would take 'free' in the narrower sense of 'free' as opposed to 'slave'.

The period of Ephebic training lasted for two years, and had been modified just before Aristotle wrote; exactly what it involved is controversial. From the age of eighteen, all Athenians were liable to military service, and it appears that from perhaps as early as the second quarter of the fifth century the first two years of this liability involved the young men in some form of service which included training to fit them to take a full place in the defence of their city thereafter. Aristotle describes the duties of the Ephebes as 'patrolling the countryside and manning the guard posts'; similarly, Thucydides says that the 'youngest' of the citizens were involved in defence against invasions (II,13,7). On the other hand, this training was not continuous, for we know of many young Athenians who continued their ordinary lives when they would have been Ephebes, for example Glaukon, who is recorded as having tried to speak in the *Ekklesia* when he was not yet twenty (Xenophon, *Memorabilia*, III,6,1). In other words, the liability of the Ephebes was very similar to, and perhaps identical with, that of every other adult male citizen: to serve in the armed forces when required. This had

* A. W. Gomme, *Essays in Greek History* 75ff; apart from attempted false enrolment as a citizen, a man could also be sold into slavery for failure to repay a ransomer if he had been captured, enslaved and then redeemed as, for example, Plato was.

changed by Aristotle's own day, when the Ephebes were required to serve continuously for their two-year period of training; the change may have been instituted by a law of Epikrates in 336/5.*

Under the new system, the Ephebes during their training garrisoned the two forts mentioned in the text which protected the harbour of the Peiraeus (cf. LXI,1), and, after completing a year's basic instruction, other guard posts near the land frontiers of Attica. They learnt the basic skills necessary to make them useful members of the mainly hoplite army, though some will have started to acquire these skills earlier in the gymnasia. The whole process, and their way of life, is reminiscent of the training of the young Spartans, though, of course, it lasted for only a short period. The care with which they were relieved of all outside calls on their time indicates how important this period was felt to be. It should be noted that although technically all citizens, that is all adult males enrolled on the deme lists, were entitled to attend the *Ekklesia*, in practice the Ephebes were now not free to do so.

An exception to their concentration on military affairs was made in the case of lawsuits concerned with inheritance and *epikleroi*, as well as the obvious and expected case where a man had to take up a family priesthood. *Epikleroi* were daughters of a family where there were no male children; the family property passed through them, though they were not what we would describe as heiresses, for they could not dispose of the property in their own right—women in most states in Greece had no right to own property in the fullest sense, the most notable exception being Sparta. Property was vital, and had to stay within the family group if possible.† The laws about *epikleroi* were designed to ensure this, and also to protect a woman if her father died. In that case, the nearest male relative could claim the orphaned girl in marriage, and the property would pass to the offspring of the marriage; male relatives were required by law to provide a girl with a dowry if one of them did not marry her himself. A dowry was normal, and had to be repaid if there was a divorce; it was regarded as part of the father's estate set apart for the maintenance of the daughter, and it is important that Athenian law always required a man in possession of his wife's dowry to maintain her. It seems probable that more girls than boys survived infancy, and this combined with battle casualties must have ensured that there was some competition for girls to marry—hence the dowry became more important. In practice both divorce and remarriage were apparently quite common, and young widows were normally expected to marry a second time.

XLIII The standard democratic principle that officers responsible for administration should be selected by lot was not impractical because

* See O. W. Reinmuth, 'The Ephebic Inscriptions of the Fourth Century B.C.', *Mnemosyne* Suppl. B. 14, 1971, 123–38.

† cf. W. K. Lacey, *The Family in Classical Greece*, 125ff on property, and 139–45 on *epikleroi*.

their duty was to carry out, or supervise the carrying out of, decisions made by the *Ekklesia*; they did not initiate policy themselves. The only deterrent which may have ensured a minimum degree of competence was that they had to undergo a *euthuna* at the end of their year of office; this was an investigation at which their accounts were checked and they were also answerable for their official actions during their tenure of office (cf. LIV,2). It has been suggested that this was enough to stop the really incompetent from putting themselves forward.

On the other hand, even the most extreme democrats recognised that there were certain positions in which expertise was essential; the military officers mentioned here are the clearest case, for the lives of those under their command depended on their ability. These officials were always elected, and were also exempt from the normal rule which dictated that any particular office should only be held once by any one man; cf. LXII,3. Aristotle here lists some other exceptions. The treasurer of military funds (probably a fourth-century post) worked closely with the *strategoi*. The Theoric fund was established to supply Athenians who could not afford it with the two-obol entrance fee to the theatre of Dionysus. By the mid-fourth century it was more important, since all surplus revenue of the state went into it. Separate magistrates in charge of the fund were probably instituted about this time, and were very important by Aristotle's day. Similarly, the chronic shortage of water in Athens made the supervisors of the water supply important. The phrase 'from one Panathenaic festival to the next' refers to the Great Panathenaia, celebrated once every four years; therefore these three groups of magistrates also went contrary to the usual principle that no office was held for more than a year. Meiggs/Lewis 72, lines 1–2 contains an exactly parallel period of office. The offices Aristotle lists required expertise, which explains why their holders were elected, and perhaps why they held office for four years rather than one.

A council of 500 such as the *Boule* could be democratic only if it were selected by lot; ideally, nobody would be a member more than once in his life, but in Athens it was found necessary to allow two terms in order to ensure enough qualified and willing candidates, though two consecutive terms were not allowed (cf. LXII,3).

The detailed analysis of the workings of the Prytany system is vital, for the Prytanies formed the only body that was more or less permanently on duty. Each tribe's members of the *Boule* formed the Prytany for one tenth of the year; in the fourth century the lunar year dictated that their periods of office should not be absolutely the same length, since it contained 354 days.* Before 407 the prytany year was distinct from the Archon's lunar year, and close to the solar year. The Prytanies ate together in the Tholos, a round building in the south-west corner of the Agora, next to the Bouleuterion where the *Boule* usually met. From the

---

* Periods added to the calendar ensured that the lunar year was approximately harmonised with the solar year; see *OCD²s.v.* 'Calendars' with references.

fifty members a chairman was selected each day by lot, and he was on duty for twenty-four hours, sleeping in the Tholos with one third of the Prytanies. They thus provided a standing committee who could at any time initiate action if necessary. In addition, they received messages as they arrived in the city, e.g. the embassies mentioned in §6. Details of the Prytanies' duties are given in XLIV, 1–3. There is an important distinction between the fourth century as Aristotle describes it and the fifth. Until late in the fifth, the Prytanies, and in particular each chairman, presided over all meetings summoned during his day in office. This meant that there was a very reasonable chance of a man chairing a meeting of the *Boule*, for it met on every day except public holidays;* in the normal way there were four meetings of the *Ekklesia* in each prytany, and the chairman for the day presided there as well. Since there was a better than 70 per cent chance of each member of the *Boule* presiding over the Prytanies, there was a very real possibility of any member having to preside over a vital meeting of one of the other bodies. That they did so without disaster is a high tribute to the competence of the average members of the *Boule*. The above arrangements were changed late in the fifth century to those described in XLIV,2, but this is no indication that the system had broken down; the aim seems to have been to divorce the presidents for the meetings where decisions were made from the Prytanies of the period, presumably because the Prytanies were deeply involved in the preliminary drafting of proposals, and it was therefore felt that they could be over-influential if they presided at the *Ekklesia* as well. The reform was aimed at even greater democratic equality, not at increased efficiency; it also gave all ten tribes a share in presiding throughout the year. The date when the system was changed is unknown, but may have been as late as 378/7.

   Aristotle digresses from his discussion of the mechanics of the workings of the *Boule*, which leads into a full analysis of its duties, to outline the topics discussed obligatorily once a month by the *Ekklesia*; the transition is effected naturally from the point that it was the duty of the *Boule* to include these items on the agenda which it drew up. The list itself (§§4–6) requires little comment; most of the individual topics are discussed further below; for ostracism, see above on XXII. The list which Aristotle gives does not, of course, cover all the topics discussed by the *Ekklesia*, but only those which were mandatory at particular meetings. The main function of the *Ekklesia* is implicit rather than explicit throughout his discussion: it had to decide everything of moment in all aspects of government. Discussions had usually to be initiated on the basis of a preliminary motion from the *Boule* (*probouleuma*), though this might only amount to a proposal that a topic should be discussed, and on rare occasions a discussion might take place

---

* The apparently large number of festivals in the ancient world can be misleading; there was then no seven-day week with a rest day built into it. Our modern weekends give 104 days a year when public business is not normally conducted, and it is unlikely that the total of festival days was much higher in fifth- or fourth-century Athens, high though their total was; see Ps. Xenophon, *Constitution of the Athenians* III,2.

without a preliminary motion. There was apparently a preliminary show of hands as to whether the motion of the *Boule* should be put to the *Ekklesia*; cf. §6. It was also open to the *Ekklesia* to pass a motion requiring the *Boule* to put a particular matter on the agenda for the next meeting.

The *Ekklesia* met on the Pnyx, a hill near the Acropolis, and the speakers spoke from a platform which was eleven feet high, from which both the sea and the Acropolis were visible. Meetings were well attended in the fifth century, although they involved participants in losing a day's earnings—a sign of the healthy spirit of involvement of the community in the city's affairs. The introduction of a fee for attendance about the year 400 indicates a change of mood, and must suggest that attendances had been falling; further evidence was the use of a rope covered with red chalk to 'sweep' those in the agora into meetings (Scholiast on Aristophanes, *Acharnians* 22)—anyone whose clothes were marked with the red who was not at the meeting was liable to a penalty; cf.xLI,3 and comment above. For a comic description of a meeting of the *Ekklesia* see Aristophanes, *Acharnians* 17–173.

Meetings were opened by priests purifying the assembly and reciting prayers, and the motions were then put forward, with the compulsory items listed by Aristotle coming first. The herald and the Scythian bowmen kept order, and speakers were required to keep to the point, speak on one subject at a time, and avoid scurrility, though one may legitimately doubt whether this regulation was observed meticulously. Anyone could speak, though members of the assembly were a critical audience quite prepared to shout down anyone they did not wish to listen to, or whom they regarded as incompetent. At the end of the speeches on a particular topic, a vote was if necessary taken on the motion put forward by the *Boule*; amendments were in order and could be voted on. Voting was normally by show of hands, though black and white pebbles were used for a form of secret ballot in important matters which affected individuals, particularly where loss of citizen rights or other severe punishment might result from the vote. The meeting was adjourned if any natural phenomenon occurred which could be interpreted as a bad omen, including rain, though this has an obvious practical reason for an assembly held in the open; for examples, see Aristophanes, *Acharnians* 171 (a joke?); *Clouds* 581–6; Thucydides V,45,4. If this happened, or if the business on the agenda was not completed, the meeting was reconvened the next day. Any emergency situation resulted in an immediate meeting of th *Ekklesia* outside the normal schedule.

One might easily overestimate the importance of the *Boule* and underestimate that of the *Ekklesia* from Aristotle's account; the impression is balanced by the works of the historians, who regularly talk of the *Ekklesia* and rarely of the *Boule*. The reason for this contrast is that Aristotle is concentrating on the mechanics of the constitution, and how proposals were formulated and came up for final decision, a process in which the *Boule* had a vital part to play; the historians are more interested in the actual decisions taken. One must always remember the detailed control exercised by the *Ekklesia*, not merely over major matters of policy, such as war and peace and alliances, but also over what we regard as administrative decisions. They appointed the generals for an expedition, fixed the size of the forces, and gave detailed instructions on the conduct of the campaign from which the commanders in the field diverged at their peril. For example, the generals sent to Sicily in 425–4 were convicted on their return; their offence was that they had made peace without the specific instructions of the *Ekklesia*—though they had been presented with a situation in which they had no other choice. No doubt, the political consequences for the individual *strategos* resulting from such use of initiative depended on the success or failure of the action in question. Equally, the internal control of the *Ekklesia* extended to such details as approving the designs for new temples. For a detailed discussion of the functions of the *Boule*, see the following pages.

The procedure for accusations described in §5 was used against those who had forced the illegal trial of the generals after the battle of Arginusae; cf. Xenophon, *History* I,vii,34. It is of interest that metics were entitled to lay information as well as citizens; presumably here, as in other official actions, the formalities were conducted through the Athenian citizen who looked after their interests; cf. below on LVIII. On informers see above on XXXV.

XLIV The first three sections are discussed above (see on XLIII); one small point remains. The main repository of the treasure of Athens was the 'rear room' (*Opisthodomos*) of the Parthenon; the text says 'sanctuaries', but the Greek need not imply more than one place, although it could; the public records were kept in the Bouleuterion, and later in the Metroon. Needless to say, custody of the keys does not imply that the chairman had any part in the administration of the treasure or records.

Elections were held in the seventh prytany, and, if they were not unduly delayed by bad omens, this would mean that the officers mentioned in §4 would be elected about four months before they took office. The interval was necessary for the investigation of their eligibility at the *dokimasia*, and for substitutions should any be rejected. To have a preliminary motion by the *Boule* for the elections when they came at a fixed point and were not amenable to a motion in the ordinary sense is at first sight odd, but is necessary in the light of the provision that nothing could normally be handled by the *Ekklesia* which was not the subject of a preliminary motion (XLV,4). On the individual officers mentioned, see below on LXI.

XLV The incident involving Lusimachos and Eumelides is otherwise unknown. The most plausible interpretation places it in the immediate aftermath of the overthrow of the oligarchy in 403, for in the later fifth century the *Boule* had certainly lost any powers of arbitrary arrest and execution they may have had at an earlier period; their summary jurisdiction was limited to a maximum fine of 500 drachmae, which, while not trivial, was not enormous. There were also limits on their powers of summary arrest; see the oath taken by members of the *Boule*, above on XXII. Demosthenes says that these limitations had been imposed by Solon (*against Timocrates* 148), but this cannot be so; he could not have reduced the powers of a body he created. In all probability the limitation was imposed at the time of the reforms of Ephialtes, and was included in the transference of all important judicial power to the *dikasteria*. Thereafter, if the *Boule* decided that the case demanded a more severe penalty than they were competent to inflict, they recommended accordingly, and passed the case to the *dikasteria* for a full trial and final decision. Apart from the fact that the powers of the *Boule* were probably greater before 462/1, the Areopagus certainly had wide-ranging authority at an early stage in Athenian history. It is therefore plausible to suggest that we have in the case of Lusimachos evidence that the oligarchs had revived some of these dormant powers in their recreation of the 'ancestral constitution'—witness also the 'trial' of Theramenes before the *Boule* under the Thirty—and that for a short while in a crisis situation the *Boule* of the restored democracy usurped similar powers until they were challenged and fifth-century democratic restrictions reimposed; cf. XL,2. The case of Lusimachos may well have been the moment when they were challenged. There is evidence that he had been involved with the Thirty (Xenophon, *History* II,iv,8), and the form of penalty he escaped confirms that he had been accused of being involved in the execution of citizens without trial.*

Similar restrictions are also specifically mentioned as applying to the other judicial functions of the *Boule*: the reviewing of the conduct of magistrates, and the investigation of the credentials of the next year's *Boule* and Archons at the *dokimasia*. The procedure under the radical democracy was the result of historical development. At first, the *Boule* and Archons had wide judicial powers; then appeal was introduced in serious cases under Solon; appeal by one side or the other gradually became the regular practice, until in the later fifth century the hearings before magistrates and others with similar powers became in the main preliminary formalities. Those who presided over the hearings gave a decision, but it was not binding unless both sides accepted it voluntarily. The normal function of the hearing was parallel to that of our magistrates' courts: the pleadings were heard and recorded, but the real trial was before a jury in the *dikasteria*. The effect of the preliminary hearing was to limit the field that would be disputed at the main hearing, for it was not permitted to introduce at that stage considerations

---

* The penalty was *apotumpanismos*, a cruel and lingering death by torture. Not all criminals were executed by the relatively humane cup of hemlock—indeed it is possible that hemlock did not come into use until the period of the Thirty right at the end of the fifth century; it was used in the fourth century, though by no means for all executions; cf. R. J. Bonner and G. Smith, *The Administration of Justice from Homer to Aristotle* II, 279ff.

or testimony that had not been raised at the preliminary hearing; cf. LIII with Commentary.

In XLV–XLIX Aristotle describes the functions of the *Boule* in administration and in relation to the other state officials. Individual points which need clarification will be discussed first, and the overall position of the *Boule* after the details have been clarified.

The investigation of the magistrates each prytany was conducted with the aid of auditors selected from the *Boule* (XLVIII,3); a good example of use by the people of the right of complaint against a magistrate and his subsequent deposition and fine is the case of Pericles in 430 (Thucydides II,65,2–3). Antiphon (*on the Choreutes*, 49) gives examples of actions against a number of different officials before the *Boule* initiated in this way. There was apparently no appeal from an acquittal by the *Boule* under this procedure. The process of the *dokimasia* is described in detail in LV.

The provision that everything which went before the *Ekklesia* must do so after a preliminary discussion by the *Boule* was of key importance. It prevented 'snap' decisions since it imposed a certain period of time between the raising of a subject and the final vote (as also did the requirement that the agenda should be published in advance of the meeting), and it ensured that everything was discussed in a body whose size made proper consideration of technical and complicated issues easier than it would be in the *Ekklesia*, though even 500 must have been uncomfortably large for some discussions. In complex matters the proposal of the *Boule* was often accepted as drafted. The procedure was not rigid, as implied by Plutarch, *Solon* 19, but could be circumvented. Demosthenes (*on the Crown* 169) describes how. in the crisis after the capture of Elateia, the *Ekklesia* had assembled before the *Boule* had had time to produce a proposal, and they therefore just introduced the subject for discussion; cf. above on XLIII.

The indictment for illegal proposals was introduced at some period in the fifth century as a check on the fully developed democracy. Those who argue that the Areopagus had extensive supervisory powers to preserve constitutionality before 462/1 frequently also argue that the indictment for illegal proposals was substituted at that date for the powers which had been abolished. However, the first definitely known cases are the prosecution of Speusippos by Leogoras in 415 and the prosecution of the general Demosthenes by Antiphon at about the same time. It seems unlikely that the statute was on the book for forty-five years without being used, or that it was used but we know nothing of the cases. It is more probable that it was introduced at a later date when the dangers of the unchecked democracy were becoming apparent. It covered illegality of drafting or a proposal which clashed with an existing law; the indictment could be brought against either a proposal or a motion already passed by the *Ekklesia*. The objector undertook to bring a prosecution under the statute, and the proposal was then 'frozen' until the case had been tried; the proposer of the indicted measure was only personally liable for punishment for a year, but the trial could be heard after any length of time. Thus it became a useful way of obstruction which need not involve a man in an actual penalty as long as the trial was suitably delayed. In the fourth century it was severely abused; Aristophon is said to have been acquitted seventy-five times! When properly used, it was a valuable constitutional safeguard; as abused it could be a menace.

XLVI Though, like everything else, under the general control of the *Ekklesia*, the supervision of the navy and everything to do with it was peculiarly the province of the *Boule*; the details are given here. Diodorus (XI,43,3), dealing with the period about 477, refers to the *Boule* having twenty new ships constructed, but there is no certainty that this was normal; *Anon. Argent.* 1,11 implies ten a year. Probably in Aristotle's day the vote of the *Ekklesia* (§1) specified how many were to be built. The election by the *Ekklesia* of the naval architects to build the ships is a good instance of the all-pervasive democratic control of what we should regard as technical matters. The members of a *Boule* which was judged to have done its duty well were rewarded with crowns; Demosthenes (*against Androtion* 8) confirms this, and also supports the specific point that the *Boule* were debarred from receiving the crowns unless they had had the requisite ships built. Aeschines (*against Ctesiphon* 30) implies that the board of ten who were responsible for the building of the triremes were picked by the tribes; perhaps the choice of the tribes was ratified by the *Boule*, but the instance he mentions may have been an unusual burden on the tribes, not the normal procedure.

The mention of quadriremes in the passage is of interest; their construction is first recorded at Athens in 330/29, while quinqueremes first appear in the surviving records in 325/4. The Archonship of Kephisophon is mentioned in LIV,7, and gives a terminus post quem for the *Constitution of Athens*, 329/8. Combining the two pieces of information, one arrives at a tentative date of 328–5 for the composition of at least the later section of the book.

The inspection of public buildings presumably refers to new constructions, and was aimed to detect any faults or defalcations on the part of the builder. It is not easy to see how it could have been applied to already completed structures which were in use; any faults in the administration of them would be detected at the *euthuna* of the magistrate responsible at the end of his term of office. Note that offences of this class were reported to the *Ekklesia*, not to an official or the *dikasteria*.

XLVII The theme of the next section is the supervision exercised by the *Boule*; Aristotle lists a number of boards responsible for particular aspects of the administration, and includes them here because their important actions had to take place in front of the *Boule*. Thus the *Boule* acted as the City's witnesses of what happened, and ensured that duties were carried out properly.

Treasurers were originally selected from the richest class of citizens (cf. VIII,1) because it was felt that the temptation to petty embezzlement would be less; that the law was disregarded by the late fourth century is no surprise; compare the parallel case of the Thetes mentioned in VII,4. The Treasurers of Athena were responsible for the safe-keeping of large sums of money and very considerable treasures, but, as with the other offices filled by lot mentioned in this section of the work, they had no administrative responsibility which would have required expertise. All decisions were taken by the people; the responsibility of the officials was only to ensure the safety of what was in their charge, receive what was paid in, and pay out sums when instructed to do so by the people.

The 'image of Athena' is the famous statue by Pheidias; the value of the gold on the statue was given by Thucydides (II,13,5) as 40 talents of refined gold, while Philochorus (Jacoby, *F.Gr.H.* III B 323 F 121) gives 44 talents. This represents 560 or 616 talents of silver (the normal currency unit), since the ratio between gold and silver in the later fifth century was 14:1. Although it was removable, there is no evidence that the Athenians ever used any of this gold even in the darkest days of the Peloponnesian War, and it was therefore presumably still there in Aristotle's day. Gold statues of Victory were an accepted way of 'storing' surplus revenue. Ten are known in the late fifth century, of which eight were melted down to make gold coins in 407/6; others are mentioned in the fourth century, notably those in Plutarch, *Moralia* 841D: '(Lycurgus) constructed gold and silver ceremonial vessels for the city and gold Victories'; the date was 334. The ceremonial equipment would have been chariots, jewelry and many other things used in the major festival processions to the gods. For all of this, as well as the ordinary cash reserves of the city, the Treasurers were responsible, and the accounts were handed over from one board to the next in front of the *Boule*, and subject to the normal review at the end of a man's tenure of office.

The word '*poletai*' means literally 'sellers', though from the description of their duties they appear to have been rather controllers of public contracts. The post of treasurer of military affairs was established in 338, and replaced the officials called 'Treasurers of the Greeks' who had originally been established to handle the money of the Delian League, and come to be the treasurers of Athens' war effort when the League became effectively the Athenian Empire. On the Theoric Fund, see above on XLIII; the officials of the Fund referred to here were established in the second half of the fourth century. Public contracts of whatever sort were the responsibility of the *poletai*, working in conjunction with the *Boule* and presumably also the *Ekklesia* where any policy decision had to be taken. Taxes were not collected directly by the Athenians, but the right to collect them was sold to private individuals who then recouped the price from what they collected, together with some profit, though there is no evidence of massive exploitation such as that practised at times by the Roman tax-farmers, presumably because they were collecting taxes from Athenians, not subject peoples; the collection of the tribute was never farmed out in this way.

The position about mines is obscure. They remained the property of the state, and what was sold was the right to work them for a period; the lessee had to pay a price and one twenty-fourth of the value of the precious metal mined. We do not know what lies behind the distinction between three- and ten-year contracts, but logic might suggest that the three-year contracts covered mines which were known to be profitable, while what I have translated as 'special agreements' covered the right to explore an unknown area and mine if any precious metal were discovered; the financial position in the latter case is unknown.*

In many cases those on capital charges were allowed to withdraw from Athens before the final stage was reached, and so avoid execution. Their property was forfeit and the procedure for its sale is described in §2; those exiled by the Areopagus were listed separately because they would have been guilty of crimes involving religious pollution; cf. LVII,3 with Commentary. At a time of general amnesty and recall of exiles, this class of offenders was specifically excluded. The whitened boards referred to were the normal vehicle for transitory public records, as here for lists of various forms of debts and payments which had to be recorded for a period, but did not require the permanence of a stone inscription. Lists of property sold by the state were inscribed on stone; see for example the fragmentary lists of the sale of the property of those involved in the mutilation of the Hermae (414), Meiggs/Lewis, 79.

The categories of debts which had to be repaid at various intervals are not known, though Aristotle sheds some light here. An interesting point is the arrangements for repayment of large capital sums over a period. The period allowed for the repayment of the price of a house may be compared with the statement by Isaeus (*on the Estate of Hagnias* 42) that property worth 35 minae brought in 3 minae per annum— i.e. one recovered the purchase price in under twelve years. In these terms, the period allowed for payment to the state was not ungenerous. It is not surprising that the King Archon was responsible for the collection of the rent from sacred property, for his particular preserve was the administration of religious affairs; see LVII and commentary. Again, the mechanics of all these payments were supervised by the *Boule*, and the system carefully devised to avoid anything being done in the wrong way or at the wrong time. The word translated as 'pigeon holes' is normally used of something resting on something else, for instance the architrave on the columns of a building; the exact connotation in the present passage is not certain, but the general meaning must be that given.

XLVIII The Receivers were officers instituted under Cleisthenes whose function was the corollary of the *poletai*; again, it is a typical democratic check that there were two boards of ten who effectively checked each other where a modern state might well employ the same

* On mining in Attica, see R. J. Hopper, 'The Laurion Mines; a reconsideration', *BSA* 63 (1968) 293–326; for other possible interpretations, see Rhodes, 553f.

people for both sides of the transaction. The penalties for defaulting on payment were severe; to the details given here should be added the statement of Demosthenes (*against Nikostratos* 27) and Andocides (*on the Mysteries* 73) that the debtor's property was seized and sold to cover the amount due. Thus the *Boule* 'exacts the money', and imprisonment was presumably employed only if the sum realised did not cover the debt. The division of money referred to was the allocation to magistrates of funds needed for the performance of their duties. See also LII,3.

The auditors mentioned in §3 are not to be confused with those mentioned in LIV,2; the present body handled the month-to-month accounts of officials, while the latter investigated their accounts at the end of the year. The officials selected for the *euthuna* worked with the second group of auditors on the annual investigation of the magistrates, for which see LIV,2. The detail here that those whose investigation had been concluded in the *dikasteria* were still liable to be tried if a complaint was made within three days of the first hearing is interesting; everything possible was done to make it possible for a private citizen to get an airing for a grievance. It is probable that these accusations were made in the Athenian Agora, where statues of the eponymous heroes stood, but certainty is impossible in view of the state of the text; see note in the translation *ad loc*. The provision that the official must think the charge justified before the case can be reopened is a necessary check on totally frivolous accusations; hearings before the *dikasteria* were time-consuming and cost the city money in fees to the jurors. On the deme justices, see below on LIII.

XLIX The first two sections deal with elements of the armed forces where the state gave financial assistance to those enrolled in them; there was naturally a check on the recipients to make sure that money was not being spent to no purpose. The cavalry received a grant to cover the upkeep of horses, but there were other expenses on armour and equipment, and they had to maintain a mounted servant; hence it was not possible for a poor man to serve, and poverty was accepted as an excuse if a man had been summoned for cavalry service. The infantry attached to the cavalry worked closely with them on foot, and therefore had to be very fit to keep up; hence again it was essential to ensure that they were capable of fulfilling their duty.

The remainder of the chapter covers a few minor functions of the *Boule*. The Greek word translated as 'models' probably covers the plans for any major public undertaking, for example a temple, but would probably include also less important items such as the statues of Victory mentioned in §4 (cf. XLVII,1, with Commentary). The robe was woven for the statue of Athena, and taken up to the Acropolis during the Great Panathenaia; scenes in the design included the battle between Athena and the Giants. The date of the transference of the inspection of these things to the *dikasteria* is unknown.

The maintenance of the disabled at public expense started under

Peisistratus, and was at first limited to those disabled by war wounds (Plutarch, *Solon* 31). Later anyone incapable of maintaining himself was included; the date of the change is unknown, but all were covered before the end of the fifth century when Lysias (*on the Refusal of a Disability Pension* 26) refers to a pension of this type which had been drawn for some years already; the speech was delivered shortly after 403. This rare example of 'social conscience' in the ancient world arose from the strong corporate sense of the city state: the first duty of every citizen was to do whatever the city required of him, and the corollary was that he had a claim on the city for a minimum subsistence if he was absolutely incapable of maintaining himself by his own efforts through no fault of his own.

Thus, with the first sentence of chapter L, Aristotle concludes his analysis. The prominence of the *Boule* at Athens after 462/1 was the direct result of the triumph of radical democracy, and the body itself was symptomatic of it. The principle of selection by lot combined with rotation ensured that it consisted of a cross-section of the people, and that a large proportion of the citizens would be members at least once. In this way they had a say in the detailed planning of every aspect of government by the drafting of decrees and motions for the *Ekklesia*, and in the day-to-day supervision of all officials — an aspect of the duties of the *Boule* which Aristotle rightly stresses at the beginning and end of his discussion. Their control was the only thing which stood in the way of anarchy in the administration of finance, and the regular checks on all those handling public money ensured its proper use. The *Boule* apparently had little initiative, but its role was vital; the drafting of complex decrees is a difficult operation, and once drafted they were unlikely to be frequently or radically altered in the *Ekklesia* because of the sheer practical difficulties involved in doing so. The role of the *strategoi* in guiding these detailed discussions must have been important. From the details Aristotle gives it is easy to see why the *Boule* was permanently behind schedule; cf. *Constitution of the Athenians* III,1. Above all, one must remember the part it played in the political education of the average citizen; the fact that there would have been present at any meeting of the *Ekklesia* a significant number of people with personal experience of the functioning of the *Boule* and the day-to-day administration of government through the many administrative boards selected from its members must have contributed greatly to the wisdom and good sense of the decisions taken by the people as a whole.

L After discussing the *Boule*, Aristotle turns to other boards and officers selected by lot, most of whom had minor duties; it appears that these officials were not members of the *Boule*. From the small sum allocated to those in charge of the sanctuaries, they cannot have had any very important function to perform. The city commissioners are also mentioned in Aristotle's *Politics* (1321 b 18ff), where their duties are listed in similar terms, though there he adds that they are responsible for collapsed buildings (presumably to make sure that they are safe and do not obstruct the street), for the general safety and repair of the streets, and for boundaries between property. The entertainers referred to were hired for drinking-parties given by ordinary citizens—the price is not high (cf. Plato, *Protagoras* 347 d); the wealthy presumably had their own entertainers. Civic control of prices and the way in which 'double bookings' were fairly resolved are remarkable examples out of the many instances where the Athenian state intervened in what are normally thought to be private matters.

The disposal of refuse was a major problem since there was no sewage system; it is referred to not infrequently in the surviving literature. A decree of 320 affecting the Peiraeus also deals with the problem of rubbish, though there the duty of seeing that it is cleared up rests on the householder, with the superintendents of the market responsible for ensuring that it is done (Dittenberger *Syll.* 1³,313). The building regulations are all designed to ensure the safety of passers by; the reference to windows is a trifle obscure, since Greek houses normally did not have windows on the ground floor on the street, though this may have been because of the ban mentioned. If it was a well-known regulation, it is hard to see why anyone should have thought of breaking it. There is an interesting parallel from Rome, where Plutarch records (*Poplicola* 20) the practice in Greece of knocking on a door from the inside to warn passers-by before opening it on to the street; later, doors opening outwards were banned. The removal of corpses from the streets indicates a section of the population who were destitute and without any home to go to or anyone to look after them.

LI In the markets, also, the Athenians went to some trouble to ensure fair dealing and fair prices, even specifying the size of loaves. The increase of the numbers of commissioners of the corn supply may indicate that they found plenty to do; it was vital for the survival of Athens that enough should be brought into the city, and for the individual Athenian that it should be honestly sold.

LII The death penalty was mandatory for the offences listed, and was inflicted without trial on those who admitted their guilt. The main aim of kidnapping would have been to sell the victims into slavery—hence it was a serious offence. On the *poletai* see XLVII,2; the cooperation of the Eleven in the detection of houses and land alleged to be public property shows that the passage refers to a criminal offence, presumably an attempt to take private possession of public property. Among the indictments the Eleven were responsible for bringing was a particular technical charge, that of improperly usurping political rights; the distinction between the cases brought by the Eleven and those brought by the *Thesmothetai* is unknown.

The procedure discussed in LII,2 ensured that certain classes of dispute could be brought to court swiftly, thus obviating delays for merchants and in other cases where a rapid trial was needed. It is probable that they were settled swiftly as well. The dowry was a part of the woman's family's property set aside for her maintenance; the payment referred to here was probably that required after divorce or the death of the husband, when the money would be vital for her. If it were not repaid, those who wrongfully retained it could be sued for its return together with interest at 18% per annum—a fairly high rate which shows that the offence was regarded as serious. The interest rate of a drachma per mina represents 1% per month or 12% per annum; this was regarded as a moderate and reasonable rate (as opposed to the higher rates of 16, 18 or 36% recorded in some cases), and therefore those who were wronged were entitled to get relief under the procedure of cases which could be instituted every month. Those aiming at higher returns had to wait longer if they needed to sue the debtor.

Demosthenes says that prosecutions for assault were heard before the Forty (cf. LIII) in his speech *against Pantainetos* 33; either the tribunal had changed by the time Aristotle wrote or there were different categories of assault heard by different bodies. Disputes about trierarchies arose in the fourth century much more than the fifth; in the former period an individual maintained a ship for the year, and the only usual cause for litigation was a charge that he had not taken up office on the proper day, not done his duty to the minimum standard prescribed by law, or handed over an unseaworthy vessel. In the fourth century the expense was divided amongst groups of men, and there was therefore a fruitful field for litigation arising from disputes about whether individuals had done their fair share, apart from the possible sources of dispute listed above. A good example of a case in the field of banking is Isocrates' *Trapezitikos*, where forgery and repudiation are the points at issue. That the Receivers should handle cases involving taxation is only natural; see XLVII,2 and XLVIII,1 with Commentary.

LIII The Forty had by Aristotle's day taken over the functions of the deme justices established under Peisistratus (XVI,5) who had been revived under Pericles (XXVI,3). This is a rare occasion where Aristotle gives the date of a change between fifth- and fourth-century practice; one must not assume from this that there was no change where he does not mention one, for there are many cases already noted where the system he describes was not that of the fifth century. Very little is known of the Thirty in the fifth century, though it is probable that after a while they, like the Forty later, did not go on circuit as the original deme justices had. The Forty appear to have been mainly concerned with property disputes—hence the procedure involving arbitration below—and to have held the first hearing of private suits except those which could be instituted every month; however, some private suits were heard in the first instance by the *Thesmothetai*; cf. LIX,5. It was sense that they should have the final word in really trivial cases, and not waste the time of a *dikasterion*; Aristotle (*Politics* 1300 b 33ff) approves of the principle of not having large juries for insignificant disputes.

The arbitration procedure is described in detail, and is interesting not least for the mechanism whereby an attempt was made to avoid prolonged litigation where a settlement could be arrived at without going to the *dikasteria*. If the case did go to the *dikasteria*, the hearings before the Arbitrators fulfilled the same functions of limiting the field for the final trial as were performed by the preliminary hearings before the *Boule* and the Archons discussed above; see on XLV. Voluntary arbitration seems to have existed in Athens for a long time; it perhaps became compulsory in private cases in the period 403–400; see Bonner and Smith, *The Administration of Justice* 1,346ff. Aristophanes (*Wasps* 962ff) implies that witnesses delivered their evidence in the *dikasteria* orally in the fifth century; this practice continued generally in the fourth, written depositions being used presumably to prevent witnesses changing their evidence.

The Arbitrators were those in their last year of the forty-two-year cycle of public service; from eighteen to fifty-eight men had to serve in the armed forces when required; then, when they were fifty-nine, they served as Arbitrators. Aristotle stresses that this service was as compulsory as any other part of their duties. Two distinct groups of eponymous heroes are mentioned here. First the ten of the ten tribes (XXI,6), and secondly the forty-two who gave their names to the age-groups in each year of the forty-two-year cycle. They were 'used' in rotation, so that the Ephebes of one year were enrolled under the eponymous hero of the Arbitrators of the previous year, who was 'available' since that year-group had finished their duties in this sense. Thus Athenians gave an absolute date by the Archon of the year, and placed a man in his age-group by the eponymous hero of his year.

An example of the actions against Arbitrators mentioned in §6 is referred to in Demosthenes *against Meidias* 86. Appeal from such a case lay naturally to the *dikasteria*.

LIV In this chapter Aristotle concludes the list of minor officials selected by lot. The commissioners of roads appear to overlap with the functions of the city commissioners as inferred from the *Politics* (see on L above); it may be that each body handled different roads—for example, the commissioners of roads may not have acted within the city—or it may be that the *Politics* and the *Constitution of Athens* cannot be conflated directly since the former is more theoretical.

The Auditors are much the most important officials of those listed in LIV; they are not the same body as that mentioned in XLVIII since the present group were responsible for the final investigation of accounts at the end of a year of office. The penalty for taking bribes could also be death, not merely ten times the bribe thought to have been taken. This paragraph makes it clear that all investigations under the *euthuna* had to go to the *dikasterion* before the final discharge of the official, not merely those where some crime was suspected.

'Clerk to the Prytanies' was another title for the Clerk to the *Boule*; he held an important post in which anyone bent on malpractice would have plenty of scope while checking and holding documents. It is therefore not surprising that by Aristotle's day the post was filled annually by lot; at what date this became the practice is not known, though it may have been between 367 and 363. The statement that before this the Athenians 'used to elect the most famous and reliable men' is a little puzzling since we know the names of at least sixty-six holders of the post in the fifth and fourth centuries, and hardly any of them are famous.

Proxenia was the status granted to Athenians who undertook to look after the interests of the nationals of other states resident in Athens; it was a position of considerable honour, and also involved duties, for foreigners were under certain disabilities; for example, they could go to law only with their *proxenos* bringing the case for them. The *Proxenoi* had a position in many respects parallel to modern consuls, but were always nationals of the state in which they lived. The term could also be used in an honorary sense, for example as a complement to foreign rulers and as a description of certain privileged metics, for whom see below LVIII,2 with Commentary. Grants of citizenship were rare but a field where dishonesty on the part of the Clerk would be very serious. The clerk whose duty it was to read out documents to the people and the *Boule* is mentioned (for example) in the account of Nicias' despatch from Sicily (Thucydides VII,10); later he apparently had the additional duty of reading out the official texts of tragedies to the actors (Plutarch *Moralia* 841 F).

The religious officials and their duties are largely self-explanatory. For the arrangements for the Panathenaia, see LX with Commentary; here the Great Panathenaia is referred to, not the Lesser, an annual celebration. The four-yearly mission to Delos had been revived in 425 (Thucydides III,104,2), and was different from the annual celebration; the six-year interval is obscure, but may have been introduced after 330. The Brauronia was a festival to Artemis at Brauron, while the Heracleia was celebrated at Marathon. The Eleusinia referred to are again not the regular yearly celebration, but a special festival. The archonship of Kephisophon is the latest date mentioned in the treatise —see above, Introduction and Commentary on XLVI.

Salamis was not an integral part of Attica, but partially populated by cleruchs, and was administered as a community dependent on Athens; hence the selection of an Archon. Demarchs may originally have been elected, but were probably all picked by lot in the fourth century. In any case, the Athenians may well have thought that the Demarch of the Peiraeus held such an important position that it had to be filled by lot, not election, because of its potential influence. If Demarchs were elected, it is possible that one of those chosen in the demes of the Peiraeus was picked by lot to act in some way as head of the local administration. The festivals of Dionysus referred to were 'Rural' Dionysia (as opposed to the 'City' Dionysia in Athens itself); they were celebrated in many places throughout Attica, and that at the Peiraeus was perhaps the grandest. On the *choregoi* (providers of choruses) see below, LVI,3ff and Commentary.

LV   Having discussed the *Ekklesia*, the *Boule*, the boards of administrative officials who were members of the *Boule*, and the other minor officials selected by lot, Aristotle now turns to the Archonship of his own day—an office also filled by lot, but very different in many ways from those which have been discussed up to now. The previous history of the office has been discussed already; see III,2–4; VIII,1; XXII,5; XXVI,2 with the Commentary on those passages. The first change from fifth-century practice noted is that the nine officials (the Archon, the King Archon, the Polemarch and the six *Thesmothetai*) together with their clerk were selected by lot in such a way that each tribe provided one member, and each tribe held each position in turn. Such democratic equality and rotation was applied much more rigidly in the fourth than the fifth century, though how early the principle of equal representation for all tribes was established is unknown.

Aristotle chooses the context of the Archons to give a general account of the process of the *dokimasia*, the preliminary investigation undergone by all office-holders before they could take up their position. The Archons, as opposed to other officials, had to go through the process twice, once before the *Boule* (cf. XLV,3) and again before the *dikasteria*. The questions asked appear to have been standard, and the aim was to test the basic qualifications of the office-holder elect; they established that he was a fully qualified citizen and had performed his basic civic and family duties. They did not in any sense test his capacity to perform the office for which he had been selected by lot. It may well be that the prospect of this examination was enough to deter some who would be hopelessly incompetent from standing, though the prospect of the *euthuna* at the end of their tenure and the monthly votes on their performance was more likely to do that.

The list of points investigated takes account of Pericles' citizenship law (XXVI,4), but omits the question of what class the candidate belonged to—cf. VII,4. Either this is just a slip, or the law excluding the Thetes from the Archonship had been a dead letter for so long that even the question had been dropped by Aristotle's day. The class question must have been asked for a few offices, notably the Treasurers who were nominally from the richest class—but see above XLVII,1. The cults mentioned were an essential part of Athenian life, and all citizens were enrolled; the gods mentioned had special care of the home and the hearth. Oral evidence was called to substantiate a man's answers; the Athenians used witnesses in a situation where modern society naturally turns to documentary evidence. Here, as everywhere else, the care taken to ensure that every citizen got a chance to lay any complaint he might have is manifest, and accentuated by the change noted by Aristotle, whereby the one formal vote of acquittal which had been traditional where no complaint had been offered against a magistrate elect was replaced by a full vote just in case bribery or intimidation had taken place before the hearing.

For the stone, and the golden statue to be dedicated for taking bribes, see VII,1 above with Commentary. The phrase translated as 'witnesses swear to their depositions' raises a problem in that the verb normally means 'foreswear' or 'deny on oath'. However, this seems an odd remark in the context, and it is perhaps preferable to accept the meaning given in the text despite the fact that it is not paralleled in extant literature until much later.

LVI As a conclusion to his discussion of the Archons as a body and before turning to their individual functions, Aristotle notes the appointment of two assessors for each of the three senior Archons. There was presumably a survival of primitive practice in the procedure by which the Archons picked their own men for the job; however, once selected they were subject to all the usual democratic checks. Note that the traditional division into chapters does not go back to Aristotle; it is an eccentricity of the modern printed version, not a whim of the author, that splits the first sentence of LVI from LV, where it clearly belongs.

The Archon was the official who gave his name to the year, and it was he who was the closest Athenian approximation to a modern Head of State; he had considerable ceremonial duties and some practical functions, but no real power after the reforms of the early fifth century. The oath he took on entering office must be a survival from the early period, for by it he guaranteed the population against disorder and any arbitrary action by the officers of the state; under the developed democracy his office gave him no powers by which he could take action against any who offended in this respect.

The *choregoi* were originally the men who trained and led the choruses for festivals; during the fifth century the position became one of the liturgies—a post where a wealthy man undertook a public duty at his own expense; see XXVII,3 and Commentary. The expense of the choruses lay in their costumes and training before the festival, and the Dionysia* (celebrated in Athens in late March) was a particularly fine opportunity for a wealthy man to spend heavily and thus earn prestige with his fellow citizens. Further expenditure could be incurred by hiring extras, and a generous *choregos* could make all the difference to the success of a play; it is said that Nicias never failed to win the prize when he was *choregos*. There were three groups of tragedies throughout the fifth and fourth centuries, perhaps five comedies before the Peloponnesian War, three during it as a measure of economy, and five again in the fourth century; the change of the method of appointing comic *choregoi* came in the middle of the fourth century.

Choruses were not restricted to those required for tragedies and comedies; there were choruses of men and boys for various dances and the dithyramb, which was the most expensive of all the liturgies, involving a chorus of fifty and the most expensive *aulos*-players. Five choruses of men and five of boys, each from one of the ten tribes, took part in the Dionysia as well as the choruses involved in the drama; the

* The 'Great' or 'City' Dionysia, as opposed to the rural Dionysia celebrated in December; see above LIV, with Commentary.

Thargelia, a festival to Apollo, was celebrated in late May. For a description of the duties of a *choregos* see Antiphon *on the Choreutes* 11–13.

When the Archon had appointed the *choregoi*, it was open to any of them either to claim that they were exempt or to challenge another wealthy Athenian to exchange property. The former claim was governed by complicated rules, the most important of which were that a man could not be required to perform more than one liturgy at the same time, and that the performance of a liturgy gave exemption for a fixed period of time; for example, a man could not be *choregos* until a full year had elapsed since he had completed his previous duties as *choregos*; allowing for the period of rehearsal, this meant that it was impossible to be *choregos* in consecutive years—unless, of course, a man volunteered for the job, which was not unheard of. The plea that a man had 'performed this liturgy before' is mystifying since it is known that men did on occasion perform the same liturgy more than once; perhaps a man could not be required to do so but might do it voluntarily, or perhaps this was a relatively recent change in the law in Aristotle's day. The restriction of age for the chorus leaders of boys' choruses was part of a general provision in Attic law which prevented younger men having charge of boys; cf. XLII,2.

The challenge to an exchange of property was a curious but in some ways highly egalitarian institution. It was open to somebody selected for a liturgy to allege that another citizen was wealthier and more able to bear the expense than he. He therefore challenged him to exchange property or accept the liturgy. The man challenged could either undertake the liturgy or exchange property, in which case the man originally selected had to undertake it; alternatively, an objection could be lodged to the challenge. In this case complete lists of property, except for holdings in the mines at Laurium which were exempt from assessment for the purposes of liturgies, had to be filed within three days of the challenge by both sides. Disputes, like claims for exemption, were reported to the *dikasteria* and decided there.

The *choregos* for Delos was in charge of the annual mission which happened to be absent at the time of the condemnation of Socrates, with the result that he was not executed until it returned, as the law provided; see Plato, *Phaedo* 58 a 7–c 3. This festival was different from the four- or six-yearly festival mentioned in LIV,7. The chorus taken may once have been of seven young men and seven girls, like the group which originally accompanied Theseus according to the myth, but it was presumably only young men in historical times. The vigil to Asclepius took place the night before the procession to Eleusis which fell in late September or October. The procession in honour of Zeus Soter ('the saviour') occurred in June/July, the last month of the Athenian year; there was also a sacrifice to Zeus Soter on the last day of the year, organised by the Archon. Little is known of the ten assistants of the Archon who helped to supervise these processions; selection of them by lot was a relatively recent innovation in Aristotle's day, and did not last long into the third century.

The cases coming under the Archon's preliminary jurisdiction were many, but the common element reflects his function as protector of the family in the widest sense and of those who could not look after them-themselves. The position of orphans and *epikleroi* has been discussed above, XLII, with Commentary. The immunity of prosecutors of those who illtreated their parents—that is failed to support them, were disobedient towards them, struck them, or failed to bury them—indicates how important it was to the Athenians that parents should be respected and properly treated. Normally a prosecutor who failed to get a proportion of the votes of the jury (usually a fifth) was fined, and could in certain circumstances lose the right to bring a similar case in the future. Actions for production in court arose where a man had control of property or documents which either belonged to another, or which the latter had the right to inspect; presumably here Aristotle is thinking of disputes involving inheritance, since this is the theme of the whole section. Similarly, the officials to divide up property probably dealt with inheritances in this instance, although they could also be appointed in business matters, for example on the break-up of a partnership.

Guardians for orphans were normally next of kin; if there were no directions in a will, the guardian was an adult male relative whose appointment had to be confirmed by the Archon; if there were no relatives, the Archon selected a suitable citizen. Disputes about inheritance or marrying *epikleroi* arose where more than one party laid claim; they had to be decided by the *dikasteria*, and the Archon was responsible for conducting the preliminary hearing and bringing the case to the *dikasteria*. The letting of properties belonging to minors or *epikleroi* was carefully controlled, and the Archon took securities for the property leased; the securities were valued by officials working under him. The limit of fourteen years old is restored in a damaged section of the papyrus; if the restoration is correct, the sentence indicates the age at which by Athenian custom it was appropriate to look for a husband for an *epikleros*—in a sense, the age at which Athenian girls 'came of age'. Male orphans took up their inheritance at the age of eighteen. In all these cases the final power of the Archon was small, though he does seem from the text to have had some power of imposing fines and exacting payments which had been wrongly withheld. In most cases he initiated proceedings, held the preliminary hearing, and then introduced the case to the *dikasteria* for decision.

LVII The King Archon was concerned primarily with religious matters. The unknown author of the speech *against Andocides* preserved among the works of Lysias summarises the position of the King Archon as follows (4): 'If (Andocides) becomes King Archon by lot, will he do anything other than make sacrifices and offer prayers on your behalf according to ancestral custom, some in the Eleusinion in Athens, some in the temple at Eleusis, and run the festival of the Mysteries?' That was, of course, not the sum total of his duties, but is the side with which Aristotle starts his account; the Eumolpidai and the Kerukes were two aristocratic families who were traditionally in charge of the cult at Eleusis; cf. xxxix,2. The Lenaia was celebrated about the end of January; many of the most successful comedies are known to have been produced in the contests there, including Aristophanes' *Acharnians*, *Knights*, *Wasps*, and *Frogs*. Torch-races figured in a number of Athenian festivals, including those to Theseus, Prometheus, Hephaestus and Pan, and also in the Panathenaia. The gymnasiarchs bore the expenses arising from the torch-races, and Demosthenes (*against Lakritos* 48) tells us that legal disputes between them came before the King Archon.

It would naturally be the function of the King Archon to initiate hearings concerning religious disputes and offences. Homicide also came within his province because it was regarded as a religious matter: the death brought a pollution on the state which required purification. The proclamation excluding the murderer (whether known or not) from all religious gatherings and from the Agora had the same motive—to prevent the spread of the pollution (cf. §4). The cases listed here were retained by the Areopagus at the time of the reforms of Ephialtes (xxv), together with damage to the sacred olives (LX,2). The element of pollution may explain why the democracy did not take them over, since religious conservatism was deeply ingrained, although the inclusion of arson is a little surprising. All homicide cases not tried by the Areopagus were brought by the King Archon before a jury of *Ephetai* who sat in different locations depending on the type of case they were trying. The origins of this archaic body are unknown, but by the fifth century they consisted of a jury of fifty-one persons, probably over fifty years of age; they did not apparently form a part of the ordinary *dikasteria* before which all other cases were brought by the magistrate or body which instituted the preliminary hearings. On the other hand, two cases mentioned by Isocrates and Demosthenes which were tried in the Palladion in the fourth century were both heard before juries of some hundreds. It may be that the *Ephetai* had been merged with the ordinary body of jurors, but it could equally be that the cases in question did not fall to the *Ephetai* to try, but were instances of ordinary actions before a *dikasterion* sitting in the Palladion.

Two unusual Athenian customs are noted here. First, the trials in the court of Phreatto; they arose when a man already in exile for one killing was charged with murder in respect of a second death. He was not allowed to set foot in Attica, but pleaded his case from a boat anchored just offshore before a jury seated near the water's edge. The taking of proceedings against 'the guilty party' is parallel to our coroner's verdict of 'murder by person or persons unknown', but takes the matter one step further in that a trial was actually held; again, the religious need for purification of the pollution was the motive. The same reason lay behind what seems to us the extraordinary practice of 'trying' animals or inanimate objects which had caused death; by doing so they had polluted the state, and it was necessary to remove them in full legal fashion. A passage in Plato's *Laws* (873 e–874 b) illustrates Athenian practice although it is theoretical, not written as history. 'If a baggage animal or any other beast kills someone, except if anything of this sort should happen to an athlete in the course of public contests, his relatives are to prosecute the killer for murder ... and the animal when found guilty shall be killed and cast outside the borders of the land. If any inanimate object shall deprive a man of his life, unless it be a thunderbolt or some other stroke from the gods, and where a man is killed either by something falling on him or by his falling on it, the next of kin shall appoint his nearest neighbour as judge, and thus purify himself and his whole family. The guilty object shall be cast out of the land, as was laid down for the animals above. If a man is found dead, and the killer is unknown and cannot be found after careful search, the same proclamations shall be made as in other cases, and the same ban against the murderer. A trial shall be held, and proclamation made in the Agora that the murderer of so and so, having been found guilty, shall not enter the temples nor any part of the country of the victim on pain of death; if he does, and is recognised, his body is then to be thrown out of the country of the victim unburied.' The above passage also brings out the point that there was a legal obligation on the relatives to prosecute for murder; in other cases there was no such requirement, and prosecutions were brought only if the offended party wished to do so, or a public-spirited citizen was willing to bring the case, or an informer stepped in; cf. above on xxxv.

The crown mentioned in §4 is not peculiar to the King Archon, but was part of the official regalia of all Archons. Little is known of the functions of the Tribal Kings, but they had religious duties and some legal functions which were associated with the King Archon in the Prytaneion Court in the fourth century. Their position within the tribe appears to have been analogous to that of the King Archon within the whole state.

LVIII The Polemarch was originally the commander-in-chief, and concerned with military affairs. The sacrifices to Artemis in memory of the battle of Marathon, and to Enualios (Ares) were survivals from his military functions, as also was the organisation of funeral games, in which he was assisted by the *strategoi*. He had general control of all litigation which affected the numerous metics resident in Athens. They were allowed to live and work freely in the city, but were expected to undertake military service if required, and were subject to certain disabilities, such as special taxation, and restrictions, as for example not being allowed to own land. Tax-exempt metics were a privileged group free from the normal tax on metics and taxed as citizens; the *proxenoi* mentioned here are not the same group as the 'consuls' already discussed (above on LIV), but were metics granted exceptional privileges, such as the right to own land and to sit in the front seats in the theatre. Since the metics could not by definition be members of any deme or tribe, the Polemarch divided the cases in which they were involved into ten equal parts, and allocated them to the four members of the Forty in each tribe (cf. LIII,1), who passed them to the Arbitrators; in this way the burden was evenly shared. It appears to have been a privilege to bring cases before the Polemarch; perhaps there were fewer of them, and the matter therefore came up for trial more speedily.

On Harmodius and Aristogeiton, see XVIII; on the Arbitrators, see LIII; all metics were required to have a patron who acted for them in affairs which could be handled only by a citizen, in the same way as the *proxenoi* of LIV acted for Greeks from other cities who were temporarily in Athens.

LIX   The *Thesmothetai*, the other six of the nine Archons, were probably introduced because of an increase of judicial business, and Aristotle gives here a long, though not exhaustive, list of the cases they handled. Most of the charges listed are self-explanatory; on motions for the deposition of magistrates and accusations in the *Ekklesia* (which were normally only a preliminary stage in the case) see XLIII; on the indictment for illegal proposals see on XLV, and on the chairmen and president see XLIV. The procedure for the collection of debts has been discussed above, XLVII–XLVIII, the *euthuna* of the *strategoi* at LIV,2, and the investigation of credentials at LV. For appeals about citizenship see XLII, and judicial decisions of the *Boule* XLV,1. The process whereby the *Thesmothetai* allotted courts (with the exception of cases of homicide), magistrates to individual cases, and the allocation of juries will be discussed below, LXIIIff. See all these passages with the relevant sections of the Commentary.

The charge translated as 'malicious prosecution' has no exact equivalent in modern practice, and is frequently rendered (by transliterating the Greek) as sycophancy. As noted already, the Athenian had no public prosecutor, and relied on the injured party or public-spirited citizens to bring a prosecution where it was known or suspected that a crime had been committed, with the exception of cases of homicide where the family of the dead man were under a legal obligation to prosecute. Rewards had to be offered to successful prosecutors to make the system work; they received a large part of the property confiscated, the money recovered or the fine imposed as a result of conviction—often a half, sometimes even more. This naturally led to the appearance of informers and to some trumped up charges brought in the hope of personal profit; in these cases the prosecutors relied on extraneous circumstances or personal prejudices against the defendant to get convictions. There was some check on this inherent in the provision that a prosecutor who failed to receive a stated, small proportion of the votes of the jury, usually one fifth, or one who dropped a case before it came to court, faced significant penalties. They could be a fine of 1,000 drachmae, a fine of one obol per drachma of the claim (i.e. one sixth of the claim), or the loss of the right to bring a similar case in the future, depending on the circumstances of the particular case. This was some check, but not enough, since some cases were specifically excluded and the unsuccessful prosecutor suffered no penalty however badly he did. This was particularly serious since prosecution was a recognised and accepted way of attempting to revenge oneself on one's enemies, whether political or private; the threat of such charges could also be used to extort money as a blackmail 'pay-off'.

Sycophancy was widespread in the late fifth century, and is mentioned frequently in Aristophanes. The charge of sycophancy or malicious prosecution was used as a further way of checking abuse (though in itself it could become an abuse), and a charge of misleading the people could also be used, and could be effective, for the maximum penalty under it was death. Many prosecutors undoubtedly acted from the best motives, and without them the whole administration of justice in Athens would have been hamstrung; others misused the system severely, and no totally satisfactory solution was found. The appointment of a public prosecutor, which might or might not have solved the problem, would have been regarded as very undemocratic in the unlikely event of it ever occurring to the Athenians as a possibility.

The international agreements mentioned were ultimately ratified by the *dikasteria*. Where they existed, criminal and commercial cases between individuals of differing states were governed by their provisions, which included agreed laws which would govern any settlement. The plaintiff normally had the right to sue in whichever state he chose, but would usually bring the case in the defendant's state because he would be more likely to be able to execute judgment there if he won. Such suits were often commercial. If no such international agreement existed, the suit would be heard in the state where the contract had been made or the crime committed, and in accordance with its laws. Cases where perjury was alleged were normally handled by the court where it was said to have taken place; the procedure mentioned here for cases of perjury in the Areopagus was an exception.

LX   The commissioners appointed to run the Panathenaic games are discussed separately because they held office for four years (cf. XLIII,1), and this leads Aristotle naturally to reserve his discussion of the duties of the Archon in collecting the oil from the sacred olives for this section. The musical contests were added to the Panathenaia (or revived) by Pericles (Plutarch, *Pericles* 13); contests included singing and playing the *aulos* and *kithara* (wind and string instruments). The athletic contests were the usual ones—wrestling, running, boxing, the *pankration* and the pentathlon. On the robe for Athena see XLIV,3 with Commentary. The vases for prizes contained olive oil given to the athletes (§3). Many have been found in widely scattered places in the Mediterranean world; on one side is a representation of Athena, and on the other a picture of the event for which the prize was awarded. By Aristotle's day, the olive oil was not taken specifically from the trees dedicated to Athena, but was a general charge on the harvest from the estate on which the trees stood; the date of the change is unknown, but was later than 395. The speech of Lysias (*about the Sacred Olive*) also suggests that the penalty for destruction of the sacred trees had before that time ceased to be death and become exile with confiscation of property. The treasurers who received and stored the oil were the Treasurers of Athena (cf. XLVII,I). Prizes for all contests included a crown; the musical contests also carried a cash prize; the contests in manliness had carried a prize of an ox in the early fourth century—the date of the change to a shield is not known. The contest itself was a considerable test of physical fitness, involving running in full armour and horse-riding.

LXI The 'also' in the first sentence has nothing to refer to, and this has led scholars to suggest plausibly that some text is missing between chapters LX and LXI. The inference is supported by consideration of the content. Despite their importance, there is no detailed discussion of the treasurer of the military funds, the controllers of the Theoric Fund, or the supervisors of the water supply. All these offices were filled by election probably for a period of four years, and are mentioned in XLIII,I just before the *strategoi*; one might therefore expect some discussion of their duties precisely here, in between the commissioners of the games, who were also appointed for four years, and the *strategoi*.

Aristotle now turns his attention to military offices which were filled by election. The institution of the *strategoi* in 501/0 was described in XXII,2, and Aristotle now indicates an important change: instead of being elected one from each tribe, they were 'now' elected from the whole people; thus there were no longer necessarily representatives of all ten tribes among the ten *strategoi*. The date of the change is unknown; it was probably motivated by the realisation that, with the increasing importance of the post in every aspect of politics, it was vital to have able men filling it, and it would be foolish always to restrict each tribe to one member. This does not mean that one has to hypothesize any complicated system whereby only one tribe in any one year could have two members of the board, and no tribe was without a member for more than one year consecutively. We know that in 441 there were two *strategoi* from the tribe Akamantis, and in 432 there were two represrntatives of the tribe Akamantis and perhaps two from the tribe Kekropis; there are other similar examples. Thus from about the middle of the fifth century, the Athenians appear to have been able in certain circumstances not as yet fully understood to elect more than one man from a tribe; it should always be born in mind that tribal loyalty was by no means non-existent, and would have ensured a reasonable 'spread' of *strategoi* in normal circumstances.* Perhaps the most interesting single feature of the fully developed system of *strategoi* at Athens is the divorce of the individual *strategoi*, who were in origin commanders of their tribal contingents, from these units; this is a startling innovation,

---

* This is a highly controversial topic, and space does not allow a lengthy discussion here; for an extreme thesis with excellent negative arguments but slightly more dubious positive points, see C. W. Fornara, *The Athenian Board of Generals from 501 to 404.*

much more likely to belong to the fifth century than the period of the original institution of the office.

The allocation of *strategoi* to particular duties or particular areas for their year of office was not a fifth-century practice—then they were sent by the *Ekklesia* to deal with crises as they arose, as was done in Aristotle's day with the five who had no specific sphere allotted to them. The innovation appears to have been made very recently, probably between 334 and 325. For the garrisons in the Peiraeus, cf. XLII,3.

The symmories were a fourth-century institution replacing some of the liturgies undertaken by individuals in the fifth; instead of the burden falling on a single wealthy man, it fell on groups. Symmories were created in 378/7 in connection with the capital levy (*eisphora*), and henceforth almost all tax-paying Athenians were involved, as also were the metics in separate groups. In 357/6 symmories were set up to replace the trierarchy; the twelve hundred richest citizens were divided into twenty equal sections each responsible for the maintenance of a portion of the fleet. The reform was aimed at spreading the burden of taxation more fairly, and probably also reflected a reduction in the number of really wealthy men compared with the fifth century. It should be noted that the text makes it clear that men were still appointed as trierarchs even after the institution of the symmories of 357/6; exactly how the two systems interlocked is not clear. For exchanges of property, see above on LVI.

The vote on the conduct of the *strategoi* was part of the proceedings at the plenary session of the *Ekklesia* (XLIII,4). It was of great importance for the democracy to keep a close check on their conduct, not merely for obvious wider reasons, but also because of the summary powers they had on campaign which are listed in the last sentence of §2. There is evidence that in the fifth century *strategoi* on campaign even inflicted the death penalty in extreme cases without trial. The importance of the check on the *strategoi* may be indicated by the detailed description given of the process; however, it would be unwise to read too much into it, since this is the only description which Aristotle gives of the procedure followed when an accusation was brought against a man in the course of his tenure of public office; he may have chosen this as the most appropriate place to include a description which he intended his readers to take as a type for all the other occasions when a similar procedure was appropriate.

The regimental commanders each had charge of one tribe's contingent of hoplites, usually his own. The post was instituted after 490, and it is tempting to associate its origin with the increasing importance of the ten *strategoi* after 487/6; perhaps their existence facilitated the development whereby the *strategoi* ceased to be tied to their own tribal units. It is of some interest that the subordinate officers were appointed by them, not by the *strategoi*—another sign of the divorce of the *strategoi* from their original function of tribal commanders. The two cavalry commanders held positions of considerable prestige—their post is linked with the office of *strategos* and ambassador as 'the greatest honours' by Lysias *on the* dokimasia *of Euandros* 20) ; the monthly vote on their conduct also shows that they were on a par with the *strategoi* at least in some respects. The position of the ten tribal cavalry commanders is strictly parallel to that of the ten regimental commanders. The cavalry commander in Lemnos commanded a detachment stationed there to protect the Athenian cleruchs on the island.

The 'Paralos' and the 'Ammonis' (or 'Ammonias') were the two state triremes which were used to send official despatches, carry ambassadors and for other public business; they were always manned by citizens, and were supposed to be the fastest ships of the fleet. In the fifth century the two state ships had been the 'Paralos' and the 'Salaminia'. The date when the 'Ammonis' was substituted for the 'Salaminia' as one of the two state vessels is unknown; interest in the oracle of Zeus Ammon may well have been increased by the visit of Alexander the Great in 331, but Athens is known to have consulted it as early as the late fifth century.

LXII   The details lying behind the discussion of where and exactly how the selection for offices filled by lot took place are unknown; the text indicates that it was suspected or proved that the casting of lots for office in as small a group as those members of one deme who attended any particular election was open to abuse, and therefore most offices were allocated by tribe. It is a not unreasonable guess that at least all boards of ten were selected by lot by tribes, since one may presume that the existence of a board of ten implies one member from each tribe except where there is specific evidence to the contrary as in the case of the *strategoi*. The text is confirmed by the evidence of the inscriptions containing lists of the Prytanies of the fourth century: membership of the *Boule* was proportional to the size of the deme, and the preliminary selection must therefore have been made at the deme level. It is probable that each deme selected twice as many men as were required, half of whom were then selected as members, and half as reserves. The guards mentioned may have been the guards of the docks mentioned in XXIV,3 or may have been used abroad when required; see above on XXIV.

Pay for attendance at meetings of the *Ekklesia* was first introduced at the very beginning of the fourth century; see XLI,3 with Commentary. The highest fee mentioned in that passage is half a drachma; by Aristotle's day it had been doubled, and represents a fairly large sum, for the jurors still received only half a drachma — the level to which Cleon had raised the original two-obol fee which Pericles had introduced (XXVII,3). The nine-obol fee for the plenary sessions of the *Ekklesia* shows what fee was needed to encourage a good attendance at the most important meeting of each prytany rather than what the average citizen would lose by missing a day's earnings. Most of the rest of the officials mentioned have already been discussed: for the Prytanies, see XLIII–XLIV, for the Archons LV–LIX, and for the commissioners of the games LX, with the relevant section of the Commentary in each case. The sacred commissioners to Delos were in charge of the temple funds there, while the officials sent to Samos, Scyros, Lemnos and Imbros were all employed in government; one of them has already been mentioned, the cavalry commander for Lemnos in LXI,6. As already noted, fees were designed primarily as compensation for loss of earnings, with the purpose of enabling anyone to take an active part in politics; they were not intended to enable a man to make his living by doing his civic duty, and it is most unlikely that this would have been possible even with the higher fees paid in Aristotle's day; cf. above on XXIV.

The provision for repeated tenure of military positions is good sense; Pericles was *strategos* for some fifteen years, and Phocion held the position forty-five times. On the need for it to be possible to be a member of the *Boule* twice rather than once only (which was the rule for all other democratic offices) see above on XXXI.

LXIII–LXV Aristotle devotes the next three chapters to a very detailed account of the process of empanelling an Athenian jury. The highly complicated series of steps involved resulted from the passionate interest of the Athenians in ensuring that the system should be as fair as possible and that bribery or 'packing' of a jury should be prevented. The following discussion will first look at the process, and then deal with other details raised by Aristotle which have not been covered in the main discussion.

In the fifth century a body of 6,000 *dikastai* were selected each year by lot from those who put themselves forward; from this group juries were constituted each day as required. Up to ten courts might sit, and the juries might consist of any multiple of 100 members from 200 upwards (cf. LIII,3); the largest might even include all the 6,000. In the fourth century there is something to suggest that odd numbers (e.g. 501) were used to avoid a tied vote, but this cannot have been universal since Aristotle mentions a specific provision for the acquittal of the defendant in the event of a tie (LXIX,1). It was by no means certain that all the 6,000 would appear for service every day, especially since they tended to include a high proportion of the older members of the community—the fee was not as much as the average labourer would earn for a day's work, and was therefore more attractive to the infirm as 'pocket money' than to an able-bodied citizen. By Aristotle's day, the specific body of 6,000 had been discontinued, and the juries were drawn from all those who had put themselves forward for service that year; there might be as many as 10,000. However, the fact that the fee remained at 3 obols from at the latest 425 until Aristotle's day argues that there was no shortage for any sitting—otherwise it would have been necessary to raise the fee to make service more attractive.

Proceedings started early in the day; Aristophanes (*Wasps*) shows that the *dikastai* arrived so early that some at least had to leave home while it was still dark. Each man had a ticket with his name on it, and one of the first ten letters of the Greek alphabet, A–K; the *dikastai* from each tribe were divided into ten sections of roughly equal size (LXIII,4). When the *dikastes* arrived at the place where the allotment was to take place, he went to whichever of the ten entrances corresponded to his tribe; there he placed his ticket in whichever of ten boxes corresponded to the letter on his ticket. The whole process of selection was presided over by the nine Archons with the secretary of the *Thesmothetai*, each presiding over one tribe at one entrance (LIX,7; LXIII,1). After the boxes containing the tickets had been shaken, the presiding magistrate drew out one from each box; the man so selected acted as 'ticket-inserter', and was automatically selected for jury service that day (LXIV,2–3). The next stage of the selection was conducted with the aid of an allotment machine, which was a tall block with five vertical rows of slots in it; there were two of these machines at each entrance, the rows of slots being labelled with the letters A–E and Z–K respectively.* The ticket-inserter drew the tickets of the *dikastai* from the box with the same letter as his own, and placed them in the column headed with this letter in the order in which they were drawn, starting at the top. The ticket-inserter was drawn each day, rather than being appointed for a period, because it must have been possible for him at least sometimes to see the names on the tickets he was drawing. It will be shown later that the last few drawn would on most days not serve on a jury, and it therefore follows that the ticket-inserter was potentially in a position where he could victimise some *dikastai*; hence, it would be wrong and dangerous for a man to hold this post for a period (LXIV,2).

Each presiding officer knew how many courts were to be filled and what size of jury was required for each; he therefore had to produce one-tenth of the total number of *dikastai* required from each tribe, and did this with the allotment machines. Naturally, not every column had the same number of slots filled, since the same number of men would not have appeared from each of the ten divisions of the tribe; he therefore automatically ruled out all those below the length of the shortest column. Assuming (purely as an illustrative example) that a total of 2,000 *dikastai* were required; 200 were therefore needed from each tribe, 100 from each of the allotment machines. *Dikastai* were accepted or rejected in horizontal rows of five; he therefore needed nineteen rows in addition to the ticket-inserters. The rows which were successful were decided by a device attached to the side of each allotment machine; this consisted of a long, narrow tube, into which cubes were placed, with a device to let them out one by one at the bottom. Assuming in the hypothetical example that there were 37 completed rows in a particular allotment machine, while 19 were needed to produce the hundred *dikastai* (allowing for the ticket-inserters), the presiding officer put 19 white cubes and 18 black cubes into a funnel at the top of the tube, and they fell into it in a random order. They were then released one at a time; if the first cube was white, the first horizontal row of five were selected for that day, if black they were rejected; the process decided the fate of each complete row (LXIV,3). Those unsuccessful in the ballot took their tickets and went home (LXV,3). This process was

---

* Z is the sixth letter of the Greek alphabet, and K the tenth.

1. Voting tokens

2. Jurors' ticket

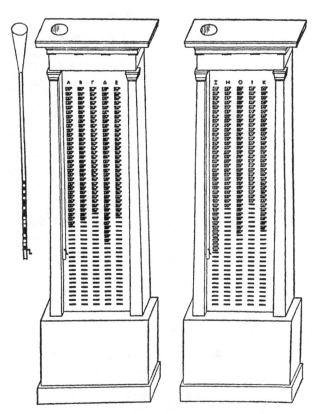

3. Reconstruction of an allotment machine

used for each machine of each tribe, the number of white cubes remaining constant, the number of black varying according to the length of the shortest column in each machine.

The juries having been selected, there was a second allotment which decided which court they sat in. Before the draw for seats on the juries had begun, one of the *Thesmothetai* had drawn lots which decided which letter (from Λ onwards) should be placed at the door of each court to be manned (LXIII,5). When the names of the successful *dikastai* were called by the herald, they stepped forward and drew a ball from an urn. This urn contained the same number of balls as there were *dikastai* required from that tribe, and each ball had a letter on it; the letters corresponded with those put up at the entrance of each court, and each tribe's urn contained one-tenth of the number of balls with each letter, the total number of balls with each letter corresponding to the size of the jury required in that court. Thus the jury contained an equal number of members of each tribe, and was of the requisite size. The letter was shown to the presiding magistrate, and the man's ticket was placed in a box with the same letter on it as was on the ball; since this ticket was returned to him at the end of the sitting when he drew his fee, this ensured that he sat in the right court, for he could not draw his fee unless he was sitting in the court to which his ticket was taken (LXIV,4–5).

The ball entitled the *dikastes* to pass through an inner door, presumably into a corridor off which the actual courts opened; at the same time, he received a staff with a colour on it which corresponded to a colour painted over the door of the court to which he had been allocated; this formed a further check to ensure that he went to the right court, for the colour would be plain for all to see. As he entered the court, the *dikastes* received an official token. This was not the token which entitled him to his fee at the end of the day (LXV,1–4; LXVIII,2). Aristotle does not make it clear what it was for, but it may have been connected with the allocation of seats in the court.

The system outlined above made it impossible for any man to know for which case he would be selected on any day, or even to know whether he would sit or not; thus it was out of the question for a litigant to ensure that his friends sat to hear his case, and almost equally difficult to bribe a jury. The case mentioned above (XXVII,5) shows that bribery was not totally impossible in the fifth century, though it appears to have been difficult. The system just described was the result of over a century's development, and it may well be that it was easier to know who would be on a jury in the fifth century, and that further precautions were taken as a result of such cases, with the near fool-proof system described by Aristotle as the end-product. The system was equally remarkable for its fairness. The one element in it which was not totally equitable was the rejection of *dikastai* who were drawn in such a position that they occupied slots in the allotment machine lower than the last position filled in the shortest column. The most equitable form of draw would have involved using the black and white cubes in their tube to decide the representation of each column separately; thus the required number of *dikastai* would have been selected from those present in each letter-group of each tribe. However, this would have involved drawing ten times for each tribe; the process as described by Aristotle must have been time-consuming, and to draw ten times instead of twice for each tribe would probably have made it impossibly so. This consideration, in fact, explains the one odd feature not so far discussed: on the face of it, it seems strange that there were two allotment machines of five columns instead of one of ten, but this ensured that an unusually poor attendance by one section affected only four other sections of a tribe instead of nine. Thus the Athenians made an important step in the direction of total equity without going so far that they imperilled the working of the whole process.*

There remain some details which require comment. That the position of *dikastes* was regarded as a public office, not merely part of the everyday functions of citizenship, is proved both by the minimum age limit of thirty, which was normal for all public office, and also by the exclusion of public debtors; they were deprived of many active political rights until they had cleared the debt. The penalties for sitting when disqualified were severe; they were apparently assessed by the court where a man had wrongly sat (Demosthenes, *against Meidias* 182).

The exact geography of the courts is not known, and a final solution will have to wait on the excavation of the *dikasteria*. It is clear that there was a general assembly area with a separate entrance for each tribe; that there was an 'inner door' through which the *dikastes* passed on his way to the court which he had drawn; and that there was a further door at the entrance to the court itself, on the lintel of which a colour was permanently painted, and by which the letter drawn at the beginning of the day was hung. The exact shape and disposition of the courts is not certain. The name of one implies that it was triangular, which implies further that it had been fitted into an awkwardly shaped space at the time of its construction. The most economical theory would suggest a row of courts joined to each other, but this is not acceptable since the orators imply not merely that crowds could gather round the court and hear and see what was going on (which is easy enough), but that this crowd surrounded three sides of the place where the court sat. This in turn implies that the crowd could assemble between one court and the next, which poses difficulties for the supposed corridor down which the *dikastai* apparently passed from their tribe entrance to the entrance of the individual court in which they were to sit. All that one can be certain of is that the courts were surrounded only by low walls on one side at least, and perhaps on three; they may have been only partly roofed.

---

* The above note is deeply indebted to the definitive publication on the allotment machines: S. Dow, 'Aristotle, the Kleroteria and the Courts', *HSCP* L (1939) 1–34. A well-illustrated and brief summary may be found in the American School at Athens' Agora Picture Book no. 4, 'The Athenian Citizen'.

LXVI   Once the juries had been allotted to their courts, the magistrates were allotted to the courts they would preside over; the allotment machines described here were very different from those used for the allotment of the juries, and probably consisted only of two of the tubes used to decide the fates of the rows of jurors whose tickets had already been inserted into the jury machines. Note that the element of lot went so far as to pick two of the *Thesmothetai* by lot to put the colours of the courts and the names of the magistrates into the machines; the Athenians were determined that it should not be at all possible for anyone to know in advance where he would be sitting.

When the presiding magistrate reached his court, he then drew one member of each tribe to serve as a court official; he drew the names from the boxes containing the original tickets of the *dikastai* which had been brought to the court where they were sitting. There was then a further draw to produce one of the ten to supervise the water clock which controlled the length of the speeches, four to supervise the voting procedure, and five to distribute fees to the jury at the end of the hearing. On the first five see further LXVII–LXIX with Commentary below; the fact that there were five distributing the fees suggests that the figure missing at LXV,4 was five.

LXVII   The papyrus of the *Constitution of Athens* is in reasonably good condition until the beginning of chapter LXIV, but from there on it becomes increasingly fragmentary. Towards the end of LXVII the papyrus is so mutilated that it is impossible to make anything very useful of it for a number of lines; the same is true of the opening of LXVIII. In the translation, I have used the text as restored by editors without indication of how much has been added by conjecture; to do that would produce a forest of brackets or italics in the worst areas. Restorations of LXIV and LXV are on the whole convincing, and confirmation can be drawn from the reconstruction of the processes involved in the allotting of jurors to courts. LXVI and LXVII are less certain, while LXVIII and LXIX are better preserved. Those who wish to study the exact authority behind the translation are referred to the Oxford Classical Text (Kenyon) or the standard editions; Von Fritz/Kapp also indicate restorations by italics and brackets in their translation.

The cases were called by the presiding magistrate in each court, though it should be stressed that his function bore almost no relation to that of a judge in a modern court; he was responsible for 'chairing the meeting' and preserving good order, not for expounding the law or giving any sort of judgement. The four types of private cases referred to in §1 are probably those defined in §2, three being distinguished by the value of the property at issue; the 'disputed claims' would be to inheritances or wardships and the like.

The water clock was a standard way of measuring time in Greece. It consisted of two large jars; the upper one had a minute copper pipe at the bottom, and water ran from the upper through this pipe into the lower. The rate of flow was known, and the number of measures allowed for each type of case thus told the speaker how long he was allowed to speak for. In private cases the clock was stopped for the reading of evidence, laws and other relevant documents, which were read to the court by the clerk of the court, but in public cases, that is crimes alleged against the state, the whole day was allocated in equal sections to the litigants. In no circumstances did a case last more than one day. The fragments surviving from §§4–5 probably show that the public cases in which the day was divided into sections were the most serious cases, and that the division of the day did not mean precisely what it says. Poseideon fell in December–January, and the standard adopted was therefore that of the shortest days of the year. The text implies that the length of time that it was possible to allocate to each side during the period of daylight at this time of year was the length of time allocated to them at all times; it also must therefore have been measured by the water clock.

The primary speech on each side had to be delivered by the prosecutor and defendant respectively. They were allowed to employ professional orators to deliver the supporting speeches, and could also employ speech writers to compose what they delivered themselves. Thus the requirement for a man to deliver the main speech himself was not such a severe challenge as it sounds at first, but could still have been a major ordeal; it cannot have been without its effect on the outcome in some cases.

LXVIII The discussion of the size of juries (§1) is so fragmentary as to add very little to our knowledge; 'the majority' is, all but the last letter, a restoration, and must be treated with caution, plausible as it may be. *Heliaia* was originally used in Athens to mean the people sitting as a court as instituted by Solon (above, IX with Commentary); here the term appears to be used of any jury of over 500, though the text is too fragmentary to allow certainty.

Examples of the voting tokens used by *dikastai* have been found in Athens; they consist of a disc of bronze with a pipe or bar running through them, rather like a small wheel centrally placed on a short axle. Some are pierced, that is the 'axle' is hollow, others solid, that is the 'axle' is solid; pierced tokens were for the prosecution, solid for the defence (LXIX,1). Every man received one of each, and cast *both*, one into the container which would be counted, and one into the container for discards; thus the secrecy of the ballot was ensured, for by holding the 'axle' of the token between his finger and thumb (§4) and thus covering its ends, he could ensure that nobody knew which he put into which container. The fact that he voted in both rather than casting a vote *either* into a container for condemnation *or* a container for acquittal also ensured secrecy. Equally careful precautions were taken to ensure that the litigants saw that justice was done, to make certain that there had been no previous 'planting' of votes, and to make sure that the *dikastai* actually voted—otherwise they would not receive the tag which had to be handed in when they received their fee.

The exact significance of the process of protesting at evidence is not known; it may be that this was the moment at which allegations of perjury had to be made, though it seems unlikely that perjury could not be alleged and lead to prosecution at a later date. Perhaps this was the last moment at which protests could be made which would be discussed before the voting, and the proviso was solely aimed at preventing a man from disrupting proceedings by issuing a desperate challenge against some piece of evidence if he suspected half-way through the voting that he was losing. If this was so, logic would suggest that the procedure had arisen before the institution of quite such carefully devised secrecy for the ballot, so that it was possible for a man to know how the votes of the jury were being cast.

LXIX The procedure for counting votes is self-explanatory; the men in charge were the four picked by lot (LXVI,2). There was no parallel in Athens to the modern judge who assesses a penalty: either the penalty was prescribed in the statute under which the defendant was accused, or there was a second 'trial' in which each side proposed penalties. The defence naturally proposed a milder penalty than the prosecution; both sides were allowed to deliver brief speeches, and the *dikastai* then voted for the penalty they thought more suitable in exactly the same way as they had voted for the verdict. The most famous instance of this procedure is described in Plato's *Apology*, though there the alternative proposed by Socrates was manifestly too mild, and known to be so; hence the higher vote for the prosecution's penalty than was originally given for Socrates' condemnation.

The treatise ends very abruptly, but the lay-out of the last page of the papyrus shows that the scribe who copied it had copied all the text which he had in front of him, and it seems quite probable that the original did conclude at this point. It is by no means an unsuitable end; one would not expect a technical work of this sort necessarily to have a peroration or summing-up, and the detailed account of the many ways in which the Athenians attempted to ensure that the administration of justice was as fair and uncorruptible as possible makes a suitable end in view of the central and vital role which the Athenians always assigned to the *dikasteria* in the maintenance of the democracy.

APPENDIX TO PART II

A manuscript in Paris preserves a very brief summary which gives every appearance of being derived from Aristotle's *Constitution of Athens*; it is referred to as the *Epitome of Heraclides*. This work summarises the lost opening chapters of Aristotle's work as follows:

1 The Athenians initially were ruled by kings; after Ion had united them into one state, they were called Ionians.

Pandion, who was king after Erechtheus, divided the rule between his sons, and they ended by quarrelling. Theseus reunified the people by proclamation on terms of equality. He went to Scyros, and was killed when he was pushed over a cliff by Lukomedes who was afraid that he might seize the island. At a later period, after the Persian Wars, the Athenians brought his bones back to Athens.

From the time of the sons of Codrus the Athenians no longer chose kings because they thought that they were living in luxury and had become soft. One of the sons of Codrus, Hippomenes, wished to dispel the slander, and when he caught an adulterer with his daughter Leimone, he killed him by tying him under his chariot, and shut her up with a horse until she was dead.

2 Megacles and his associates killed the supporters of Cylon in his attempt to establish a tyranny after they had taken refuge at the altar of Athena; those responsible were exiled as accursed.

The historical value of the information contained in this section must have been highly dubious even in Aristotle's original version, and the situation is not made any better by the fact that we have only a summary of what he wrote; comparison of later parts of the *Epitome* with the surviving text is not encouraging. Ion himself was not a historical character, but the connection of Athens with the Ionian branch of the Greek people is confirmed archaeologically. The story of Theseus is also probably largely mythical as represented here and in Plutarch's *Theseus,* though there may well be a substratum of truth lying beneath it which refers to an important step in the process of the unification of Attica. Plutarch ascribes to Theseus the establishment of the old aristocratic classes of the *eupatridai,* the *geomoroi* and the *demiourgoi,* and assigns to the *eupatridai* control of religious ceremonial, the provision of the Archons, the exposition of the laws, and general control of things sacred and profane. He quotes Aristotle specifically for the statement that Theseus was the first to show favour to the common people; see Plutarch *Theseus,* 25. Thucydides (II,15,2) says that Theseus established one Council for the whole of Attica—presumably the Areopagus.

SELECT BIBLIOGRAPHY

The translation is based on *Aristotelis Atheniensium Respublica*, edited by F. G. Kenyon, (Oxford, Oxford University Press, 1920). I have also consulted extensively J. E. Sandys, *Aristotle's Constitution of Athens*, (London and New York, Macmillan, 3rd edition 1912) and less extensively Kenyon's own edition with commentary, *Aristotle on the Constitution of Athens*, (London, British Museum, 3rd edition 1892). Both Sandys and K. von Fritz and E. Kapp, *Aristotle's Constitution of Athens and Related Texts*, (New York and London, Hafner, 1966) (cited as Von Fritz/Kapp) contain much useful material in their commentaries. For the second edition I have had the great advantage of being able to consult P. J. Rhodes, *A Commentary on the Aristotelian Athenaion Politeia* (Oxford, Clarendon Press, 1981); a mine of information, cited as Rhodes.

Of the most important ancient sources which touch on subjects covered by Aristotle in the present work, Herodotus, Thucydides, Xenophon, some Demosthenes speeches, and sundry Lives of Plutarch are available in Penguin translations; most of the remainder are included in the Loeb Classical Library; useful parallel material in translation will be found in Lactor 5, *Athenian Politics, Democracy in Athens from Pericles to Cleophon*, (London Association of Classical Teachers, 1969). For [Xenophon] *The Constitution of the Athenians* see Part 1 of this volume.

The standard histories of the period provide a very adequate background to Aristotle's text; in general, see also:

J. K. Davies, *Democracy and Classical Greece* (London, Fontana, 1978).

W. G. Forrest, *The Emergence of Greek Democracy* (London, Weidenfeld, 1966).

C. Hignett, *A History of the Athenian Constitution to the end of the Fifth Century BC* (Oxford, Oxford University Press, 1952); sometimes over sceptical.

A. H. M. Jones, *Athenian Democracy* (Oxford, Blackwell, 1957).

On particular points, the following books may be found useful:

R. J. Bonner and G. Smith. *The Administration of Justice from Homer to Aristotle*, (Chicago, University of Chicago Press, 2 Vols., 1930, 1938).

T. J. Cadoux, 'The Athenian Archons from Kreon to Hypsichides', *JHS* 68 (1948).

W. R. Connor, *The New Politicians of Fifth-Century Athens* (Princeton, Princeton University Press, 1971).

A. French, *The Growth of the Athenian Economy*, (London, Routledge and Kegan Paul, 1964) to be used with caution.

A. Fuks, *The Ancestral Constitution* (London, Routledge and Kegan Paul, 1953).

C. W. Fornara, *The Athenian Board of Generals from 501 to 404*, Historia einzelschriften 16, 1971; the negative arguments here are more convincing than the positive theses.

D. M. MacDowell, *The Law of Classical Athens* (London, Thames and Hudson, 1978).

R. Meiggs, *The Athenian Empire*, (Oxford, Oxford University Press, 1972).

R. Meiggs and D. M. Lewis, *A Selection of Greek Historical Inscriptions to the end of the Fifth Century*, (Oxford, Oxford University Press, 1969) (cited as Meiggs/Lewis).

P. J. Rhodes, *The Athenian Boule*, (Oxford, Oxford University Press, 1972).

R. S. Stroud, *Drakon's Law on Homicide*, University of California Class.

The Athenian Agora; a Guide to the Excavations and Museum, (3rd edition, Athens, American School of Classical Studies, 1976).

The Oxford Classical Dictionary, (2nd edition, Oxford, Oxford University Press, 1970) (cited as OCD²).

Index

This is a selective index, designed as a guide to the Introductions and Commentaries; it includes only the more important references. In general, references to the Commentaries should be used to lead to the relevant sections of the texts translated in the volume. A very few page references to the actual texts have been included where the discussion of a particular passage might not lead readers to look for the point indexed.

Page references to key discussions are printed in **bold type**.

The index includes a complete list of passages from ancient authors referred to; where such passages are translated, the page references are given in *italics*.

Words defined in the Glossaries are marked (g) indicating the Glossary to the *Politeia of the Spartans*, and (G) the Glossary to the *Constitution of Athens*.

317

INDEX

INDEX

Printed in the USA
CPSIA information can be obtained
at www.ICGtesting.com
LVHW052239300823
756645LV00001B/163